CHIAPAS

LIZA PRADO & GARY CHANDLER

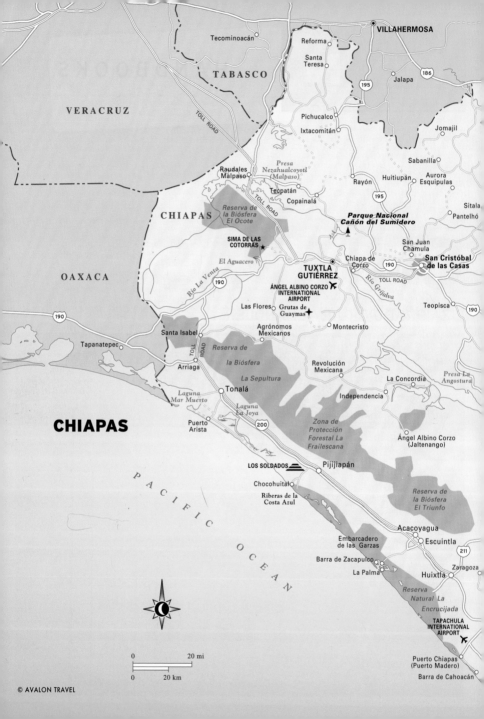

Contents

Discover Chiapas

Along a winding highland road in Chiapas is a tidy 18th-century chapel called Templo Carmen Arcotete. Built as a retreat for the state's local bishop, the chapel overlooks a picturesque valley, a patchwork of corn and cabbage fields dotted by low adobe homes. Down the road is a towering stone arch, the remnants of an ancient cave system, complete with dangling stalactites; a clear icy river burbles through the vaulted stone, great for swimming if you can stand the cold.

A short distance up the road is the Maya village of El Romerillo, where every November 1 – *Día de Todos Santos* – families gather at the local cemetery to speak with loved ones through wood doors placed over their mounded graves. A few kilometers away is San Cristóbal de las Casas, one of Mexico's finest colonial cities, known for its rich history and bohemian air; and beyond that, the modern state capital of Tuxtla Gutiérrez, whose gleaming new airport connects travelers to Mexico City and beyond.

Neither Templo Carmen Arcotete, the archway, nor El Romerillo are major tourist attractions, even for those visiting San Cristóbal. But that's the amazing thing about Chiapas – whether it's a marquee attraction or a quiet stretch of mountain road, the state bursts with natural beauty, intriguing history, and fascinating culture. Of course, for many people Chiapas is synonymous with the armed uprising that broke out in 1994,

and the movement's charismatic pipe-smoking spokesman Subcomandante Marcos. But it doesn't take long to discover just how remarkable (and peaceful) the state really is.

Chiapas has gorgeous colonial cities, a prominent and highly independent indigenous population, and some of Mesoamerica's most stunning ancient Maya ruins, including Palenque and Yaxchilán. Chiapas's landscape ranges from scenic beaches to jagged peaks cloaked in cloud forest – and just about everything in between, even an active volcano. The state's massive Lacandón rainforest forms part of one of the largest tropical rainforests north of the Amazon, and, unbeknownst to many, Chiapas is one of the most biologically diverse places on the planet.

Best of all, Chiapas is as charming and pleasant as it is fascinating and engaging, full of quiet coffee shops and tree-lined plazas, and home to a diverse and gracious population. It is a place to linger – and a place that will linger in you, long after you've left.

Planning Your Trip

▶ WHERE TO GO

Palenque

The main attraction in this area, of course, is Palenque Archaeological Zone, one of the Maya world's most important ancient cities, and a perennial favorite among travelers. Just south of Palenque are the beautiful waterfalls of Agua Azul and Misol-Há, and beyond those, the remarkable but little-visited Toniná Archaeological Zone.

The Río Usumacinta Valley

This region is best known for Bonampak and Yaxchilán Archaeological Zones, the former boasting some of the Maya world's finest murals, the latter rising regally from the Río Usumacinta riverbank. This region also serves as a gateway to the state's vast central rainforest, and the fascinating Lacandón villages Lacanjá Chansayab, Metzabok, and Nahá. Improved roads and security have made it possible to connect directly to eastern Chiapas and the Lakes Region.

IF YOU HAVE . . .

- **ONE WEEK:** Visit Palenque, the Río Usumacinta Valley, and San Cristóbal de las Casas
- **TEN DAYS:** Add Toniná, San Juan Chamula, Cañón del Sumidero, Comitán, and Lagunas de Montebello
- **TWO WEEKS:** Add Las Guacamayas and Laguna Miramar
- **THREE WEEKS:** Add Tuxtla Gutiérrez, Sima de las Cotorras, Barra de Zacapulco, and Ruta del Café

San Cristóbal de las Casas

One of Mexico's most appealing cities, San Cristóbal de las Casas has gorgeous colonial architecture, an engaging bohemian atmosphere, and a cool energizing climate. There's also a strong indigenous presence, and the

Palenque isn't the biggest Maya ruin, but many consider it the most beautiful.

city is surrounded by vibrant and interesting Maya villages, like San Juan Chamula and Tenejapa, where traditional customs and language are still in wide use.

The Lakes Region

The Lakes Region gets its name from Lagunas de Montebello, a popular national park containing dozens of lakes. But it's got much more than that, beginning with the highly underrated city of Comitán, with museums, churches, and charm to rival San Cristóbal's. East toward the Guatemalan border are two popular eco-centers, Las Guacamayas and Las Nubes, plus backdoor access to Laguna Miramar, one of the state's most isolated and picturesque spots.

The mustard-yellow cathedral in San Cristóbal de las Casas seems to glow in the late afternoon light.

Tuxtla Gutiérrez

Most travelers prefer Chiapas's rural areas over its bustling state capital, but Tuxtla Gutiérrez does have a terrific zoo and museums, and the surrounding area includes some true must-sees, including Cañón del Sumidero and Sima de las Cotorras. Tuxtla is also the main gateway to the Pacific coast and the state's little-visited northwest region.

The Pacific Coast

The broad grey-black beaches at Puerto Arista and Boca del Cielo are popular weekend getaways from Tuxtla, but the rest of Chiapas's scenic Pacific coast is far less visited, including the peaceful Riberas de la Costa Azul and Barra de Zacapulco, home to Latin America's tallest mangrove forests. The region's largest city, Tapachula, is a jumping-off point for hiking Tacaná Volcano and exploring the gorgeous Ruta del Café (Coffee Route), as well as an important border crossing with Guatemala.

► WHEN TO GO

The weather in Chiapas varies considerably from region to region, especially those at different altitudes. Most travelers prefer the dry season (roughly November to May), when the state's famously blue rivers are clear and rural roads more passable. (It can be quite cold then, however, especially in the highlands.) If you want to beat the crowds, avoid the peak travel periods around Christmas and New Year's, Semana Santa (the week before Easter), and July and August. That said, it can be interesting to visit during local holidays, like December 12 (saint's day for the Virgin of Guadalupe) and Carnaval (end of February).

► BEFORE YOU GO

Passports and Visas

American travelers are now required to have a valid passport to travel to and from Mexico. Tourist visas are issued upon entry; you are allowed to stay up to 180 days, but agents sometimes issue visas for just 30 or 60 days. If you want the maximum period, request it when you present your passport. To extend your visa, visit the immigration offices in San Cristóbal or Tuxtla Gutiérrez.

Vaccinations

No special vaccines are required for travel to Chiapas, but it's a good idea to be up-to-date on the standard travel immunizations, including Hepatitis A, MMR (measles-mumps-rubella), tetanus-diphtheria, and typhoid.

Transportation

Chiapas is blessed with a reliable and far-reaching network of buses and smaller colectivos (aka combis). Combining public transportation with day trips offered by local tour agencies, most travelers find they do not need a rental car. That said, public transportation can be infrequent or unreliable in remote areas, and having a car can dramatically cut your travel time, leaving more time to see and do the stuff that drew you here in the first place.

Tuxtla's Ángel Albino Corzo International Airport (TGZ) is the state's main airport. Tapachula's airport also has commercial service, while those in San Cristóbal, Comitán, and Palenque are used for charter flights only.

What to Take

Chiapas has a highly varied landscape and climate; in Palenque you'll need light clothing and a billed hat, while in San Cristóbal you'll appreciate having a winter hat and thermal underwear. Sunscreen, insect repellent, and a swimsuit all come in handy, and a good pair of shoes are vital for exploring Maya ruins safely. During the rainy season, be sure to bring an umbrella or raincoat. And if you wear contacts or glasses, bring a replacement set.

Volkswagen bugs are a mainstay of Mexican roads and highways, including in Chiapas.

Explore Chiapas

▶ THE BEST OF CHIAPAS

If you're visiting Chiapas for the first time and want to be sure to hit all the must-sees, this is the tour for you. It covers a little of everything—Maya ruins, indigenous villages, colonial cities, and some jaw-dropping natural attractions—all in just over two weeks. You won't need a rental car for most of this trip; with the exception of Aguacero and Sima de las Cotorras (west of Tuxtla Gutiérrez) everything is easily accessible by public transportation or organized tour.

Day 1
Stretch your legs with a stroll through the town of Palenque, ending up at the *zocalo* (central park), where there's occasionally live marimba music. Enjoy dinner at Las Tinajas.

Day 2
Spend the day visiting the Palenque Archaeological Zone and museum. It's not a big site, but many travelers find themselves lingering over it, and the museum is terrific. Have lunch at Mayabell or Café Restaurante Don Mucho in El Panchán, near the entrance to the ruins. That evening, set up tomorrow's tour of Agua Azul and Misol-Há.

Day 3
Take a tour of the Parque Nacional de Agua Azul and Cascada de Misol-Há waterfalls. You'll be back by mid-afternoon, leaving time to relax and make arrangements for a tour of Yaxchilán and Bonampak archaeological sites tomorrow.

Day 4
Take an all-day round-trip tour of Yaxchilán and Bonampak Archaeological Zones. It's

The path behind Misol-Há offers a unique (and mist-drenched) view of this gorgeous waterfall.

San Cristóbal's *andador*, or pedestrian walkway.

a long day, leaving Palenque at 6 A.M. and returning just before dark, but the tour typically includes stops for breakfast and lunch.

Day 5

Catch a bus to San Cristóbal de las Casas. If you enjoy ancient ruins, consider stopping off in Ocosingo to visit Toniná Archaeological Zone, an excellent but little-visited site with a first-rate museum. Stay the night in Ocosingo, or simply stow your bags at the bus station while you see the ruins, then catch a later bus onward to San Cristóbal.

Day 6

Spend the day in San Cristóbal. Favorite sights include La Catedral de San Cristóbal and El Zócalo (the central plaza). Browse the *artesanía* market at Templo y Ex-Convento de Santo Domingo de Guzmán, admire the amber collection at Museo del Ámbar de

Chiapas, and discover Maya medical practices at the Museo de la Medicina Maya.

Day 7

Take a regional tour of the Maya villages of San Juan Chamula, Chiapas's largest indigenous town, and nearby Zinacantán. You'll be back in San Cristóbal around 2 P.M., in time for a late lunch and coffee.

Day 8

Catch an early *combi* to Chiapa de Corzo for a tour of stunning Cañón del Sumidero, one of Chiapas's most impressive natural wonders. Plan to eat lunch in town, and spend a few hours in the afternoon visiting the colonial structure of La Pila, the Museo de Laca (a lacquerware museum), and other sights before returning to San Cristóbal. Consider heading into Tuxtla Gutiérrez to pick up a rental car.

Day 9

Spend another day touring around San Cristóbal. With a rental car, explore outlying

Santo Domingo church, one of San Cristóbal's most ornate and striking structures

Parque Nacional Lagunas de Montebello has nearly 60 lakes, each more beautiful than the last.

indigenous villages like El Romerillo or Tenejapa.

Day 10
Drive or take a bus to the friendly city of Comitán. Visit the sights around town, including two excellent museums: Museo Arqueológico de Comitán (archaeology) and Museo de Arte Hermila Domínguez de Castellanos (modern art). If you don't have a car, arrange a tour to Lagunas de Montebello and Tenam Puente the next day.

Day 11
Visit Parque Nacional Lagunas de Montebello, a colorful array of lakes, lagoons, and ponds. Stop to admire the ruins at the Tenam Puente Archaeological Zone, returning to Comitán by late afternoon. Enjoy the evening in town, where there's usually live music in the *zócalo* (central plaza).

Day 12
In the morning, visit Cascada El Chiflón, one of the highest and most powerful waterfalls in Chiapas. Make your way to Tuxtla Gutiérrez by the afternoon and rent a car, if you haven't done so already.

Day 13
Drive to Aguacero waterfall, then backtrack slightly to view the enormous caves and sinkholes at Sima de las Cotorras. Definitely plan to be there between 4 and 5 P.M. so you can watch thousands of *cotorras,* or green parrots, return to their nests.

Day 14
Get up at 5:30–6 A.M. to see the parrots again, then return to Tuxtla Gutiérrez. Time permitting, consider visiting the ZOOMAT, one of the best zoos in Latin America, or drive the rim of Cañón del Sumidero before returning home.

▶ PYRAMIDS AND PALACES

Chiapas doesn't have as many ruins as, say, the Yucatán Peninsula, but the ones it does have are almost uniformly magnificent, many ensconced in the tropical rainforest. The state also has a number of excellent archaeological museums, which are oddly lacking at most Maya ruins.

Palenque

Palenque is the all-time favorite ruin of many travelers, thanks to its elegant architecture, intricate carvings, and superlative museum. Much of what archaeologists know about the Maya calendar, hieroglyphics, and astronomy emerged from studies conducted here.

Toniná is a terrific hillside ruin, featuring a labyrinthine palace and temples, morbid stucco friezes, and impressive views from its high-reaching summit. The site museum here is outstanding.

Yaxchilán is famous for its beautiful and well-preserved lintels.

The Río Usumacinta Valley

Yaxchilán is one of Chiapas's most enchanting ruins, an ancient city built on a lush hillside

Take time to explore Palenque's remarkable palace, including its iconic tower and the Patio of the Captives, where large panels are engraved with images of rival leaders taken prisoner.

LIVING MAYA

Visiting ancient Maya ruins, and reading about the sudden "collapse" of Maya cities a thousand years ago, you might get the impression that Maya civilization is a thing of the past. In fact, Maya people, communities, and culture are very much alive and thriving – some six million people speak a Maya language, from the Yucatán Peninsula to Honduras, including, of course, Chiapas. Outside of big cities, the Chiapanecan population is mostly Maya, making it possible for travelers to learn about, experience, and appreciate their cultures.

SAN CRISTÓBAL DE LAS CASAS

A number of excellent museums in town offer an introduction to living Maya cultures. **Museo Na Bolom** is dedicated to preserving Lacandón culture; it is housed in the former home of an anthropologist-photographer couple who were among the first foreigners to maintain contact with the reclusive group. **Museo de la Medicina Maya** has excellent displays on traditional Maya medicine, including medicinal plants and different types of healers. **Museo de Trajes Regionales Sergio Castro** is a private collection of the different shawls, tunics, and other traditional garb used throughout Chiapas, each specific to a particular region. San Cristóbal also is home to thousands of indigenous Maya, whom you'll encounter on a regular basis in the plaza, markets, and city streets.

SAN JUAN CHAMULA AND ZINACANTÁN

Just a few kilometers from San Cristóbal, these Tzotzil Maya towns are the easiest and most popular indigenous communities to visit, whether by tour or on your own. San Juan Chamula is especially intriguing – among other things, the town church has no pews or priest, and is used for traditional healing ceremonies that mix pre-Hispanic customs, Catholic saints, and modern accoutrements, like paraffin candles and Coca-Cola. In Zinacantán, you'll be invited into local homes to see how textiles are woven by hand or using a back-loom.

OUTLYING TOWNS AND VILLAGES

As fascinating as Chamula and Zinacantán

The Maya revered a cross-like symbol long before Spanish missionaries arrived.

can be, they also are quite touristed. Not so in the outlying towns and villages, where you may well be the only foreign visitor in town. **Oxchuc** is a bustling Tzeltal Maya community, with a historic church and vibrant Saturday market. **El Romerillo,** a tiny Chamulan village with an intriguing Maya cemetery, is on the way to **Tenejapa,** a Tzeltal town with an excellent Thursday market. Other villages to check out include **Chenalhó** and **San Andrés Larrainzar.**

LACANDÓN VILLAGES

The Lacandónes are one of the best known Maya groups, as well as one of the smallest – numbering only around a thousand people in all, they are descendants of Yucatec Mayas who fled into the Chiapanecan rainforest to escape Spanish domination. For travelers, the village of **Lacanjá Chansayab** is the easiest to reach, but isolated communities like **Nahá** and **Metzabok** offer a more traditional ambience and experience.

Getting to Yaxchilán ruins is half the fun and includes an hour-long trip down the Río Usumacinta on arrow-like river boats.

overlooking the Río Usumacinta. Getting there is half the fun: an hour-long boat ride down the river, with beefy crocs along the banks and howler monkeys in the trees.

Yaxchilán's sister city is Bonampak, which has only modest structures but boasts some of the finest murals yet discovered in the Maya world. Housed in an innocuous-looking temple, the brightly colored frescoes depict events like the crowning of a boy king and a fierce jungle battle.

Plan de Ayutla is a unique off-the-beaten-path ruin that has not been formally restored (so there's no ticket booth or even any signs). It is excavated enough to explore and appreciate the structures, including high vaulted sanctuaries, numerous temples, and a multi-level palace. Best of all, you're almost certain to have the place to yourself.

The Lakes Region

Tenam Puente is built on a series of broad terraces, which mask the site's true size and complexity. What looks like a low tree-covered hill in fact contains numerous impressive structures, making it a fun place to explore.

Cross your fingers that Chinkultik will be open—an impressive site, it's at the center of a bitter dispute between local residents and federal overseers, and is often closed. The site is built on a rocky bluff overlooking a cenote where ceremonial items, and occasionally sacrificial victims, were cast.

The Museo Arqueológico de Comitán has an excellent collection of artifacts from nearby ruins, with a particular focus on funerary items—urns and incense burners, fine jade and obsidian carvings, and small ceramic figurines—all intended to adorn bodies and accompany departed souls into the next realm. A separate room, the Sala Tenam Puente, showcases items from Tenam Puente archaeological site.

Tuxtla Gutiérrez

Though not strictly an archaeological museum—and badly in need of a face-lift—the Museo Regional de Chiapas has a terrific section on ancient Maya development in Chiapas, including the most extensive and varied collection of artifacts in the state. Displays provide a great overview of the state's

Tenam Puente makes for fun exploring.

main Maya centers and advancements, from prehistoric times to the present.

The Pacific Coast

Izapa dominated the coastal region for nearly a thousand years, so it's no surprise that it's the Pacific coast's most important ruin. Though not as arresting as Palenque or Yaxchilán, Izapa is intriguing for its possible connection to the Olmecs (Mesoamerica's first major civilization) and the high quality of its stelae and other carvings.

Museo Arqueológico del Soconusco, Tapachula's archaeological museum, has an excellent collection of ancient Maya artifacts, including musical instruments and finely carved stelae, most from the nearby site of Izapa. It's even got kid-friendly exhibits, like stelae rubbings and Náhuatl (Aztecan) vocabulary games.

▶ A TWO-WEEK ECOTOUR

Chiapas's landscape ranges from rugged mountains to steamy coastal lowlands, and includes vast swaths of tropical rainforest, temperate woodland, estuaries, and mangrove forests, and countless rivers and lakes. There's far more to do than can be squeezed into two weeks, without running yourself ragged, but this tour covers the highlights. Definitely consider adding additional stops, depending on your time and interests. With an ever-growing tourism infrastructure, Chiapas is a great place for active, eco-minded travelers.

Day 1

Arrive in San Cristóbal de las Casas and take a mountain bike tour of the surrounding countryside, either to the Huitepec Reserve, Arcotete (a natural archway), or through isolated indigenous villages.

WATER WORKS

If there's anything that Chiapas has plenty of, it's water. The state contains 40 percent of Mexico's freshwater supply, and a series of massive dams generate over 50 percent of the country's hydroelectric power. Water also helps paint some of Chiapas's most picturesque scenes, including waterfalls, lakes, rivers, and seascapes. Some of the watery highlights include:

- **Lagunas de Montebello:** Sixty lakes, sixty different colors – or so it seems at this pine-swathed national park east of Comitán. You can visit a dozen or so by car, a popular day trip on your own or on a package tour.

- **Cascada El Chiflón:** At 120 meters, the main waterfall here is one of Mexico's highest, yet is just one of a series of cascades extending more than a kilometer, flanked by trails, observation platforms, and even a zip line.

- **El Aguacero:** Located at the bottom of an isolated river canyon west of Tuxtla, this is arguably Chiapas's most beautiful waterfall, with countless rivulets pouring over a long ledge and down natural stair-steps.

- **Agua Azul:** A series of powerful waterfalls separated by pools of luminescent teal-blue water – it's a remarkable sight, and a great day trip from Palenque, usually paired with a stop at the serene **Misol-Há** waterfall.

- **Laguna Miramar:** Said to be Mexico's purest body of water, and certainly among its most enchanting, this huge lake is nestled in thick rainforest, accessible only by a long bus ride or a boat trip through Zapatista territory.

- **Barra de Zacapulco:** Enjoy the scenic and expansive dark-sand beach, or tour the winding inland waterways teeming with birds and home to Latin America's tallest mangrove trees.

You can stroll Barra de Zacapulco's long scenic beach for hours without seeing another soul (unless you count shore birds and sand crabs).

Templo Carmen Arcotete is a little-visited jewel outside San Cristóbal.

Day 2

Catch an early *combi* to Chiapa de Corzo for a boat tour of Cañón del Sumidero. Eat lunch and check out some of the sights around

the sheer stone walls at Cañón del Sumidero

town before continuing to Tuxtla Gutiérrez, where you'll spend the night and arrange a rental car.

Day 3

First thing in the morning, drive to magnificent El Aguacero waterfall, then to Sima de las Cotorras. On weekends, you can rappel 140 meters down to the bottom of the *sima* (sinkhole). Stay to watch thousands of parrots return to the *sima* in the evening (4–5 P.M.).

Day 4

If you missed the evening parrot show, get up early (5:30–6 A.M.) to catch the parrots leaving Sima de las Cotorras, then hit the road for a long drive to Barra de Zacapulco, on the Pacific coast. The drive over the Sierra Madre mountains is gorgeous; be sure to take the new *cuota* (toll road) and upon arrival arrange a boat tour for tomorrow.

Day 5

Visit the La Encrucijada mangrove forest in the morning, and spend the afternoon relaxing on the town beach. In the evening, volunteer at the Campamento Tortuguero de Barra de Zacapulco, a sea turtle protection and preservation center that searches the beach for turtle eggs and releases newborns into the ocean.

Day 6

Catch an early boat back to your car, then drive to Union Juárez and set up a hike of Volcán Tacaná for the following day.

Days 7-9

Climb the Volcán Tacaná. Strong hikers can make the whole trip in two days; others may need or want to budget three days. Upon your return, treat yourself to a nice hotel or B&B in Tapachula.

Day 10

Get an early start so you can reach Las Guacamayas, an eco-center in eastern Chiapas across the river from the Montes Azules biosphere reserve.

Day 11

Take a morning hike or boat ride in the reserve, and a macaw-spotting walk in the afternoon. Between outings, take a dip in the river or relax in a hammock on your cabin porch.

Day 12-13

Drive to La Democracía and catch a motorboat to Laguna Miramar, the largest lake in the Lacandón rainforest. Be sure to arrange for the boatman to pick you up in two days.

Camp or sleep in hammocks along the lakeshore, or in simple cabins in the nearest town, seven kilometers away. Rent a kayak the next day and explore Laguna Miramar, one of the most picturesque spots in Chiapas.

Days 14

Take a boat back to La Democracía, returning to San Cristóbal. On the way, consider a quick stop to admire the lakes, lagoons, and ponds of Parque Nacional Lagunas de Montebello or to enjoy the cascading power of Cascada El Chiflón.

the thundering main waterfall at Cascada El Chiflón

OFF THE BEATEN PATH

Seldom visited and only partially excavated, Plan de Ayutla ruins may be a 'lost' city long sought by archaeologists.

Some would say Chiapas as a whole is off the beaten path, but within each of the state's regions are a few priceless locations that are especially harder to reach, but all the more rewarding for those who do.

PALENQUE

For some reason, the beaten path hasn't reached the Maya ruins at **Toniná Archaeological Zone,** despite their being conveniently located midway between Palenque and San Cristóbal. It's a gorgeous hillside ruin, with macabre stucco friezes and a must-see museum.

THE RÍO USUMACINTA VALLEY

For sheer isolation, you can't beat the Lacandón village of **Metzabok,** where the nearest bus stop is six hilly kilometers away and once there you can take canoe rides through pristine lagoons to see prehistoric paintings.

Maya-ruin junkies will love the partially excavated sites of **Plan de Ayutla Archaeological Zone** and **Piedras Negras;** the former is easier to reach than the latter, but both exude a mysterious otherworldly charm.

SAN CRISTÓBAL DE LAS CASAS

Surrounding San Cristóbal are seldom-visited Maya communities like **Chenalhó** and **Tenejapa,** both with colorful markets and a scenic drive to reach them. Another town, **Oxchuc,** is actually right along the highway to Ocosingo, yet sees very few foreign visitors.

THE LAKES REGION

Laguna Miramar is one of the jewels of Chiapas, and all the more appealing for its remote location in the Lacandón rainforest, reached by bus or via a more scenic and adventuresome river route from the south.

TUXTLA GUTIÉRREZ

Chiapas has few places more isolated than **El Triunfo,** a rugged biosphere reserve in the Sierra Madre mountain range, and an excellent place to spot wildlife, like the reclusive resplendent quetzal.

THE PACIFIC COAST

It takes two days to reach the summit of **Volcán Tacaná,** an imposing 4,100-meter active volcano with awesome views of the ocean and the volcanoes of Guatemala. In the shadow of the volcano is the **Ruta del Café** (Coffee Route), comprised of small coffee farms and vast plantations accessible only by steep rocky roads.

► COLONIAL CHIAPAS

Travelers interested in colonial architecture will not leave Chiapas disappointed. San Cristóbal de las Casas is easily one of Mexico's finest colonial cities, boasting a beautiful cathedral, elegant Dominican priory and convent, and numerous well-preserved colonial-era structures. Nearby are the smaller, but no less significant, colonial towns of Comitán and Chiapa de Corzo. There also are a number of indigenous villages that are not colonial in an overall sense but that contain superb colonial structures, especially churches and convents. A rental car is recommended for this route, which includes leap-frogging from town to town.

Day 1

Arrive in San Cristóbal de las Casas and settle into your hotel. Walk down to the central plaza in the afternoon, when the sun lights up the cathedral's striking yellow facade.

Comitán has numerous striking colonial churches.

Chiapas's rich colonial history can be seen not only in its soaring churches and broad plazas, but also in artful details, like weatherworn doors and centuries-old ironwork.

La Pila in Chiapa de Corzo is one of the state's oldest and most exquisite colonial structures.

Day 2

Visit San Cristóbal's colonial gems, including La Catedral de San Cristóbal, Casa Sirena, and Templo y Ex-Convento de Santo Domingo de Guzmán. Book a rental car for the following days.

Day 3

Visit outlying indigenous villages known for their colonial churches, including San Juan Chamula and Tenejapa. Time permitting, the church in Oxchuc is also superb. (Remember that taking pictures of indigenous people or inside any of the town churches is strictly forbidden.)

Day 4

Drive east toward Comitán, stopping to admire colonial churches and plazas in Teopisca, Amatenango del Valle, and Soyatitán. In the evening, enjoy a meal and live music at Comitán's lovely central plaza.

Day 5

Visit Comitán's churches, Templo Santo Domingo de Guzmán and Iglesia de San Caralampio, and wander the town's carefully restored colonial neighborhoods. Stay the night, or drive to Chiapa de Corzo.

Day 6

Take a tour of Cañón del Sumidero—not a colonial attraction, but a must-see nonetheless—and spend the afternoon enjoying colonial gems around Chiapa de Corzo, including La Pila, a superb 16th-century public fountain.

Day 7

Get an early start on the Ruta de Zoques, including stops at Chicoasén, Copainalá, and especially Tecpatán, home to one of the state's most magnificent Dominican monasteries. Return to Tuxtla Gutiérrez and enjoy the live music at Parque Marimba before returning home.

CHURCHGOING CHIAPAS

Between San Cristóbal de las Casas and Comitán are a number of small towns boasting outstanding Dominican churches and missions, some in use, others long abandoned. They make for interesting detours – or even a complete day trip – if you've got a car and an interest in colonial architecture.

TEOPISCA

The cavernous nave of Teopisca's **Iglesia San Agustín** is the second-largest in the state, after San Tomás in Oxchuc. The floors are covered in beautiful pink and white tile, while the lofty ceiling is spanned by ornately carved wood beams. But the church's most remarkable feature is its massive *retablo* altar, the oldest in Chiapas (dated 1708) and by most accounts the finest. It was originally installed in the San Agustín church in San Cristóbal, but transferred here, along with two excellent

Many of Chiapas's small towns are home to stunning colonial-era churches.

flanking *retablos*, to replace ones destroyed by an earthquake in 1817. The altarpiece has 18 niches in all, the center ones filled by sculptures of saints (including San Dominic at the top, and San Agustín at the bottom), and outer ones with paintings of religious scenes; it is framed by gilded and ornately carved columns and a large base with carvings of animals, angels, and other figures.

SOYATITÁN

The imposing facade and thick stone walls attest to the former grandeur of this 16th-century church, known as **Asunción Soyatitán.** Unfortunately it is severely deteriorated, with the nave's roof having long since collapsed and pigeons roosting in holes meant to anchor the main altarpiece against the back wall. The sober facade rises in three levels, divided by plain stone columns, topped by a grand but decaying bell gable, and facing a small grassy patio.

AMATENANGO DEL VALLE

Amatenango del Valle has a lovely and unique **colonial church.** The brilliant white facade gives way to a long simple nave with pink and white tile floors. The *retablo* altarpiece is set quite far back, beneath a polygonal wood cupola. The altar is notable for being painted a deep red with white and gold floral patterns; the niches feature scenes from the life of San Francisco de Asis, Amatenango's patron saint. A spiral staircase near the entrance leads to the church's choral balcony, with small windows overlooking the town's plaza.

SAN JOSÉ CONETA

San José Coneta, located near the Guatemalan border, was founded in the late 1500s but abandoned in 1804 in the face of a dwindling population. The **mission church,** a lonely monument surrounded by corn fields and cow pastures, has proved remarkably resilient. The facade features an eclectic array of columns, niches, arches, and decorative frames and figures. Tall trees grow out of the spacious (and roofless) nave, adding to the ghost-town atmosphere.

PALENQUE

For all its rich indigenous culture and history, Chiapas has surprisingly few ancient ruins open to the public. But what it lacks in quantity it more than makes up for in quality, boasting some of the most stunning examples of Maya architecture, design, carvings, and paintings. The Palenque archaeological site is the crown jewel, of course, not only of Chiapas but of the entire Maya world. Though fairly modest in size and scale, Palenque exudes a sense of class and sophistication that has captivated visitors for decades, even centuries. (The town of Palenque, unfortunately, is decidedly less lovely, and the difference can be jarring.)

South of Palenque, the Río Tulijá flows out of the mountains on a limestone riverbed that gives the water a radiant turquoise color. Three popular attractions—the 30-meter Misol-Há waterfall, Agua Clara swimming and recreation area, and especially Agua Azul National Park, an impressive series of powerful waterfalls and blue-hued swimming holes—are great for escaping Palenque's sticky lowland heat. Tour agencies in Palenque offer recommended day trips there.

Further south, the medium-sized city of Ocosingo is home to the terrific Maya ruins of Toniná, easily one of the best-kept secrets in Chiapas. The ancient city climbs a steep hillside, with elaborate temples, impressive stucco friezes, and expansive views of the surrounding countryside; there's an excellent museum, too, a rarity among Maya sites. Located halfway between San Cristóbal and Palenque, Toniná is an easy and logical layover—welcome, even, if the corkscrew highway has you feeling green—yet amazingly few people stop.

HIGHLIGHTS

◖ **Palenque Archaeological Zone:** One of the most important Maya ruins for the many discoveries and breakthroughs made there, Palenque also happens to be among the most beautiful, with graceful structures and well-preserved carvings and hieroglyphics. Although not a very big site, it's a favorite for many (page 28).

◖ **Museo Arqueológico de Palenque:** Only a handful of Maya archaeological sites have museums, and most aren't too inspiring. Not so with Palenque's museum, home to a small but stunning collection of artifacts, from huge panels of stucco glyphs to intricate funerary urns, plus a fascinating full-size replica of Lord Pakal's tomb (page 35).

◖ **Cascada de Misol-Há:** As serene as it is impressive, Misol-Há waterfall leaps 30 meters (98 feet) from the top of a crescent-shaped cliff to a large pool below. It's perfect for swimming or just admiring, with a path that leads behind the crashing water to a small cave (page 46).

◖ **Parque Nacional de Agua Azul:** Pictures don't do justice to this remarkable natural phenomenon – luminescent blue water tumbling over a series of powerful waterfalls and gathering in calm clear pools, perfect for swimming. This is a great day trip from Palenque, but plan on going on an off day – this place definitely draws a crowd (page 47).

◖ **Toniná Archaeological Zone:** Beautiful temples, amazing stucco murals, imposing hill-

side perch, intriguing history, a fascinating museum, and convenient location between San Cristóbal and Palenque – the only thing missing from this gorgeous and overlooked archaeological site are the crowds (which is all the more reason to visit!) (page 50).

LOOK FOR ◖ TO FIND RECOMMENDED SIGHTS, ACTIVITIES, DINING, AND LODGING.

Ocosingo is also the starting point for an arduous but rewarding journey to Laguna Miramar, a pristine lake deep in the Lacandón rainforest.

PLANNING YOUR TIME

Plan to spend a full day at Palenque archaeological site and its excellent on-site museum—you don't need quite that much time, but it's hard to squeeze it into just a morning or afternoon. Budget another day for the waterfalls on the Río Tulijá; most people book day trips from

Palenque town, but some agencies offer onward service to San Cristóbal, a convenient option if you're headed that direction. Better still, plan to stop for a few hours, or even stay overnight, in Ocosingo to visit the excellent but little-visited ruins of Toniná. Located almost exactly halfway between Palenque and San Cristóbal, it's a great way to break up the trip. Palenque is the most common jumping-off point for visiting ruins and indigenous villages in the Río Usumacinta Valley; definitely worth figuring into your plans.

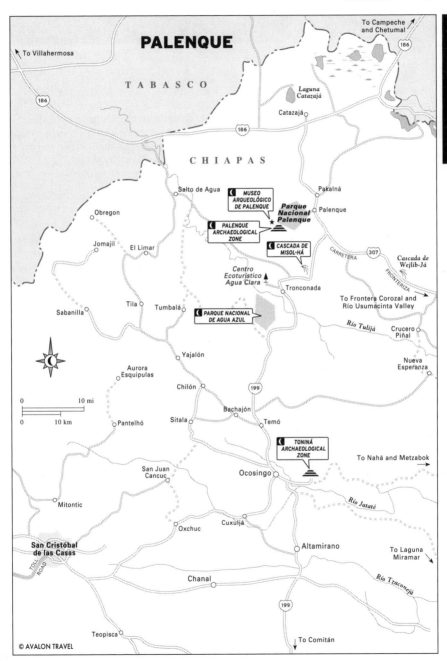

© AVALON TRAVEL

Palenque Archaeological Zone and Town

The town of Santo Domingo de Palenque, usually just called Palenque, is eight kilometers (5 miles) from the Palenque archeological zone. The town itself is rather grubby and nondescript, but it bulges at its seams with tourists here to visit the ruins. Avenida Juárez is the main drag, where you'll find the bus terminal, tour agencies, and other services, plus a number of no-frills hotels. Many travelers find the leafy neighborhood of La Cañada and the hotels along the road to the ruins to be more pleasant spots to spend the night, though they cost a bit more. There's a small, little-used plaza at one end of Avenida Juárez, and a large sculpture of a Maya warrior's head (and the turnoff to the ruins) at the other.

ℂ PALENQUE ARCHAEOLOGICAL ZONE

Palenque is a must-see on any itinerary of Maya ruins. It is a relatively small site—by no means as large as Chichén Itzá or Tikal—but considered by many to be the Mona Lisa of Maya ruins, with a particularly graceful design and construction. Its setting, on a lush green shelf at the edge of the Sierra de Chiapas forest, perfectly complements its elegant design and ornate carvings. And unlike many archaeological sites, Palenque's museum is terrific, with a small but exquisite collection of stone, ceramic, and stucco artifacts, accompanied by well-written explanations.

History

The name Palenque, Spanish for fortification, is a rough translation of the Ch'ol Maya term Otolum (Strong Houses); that's how local residents described the mysterious stone ruins to Spanish explorers at the time of the conquest. The ancient city's true original name was Lakam Ha, or Big Water, surely a reference to the many springs and streams found in the area. It was the capital of a city-state known as B'aak (Bone Kingdom).

Scholars have been able to decipher enough Maya glyphs to construct a reasonable genealogy of the Palenque kings, from the rule of Chaacal I (A.D. 501) to the demise of Kuk (A.D. 783). But it was the period from A.D. 615 to 702, during the glorious reigns of Pakal the Great and his eldest son, Kan Balam, that Palenque grew from a minor city to an important economic and political center.

Palenque's most distinguished leader, Pakal the Great (properly called K'inich Janaab' Pakal, or Great Sun Shield, but also referred to as Lord Pakal or Pakal II) was born in A.D. 603 and ascended to the throne in A.D. 615, when he was just 12 years old. Pakal lived to be 81 years old—remarkable for that time—and during his long rule expanded Palenque's influence throughout the western Maya lowlands. He built the Temple of the Inscriptions to house his own elaborate tomb, and commissioned many of the most notable structures and artwork in the palace.

Pakal was succeeded by his eldest son, Kan Balam (Serpent Jaguar, also written as Kan Balamok) who was noteworthy for having six digits on his hands and feet. (To maintain the royal bloodline, Maya rulers often took relatives as wives, eventually leading to birth defects. Pakal himself had a clubfoot, and some archaeologists believe his mother and father were siblings. Likewise, Pakal may have married his sister, leading to his son's defects.) Kan Balam reigned for 18 years and built the Temples of the Cross, Foliated Cross, and Sun, which emphasize the preordination of his rule.

When Kan Balam died in A.D. 702, his younger brother, Kan Xul, took the reins of power. His rule was Palenque's apogee in terms of population—over 50,000 by some estimates—and political power, controlling a region that extended nearly from the Sierra Madre to the Gulf of Mexico. But the glory was not to last; in A.D. 711, Palenque attacked its traditional rival, Toniná, but was unexpectedly defeated by the much smaller kingdom. Palenque's king was captured and

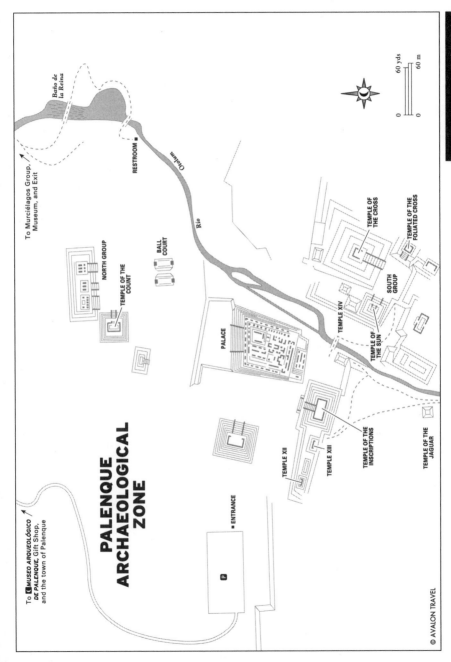

PALENQUE ARCHAEOLOGICAL ZONE

To **MUSEO ARQUEOLÓGICO DE PALENQUE,** Gift Shop, and the town of Palenque

To Murciélagos Group, Museum, and Exit

Baño de la Reina

RESTROOM

Río Otolum

NORTH GROUP

TEMPLE OF THE COUNT

BALL COURT

PALACE

TEMPLE XII

TEMPLE XIII

TEMPLE OF THE INSCRIPTIONS

TEMPLE OF THE JAGUAR

ENTRANCE

P

TEMPLE XIV

TEMPLE OF THE CROSS

TEMPLE OF THE FOLIATED CROSS

SOUTH GROUP

TEMPLE OF THE SUN

0   60 yds
0   60 m

© AVALON TRAVEL

DECIPHERING THE GLYPHS

For years, scholars could not agree whether the fantastic inscriptions found on Maya stelae, codices, and temple walls were anything more than complex records of numbers and dates. Many thought the text was not "real writing," as it did not appear to reproduce spoken language. Even those who believed the writing to be more meaningful despaired at ever reading it.

Mayanist and scholar Michael D. Coe's *Breaking the Maya Code* (Thames and Hudson, 1992) is a fascinating account of the decipherment of Maya hieroglyphics. He describes how, in 1952, a reclusive Russian scholar named Yuri Valentinovich Knorosov made a crucial breakthrough by showing that Maya writing did in fact convey spoken words. Using a rough syllabary recorded by Fray Diego de Landa (the 16th-century bishop who, ironically, is best known for having destroyed numerous Maya texts), Knorosov showed that ancient texts contain common Yucatec Maya words such as *cutz* (turkey) and *tzul* (dog). Interestingly, Knorosov conducted his research from reproductions only, having never held a Maya artifact or visited an ancient temple. (When Knorosov did finally visit Tikal in 1990, Coe says the Russian wasn't very impressed.)

But Knorosov's findings were met with staunch resistance by some of the field's most influential scholars, which delayed progress for decades. By the mid-1980s, however, decipherment picked up speed; one of many standouts from that era is David Stuart, the son of Maya experts, who went to Cobá with his parents at age eight and passed the time copying glyphs and learning Yucatec Maya words from local playmates. As a high school student, he served as chief epigrapher on a groundbreaking exploration in Belize, and at age 18 he received a US$128,000 MacArthur Fellowship (aka "Genius Award") to, as he told Michael Coe, "play around with the glyphs" full-time.

Researchers now know that Maya writing is like most other hieroglyphic systems. What appears at first to be a single glyph can have up to four parts, and the same word can be expressed in pictorial, phonetic, or hybrid form. Depending on context, one symbol can have either a pictorial or phonetic role; likewise, a particular sound can be represented in more than one way. The word cacao is spelled phonetically as "ca-ca-u" but is written with a picture of a fish (*ca*) and a comblike symbol (also *ca,* according to Landa) and followed by -u. One of David Stuart's great insights was that for all its complexity, much of Maya glyphic writing is "just repetitive."

But how do scholars know what the symbols are meant to sound like in the first place? Some come from the Landa alphabet, others are suggested by the pictures that accompany many texts, still others from patterns derived by linguistic analyses of contemporary Maya languages. In some cases, it is simply a hunch that, after applying it to a number of texts, turns out to be right. If this seems like somewhat shaky scientific ground, it is – but not without a means of being proved. The cacao decipherment was confirmed when the same glyph was found on a jar with chocolate residue still inside.

Hundreds of glyphs have been deciphered and most of the known Maya texts can be reliably translated. The effort has lent invaluable insight into Maya civilization, especially dynastic successions and religious beliefs. Some archaeologists lament, not unreasonably, that high-profile glyphic studies divert attention from research into the lives of everyday ancient Maya, who after all far outnumbered the nobility but are not at all represented in the inscriptions. That said, it's impossible not to marvel at how one of the world's great ancient civilizations is revealed in the whorls and creases of fading stone pictures.

killed—described in victorious carvings and texts in Toniná—leaving Palenque in disarray, with no supreme ruler for over a decade. A new king named K'inich Akal Mo' Nab'—presumably a descendant of the Pakal dynasty but possibly not—emerged in A.D. 722, and was succeeded by his son and grandson. Several new structures were commissioned under their reigns, and Palenque appeared to be on the rise once again. However the historical record abruptly ends in A.D. 799, after which the city underwent a rapid and lasting decline, part of a widespread Maya collapse during that period.

The first detailed account of Palenque by Europeans was made by a Spanish army captain, Antonio del Río, who passed through in March 1785. (Two centuries earlier, Hernán Cortés came within a few dozen kilometers of the ruins but apparently never knew they were there.) Del Río drew maps and plans and eventually received a royal order to excavate the site for a year. But the Spaniard's "excavation" was amateur and brutish and led to the destruction of a number of structures. Captain del Río also broadcast wild and fantastic assumptions about the beginnings of the Mayas, and it wasn't long before visions of Palenque as the lost city of Atlantis or a sister civilization to the ancient Egyptians circulated in Europe. A true picture of Palenque didn't emerge until the mid-1800s, when the American diplomat John L. Stephens and English artist Frederick Catherwood visited the site and wrote and drew realistic and detailed accounts of what they saw.

For detailed reports and photos of current and past archaeological digs, check out www.mesoweb.com/palenque.

Temples XII and XIII

Through the entrance you follow a short road and a few steps up to Palenque's main plaza. The first two temples on your right are Temple XII and XIII, known as Funerary Corridor for their deathly ornamentation and content.

Temple XII is also known as Temple of the Skull, so named for the stucco relief of a rabbit skull, visible at the base of one of the pillars on the upper temple, and probably representing

a god of the underworld. (Unfortunately, you can't climb the stairs to get a better look.) In the 1990s, archaeologists uncovered a passageway leading from that same upper patio to a sarcophagus deep in the structure's interior, just as was famously discovered in the site's Temple of the Inscriptions. Inside the tomb were the remains of a leader, as yet unidentified, plus several other bodies, most likely the leader's servants. Alas, the passage and tomb are also off-limits to visitors.

To the left is Temple XIII, which also contains a newly discovered crypt. Dubbed the Tomb of the Red Queen, the three-room chamber has a large stone sarcophagus in which archaeologists discovered the remains of a woman. The woman had been interred with a rich collection of jade jewelry and was covered in cinnabar powder, a prized red pigment, hence the evocative name. The woman's identity hasn't been determined, thanks to the lack of inscriptions of any kind, but archaeologists suspect it was the mother of Pakal the Great, Palenque's most influential leader. The remains of the mysterious Red Queen have been removed, but visitors can see the tomb and sarcophagus (which is itself painted red) via a passageway near the bottom of the stairs. This is not the original entryway, however; it was created to study—and now showcase—the inner tomb. The original entry has not yet been discovered.

Temple of the Inscriptions

Just beyond Temple XIII is the Temple of the Inscriptions, a 24-meter-high (79-foot) pyramid and Palenque's most famous structure. Its name derives from the magnificent glyph-covered tablets found in the spacious temple at its summit, which tell the ancestral history of Palenque's rulers. It was toward the rear of that lofty gallery that Mexican archaeologist Alberto Ruz L'Huillier first uncovered, in 1949, a secret stairway cleverly hidden under a stone slab. The stairs were intentionally jammed with rubble and debris, clearly to prevent access to whatever lay beneath.

It took Ruz three years to excavate the

stairway, which descended in several sections all the way to ground level. At the foot of the stairs Ruz found another sealed passage, in front of which were clay dishes filled with red pigment, jade earplugs, beads, a large oblong pearl, and the skeletons of six sacrificial victims. A final large stone door was removed, and on June 15, 1952, Ruz made what many consider to be the greatest discovery of Maya archaeology: the untouched crypt of Pakal the Great, or K'inich Janaab Pakal, Palenque's most revered leader.

The centerpiece of the chamber is the massive sarcophagus, hewn from a single stone and topped by a flat four-meter-long (13-foot) five-ton slab of stone. The slab is beautifully carved with the figure of Pakal in death, surrounded by monsters, serpents, sun and shell signs, and many more glyphs that recount death and its passage. The walls of the chamber are decorated with various gods, from which scientists have deduced a tremendous amount about the Palencanos' theology.

Working slowly to preserve everything in its pristine state, Ruz didn't open the lid of the sarcophagus for six months. It then took a week of difficult work in the stifling, dust-choked room to finally lift the five-ton slab. On November 28, 1952, the scientists had their first peek inside. In the large rectangular sarcophagus they found another, body-shaped sarcophagus, within which was Pakal's skeleton, with precious jewelry and special accoutrements to accompany him on his journey into the next world. A jade mosaic mask covered the face, under which his teeth had been painted red. (The mask was exhibited at the Museo Nacional de Antropología in Mexico City until December 24, 1985, when it was stolen along with several other precious historical artifacts. The mask was recovered in an abandoned house in Acapulco in 1989, mostly undamaged.)

The excavation of the Temple of the Inscriptions forced a revision of archaeologists' conception and understanding of the ancient Maya. It was long believed that the pyramids had served a single function: to provide a platform for ceremonial temples and rituals to be closer to the heavens. But the discovery of Pakal's tomb revealed that pyramids were used as tombs for revered leaders as well, and numerous other such temple-crypts have since been discovered.

The Temple of the Inscriptions and the passageway to Pakal's tomb have been closed for several years; erosion caused by hundreds of thousands of visitors had become increasingly severe. In fact, access to major structures has been restricted at many Maya sites, including Uxmal, Chichén Itzá, and Tulum, with no sign of reopening any time soon.

The Palace

Palenque's palace is one of the Maya world's most compelling and impressive complexes. Built atop a platform 10 meters (33 feet) high and covering an area larger than a city block, it is composed of thirteen vaulted "houses," four enclosed patios, and three spacious underground arcades. It was built in phases over the course of nearly four centuries, and served as residential quarters for the city's elite and as an exclusive administrative and ceremonial center. The iconic tower is singular in Maya architecture—only a handful of minor tower-like structures even compare—and archaeologists have speculated that it was built to provide a ceremonial observation point of the winter solstice (December 22), when the sun appears to drop directly into the Temple of the Inscriptions. It may also have been used to make astronomical calculations, an important part of Maya religious rites, or simply as a watchtower. Unfortunately, the top of the tower had collapsed by the time it was rediscovered, so the structure's original height and appearance—and therefore function—could only be guessed from the pattern of rubble.

Two sunken patios on the palace's northern half are each dedicated to a different purpose. The Patio of the Captives, in the northeast corner, contains large stone panels depicting important prisoners captured in war; notice how each has his hand on the opposite shoulder, a common gesture of submission.

THE MAYA COLLAPSE

Something went terribly wrong for the Maya between the years A.D. 800 and A.D. 900. Hundreds of Classic Maya cities were abandoned, monarchies disappeared, and the population fell by millions, mainly by death and plummeting birth rates. The collapse was widespread but was most dramatic in the Southern Lowlands, a swath of tropical forest stretching from the Gulf of Mexico to Honduras and including once-glorious cities such as Palenque, Tikal, and Copán. (Archaeologists first suspected a collapse after noticing a sudden drop-off in inscriptions; it has been confirmed through excavations of peasant dwellings from before and after that period.)

There are many theories for the collapse, varying from climate change and epidemic diseases to foreign invasion and peasant revolt. In his carefully argued book *The Fall of the Ancient Maya* (Thames and Hudson, 2002), archaeologist and professor of anthropology at Pennsylvania State University David Webster suggests that it was a series of conditions, rather than a single event, that led to the collapse.

To a certain degree, it was the very success of Maya cities during the Classic era that set the stage for their demise. Webster points to a population boom just before the collapse, which would have left agricultural lands dangerously depleted just as demand spiked. Classic-era farming techniques were ill-suited to meet the challenge; in particular, the lack of draft animals kept productivity low, meaning Maya farmers could not generate large surpluses of corn and other food. (Even if they could, storage was difficult given the hot, humid climate.) The lack of animals also limited how far away farmers could cultivate land and still be able to transport their crops to the city center; as a result, available land was overused. As Webster puts it, "too many farmers [growing] too many crops on too much of the landscape" left the Classic Maya world acutely vulnerable to an environmental catastrophe, such as drought or crop disease.

Certain kingdoms reached their tipping point before others (prompting some to launch eleventh-hour military campaigns against weakened rivals), but few escaped the wave of malnutrition, disease, lower birthrates, and outright starvation that seems to have swept across the Maya world in the 9th century. Kings and nobility would have faced increasing unrest and insurrection – after all, their legitimacy was based on their ability to induce the gods to bestow rain, fertility, and prosperity – further destabilizing the social structure and food supply.

The collapse was not universal, of course, and the fall of lowland powers (like Palenque and Yaxchilán) gave other city-states an opportunity to expand and gain influence (like Tenam Puente and Chinkultik). But the Maya world was dramatically and permanently changed by it; the grand cities built by the Classic Maya were abandoned to the jungle, most never to be reoccupied, and the population plummeted. As Webster notes, "[Hernán] Cortés and his little army almost starved in 1525 while crossing a wilderness that had supported millions of people seven centuries earlier."

In the northwest corner, the smaller Patio of Warrior Chiefs is believed to have served as a meeting place for military leaders. Pillars facing into this patio have remnants of stucco moldings depicting figures in elaborate militaristic regalia.

The southern half of the palace is more residential and ceremonial in nature, with enclosed rooms and small tidy patios. In the southwest corner, two holes marked with notched stones probably served as toilets, and are connected to a surprisingly sophisticated drainage and plumbing system built beneath the stone floors. It still works, too—after heavy rain, maintenance works sweep standing water into the holes to drain it out. Also look for a narrow flight of stairs leading down into a maze of underground rooms that likely served as royal sleeping quarters.

Dividing the southwest and southeast

sections is the palace's most notable temple, the Casa de Ascensión de Poder (House of Enthronement). It was here that Palenque's supreme *ahau* (high lord or kings) were officially throned, likely in elaborate ceremonies attended by a small cadre of religious, military, and political leaders. On the western exterior wall is the Oval Tablet, which depicts the city's best-known ruler, Pakal the Great, receiving the insignias of power from his mother in A.D. 615. Also look for paintings of flowers on the same wall—they're originals.

Even the palace's exterior facades are fascinating, and easy to miss while exploring the labyrinthine interior. The West Gallery, atop a long bank of stairs facing the main plaza, has six stout pillars, four of which are still decorated with large stucco reliefs. A plaque at one end describes what's depicted there, including a man holding a serpent and dancing with a woman dressed in a traditional *huipil* and an incarnation of Chaac, the god of rain, decapitating captives. The East Gallery has similarly elaborate relief carvings, including several circular frames that probably contained images of assorted gods (but which were destroyed or looted long ago). A dramatic triple-layered vaulted archway leads into the Patio of the Captives.

South Group

Across a small stream from the Temple of the Inscriptions and the palace, the South Group, also known as the Crosses Group, rises from an elevated bluff. The group contains three temples, all built during the reign of Kan Balam, the son and heir of Pakal the Great.

The largest and most prominent structure in the group is the **Temple of the Cross,** standing atop a nine-level pyramid-like base and crowned by a grand roof comb. Inside the upper structure—unfortunately you are not permitted to climb the stairs—is a shrine where archaeologists discovered a remarkable relief carving relating the ascension of Kan Balam to the throne, and his place among a long line of rulers. In the carving, Kan Balam is pictured with his father, Pakal the Great, on either side of an ornate "world-tree," a stylized

cross symbolizing a sacred ceiba tree, which in Maya cosmology joins the corporal world to the mythic upper and lower realms. Pakal is dressed in funerary clothes, suggesting he has already died, and indeed the text describes Kan Balam visiting his deceased father to receive the accoutrements of power. The two figures are flanked by extensive hieroglyphic text telling of ancestors, gods, and former rulers, meant to legitimize Kan Balam's claim to power. Side panels depict Kan Balam wearing the full paraphernalia of royalty after his accession as well as a wizened figure archaeologists classify as God-L, a lord of the underworld, shown smoking a cigar and wearing an owl-feather headdress. Archaeologists also discovered a major tomb at the base of the Temple of the Cross, containing the headless body of an official, perhaps the governor of a neighboring city, and hundreds of pieces of jade. They also found a collection of extremely fine ceramic figurines and incense burners, many of which are on display in the museum.

On the South Group's east side, a winding path leads up a steep incline to the **Temple of the Foliated Cross.** The structure is much deteriorated, but notable for the large keyhole-shaped niches in the corners of its upper facade. And like the Temple of the Sun, the enclosed gallery contains a terrific relief carving depicting Kan Balam assuming kingly power and duties from his deceased father, this time in the form of a bloodletting tool. The cross between them is adorned with corn leaves (hence the temple's name), symbolizing life and the birth of mankind, and a striking forward-facing deity representing rebirth.

The **Temple of the Sun** is the smallest of the three temples, but in many ways the best preserved. Built atop a modest platform on the grouping's west side—climbing is prohibited here as well—its pillars, facade, and roof comb have elaborate stucco decoration. Although you can't see it from below, the temple contains yet another relief carving depicting Kan Balam and Pakal the Great at the former's enthronement. Instead of a cross between them, however, there is a disk-like shield, held up by two kneeling deities and representing the sun and warfare.

The Ball Court and North Group

A large grassy plaza on the palace's north side is flanked by several structures. Closest to the palace is Palenque's ball court, notable for its I-shaped playing area and believed to have doubled as a site for ritual sacrifices. Perpendicular to the ball court is the North Group, made up of five temples, most quite deteriorated. Temple II is the best preserved, a sturdy stone structure crowning a terraced platform; at the foot of the stairs is a well-preserved stucco molding depicting Tláloc, a deity most likely introduced to the Maya by emissaries from the great central Mexican city of Teotihuacán, near present-day Mexico City. Finally, the Temple of the Count is a similarly stout structure atop a supporting pyramid, so-named for Jean-Fréderic Waldeck, an eccentric French count who lived there in the early 1830s, and whose embellished drawings and wild speculations

fostered lasting misconceptions of the Maya, especially regarding an alleged connection to ancient Egypt.

A well-marked path leads from the palace, past the Ball Court, and down a steep hillside to the main road. Along the way you'll pass the **Grupo Murciélagos** (Bats Group), a maze of low foundations that most likely served as elite residential quarters, and **Baño de la Reina** (Queen's Bath), a scenic waterfall and pool; swimming is no longer permitted, however. This is a good way to exit the ruins (assuming you came by *combi*)—the path emerges from the trees not far from Palenque's museum.

◖ Museo Arqueológico de Palenque

After you see the ruins, be sure to leave time to visit Palenque's museum (10 A.M.–4:30 P.M. Tues.–Sun.), which contains a truly incredible collection of stucco and stone artifacts found at Palenque, including ornate incense burners and perfectly preserved relief carvings and

© LIZA PRADO

Palenque's must-see museum includes stellar artifacts like this panel of hieroglyphics, plus ornate vases, masks, and more.

DETOUR: COMALCALCO

If you're headed to Chiapas from the Yucatán Peninsula, or just can't get enough of Mexico's ancient ruins (we feel your pain), the state of Tabasco makes for a quick and rewarding detour. There you'll find the Maya ruins of Comalcalco, notable for being constructed of adobe-like brick instead of stone, and located just an hour beyond the state capital of Villahermosa and three hours from Palenque. Comalcalco is also the heart of chocolate country, and you can visit working plantations to learn how cacao is grown and processed.

COMALCALCO ARCHAEOLOGICAL ZONE

The ruins (8 A.M.–5 P.M. daily, US$4) are set in a lush agricultural area a short distance from a small town of the same name. The site's earliest structures date to around A.D. 250 and are large mounds made from dirt mixed with crushed oyster shells for strength and cohesion. Around A.D. 500-700 distinctive bricks were developed as an alternative to stone, which is rare and difficult to quarry in Tabasco's swampy environment. The bricks were made of a mixture of dirt and crushed oyster shells and fired in kilns; they were then used to cover and expand the earlier packed-dirt temples and in some cases incised with designs, including animals, humans, glyphs, and patterns.

Temple 1, the immense structure on the left as you walk in from the entrance, has the best remaining example of the stucco high relief that once covered most of the structures. Look for the animal figures along the pyramid's southeast corner as well as a molded skull about halfway up the main stairway. Opposite Temple 1, the **Great Acropolis** is 80 meters (260 feet) long and has a stucco mask of Kinich Ahau, the sun god. To the right, walk up a hill to the **Palace,** which reveals a panoramic view of the countryside, including unexcavated mounds and a chocolate plantation in the distance.

A small but interesting **museum** sits at the entrance to the site. Inside you'll find excellent artifacts as well as a few human skeletons found by workers while excavating the site.

CHOCOLATE HACIENDAS

About half a kilometer (0.3 mile) beyond the road to the ruins, **Finca Cholula** (Carr. Comalcalco-Paraíso, tel. 933/334-3815, www.fincacholula.com.mx, 9 A.M.–4 P.M. Tues.-Sun., US$3.50) offers an interesting hour-long guided tour of its cacao plantation. You'll stroll through the orchard, then visit the factory where the cacao seeds are processed and turned into chocolate candies.

PRACTICALITIES

In Villahermosa, **Comalli Plus** (Calle Reforma at Calle Bravo) and **Transportes Torruco**

hieroglyphic panels, with excellent explanations in both Spanish and English. It's not a huge museum—an hour should suffice—but absolutely worth visiting, and for many people a highlight of their visit to Palenque. A new exhibit called "The Tomb of Pakal" includes a life-size reproduction of the sarcophagus and elaborately carved lid, installed in an exact replica of the crypt made of Plexiglas so you can see through to appreciate its unique design. (It's more effective than it sounds.) Professionally produced videos and wall displays describe the tomb's discovery and explain the symbols and imagery found within. Two gift shops at Palenque's museum have reasonably good selections of books and locally produced *artesanía.*

Admission to the museum is included with admission to the ruins—be sure to hang on to your ticket! Also note that although the ruins are open daily, the museum is closed on Monday.

Practicalities

The archaeological site is open 8 A.M.–5 P.M. daily (US$4.75, free after 4 P.M., last entry at 4:30 P.M.). The museum is open 10 A.M.–4:30 P.M. Tuesday to Sunday only. Guides

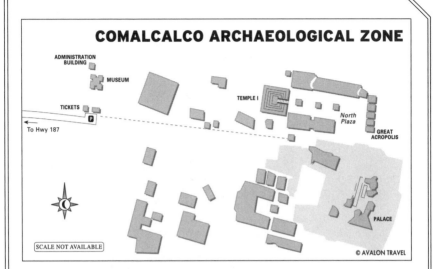

COMALCALCO ARCHAEOLOGICAL ZONE

ADMINISTRATION BUILDING

MUSEUM

TICKETS

P

To Hwy 187

TEMPLE I

North Plaza

GREAT ACROPOLIS

PALACE

SCALE NOT AVAILABLE

© AVALON TRAVEL

(Calle Reforma at La Arboleda) provide identical service to and from Comalcalco, from terminals a block apart near the ADO bus station. Vans run every 20 minutes 4:30 A.M.–9 P.M. daily (US$2.25, 45 mins).

To get to the ruins, take any bus headed north on Carretera Comalcalco–Paraíso (US$0.50, 10 mins). From the highway drop-off, it's about a 10-minute walk to the entrance of the ruins. Finca Cholula is about 500 meters (0.3 mile) further down the main road. A cab from town to either place costs about US$3.

Comalcalco's best hotel is **Hotel Plaza Broca** (Blvd. Adolfo López Mateos at Nicolas Bravo, tel. 933/334-4060, US$24-29 s/d with a/c), offering simple but very clean lodging in the heart of town. All rooms have air-conditioning and cable TV, and there's a private parking garage to boot. Villahermosa has many more options, in all price ranges.

can be hired at the entrance to the ruins; official trained guides charge US$85 for a two-hour tour in English or US$60 in Spanish, or you can test your luck with one of the freelance guides hanging out near the entrance, who charge US$20–25 for a somewhat shorter tour, and who typically speak Spanish only.

Palenque is technically part of a national park, and there's a park-service gate a kilometer or so before reaching the ruins; admission is US$2 per person. There is parking at the ruins, although on busy days drivers end up parking well down the access road.

It is possible to enter the archaeological site at a smaller gate just past the museum, but from there it's a steep uphill walk to the main structures. A better idea, if you're arriving by *combi*, is to enter at the main gate and exit through the lower one, where it's just a short walk to the museum.

MUSEO DEL TEXTIL

The Museo del Textil (central plaza, 9 A.M.–1 P.M. and 5–9 P.M. Mon.–Fri., US$0.50) is a small museum in the heart of Palenque town showcasing the variety of traditional dress found throughout Chiapas. Each

outfit is displayed on a mannequin with signage explaining a bit about its background—the material used, the time it took to create, the town or region where it's worn, the language spoken, and some population stats. Signage is in Spanish only.

ACCOMMODATIONS

Hotels in Palenque proper tend to be quite bare-bones, adequate for a night or two while visiting the area but not especially pleasant. The advantage is having easy access to the bus terminal and tour agencies, plus banks, Internet, and restaurants. In the northwest corner of town, a neighborhood called La Cañada has better lodging options in a more serene setting, but is somewhat less convenient thanks to a longish walk into town. (That may be improved, however, with a new shortcut that's reportedly being built.) There are also several pleasant mid- and high-end resorts on the road to the ruins, and a neighborhood called El Panchán, nestled in the forest, with eco-minded accommodations and a distinctly bohemian air. Getting back and forth to town can be somewhat inconvenient if you don't have a car, especially at night after *combi* service ends; then again, the relaxing atmosphere may convince you there's not much reason to go into town anyway.

In Town
UNDER US$25
Posada Kin (Abasolo near Calle 5 de Mayo, tel. 916/345-1714, posada_kin@hotmail.com, US$20–23 s, US$23–26 d) is a charming place offering white tiled rooms with stenciling on the walls. Each has a private bathroom, fan, and decent bed. Those at the front of the building have tiny balconies, which let in a good breeze. It's a simple but nice place to stay.

The no-frills **Posada Canek** (Av. 20 de Noviembre near Abasolo, tel. 916/345-0150, posada_canek@hotmail.com, US$7.50 dorm, US$15 s, US$20 d) offers a decent dorm option with twin and queen beds (no bunks here!) set up in spacious rooms. All include sheets, towel, soap, and toilet paper. The only bummer here

is that there is only one fan per room—arrive early to get the bed nearest to it. There are no lockers, but small safes at the reception desk are assigned to each guest to store their valuables. If this is full, try the dorm at Posada Shalom II (Corregidora at Calle Abasolo, tel. 916/345-2641, US$8 pp).

US$25-50
An excellent deal if you don't mind the longish walk into town, **Hotel Posada Quiroga** (Av. Manuel Velasco Suárez 77, tel. 916/345-0174, US$25–35 s/d) has spotless if somewhat sterile rooms, with cheery lime-green paint inside and out; all have comfy beds, TV, and air-conditioning but no Internet. Definitely ask for a 2nd-floor unit, as they're larger and brighter. Parking and complimentary coffee are included. The market area east of there is a bit dodgy, especially at night—better to walk along the highway to get to and from town (there's a sidewalk).

Posada Ysolina (Av. Manuel Velasco Suárez 51, tel. 916/345-1524, US$25/US$30 s with fan/air, US$28–35 d with fan, US$35–38 d with a/c) is across the street and virtually identical in category. It has clean tidy rooms decorated with simple Mexican furniture, *talavera* tiles, and stenciled walls. Rooms 5, 6, 12, and 13 have corner balconies and better light; others are a bit dimly lit but otherwise perfectly comfortable. The lone "suite" is more spacious, but located right behind the reception desk. There are TVs and parking, but no Internet; coffee and bread are available each morning in the lobby.

Hotel Lacandonia (Calle Allende at Av. Hidalgo, 916/345-0057, hotel-lacondia@hotmail.com, US$40 s with a/c, $45 d with a/c) faces a hectic and somewhat grubby street corner but offers surprisingly comfortable and tasteful rooms, making it one of Palenque's best values. Rooms have new mattresses, with pretty iron lattice headboards and matching vanities. All have air-conditioning and cable TV, and those facing Avenida Hidalgo have small balconies as well. The hotel café is also unexpectedly appealing, with an upstairs section that offers a bit of separation from the bustle of traffic outside. The upside to the location is that *combis* to the ruins are across the street, and those to Agua Azul/Misol-Há and Bonampak/Yaxchilán just around the corner.

Hotel Chablis (Calle Merle Green 7, Barrio La Cañada, tel. 916/345-0870, toll-free Mex. tel. 800/714-4710, www.hotelchablis.com, US$48 s/d with a/c) is a simpler, less expensive alternative to its sister hotel, the Maya Tulipanes, just up the street. Rooms in the new section have tile floors, two queen beds, modern bathrooms and amenities, and small balconies, albeit facing the street. All have cable TV, air-conditioning, and free wireless Internet. (The older rooms aren't recommended, thanks to saggy king beds and a musty smell.) The reception area doubles as an open-air lounge, with armchairs and a high *palapa* roof. During low season guests can use the pool at the Maya Tulipanes.

Posada Shalom I (Av. Juárez btwn. Calles Allende and Aldama, tel. 916/345-0944, www .hotelesshalom.com, US$25–30 s/d, US$35–40 s/d with a/c) is in the heart of downtown and offers sparse, clean rooms with hot-water bathrooms and cable TV. Most have windows that open onto an interior hallway, so units are dark but quiet. If it's full, try its sister hotel, **Posada Shalom II** (Corregidora at Calle Abasolo, tel. 916/345-2641), which has almost identical prices and facilities and a bare-bones dorm (US$8 pp) with 15 queen beds and just two fans for the lot; BYO towel, soap, and toilet paper.

Once you get past the dingy lobby at **Hotel Avenida** (Av. Juárez 173, dmarcohj@hotmail .com, US$20 s, US$25 d, US$30 s with a/c, US$35 d with a/c), you'll see the main reason to stay here: the well-kempt free-form pool with a jungle backdrop. It makes a great place to relax and cool off after a day at the ruins. Rooms themselves are simple, all with television and screened windows. The best rooms are in the back, most with a private porch overlooking onto the thick forest.

US$50-100

Maya Tulipanes (Calle Merle Green 6, Barrio La Cañada, tel. 916/345-0201, www.maya tulipanes.com.mx, US$75–90 s/d) is a large modern hotel with excellent service and a prime location. Rooms are a bit sterile but perfectly comfortable and the leafy forest setting of La Cañada is a definite plus. Amenities include air-conditioning, cable TV, in-room telephones, and free wireless Internet, and the hotel has a small pool and children's play area, a good restaurant, and secure parking. Tour groups often stay here, but it typically doesn't affect the service that independent guests receive, other than some hustle and bustle at breakfast. It's a fine choice, budget permitting.

Hotel Xibalba (Calle Merle Green 9, Barrio La Cañada, tel. 916/345-0411, www .hotelxibalba.com, US$55 s/d) is La Cañada's best small hotel, with modern comfortable rooms, friendly personalized service, and a recommended restaurant. Rates have jumped, so it's not the hands-down top pick it used to be, but still a good mid-range value. All rooms have a/c, fans, Wi-Fi, and small flat-screen TVs; those in the main building are reasonably spacious with low-key decor, save those curiously robust stone mantels. A second building has a high Maya-esque entryway, and rooms that are smaller but with a certain coziness and isolation that some guests prefer. The upper floors in both buildings get better light, and are worth requesting.

Hotel Chan-Kah Centro (central plaza, Av. Juárez at Independencia, tel. 916/345-0318, www.chan-kah.com.mx, US$47 s with a/c, US$53 d with a/c) is a modern hotel offering pleasant accommodations with whitewashed brick walls and stone-inlaid floors; some also have balconies overlooking the central plaza, which is nice for people-watching and even nicer for the breeze. All the rooms have air-conditioning and cable TV. Wireless Internet is available in the 2nd-floor rooms and the lobby too.

OVER US$100

Located on 50 acres of lush grounds, **Misión**

Palenque (Periférico Oriente s/n, tel. 916/345-0241, toll-free Mex. tel. 800/900-3800, www.hotelesmision.com.mx, US$151 s/d with a/c) is the most upscale hotel in town. It boasts a full-service spa, lighted tennis courts, two pools, and a *palapa*-roof restaurant with an international menu. The 180 rooms are spread out over two floors, all opening onto open-air walkways. They're comfortable and sparse, with splashes of color here and there. Be sure to ask for one of the remodeled ones when you reserve. There also is complimentary shuttle to and from the ruins.

Near the Ruins
UNDER US$25

Named after the welcoming owner, **Chato's Cabañas** (El Panchán, Carr. Ruinas Km. 4.5, www.elpanchan.com, US$16 s, US$20 d) offers *cabañas* of various sizes and styles, all set deep in the jungle of El Panchán. All have private bath and fans. Be sure to ask for a newer *cabaña,* as the older ones are showing their age.

Although it sounds like a Vegas casino, **Jungle Palace** (El Panchán, Carr. Ruinas Km. 4.5, www.elpanchan.com, US$10 s with shared bathroom, US$12 d with shared bathroom, US$15 s, US$20 d) is a *cabaña* hotel offering 18 basic units in a manicured section of the jungle. Some have porches and hammocks that overlook a gurgling river, which is especially relaxing after a day at the ruins. During the rainy season, stay elsewhere—the river often overflows, flooding the grounds.

If El Panchán isn't quite your scene but you'd like to stay near the action, consider staying across the highway at **Cabañas El Jaguar** (Carr. Ruinas Km. 4.5, tel. 916/103-1983, www.elpanchan.com, US$10 s with shared bathroom, US$12 d with shared bathroom, US$16 s, US$20 d). Although not as alluring as sleeping in the thick of the jungle, the *cabañas* are modern and comfortable and the cleared grounds offer spectacular stargazing.

If every penny counts and you don't mind a little grime, try **El Mono Blanco del Panchán**

© LIZA PRADO

The entrance to the national park that houses Palenque Archaeological Zone is just beyond the boho community of El Panchán.

(El Panchán, Carr. Ruinas Km. 4.5, US$3 pp hammock, US$3 pp camping, US$4–5 dorm, US$10 s with shared bathroom, US$15 d with shared bathroom, US$15 s, US$20 d). Offering a wide range of very rustic accommodations, it's best as a place to just hang your hammock. Dorm rooms include a locker, toilet paper, and soap.

US$25-50

Margarita and Ed (El Panchán, Carr. Ruinas Km. 4.5, tel. 916/348-4205, US$24–26 s/d *cabañas,* US$27 s/d, US$36 s/d with a/c) is a good option if you like being in the wild but prefer modern comforts. Rooms are reminiscent of a mid-range hotel room in town—tile everywhere, spotless bathrooms, decent beds, and fans or air-conditioning—and not much else. A couple of rustic *cabañas* are also available near the entrance—for the price, however, you're better off elsewhere.

Just 2.5 kilometers from the ruins, **Mayabell** (Carr. Ruinas Km. 5.5, tel. 916/348-4271, www.mayabell.com.mx, US$2 pp hammock, US$4 pp camping, US$15 trailer, US$25 s/d with shared bathroom, US$55 s/d, US$75 s/d with a/c) has shady grounds and super-mellow atmosphere, plus great options for budget and mid-range travelers alike. A string of open-air *palapas* serve for tents and hammocks, while RVs park on a grassy area near the entrance. *Cabañas* with private bath (and optional a/c) are surprisingly pleasant, with low comfortable beds, small shady patios, and a creek burbling nearby. The restaurant serves ample well-priced meals and has live music every night. A large swimming pool is in serious need of resurfacing, but it still hits the spot on hot muggy days.

OVER US$50

Palenque's most upscale accommodations are at █ **Chan-Kah Resort Village** (Carr. Ruinas Km. 3, tel. 916/345-1134, toll-free Mex. tel. 800/714-3247, www.chan-kah.com .mx, US$145 s/d with a/c), boasting 83 spacious *casitas* in a manicured jungle setting. The units have stone-encrusted floors, shaded patios with chairs, new firm beds, and large bathrooms, and modern amenities like mini-air-conditioners, flat-screen TVs, and wireless Internet. Families or foursomes might consider booking a "suite," which means two identical rooms with connecting doors and a large shared sitting room in back. The resort's huge main pool and restaurant-bar area are oddly ostentatious, but units at the rear of the property (Nos. 71 through 83) and a smaller second pool exude the natural peacefulness of their surroundings.

Hotel La Aldea (Carr. Ruinas Km. 2.8, tel. 916/345-1693, www.hotel-la-aldea.com.mx, US$75 s/d with a/c) is a decent mid-range option on the road to the ruins, not as expensive as Chan-Kah, but less rustic (and less likely to be booked up) than most hotels in El Panchán. Set on a forested hillside, the *cabañas* are spacious, with air-conditioning, high ceilings, and shaded patios with hammocks. Unfortunately they're squeezed too close together, and details like hard beds, dim lighting, and unreliable hot water can add up. The hotel was undergoing a major renovation at the time of research, removing older cabins, upgrading the restaurant, and installing a large new pool, all of which will help the overall value.

FOOD

As with hotels, Palenque has a large but not particularly inspiring selection of restaurants. With a few exceptions, most offer standard Mexican dishes at moderate prices.

In Town

Restaurante Maya (Av. Independencia at Av. Hidalgo, tel. 916/345-0042, www.maya restaurante.com, 7 A.M.–11 P.M. daily, US$4–12) is an old standby, with bright tablecloths and a mural of Palenque on the back wall. Reputation lets it get away with somewhat inflated prices, but the location facing the plaza is good and the meals—standard chicken, fish, and beef dishes—reliable. A classy sister restaurant of the same name in the La Cañada neighborhood has similar fare plus live marimba music most nights.

◖ Las Tinajas (Calle 20 de Noviembre at Calle Abasolo, 7 A.M.–11 P.M. daily, US$5–10) is one of the better options in town. In addition to standard fish, chicken, and beef dishes, there are also pasta dishes, sandwiches, and salads. The main dining area is right on the corner with tables looking onto both streets. Portions are hefty—*jarras* (pitchers) of fruit drinks are a good deal for the very, very thirsty.

Lakan-Ha (Av. Juárez btwn. Calles Abasolo and Independencia, 7:30 A.M.–10 P.M. daily, US$4–10) is a breakfast favorite, with a variety of inexpensive combo plates, but it can be counted on for a decent, reasonably priced meal anytime. The pleasant dining room is on the 2nd floor, away from the hubbub on Avenida Juárez.

If you're tired of Mexican food, **Pizzería Palenque** (Av. Juárez near Calle Allende, tel. 916/345-0332, 1–11 P.M. daily, US$8–15) offers decent pies in a breezy locale. The selection is standard pizzería—vegetarian, meat lovers, Hawaiian—so you're sure to find one that's appealing, or at least familiar. Delivery is available.

In La Cañada, the restaurant at **Hotel Xibalba** (Calle Merle Green 9, tel. 916/345-0411, 7 A.M.–10:30 P.M. daily, US$4–12) has a variety of vegetarian, Italian, and Mexican dishes, all well prepared and graciously served. The heavy wood tables and chairs are set up somewhat incongruously in the hotel's reception area, but it remains a peaceful, low-key spot. In high season, the restaurant across the street occasionally has live marimba music, which can be heard quite well here (and on the entire block, for that matter).

Also in La Cañada, **Cafetos Café** (corner of Calle Merle Green and 6a Calle Pte., 7 A.M.–11 P.M. daily, US$2–8) is technically part of Maya Tulipanes, but isn't your typical hotel coffee shop. Stainless-steel tables and chairs, free Wi-Fi, and a long menu of drinks, sandwiches, and other snacks—not to mention a separate corner entrance—give it a youthful, independent air.

On the highway next to the Super Che grocery store, **Plaza Chulavista** (5a Av. Nte. Pte.

at Hwy. 199, no phone, 8 A.M.–10 P.M. daily) is a tiny commercial center with a food court on the 2nd floor, including a coffee shop and pizza place. More importantly, it's air-conditioned and has public restrooms and a small indoor children's play area (up to five years old)—it's not much, but the only such place in town.

Near the Ruins

◖ Café Restaurante Don Mucho (El Panchán, Carr. Ruinas Km. 4.5, tel. 916/341-8209, 7 A.M.–midnight daily, US$3–12) is a popular spot in the jungle neighborhood of El Panchán. Italian and Mexican dishes fill the menu, mostly homemade pastas, wood-oven pizzas, and *comida típica*. There's often live music and fire dancers too, which keeps the place hopping 8–11 P.M.

Mayabell (Carr. Ruinas Km. 5.5, tel. 916/348-4271, www.mayabell.com.mx, 8 A.M.–9 P.M. daily, US$5–10) is a short walk from Palenque's site museum and a great spot for lunch after a long morning visiting the ruins. Order at the counter from a menu that ranges from spaghetti to sandwiches to grilled chicken and beef. Portions are generous, and there are plenty of vegetarian options. A *jarra* (jug) of cold fruit juice is a bargain at just US$4, and a godsend on hot muggy days.

Groceries

Super Che (5a Av. Nte. Pte. at Hwy. 199, no phone, 7 A.M.–10 P.M. daily) is the name given "small" Chedraui supermarkets, though by any other standard this is a huge store, with fruit, veggies, canned goods, nonperishables, and more.

INFORMATION AND SERVICES
Tourist Information

The state tourist office (Av. Juárez at Abasolo, tel. 916/345-0356, 9 A.M.–9 P.M. Mon.–Sat., 9 A.M.–1 P.M. Sun.) hands out decent maps and can answer basic questions. The city tourism office (9 A.M.–9 P.M. Mon.–Sat., 9 A.M.–1 P.M. Sun.) is operated out of a kiosk on the central plaza; service here is hit or miss.

Emergency Services

The **Hospital General** (Av. Juárez s/n, tel. 916/345-1443, 24 hours) is just west of the bus station. For meds, try **Farmacia Similares** (Av. Juárez at Calle Allende, tel. 916/345-2250, 8 A.M.–9 P.M. daily), which is well stocked. The **police station** (Av. Independencia near Hidalgo, tel. 916/345-0141, toll-free Mex. tel. 066, 24 hours) is in the Palacio Municipal.

Money

Located on Avenida Juárez, **Bancomer** (8:30 A.M.–4 P.M. Mon.–Fri., 9 A.M.–4 P.M. Sat.) and **Banamex** (9 A.M.–4 P.M. Mon.–Fri.) have reliable ATMs.

Media and Communications

The **post office** (Av. Independencia at Calle Bravo) is open 9 A.M.–6 P.M. Monday–Friday and 9 A.M.–1 P.M. on Saturday. For Internet, **Internet Online** (Av. Benito Juárez btwn. 1a and 2a Calles Sur, 8 A.M.–10 P.M. daily) is one of myriad Internet cafés in town, charging US$0.80 an hour. Computers are loaded with Skype and the major messaging programs. For telephone calls, try the **Caseta Telefónica** (Artesanía El Yugo, Av. Juárez near Calle Allende, 7 A.M.–10:30 P.M. daily), which charges US$0.20 for calls to the U.S. and Canada and US$0.50 everywhere else.

In El Panchán there is just one **Internet café** (El Panchán, Carr. Ruinas Km. 4.5, 10 A.M.–10 P.M. Mon.–Sat., 2–10 P.M. Sun., US$1.50/hr). There is no place to make calls out there.

Travel Agencies

A great many travel outfits want your business in this town. Almost all offer the same tours at pretty much the same prices—none, however, include guides or entrance fees. The most popular trips are to Misol-Há, Agua Clara, and Agua Azul (US$10–15 pp, 9 A.M.–4:30 P.M.); day trips to Bonampak and Yaxchilán ruins (US$50–60 pp, 6 A.M.–7:30 P.M.); and two-day excursions to Bonampak, Yaxchilán, and the Lancandón forest (US$100–110 pp, including meals and lodging).

Tour operators also offer combination trips, such as a morning tour of Palenque ruins followed by an afternoon at Misol-Há and Agua Azul (US$12–15 pp). Convenient drop-off tours include spending the day visiting Bonampak and Yaxchilán, spending the night near the border, then the following morning taking a 30-minute boat ride to Betel, Guatemala, where a shuttle takes you to Flores (US$100–110 pp, including all transport, meals, and lodging).

In town, reliable operators include **Na Chan Kan** (next to Hotel Avenida, Av. Juárez s/n, tel. 916/345-0263, www.nachankan.com, 6 A.M.–10 P.M. daily), **Kukulcán Travel Agency** (Av. Juárez 8 next to the bus station, tel. 916/345-1506, www.kukulcantravel.com, 7 A.M.–10 P.M. daily), and **Transporte Chambalú** (Av. Miguel Hidalgo btwn. 3a and 4a Calle Pte. Nte., tel. 916/345-2849, 7 A.M.–9 P.M. daily). In El Panchán, **El Mono Blanco del Panchán** (El Panchán, Carr. Ruinas Km. 4.5, 7 A.M.–10 P.M. daily) has a travel agency that books the same tours, at the same prices, as those offered in town. Look for it under a *palapa* facing the hotel's café.

Laundry and Storage

Lavandería Mundo Maya (Calle Jiménez near Av. 20 de Noviembre, 8 A.M.–9:30 P.M. Mon.–Sat., 10 A.M.–3:30 P.M. Sun., US$1 per 1 kg/2.2 lbs) offers same-day service if you bring your clothes in early.

In El Panchán, **Jungle Palace Lavandería** (El Panchán, Carr. Ruinas Km. 4.5, 7 A.M.–3 P.M. Mon.–Sat.) provides laundry service for US$2.50 per three kilograms (6.6 pounds).

There is **storage service** at the bus station (Av. Juárez s/n, tel. 916/345-1344, 6 A.M.–10 P.M. daily) for US$0.50 per bag per hour.

GETTING THERE
Air

The tiny Palenque International Airport (PQM) is located about five kilometers (3 miles) north of town; there was no regular passenger service there at the time of research.

Bus

The ADO bus terminal (Av. Juárez s/n, tel. 916/345-1344) is about 100 meters (328 feet) from the turnoff to the Palenque ruins. Tickets can be purchased at the terminal or at **Ticket Bus** (central plaza, tel. 961/345-5302, toll-free Mex. tel. 800/702-8000, www.ticketbus.com .mx, 8 A.M.–10 P.M. daily). Destinations include:

- Campeche: (US$23, 5–5.5 hrs) 8 A.M., 9 P.M., 10 P.M.

- Cancún: (US$53, 12.5–13.5 hrs) 5:20 P.M., 7:35 P.M., 8 P.M., 8:35 P.M., and 9 P.M.*

- Mérida: (US$34, 7.5–8 hrs) 8 A.M., 9 P.M., 10 P.M., and 11:25 P.M.

- Mexico City: (US$70–72, 10–11 hrs) 6:30 P.M. (TAPO) and 9 P.M. (Norte)

- Ocosingo: (US$7.60–9, 2.5 hrs) take any San Cristóbal bus

- San Cristóbal: (US$12–14.60, 5 hrs) 4:35 A.M., 6:50 A.M.*, 8:50 A.M., 9 A.M., 11:40 A.M. and 2:10 P.M.; 11 P.M.–2 A.M. departures not recommended for safety reasons

- Villahermosa: (US$9.50, 2–2.5 hrs) 10 departures 7 A.M.–9 P.M.

An asterisk denotes first-class service.

Combi

Autotransporte Chamoan (Av. Miguel Hidalgo btwn. Calles 1a Pte. and Allende) provides *combi* service to destinations in the Río Usumacinta Valley, including to the Lacandón community of Lacanjá Chansayab (US$7, 3 hrs); Crucero Bonampak (US$7, 3 hrs), where you can catch another *combi* to Bonampak ruins; and finally to Frontera Corozal (US$7, 3.5 hrs), where you can catch boats to Yaxchilán ruins. *Combis* leave the Palenque terminal every hour on the hour from 5 A.M. to 5 P.M. daily, and leave Frontera Corozal at 4, 4:30, 5, 5:30, 6, 7, and 8 A.M., and then hourly from 11 A.M. to 4 P.M.

To get to Las Guacamayas ecocenter in Reforma Agraria, **Lineas Montebello** (Av.

Manuel Velasco Suárez near Coppel department store, tel. 916/345-1260, US$9, 5–6 hrs) offers service to the village turnoff every 60–90 minutes 3:30 A.M.–1:30 P.M. daily. From there, it's about one kilometer (0.6 mi) to the ecocenter. Be aware that some departures only go as far as Benemérito de las Américas (US$7.50, 4 hrs) where you can catch a connecting *combi*.

Car

There are still no car rental agencies in Palenque. The nearest one is in Villahermosa, which is about 150 kilometers (93 miles) away; it is a safe and pleasant ride. You also can rent in San Cristóbal de las Casas, about five hours away. If you do rent a car, plan on driving during daylight hours only; security has improved immensely in this area, but the occasional robbery does occur, almost always after dark. Also, get in the habit of filling your gas whenever you can, as gas stations are few and far between. In a pinch, look for roadside gasoline stands, which typically sell gas in semi-transparent jugs of 5, 10, or 20 liters.

GETTING AROUND

Palenque town is easy to navigate on foot. To get to the ruins or accommodations outside of town, though, you'll either have to take a *colectivo* or a taxi.

Colectivo

Local shuttle companies provide *colectivo* service to and from the ruins (every 10–15 mins, 6 A.M.–6 P.M. daily, US$1). You can board at their terminals in town, at the Maya Head monument, or anywhere along the road to the ruins. Be aware that if you buy your ticket at the terminal, the cashier may try to sell you a round-trip ticket. Don't bother—this saves no money and no time; on the contrary, it means you'll have to wait for a *colectivo* from that specific company when you're ready to leave.

Taxi

A taxi between town and the ruins costs around US$4. Within the town limit (the *periférico*), a cab ride costs US$2.50.

Tours

Maya Exploration Center (El Panchán, Carr. Ruinas Km. 4.5, U.S. tel. 512/350-3321, www .mayaexploration.org) is a U.S.-based agency that specializes in sophisticated tours of various Maya sites and themes, often led by professors. While advance reservations are required for most tours, the group sometimes offers lectures and day tours that are open to walk-ins. Stop by the office in El Panchán for more information.

Along the Río Tulijá

There's no mistaking the Río Tulijá, a ribbon of luminescent turquoise water wending through farmland and dense tropical forest and visible from parts of Highway 199 between Palenque and Ocosingo. Known to local Maya as Yaks-Ha (Blue Water), the river was described by Chiapanecan poet Elva Macías as "a peacock dragging its watery tail," and you'd be forgiven if at first glance you thought it was the result of contamination or a mineral dissolved in the water. In fact, the water is not only clean but perfectly transparent, and the unusual color is the result of sunlight reflecting off the limestone riverbed. (For that reason, the effect isn't visible all year; during rainy season—roughly August to January—sediment washes into the river and turns the water a turbid brown.)

VISITING THE SITES

There are three popular and impressive sites along the Río Tulijá: **Misol-Há** (a high beautiful waterfall), **Agua Clara** (a large picturesque pool), and **Agua Azul** (a series of powerful waterfalls). All three are reached by way of access roads (3–5 km long) that are well-marked on Highway 199. Tour operators in Palenque offer popular and affordable tours, either stopping at all three or just Misol-Há and Agua Azul. The trips typically include a half hour at Misol-Há and Agua Clara (if included) then three hours at Agua Azul. You can also visit them independently, preferably by car, as there's little public transport along the access roads.

At the time of research, members of the local *ejidos* (land cooperatives, ostensibly affiliated with the Zapatistas in this case) had set up road blocks at Agua Clara and Agua Azul, and were charging US$5 per vehicle to pass. Agua Azul remained open as normal, but Agua Clara was shut down while the situation was negotiated. Ask tour operators in Palenque for the latest.

◖ CASCADA DE MISOL-HÁ

Maya for waterfall, Misol-Há (21 km/13 mi south of Palenque, 7 A.M.–6 P.M. daily, US$1.50) is definitely that, and a beautiful one to boot, falling some 30 meters (98 feet) from an overhanging semicircular cliff down into a broad shimmering pool. The water doesn't appear blue here—the pool is too deep—but it's a gorgeous sight nonetheless, and fantastic

© GARY CHANDLER

the stunning 30-meter waterfall at Misol-Há

for swimming, especially on hot afternoons. (Unfortunately most tours stop here in the morning, before you've had a chance to get hot and sweaty!) There's a fairly deep cave on the far side, but getting there is the most memorable part—by way of a slippery path along the base of the cliff and behind the falls, buffeted by mist from the falling water.

A newly expanded welcome center includes a large restaurant (7 A.M.–8 P.M., US$5–15), bathrooms, and expanded parking. From there, it's just 50 meters to the falls.

Accommodations

Misol-Há has a bevy of wood *cabañas* (tel. 55/5329-0995, ext. 7006, US$29 d, US$63 1–5 people with kitchen) built in a stand of thick trees within earshot of the crashing waterfall. Surprisingly well outfitted, all have hot water, fans, and one or two queen beds; family units have separate bedrooms and dining area, and you have the falls all to yourself in the early morning and late afternoon. Still, with Palenque and Ocosingo on this same road, it's hard to imagine a travel itinerary that includes a night here.

Getting There

Misol-Há is the closest of the three Río Tulijá sites to Palenque. The welcome center and falls are about two kilometers from the highway turnoff.

CENTRO ECOTURÍSTICO AGUA CLARA

Agua Clara (40 km/25 mi south of Palenque, 7 A.M.–6 P.M. daily, US$1.50) is a pretty spot where the Río Tulijá slows into a long, wide pool between sloping stone banks. It's a good place to appreciate the river's famous turquoise color. A long rope bridge spans the river from a high bluff, and one or two tourists usually dare each other into making the long, whooping plunge from the middle of the bridge into the water below. Though peaceful and picturesque, Agua Clara has the least "wow" factor of the three riverside sites, and some tours skip it in favor of having more time at the other two.

Near the entrance are a restaurant and bathrooms, and you can rent kayaks to ply the tranquil waters, or arrange guided hiking and horseback tours further along the river.

Getting There

Agua Clara's access road was closed at the time of research, but will likely reopen by the time you read this. It is about three kilometers from the highway to the falls.

◀ PARQUE NACIONAL DE AGUA AZUL

The churning cascades and serene pools of Agua Azul National Park (60 km/37 mi south of Palenque, 7 A.M.–6 P.M. daily, US$1 pp, US$0.50 restrooms and changing area) are reason enough to visit, but the blue-teal color of the water is what makes it especially impressive. The Tulijá is quite powerful here (having been joined upstream by another river, the Río Shumuljá) and tumbles down several kilometers of stair-stepped limestone, variously splintering and rejoining and forming hundreds of waterfalls in the process. Between the falls—which range from just a few feet to several stories high—are pools of water where the water's teal hue can be appreciated. Several of the largest pools have been shored up to allow swimming and wading, and various *miradores* (vista points) afford fine views of the falls from above and below.

A wide paved path leads from the parking area up alongside the falls, with smaller trails leading to the observation points and designated swimming areas. Unfortunately, there are also myriad stalls crammed along the pathway, hawking food, T-shirts, souvenirs, and more. The first several hundred meters have the most shops—also the largest falls and most accessible pools, not coincidentally. However, even on busy days (it's a madhouse during Christmas and Semana Santa) the park's upper section remains much quieter and less crowded, and a number of scenic pools are great for cooling off. The upper section starts about a kilometer from the entrance, where the path turns to dirt. Even further (about an hour's hike) is El Cañon

Iridescent blue waters mark the impressive waterfalls at Agua Azul.

© GARY CHANDLER

(The Canyon), where the valley narrows and a number of additional falls are located.

Be cautious when swimming or wading in Agua Azul, as the current is deceptively strong in many places, even those that look placid. Drownings have occurred, and there are relatively few signs warning of the danger.

Accommodations

The **Comisión Federal de Electricidad** (Federal Electricity Commission, no phone), of all places, allows camping on its grassy enclosed yard, charging US$10 per tent (up to four people). The white cinder-block building is located just past where the path turns to dirt, or you can drive there through the small community; ask at the park entrance for directions. Several local homes also allow camping—look for signs.

Getting There

Agua Azul is located four kilometers (2.5 miles) down a windy road from a well-marked turnoff on Highway 199. Taxis are often waiting at the turnoff to ferry passengers who arrive by *combi* (US$1.50); otherwise it's an hour's walk down, and an even longer walk back up.

Ocosingo

Thousands of people visit Ocosingo every year—for about 15 minutes. That's how long buses stop here on their way to and from must-sees San Cristóbal de las Casas and Palenque. But this small city is well worth a longer stop, principally to visit Toniná, a remarkable yet little-visited Maya archaeological site just outside of town. The city itself doesn't have much appeal, and many people simply get back on the bus and continue onward after visiting the ruins. Others stay the night to enjoy Ocosingo's small-town atmosphere, or to catch early buses to remote destinations in the Lacandón rainforest, including Laguna Miramar. Ocosingo also happens to be famous

for its cheese—once a cow town, always a cow town—and some aficionados come here expressly for the tasty *doble crema* or the spicy spreadable *queso botanero.*

Ocosingo was one of the primary targets of the Zapatista army on its New Year's Day uprising in 1994. The radio station was taken over, and used to broadcast the rebels' message of political and agrarian reform. The Zapatistas eventually retreated back into the forest, but the Mexican army has remained, establishing a massive military base just outside of town, and even maintaining checkpoints and armed patrols around town. More than 15 years after the uprising, the military presence strikes many as

© AVALON TRAVEL

excessive, and the army is the cause of as much local grumbling as the Zapatistas ever were.

◖ TONINÁ ARCHAEOLOGICAL ZONE

Toniná (9 A.M.–4 P.M. daily, museum closed Mon., US$4) is one of the best Maya archaeology sites that no one seems to know about. Easy to reach from both Palenque and San Cristóbal (or as a stop-off between the two) and boasting an excellent museum, this impressive site nevertheless sees only a trickle of tourists.

History

Archaeologists believe that Toniná (Tzeltal Maya for House of Stone) was the last major city-state to succumb to the abrupt and widespread collapse that struck the Classic Maya in the 9th century. While Palenque collapsed in A.D. 799 and Yaxchilán a decade later, Toniná hung on until A.D. 909, the latest Long Count calendar inscription yet to have been uncovered. With the Maya world collapsing all around them, it's not surprising that Toniná's leaders were obsessed with death and sacrifice,

as dramatically depicted in their monuments and stelae.

Most of Toniná's major structures date to the Late Classic period, though the area was surely populated well before that. A stone monument dated A.D. 583 is the first to have been established, and marks Toniná's emergence as a regional power. It was also the beginning of a long rivalry between Toniná and Palenque, marked by numerous skirmishes and shifting power. (The rivalry is even depicted in Toniná's huge ball court, where a carving shows a ruler of Palenque as a prisoner.) Toniná was defeated by Palenque in A.D. 687, and its king captured or killed, but the defeat helped bring to power Toniná's most accomplished leader, K'inich B'aaknal Chaak. He would later score a surprise win over Palenque in A.D. 711, a victory that is gleefully recounted in one of Toniná's best-known relief carvings. (For Palenque, the loss marked the beginning of the end for the kingdom, one of the Maya world's great city-states.)

Visiting the Ruins

The first structure you come to on the path

The ancient Maya city of Toniná uses a series of terraces and staircases to climb nearly 80 meters up a steep hillside. Bring your hiking shoes!

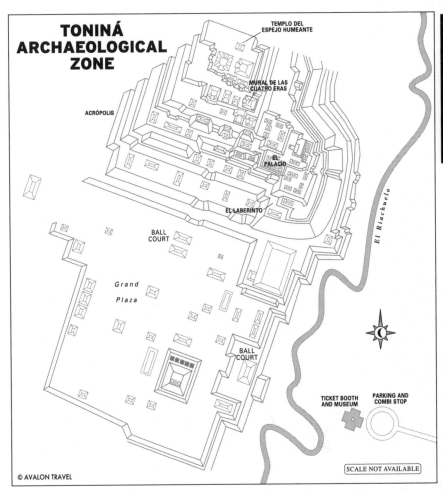

TONINÁ ARCHAEOLOGICAL ZONE

TEMPLO DEL ESPEJO HUMEANTE

MURAL DE LAS CUATRO ERAS

ACRÓPOLIS

EL PALACIO

EL LABERINTO

BALL COURT

Grand Plaza

BALL COURT

El Riachuelo

TICKET BOOTH AND MUSEUM

PARKING AND COMBI STOP

SCALE NOT AVAILABLE

© AVALON TRAVEL

from the entrance is Toniná's unique **ball court;** at 60 meters long, it's one of the Maya world's largest, and has a unique "sunken" construction and is decorated with images of prisoners. Stairs lead up to a massive raised plaza known as the **Grand Plaza,** also one of the biggest of its kind and dotted with several structures, including a second ball court, this one decorated with images of Toniná's rulers—and an altar believed to have been used for sacrificing ball-game players (though whether it was the winners or losers remains uncertain).

But by far the most arresting feature of the Grand Plaza is the view it affords of Toniná's city center, or **Acrópolis,** a spectacular complex of temples, terraces, and stairways climbing a steep hillside. Nearly 80 vertical meters (260 feet) from top to bottom, the Acrópolis has more vertical gain than any known Maya structure, but is not considered a true pyramid, as it uses the hill to gain height.

The Acrópolis has a total of seven terraces, each with various temples or other structures built on either end. Some visitors take their

ZAPATISTAS

On January 1, 1994, masked soldiers belonging to the **Ejército Zapatista de Liberación Nacional** (Zapatista National Liberation Army, or EZLN) stormed town halls in seven cities in eastern and central Chiapas, including San Cristóbal de las Casas, Ocosingo, and Oxchuc. Using a captured radio station in Ocosingo, they declared themselves in rebellion against the national government, calling for reforms to Mexico's treatment of its marginalized peasant population.

The Mexican government responded with 12,000 troops, plus air strikes against rebel positions, including several indigenous villages. Within days, the Zapatistas had retreated into remote hideouts in the eastern jungles. Meanwhile, mass demonstrations erupted across Mexico, mostly in support of EZLN demands, and the government declared a cease-fire on January 12. In all, about 145 people, mostly Zapatistas, died in the initial uprising.

The Zapatista rebellion took most observers by surprise, though the conditions that sparked it were neither new nor unfamiliar. Often referred to as a Maya uprising, it was really more a peasant or agrarian revolt – albeit in a place where most peasants happen to be indigenous. The uprising was launched on the day the North American Free Trade Agreement (NAFTA) took effect, an agreement which critics rightly believed would disenfranchise Mexico's peasant farmers, indigenous and non-indigenous alike, by flooding the country with cheap U.S.-produced crops. (January 1 also was a national holiday, when city halls were unoccupied and the police and army presence minimal.)

But the seeds of the conflict were sown long before NAFTA came about. Following the debt crisis in 1982, international banking institutions pressured Mexico to adopt strict austerity measures, including reductions in subsidies and land grants for poor farmers. The ruling PRI was only too willing to comply; in Chiapas alone, nearly 8,000 "certificates of nonaffectability" – which exempted certain lands from being redistributed to campesinos – were issued between 1982-1987, compared to just over 1,400 in the previous 48 years, most benefiting powerful cattle ranchers. During the same period, Chiapas's governor – Ábsalon Castellanos Domínguez, a rancher and former army general named – oversaw a brutal crack-down on farmers and activists involved in land conflicts, with hundreds arrested, tortured, and killed. (During the 1994 uprising, Castellanos Domínguez was abducted by the Zapatistas and convicted of human rights violations by a revolutionary tribunal; he was released six weeks later, following negotiations.) The coup de grace came in 1992, when PRI legislators

time reaching the top, visiting the notable structures along the way; others bee-line to the top, then take their time descending. Either way, be aware that the stairs are extremely steep in places, and proper shoes are a must.

On the ground level is a warren of winding passages and tunnels aptly called **El Laberinto** (The Labyrinth), which connects to **El Palacio,** one level up. But Toniná's most famous artifact is a stunning stucco codex known as the **Mural de las Cuatro Eras** (Mural of the Four Eras) located on the sixth platform. Feathered X-patterns divide the panel into four parts within which are images representing the four eras, or suns, the world was believed to have passed through

in Maya cosmology. The images are dark and deathly, including a skeleton holding a human head, an anthropomorphic rat representing a lord of the underworld, and severed human heads representing the passing eras, with feathers protruding from their neck stumps. Parts of the frieze are damaged or destroyed, but those that remain are quite remarkable.

The seventh and final platform is packed with structures, including the **Templo del Espejo Humeante** (Temple of the Smoking Mirror). The stairs here are incredibly steep, but the view from the summit is breathtaking, albeit somewhat marred by the massive military compound plopped in a sea of farmland.

and then-President Carlos Salinas de Gortari amended Article 27 of the Constitution, effectively ending Mexico's 75-year commitment to land redistribution, and even allowing for the privatization of *ejidos* (communally held lands). Many Zapatista militants were landless farmers who had long held out hope of receiving a government land grant; the amendment of Article 27 officially dashed those hopes, prompting many farmers to join the EZLN. (Relatedly, the Zapatistas are also highly critical of ecotourism and even many environmental conservation efforts, viewing both as a means for the government to control use of prized lands.)

Contrary to popular notions, the Zapatistas were not universally supported by Chiapas's indigenous communities. Chamulan, Lacandón, and other prominent entities viewed the Zapatistas as troublemakers. For their part, the Zapatistas drew considerable support from *los expulsados*, the vast numbers of indigenous people who have been expelled from their lands and communities for having joined a Protestant church or voting for a non-PRI candidate.

Today, tens of thousands of Mexican troops patrol central and eastern Chiapas, conducting "low intensity" warfare aimed at disrupting Zapatista strongholds without engaging in actual combat. However, the brutal massacre of 45 Zapatista sympathizers – mostly women and children killed by paramilitaries during a prayer service – in 1997 in the town of Acteal raised the troubling suggestion that the government also is pursuing a covert dirty war.

The EZLN – believed to still have around 3,000 armed soldiers – has struggled to maintain the world's focus and attention. It formed a political wing in 1997 (the FZLN), addressed the national congress in 2001, and in 2005 launched La Otra Campaña (The Other Campaign), intended to refocus popular support for agrarian and democratic reform. Subcomandante Marcos – the EZLN's iconic pipe-smoking spokesperson, identified by the government as a former university professor named Rafael Guillén, also known as the Sup, but currently calling himself Delegado Zero – has been criticized by some for abandoning the cause and by others for cultivating a cult of personality. (He co-wrote a novel, got married, and toured Mexico by motorcycle, among other things.) It is tempting to call the Zapatista uprising a failed revolution – certainly they did not "advance to the capital of the country" as their first declaration promised. Then again, as Marcos put it to reporter Alma Guillermoprieto, "Weren't we there already by January 2nd? We were everywhere, on the lips of everyone – in the subway, on the radio. And our flag was in the *zócalo*."

Museum

Definitely leave time to visit the museum (9 A.M.–4 P.M. Tues.–Sun.), which is one of the best at any Maya site. Opened in September 2002, it contains fantastic artifacts and carvings, including figures that were deliberately decapitated (which was probably done when the personage depicted was himself decapitated) and distinctive round obelisks marking important dates.

SPORTS AND RECREATION

Horseback riding tours of Ocosingo's countryside can be arranged through Hospedaje y Restaurant Esmeralda (Calle Central Nte. near Av. Central, tel. 919/673-0014). Tours are led by an experienced guide and can include stops in working ranches. Excursions typically last 1.5–2 hours.

ACCOMMODATIONS

As the name suggests, **Hotel Central** (Av. Central near Calle Central Nte., tel. 919/673-0024, US$20 s, US$25 d) is centrally located—in fact, it faces the central plaza. Rooms are small and simple but all have private bathroom, cable TV, and wireless Internet. Some 2nd-floor rooms open onto a wide veranda that overlooks the plaza, which is great for people-watching if you don't mind the early-morning hubbub.

Just around the corner, **Hospedaje y Restaurant Esmeralda** (Calle Central Nte. near Av. Central, tel. 919/673-0014, US$14 s with shared bathroom, US$23 d with shared bathroom, US$22 s, US$28 d) offers five large rooms in a remodeled historic home. Accommodations are a little run-down but colorful Chiapanecan bedspreads, lots of plants, and friendly service make up for it. The heart of the hotel is clearly in the common areas, which include a breezy terrace and a homey restaurant and bar. In the latter, you'll find loads of traveler information and a decent book exchange too.

Hotel Margarita (Calle Central Nte. near 2a Av. Nte. Pte., tel. 919/673-0280, hotel margarita@prodigy.net.mx, US$25 s, US$30 d, US$50 s/d with a/c) offers ample rooms with two queen beds, cable TV, and wireless Internet. They lack charm, but if you're lucky you may get one with views of the surrounding hills. Better yet, ask to see a few before committing.

FOOD

Hospedaje y Restaurante Esmeralda (Calle Central Nte. near Av. Central, tel. 919/673-0014, 7:30 A.M.–9:30 P.M. daily, US$5–10) has perhaps the best restaurant in town. International and Mexican dishes are served on large wooden tables in the hotel's homey dining room—the fajitas and chicken curry are tasty options.

Restaurante El Desvan (tel. 919/673-0117, 7 A.M.–11 P.M. daily, US$4–10) is one of many simple restaurants set around the central plaza. Most serve standard Mexican fare; here you can also get pizza.

For a hearty breakfast, try **Las Delicias** (Av. Central at Calle Central Nte., tel. 919/673-0024, 7 A.M.–11 P.M. daily, US$4–8), an airy restaurant with outdoor seating and great views of the plaza.

Just a block north of the plaza, **Fábrica de Quesos Santa Rosa** (1a Calle Ote. Nte. 11, tel. 919/673-0009, 8 A.M.–2 P.M. and 4–8 P.M. Mon.–Sat., 8 A.M.–2 P.M. Sun.) is a recommended shop offering a half dozen or more varieties of Ocosingo cheese. If you can't decide which to buy, try the smooth *doble crema* (double cream).

INFORMATION AND SERVICES
Tourist Information
There is a tourist information kiosk (9 A.M.–3 P.M. and 6–8 P.M. Mon.–Fri.) on the central plaza that doles out general information about Ocosingo and the state of Chiapas.

Emergency Services
For meds, **Farmacias Similares** (2a Calle Ote. Sur at 1a Sur Ote., tel. 919/673-1515, 8 A.M.–8 P.M. Mon.–Sat., 8 A.M.–2 P.M. Sun.) is around the corner from the town church, Templo de San Jacinto. If you need to contact the **police** dial toll-free 066 from any telephone.

Money
Banamex (central plaza, 9 A.M.–4 P.M. Mon.–Fri.) and **Santander** (Calle Central Nte. near Calle 2a Nte. Pte., 9 A.M.–4 P.M. Mon.–Fri., 10 A.M.–2 P.M. Sat.) have 24-hour ATMs.

Media and Communications
The **post office** (2a Calle Ote. Nte. at 2a Av. Nte. Ote.) is open 8 A.M.–4:30 P.M. Monday–Friday. For email, the conveniently located **Planeta Azul** (central plaza, 8 A.M.–10 P.M. daily, US$0.80/hr) has flat screens and fast connections. If it's full, there are easily half a dozen more Internet cafés within a Frisbee throw, many on Calle Central Norte; all charge about the same and have similar hours.

Laundry and Storage
Half a block north of the central plaza, **Lavandería La Paz** (Calle 1a Ote. Nte. near Av. Central, 8 A.M.–8 P.M. Mon.–Sat.) charges US$1.20 per kilogram (2.2 pounds) to launder your threads; they offer same-day service. For **luggage storage,** the bus terminal (Hwy. 199, tel. 916/673-0431) charges US$0.50 per hour.

GETTING THERE
Bus
Ocosingo's bus terminal (Hwy. 199, tel. 919/673-0431) is on the highway about seven

blocks from the center of town. Most departures are *de paso* (mid-route), so be sure to arrive a half hour early in case the bus arrives ahead of schedule. Destinations include:

- Palenque: (US$7.50, 3 hrs) 9:30 A.M., 1:40 P.M., 2:35 P.M., 4:50 P.M., 5:50 P.M., 6 P.M., 8:15 P.M., and 10:40 P.M.

- San Cristóbal: (US$3.75, 2 hrs) 5:35 A.M., 5:40 A.M., 7:20 A.M., 12:10 P.M., 2:25 P.M., 3:45 A.M., and 4:55 P.M.

- Tuxtla Gutiérrez: (US$10.50, 4 hrs) take any San Cristóbal bus.

GETTING AROUND

Ocosingo is small enough that you can easily get around on foot. If you are coming or going to the bus station or are headed to Toniná, *combis* (vans) and taxis are your best option.

Combi

To get to Toniná Archaeological Zone, take a *combi* (US$1) marked Predio-Ruínas; they leave from 3a Avenida Sur Oriente in front of the market. *Combis* leave whenever they are full, usually every 15–45 minutes. To return to town, catch the same *combi* back.

Taxi

Taxis around town cost US$2. To the Toniná ruins, a cab runs about US$7 from the bus terminal, US$5 from the central plaza; you also can arrange for the driver to pick you up after you've toured the site.

THE RÍO USUMACINTA VALLEY

The Río Usumacinta Valley extends southeast from Palenque almost 200 kilometers, following the winding path of its namesake river and forming a natural border between Mexico and Guatemala. For travelers, the valley's main attractions have long been two fascinating and well-excavated Maya ruins: Bonampak, home to a stunning set of thousand-year-old fresco paintings; and Yaxchilán, a grand city rising dramatically from the banks of the Río Usumacinta, along which you are sure to spot crocodiles and howler monkeys in the trees.

Not long ago, the only way to visit the ruins was by a rutted one-track road, followed by a long hike through the rainforest. Nowadays, a paved highway—the Carretera Fronteriza, or Border Highway—and reliable boat service make visiting Bonampak and Yaxchilán easy

and secure, whether by tour or on your own. (Roadside robberies, once a problem, are now quite rare, especially in daylight hours.)

That's not to say there aren't out-of-the-way places to visit. The still-traditional Lacandón villages of Nahá and Metzabok are nestled in forest reserves, 40-plus kilometers down a rough dirt road. Both have simple accommodations and terrific boating and hiking. Easier to reach, but no less impressive, is Plan de Ayutla Archaeological Zone, a partially excavated and rarely visited ruin outside the town of Nueva Palestina.

Greater accessibility has been less kind, or perhaps too kind, to the Lacandón village of Lacanjá Chansayab. Just a few kilometers from Bonampak ruins, the village has been given over almost entirely to mass tourism, at the

HIGHLIGHTS

Nahá: Deep in the rainforest, this Lancandón Maya village isn't easy to get to, but all the more rewarding when you do. Sleep in simple cabins, explore pristine lakes and forest trails, and experience ancient Maya ceremonies, all in a welcoming but unadulterated atmosphere (page 60).

Plan de Ayutla Archaeological Zone: This site's twin pyramids, still covered in trees, are easy to mistake for hills. But climb to their tops to discover wondrous semi-excavated temples, some with high peaked ceilings, others with ancient glyphs painted on their walls. Best of all, there's not a soul in sight (page 65).

Bonampak Murals: Inside an otherwise innocuous temple halfway up Bonampak's main staircase are some of the finest and best-preserved Maya murals yet discovered. In brilliant colors they tell of jungle warfare, ritual bloodletting, and the ascension of a boy king (page 70).

Yaxchilán Ruins: Perched on a leafy riverbank, Yaxchilán exudes a regal bearing, as if waiting assuredly for its glory days to return. When you're not admiring the gorgeous carvings and complex layout, keep an eye out for beefy crocs in the river and howler monkeys in the trees (page 74).

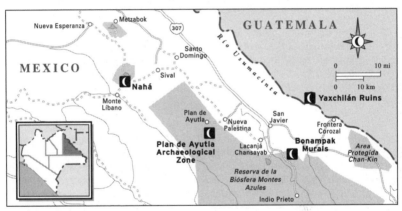

LOOK FOR **(** TO FIND RECOMMENDED SIGHTS, ACTIVITIES, DINING, AND LODGING.

cost of much of the community's traditional customs and independence.

PLANNING YOUR TIME

The vast majority of travelers here visit Bonampak and Yaxchilán on round-trip shuttles from Palenque; if you've only got a day to spend here, it's the easiest and cheapest way to go, as you don't spend time or money organizing the transfers, particularly the boat to Yaxchilán.

With more time, you might consider staying the night, and taking the next day to visit places like Lacanjá Chansayab or Nueva Palestina.

Two nights or more are recommended for visiting Nahá or Metzabok, to leave plenty of time for the long drive in and out, plus at least one full day for the various excursions and other activities available there.

It's possible to explore the Río Usumacinta Valley by public transportation, though service anywhere off the main highway can be pretty spotty. A rental car or truck, if it's in your budget, makes visiting the area simpler and much more efficient.

The Carretera Fronteriza now loops all the way around to Comitán and onward to San

Cristóbal de las Casas, with turnoffs to popular ecotourism destinations like Las Guacamayas, Las Nubes, and the Lagunas de Montebello—a great option that avoids any backtracking.

Frontera Corozal also offers a back-door route to Tikal, the stellar Maya ruins outside of Flores, Guatemala, if you're considering heading there.

Along the Carretera Fronteriza

The Carretera Fronteriza (Border Highway) runs from Palenque southwest along Río Usumacinta and the Guatemalan border to the town of Frontera Corozal; from there it loops down and westward, eventually reaching the city of Comitán in central Chiapas.

The first section, from Palenque to Frontera Corozal, is covered here, including a variety of villages, detours, and roadside attractions, roughly in the order you'd encounter them driving from Palenque. Some make for a quick stop, others an extended side trip; some have food and lodging, others do not. It's worth reviewing the entire section before deciding how to tackle the region.

A number of agencies offer transportation from Palenque that hits the major destinations; they're recommended for their convenience and reasonable price. Alternatively, *colectivos* ply the Carretera Fronteriza throughout the day, and a rental car is very handy for places off the main road, as bus service to those areas can be very slow and unpredictable.

CASCADA WEJLIB-JÁ

Ch'ol Maya for Falling Water, Cascada Wejlib-Já (7 A.M.–7 P.M., US$1) is a large waterfall and swimming area that's popular among locals and a reasonably worthwhile stop for travelers looking for a place to cool off. From the parking area, a path follows the riverbank past several swimming holes and waterside picnic tables. (There's also a simple eatery near the entrance.) The falls are a short distance further, a thick rope of water lumbering through a limestone notch and crashing into a large pool 20 meters below. The path winds around to the bottom, where you can swim as well. The falls are most powerful in September and October, at the end of the rainy season, but the water is clearer during dry months.

THE RÍO USUMACINTA VALLEY

© GARY CHANDLER

Cascada Wejlib-Já makes for a quick cool-off on the highway between Palenque and Frontera Corozal.

Getting There

A huge sign marks the turnoff for Wejlib-Já, about 30 kilometers from Palenque. From there, it's 500 meters by dirt road to the entrance.

VALLE ESCONDIDA

More a roadside business than a village, Valle Escondida (Carr. Fronteriza del Sur Km. 61, cell tel. 044-916/100-0399, busil_h@hotmail.com) is arguably the best lodging and food between Palenque and Frontera Corozal. A fresh, well-prepared buffet breakfast (US$8 pp, daily from 7 A.M.) includes eggs, beans, coffee and juice, fresh fruit, handmade tortillas, and more, served in an open-air dining area beneath a thick forest canopy. It can get crowded—just about every tour group stops here on the way to Bonampak and Yaxchilán—but makes a great pit stop nonetheless.

PIEDRAS NEGRAS

Deep in the rain forest on the Guatemalan side of the Río Usumacinta, Piedras Negras Archaeological Zone boasts imposing tree-covered structures and magnificent sculptures and stelae, many signed by the artists who created them – a rarity in the Maya world. It's also where the great Russian-born Mayanist Tatiana Proskouriakoff is buried; some of her most important breakthroughs, especially in deciphering previously unreadable Maya hieroglyphics, stemmed from her research at Piedras Negras in the 1960s.

Though quite isolated, Piedras Negras has gotten somewhat easier to reach, thanks to the construction of a new access road near Nueva Esperanza. Day-long excursions can be arranged through **Valle Escondida** (Carr. Fronteriza del Sur Km. 61, cell tel. 044-916/100-0399, busil_h@hotmail.com); trips cost US$125 per person (four people minimum) and include round-trip transport, 2.5-3 hours at the archaeological site with a multilingual guide, and often a stop at the Cascada Busil-Há waterfall.

Valle Escondida's handful of *cabañas* (US$80–100) are on the opposite side of the highway, near the owners' ranch house. Deluxe units have king-size beds and two singles, high sloped ceilings and oversize windows, and a bathroom and shower tucked behind an attractive stone wall—truly a sight for sore eyes after a long day at the ruins. Smaller units are perfectly comfortable, but lack the same charm. Service is friendly, though there's no official reception desk; if the restaurant is closed, try knocking on the door of the main ranch house.

Getting There

Valle Escondida is easy to spot if you pass before 10 A.M., as there's always a collection of cars and tour buses pulled off along the shoulder in front. Otherwise, use the kilometer markers painted on the pavement as a reference (it's at Kilometer 61), and look for the dark-green roadside sign on your right (coming from Palenque). It's not in any particular town, but is located between Chancalá and the military checkpoint at the turnoff to Nueva Palestina.

NAHÁ

The remote Lacandón village of Nahá is situated beside a beautiful lake and surrounded by hills covered in lush rainforest. About 70 Lacandón Maya families live there, surviving in much the same way their predecessors did generations ago, mostly by fishing and small-scale farming. Tourists are a fairly new development here, and are received with cordial reserve befitting this resourceful and reclusive indigenous group. As the Lacandón village of Lacanjá Chansayab, near Bonampák ruins, grows exceedingly touristy, a small but steady number of travelers are making the far more difficult trip to Nahá (and the even smaller and less-visited sister village of Metzabok) in search of more "authentic" Lacandón culture and community. And unlike indigenous villages around San Cristóbal, residents here typically don't object to having their picture taken.

THE LACANDÓN

Early in the Spanish conquest, a small number of Yucatec Maya, facing disease and forced labor, fled the Yucatán Peninsula and settled deep in the rainforest of present-day Chiapas. Utterly isolated, the new arrivals developed a remarkable form of semi-nomadic subsistence agriculture that did not deplete the rainforest soil, involving dozens of different foods and fibers and following a careful system of limited cutting and burning, frequent crop rotation, and "rest" periods for cultivated lands. Their descendants – today's Lacandón Indians – practiced the same system well into the 20th century. (They are not descendants of Palenque's former rulers, however, as some romantically suggest.) The Lacandón's first sustained contact with the outside world was with loggers and chicle tappers in the early 1900s, and they gained wider attention as anthropologists and activists (including Frans and Gertrude Dudy Blom, founders of Na Bolom in San Cristóbal) sought to incubate this unique and essentially Stone Age culture from loggers, squatters, and other intruders.

In 1971, the Mexican government granted the Lacandón rights to over 614,000 hectares (6,140 square kilometers) of pristine rainforest, a massive swath of land for a group of just 350 people at the time. (Even today, there are only around a thousand Lacandón people.) Few contest the value of land grants to indigenous groups, but many see the Lacandón grant as too much of a good thing. Many Lacandón promptly sold logging rights on their portions – often back to the government, leading critics to question the "altruistic" motivations of the federal grant. Though paid a pittance compared to the value of the lumber there, many Lacandón nevertheless became instantly wealthy, which subsequently led to a host of predictable social vices, particularly alcohol and violence.

More critically, the land grant turned approximately 12,000 non-Lacandón farmers into illegal squatters, who were removed from the land (with little compensation) to present-day Nueva Palestina and Frontera Corozal. In fact, the grant meant there was far less land available to non-Lacandón peasants throughout the state, despite their far greater numbers and equally dire circumstances. Those same farmers – mainly landless Tzotzil and Tzeltal Maya from eastern and central Chiapas – formed the core of the Zapatista uprising in 1994 (which the Lacandón, staunch allies of the federal government, generally did not support). The Lacandón land grant did not cause the Zapatista uprising, much less the inequalities it aimed to correct, a more balanced approach might have mitigated the circumstances of many suffering peasants, Lacandón and otherwise.

Sights

Nahá is a good place to observe and learn about Lacandón culture and lifestyle, while Metzabok has somewhat richer outdoor opportunities. A highlight for many visitors is a meeting and ritual ceremony with **Don Antonio** (US$30 per group, advance notice required), an octogenarian spiritual leader and successor to the great now-deceased Lacandón shaman Chan Kin Viejo. The village also has a modest **museum** (US$1, by appointment only) with photos and artifacts explaining Lacandón history, beliefs, and practices. Signage is in Spanish, with some English translations.

Local guides lead visitors on nature outings of various types and lengths, as well, charging around US$20–50 per group, but highly variable depending on what you'd like to do. There's a short (two-kilometer) **nature trail** that leads from the village to Laguna Nahá. There, it's possible to **canoe** around the lake, whose reed-filled shallows and curving tree-shaded banks offer fine bird-watching. There's also a **waterfall** within walking distance, and plenty of numerous opportunities to see and learn more about the rich rainforest flora, including medicinal plants.

At the time of research, Nahá's tourism contacts were **Miguel and Kin García** (tel. 55/5150-5953 or 916/341-4473), who can help make advance arrangements for your visit. Alternatively, call or visit the Palenque office of the **Comisión Nacional de Areas Naturales Protegidas** (National Commission of Protected Natural Areas, Prolongación Av. Juárez 1085, Barrio La Cañada, tel. 916/345-0967, naha@conanp.gob.mx, 9 A.M.–6 P.M. Mon.–Fri.), which oversees the reserve and tourism there. It's best to go (or call) on Monday or Tuesday, as the regional specialists typically are in the field the rest of the week.

Accommodations and Food

Nahá has a handful of simple but comfortable **cabins** (US$30–40, 1–4 people) with either shared or private bathroom, one or two queen-size beds, and 24-hour electricity. There are hooks for hammocks, and mosquito nets over the beds. Reservations are recommended. There is also space for **camping** (US$6) provided you bring your own gear.

A small **comedor** serves breakfast, lunch, and dinner for US$6 apiece.

Getting There
BUS

There's bus service to Nahá from both Palenque and Ocosingo. From Palenque (US$4, 5–6 hrs), departures are at 11 A.M. and 1 P.M. daily. The return is not so agreeable, however, departing Nahá at 11 P.M. and 1 A.M.—ouch. From Ocosingo (US$5, 6–7 hrs), one bus leaves at noon–1 P.M. daily from near the market. The return bus is just as bad as Palenque's, leaving Nahá at 11:30 P.M.; worse, it starts in another village, and is frequently standing-room-only by the time it reaches Nahá.

From either direction, buy your ticket in advance to reserve a specific seat, and arrive early to claim it; the buses are frequently full and latecomers may go standing. Also keep in mind that departure and arrival times are estimates at best, and some buses are canceled altogether—plan accordingly.

CAR

Driving to Nahá on your own is a difficult but not impossible task, and affords more flexibility to come and go. A truck is definitely preferable, but it's doable in a midsize rental car as long as the road is dry. Whatever you're driving, be sure your tank is full and that you have a spare tire, and leave early to have plenty of daylight.

From Palenque, head east on Carretera Fronteriza del Sur for 44 kilometers, to the largish town of Chancalá. Turn right and continue another 14 kilometers to an intersection known as Crucero Piñal, where a sign directs you to the right again. The road is paved to there, and for another 3.5 kilometers beyond, before turning to gravel and eventually dirt. In the village of Piedrón (3.5 kilometers after the pavement ends) continue straight to the fork; from there the road is easy to follow, but increasingly rough, passing through small settlements and the town of Nueva Esperanza. Forty kilometers from Chancalá is a well-marked turnoff to Metzabok (6 kilometers); it's another 18 rutted kilometers to reach Nahá. Budget at least three hours for the trip.

Alternatively, at Crucero Piñal, where the sign points right, it is possible to continue straight to—and a short distance past—Finca Santo Domingo, then turn right onto a dirt road leading to Nahá via the villages of Sival and Jardín—ask directions as it may not be well marked. This route is longer, but paved to Santo Domingo, leaving only about 20 kilometers, or one hour, on dirt road. You do not pass the turnoff to Metzabok, however.

It is also possible to reach Nahá from Ocosingo, though the road is much longer and entirely *terracería* (dirt road). Look for the turnoff at Kilometer 14 on the road to Toniná ruins; the road goes through the Monte Líbano and San Luís Guadalupe *ejidos* before reaching Nahá.

METZABOK

Metzabok is a quiet Lacandón community of just 20 families, who live in simple wood homes in a region of numerous lakes and waterways. The community is situated on the edge of Laguna Tzibana, whose name means *casa pintada* (painted house) in Lacandón Maya and is most likely a reference to prehistoric paintings visible along the lake's edge. (The word Metzabok comes from the god of the Maya ball game, though it's unclear why the name was used here.) Laguna Tzibana is connected by a natural canal to Laguna Metzabok, a much larger lake, and the source of several of the rainforest's streams and rivers. The entire region is protected as part of a federal nature reserve, and is home to a rich array of plants, birds, and mammals.

Metzabok's residents are less accustomed to outsiders and generally more reserved than Nahá's, making it harder (but not impossible) to experience Lacandón life and culture. By the same token, the surrounding rainforest and waterways are even more pristine, and excursions longer and more varied.

There are no public telephones, Internet, or other services in Metzabok, and cabins and meal service are available with advance notice only. At the time of research, the tourism contact person in Metzabok was Enrique Valenzuela (tel. 961/341-8044); alternatively, you can call or visit the Palenque office of the **Comisión Nacional de Areas Naturales Protegidas** (National Commission of Protected Natural Areas, Prolongación Av. Juárez 1085, Barrio La Cañada, tel. 916/345-0967, metzabok_05@yahoo.com.mx, 9 A.M.–6 P.M. Mon.–Fri.), which oversees the reserve and tourism there.

Sights

Metzabok is surrounded by water, so it's no surprise that the best way to enjoy the sights is by boat. Local men and boys give paddling tours, whose length and price depends on what you see and how many people are in the group.

Basic **tours** (US$15–30, 1.5–3 hrs) typically begin by paddling across Laguna Tzibana to a set of red *pinturas rupestras* (prehistoric pictograms) on a sheer stone wall right on the edge of the lake. Though streaked and faded, various designs are discernable, including handprints, deities, birds, and monkeys. Nearby, a small cave has a clutch of ceremonial artifacts, including incense holders, urns, even a human skull, though it's unclear how old they are.

A short paddle from the paintings is an unexcavated archaeological site, also near the water's edge; very little is known about the history or origins of the site, though it's quite extensive, including numerous mounds and foundations and at least one large pyramid-like structure. The thick forest cover makes it difficult to appreciate, but clambering over and around the tree cover also adds to the appeal and mystery of this ancient site.

Looming over Laguna Tzibana is a high round butte, and tours often include climbing a winding trail to the top, where a *mirador* (vista point) offers all-embracing views of the lagoons and verdant forest beyond.

Longer excursions (US$50–70, 5 hrs) include all of the above, plus paddling into Laguna Metzabok, where there are another set of prehistoric paintings (in multiple colors), a large cave, and additional opportunities for short walks in the forest.

Accommodations and Food

Several small thatched-roof **cabañas** (US$30) are available for rent, each with two queen beds, hammock hooks, and private bathroom, and located on a grassy lot near the entrance of town. Rooms are reasonably comfortable, though far from luxurious—don't be startled by insects or even the occasional mouse, as the units are shuttered between visitors, sometimes for long periods of time. Advance notice is required to be sure the key is available and the cabin tidied up.

There are no restaurants in town, but home-cooked meals can be prepared by a local family or community member. As with the cabins, advance notice is required to allow time to buy necessary supplies.

Getting There
BUS
There is no direct bus service to Metzabok. Buses to Nahá can drop you at the turnoff (US$3, 4 hrs), which is about six hilly kilometers from town. To return, you'd have to be back at the turnoff at midnight or 2 A.M. to catch the bus from Nahá—not a good plan. A better

option would be to take the bus into Nahá (it passes the Metzabok turnoff at around 3 P.M. and 5 P.M.) and spend some time there before catching a bus back to Palenque or Ocosingo. That way, if the bus is late or canceled, you're in town instead of at a lonely crossroads.

CAR

Metzabok is some 80 kilometers from Palenque, half by dirt road. From Palenque, head east on Carretera Fronteriza del Sur for 44 kilometers, to the largish town of Chancalá. Turn right and continue another 14 kilometers to an intersection known as Crucero Piñal, where a sign directs you to the right again. The road is paved to there, and for another 3.5 kilometers beyond, before turning to gravel and eventually dirt. In the village of Piedrón (3.5 kilometers after the pavement ends) continue straight to the fork; from there the road is easy to follow, but increasingly rough, passing through small settlements and the town of Nueva Esperanza. Forty kilometers from Chancalá is a well-marked turnoff to Metzabok (6 kilometers).

NUEVA PALESTINA

Wide dusty streets and an unusually large central square make this Tzeltal Maya village seem even sleepier than it already is. Located 11 kilometers south of the main highway by paved road, the best reason to make a detour to Nueva Palestina is to visit Plan de Ayutla Archaeological Zone, a fascinating and little-visited site that researchers believe may be the remains of a long-sought Classic-era city. Other local sights, including a large natural swimming hole and a frothing waterfall, wouldn't really merit a special trip themselves, but can be a nice place to cool off after visiting the ruins.

Nueva Palestina has limited services. You'll find a handful of shops, including a minimart, pharmacy, and Internet café, around the main square and on the wide avenues leading into and away from town.

Sights

POZA PO'OP CHAN

As if the English connotation weren't concerning enough, Po'op Chan is Tzeltal Maya for Serpent in the Water—not the most enticing name for a swimming hole! Nevertheless, this large aqua-blue *poza* (pool) makes for a pleasant and cooling swim, and at 70 meters across is even big enough to navigate by kayak. A platform at the downstream end of the pool makes getting in and out easy, and there are several tables along the bank for a picnic lunch.

Poza Po'op Chan is located in the rear of Campamento Po'op Chan (tel. 55/5004-7135, campamentopoopchan@yahoo.com, US$15 pp), which charges US$1 admission and rents inflatable kayaks for US$2.50 per hour. A trail connects Po'op Chan and Cascada Las Golondrinas (each open 8:30 A.M.–6 P.M. daily), a mild and pleasant walk of about three kilometers.

CASCADA LAS GOLONDRINAS (CH'EN ULICH)

This sloping multipart falls gets its name—Swallows Waterfall—from a cave behind the main curtain of water that's a favorite nesting area for the loud energetic birds. A low wooden footbridge extends across the river at the foot of the main cascade, making for a cool and misty vista point. Several small pools are popular for swimming and wading. At the entrance are several *palapa* umbrellas with small tables beneath them, plus bathrooms and a modest eatery.

The turnoff to the falls is about two kilometers north of Nueva Palestina (before entering town, if you're coming from the highway); from there it's another kilometer down a dirt road to the parking area and entrance. You can also walk by trail to the falls from Campamento Po'op Chan, about three kilometers each way. Admission is US$1.

SENDERO RÍO CEDRO

For a more challenging excursion, Sendero Río Cedro (Cedar River Trail) connects Nueva Palestina to the Lacandón village of Lacanjá Chansayab, a 6-to-8-hour hike that ranges from cornfields to the pristine rainforest of the Montes Azules biosphere reserve, passes waterfalls and massive ceiba trees, and crosses numerous waterways. Camping is possible at Campamento Río Cedro, a small Lacandón settlement about two hours from Nueva Palestina, where local guides can lead short side trips into the forest and to nearby lagoons. From there to Lacanjá Chansayab is another 4–6 hours, mostly through dense rainforest, and across the namesake Río Cedro.

The trail splits and fades in numerous places, making a private guide or organized tour all but essential. One option is **Latitud 16** (www .latitud16.com), which offers a five-day/four-night trip including a night at Campamento Río Cedro and visiting Plan de Ayutla ruins.

◖ PLAN DE AYUTLA ARCHAEOLOGICAL ZONE

For all the attention paid to must-see archaeological sites like Palenque and Yaxchilán, the ruins of Plan de Ayutla rank as one of the most fascinating and memorable in the region and the state. Seven kilometers outside Nueva

Palestina and way off the beaten path, the ruins consist of twin pyramids, ensconced in trees and vegetation, and crowned by a complex of remarkably well-preserved structures that are a thrill to explore and clamber about. What's more, there is growing evidence that these are the remains of the ancient Maya city of Sak Tz'i', whose location has been one of the enduring archaeological mysteries of the Río Usumacinta and Lacandón region.

For decades, archaeologists have known of Sak Tz'i' (Tzeltal Maya for Perro Blanco, or White Dog) from inscriptions at Piedras Negras and Bonampák, but could never find the city's location or remains. The city seems to have played the role of ancient swing voter (or "catalyzing agent" in archaeological parlance), never a major player itself, yet capable of tipping the balance of power among the dominant cities through strategic alliances. This role is suggested in part by military defeats at the hands of various rivals, including Piedras Negras in A.D. 628, Yaxchilán and Bonampak

THE RÍO USUMACINTA VALLEY

© GARY CHANDLER

The intriguing Plan de Ayutla ruins are believed to be a long-lost rival city depicted in the murals at Bonampak.

in A.D. 726—possibly the battle portrayed in Bonampák's famous murals—and Toniná even later. But Sak Tz'i' may have had the last laugh: As the major powers collapsed one by one around the turn of the 9th century, San Tz'i' held on until at least A.D. 864, making it one of the last significant Maya cities to fall.

The buildings atop the pyramid on the left (as you enter the site) are larger and more elaborate, including several multiroom "palace structures" with original stucco and paint still visible, and two temples with stunning 10-meter vaulted ceilings. Together they form a grand multilevel complex that probably served as residential quarters for the city's elite, and today makes for fun exploring. The structures on the other pyramid are smaller, and probably related to administrative functions, but no less impressive. In particular, a small but artful building dubbed Temple of the Inscription has faint hieroglyphic text on two sides, while a nearby structure has a distinctive temple-within-a-temple design, similar to structures found at Palenque.

Beyond the two pyramids, a low structure is being excavated, which archaeologists believe may have been part of an unusually large ball court—some 65 meters long. If confirmed, this would be the largest ball court in the region, even bigger than the ones at Palenque and Toniná. Numerous additional structures await excavation; in all, the city covered over five hectares (12 acres).

To get to the ruins, continue on the main road past Nueva Palestina for 4.25 kilometers, looking for a smaller unmarked road just before a bridge and curve. Turn left there, and go another three kilometers to where the road makes a curious S-curve beneath a stand of trees—there are no signs, but you can't miss the twin pyramids looming on either side of the road. The archaeological site is technically on private property, and you may be asked to pay an admission fee of US$2 per person.

Accommodations and Food

Campamento Po'op Chan (tel. 55/5004-7135, campamentopoopchan@yahoo.com, US$15

pp) has simple wood cabins built on stilts overlooking a small stream, utilizing so-so shared toilets and showers. Cabins are reasonably clean and comfortable, each with two double beds, a patio, and mosquito screens for walls. Large holes in the screens—not to mention gaps in the floor boards—make insect repellent a good idea, especially in the rainy/buggy season.

The *campamento* receives mostly groups, which typically bring their own food supplies. Ask at reception about arranging meals at Po'op Chan (tel. 55/5004-7135, campamento poopchan@yahoo.com); otherwise there are several simple eateries in town.

In San Cristóbal, **SendaSur** (Calle Real de Guadalupe 46, tel. 967/678-3909) is an office operated jointly by several community tourism entities in order to promote and facilitate their projects. Stop by for information about the various destination, or to make reservations; a deposit may be required, and is payable at the office.

Getting There
COMBI

Combis leave Palenque for Nuevo Palestina (US$4, 2 hrs) at 10:30 A.M., 11:30 A.M., 12:30 P.M., and 5:30 P.M. To return, *combis* leave the small terminal facing the main square at 4 A.M., 5 A.M., 6 A.M., and 2 P.M. A taxi to or from Nueva Palestina's central square to Campamento Po'op Chan is US$3. Alternatively, take a taxi to the highway turnoff (US$5), where you can flag down a *combi* headed either direction.

CAR

The turnoff to Nueva Palestina is at Kilometer 107, right where a major military checkpoint is located. From there, it's 11 kilometers into town, all paved. The road turns to dirt on the opposite side of town.

LACANJÁ CHANSAYAB

For many years, the Lacandón village of Lacanjá Chansayab was once a true off-the-beaten-path destination—an adventuresome jaunt into the *selva Lacandona* (Lacandón jungle) that was occasionally added to still-nascent tours of Yaxchilán and Bonampak. How things have changed. Today, Lacanjá Chansayab more closely resembles a summer camp than it does an indigenous village, with virtually every family engaged in tourism, mainly in the form of cookie-cutter *campamentos* (rustic lodging) and overpriced tours along well-worn forest trails. Competition seems to have quickly overpowered most sense of community spirit among local residents. A visit here can still be rewarding—the rainforest remains impressive, and local residents and families, when they let their guard down, often reveal fascinating experiences and perspectives—but it's not the sublime ecological and cultural encounter many expect.

Sights

Every *campamento* offers guided walks, or *caminatas,* through the rainforest to nearby sights, typically lasting 3–5 hours and costing US$25–40 per person.

Ruínas Lacanjá (Lancanjá Ruins) is a minimally excavated archaeological site, with a small main temple with traces of the original red paint still visible and several inscribed panels and stelae, ensconced in lush rainforest.

Cascada Las Golondrinas (Swallows Waterfall) is a scenic waterfall made up of four different cascades, pouring over a long cliff. While included in most guided walks, it's easy enough to reach on your own, following a trail accessed through Parador Sak Nok' (US$3.50 entrance).

Campamento Río Lacanjá (San Cristóbal tel. 967/674-6660, www.ecochiapas.com/lacanja) arranges **rafting trips** (US$60 pp) that include two hours rafting down the Río Lacanjá and two hours hiking back, with stops at Lacanjá ruins and Cascada Las Golondrinas.

Laguna Lacanjá is described by some as a mini–Laguna Miramar; it's a gorgeous crystalline lake emerging like an oasis from the lush tropical rainforest. Unfortunately, a disagreement between local residents has halted visits there, at least officially. Still, it doesn't hurt to ask—it's a true gem, and all the more memorable for being so seldom visited.

Accommodations

Campamento Río Lacanjá (San Cristóbal tel. 967/674-6660, www.ecochiapas.com/lacanja, US$10–12 pp shared bathroom, US$45–65 private bathroom 1–4 people) is the most atmospheric of the *campamentos* in Lacanjá Chansayab. The complex includes eight simple wood cabins with mosquito nets over the beds and small porches with hammocks, built in a shady grove alongside a small river. There are no locks—nor doors for that matter, just a bolt of fabric hanging in the doorway—but the staff insists there's never been any theft. Clean shared bathrooms and showers are in a central building. For a bit more comfort, there are also three large, albeit sterile, units with private bathrooms, tile floors, and ceiling fans. Campamento Río Lacanjá is associated with Explora Ecoturismo (www.explorachiapas.com), a San Cristóbal–based tour operator that specializes in rafting trips and uses this *campamento* for its groups. To get here, turn left at the village center and continue to the end of the road.

Campamento Topche (campamento-topche @hotmail.com, US$8 pp shared bathroom, US$30 s, US$40 d/t) is run by the amiable Don Enrique Chankin Paniagua and family, and is sometimes referred to as Campamento Enrique. The shared-bath units are cheap but pretty grim, with plywood walls and grubby cement floors. The private units are more appealing, with tile floors and high sloped ceilings. The family operates a pleasant restaurant adjacent to the cabins, and has the only Internet access in town (US$1.50/hr).

Campamento Ya'aj Che (martin@send asur.com, US$8 pp shared bathroom, US$30 s, US$40 d/t) has simple wood cabins with shared bathrooms and is located within earshot of a gurgling stream. Boxy private units are more comfortable, with private bathrooms and tile floors, but lack the outdoorsy ambience.

Nearby, **Campamento Ecológico Tucán Verde** (tel. 961/102-7863, www.tucanverde .com, US$2.50 pp camping, US$6 pp dorm, US$7 pp private *cabaña,* some with en suite bathroom) has a promising website, but the *cabañas* leave a lot to be desired. Still, the host family is friendly and the large grassy area is suitable for camping.

Food

All of the *campamentos* have small restaurants, most of which are open to guests and non-guests alike and serve standard Mexican meals at moderate prices.

Parador Sak Nok'p (8 A.M.–6 P.M. daily, US$4–12) has simple wood tables set in a leafy open-air dining area. Look for the sign on your left, about halfway between the village center and Campamento Topche (aka Campamento Enrique).

Practicalities

There's **Internet access** (US$1.50/hr) at Campamento Topche, also known as Campamento Enrique. The village also has a very basic clinic, but medical issues of any severity ought to be handled in Palenque or Villahermosa.

Getting There

COMBI

Although Lacanjá Chansayab is 12 kilometers (7 miles) off the Palenque–Frontera Corozal highway, *combis* operated by **Autotransporte Chamoan** (in Palenque, Av. Miguel Hidalgo btwn. Calles 1a Pte. and Allende) are supposed to drive passengers all the way into the village, provided you inform the driver in advance. If for some reason you are dropped in San Javier, on the highway, a taxi to the village costs US$1–2.

CAR

The well-marked turnoff to Lacanjá Chansayab is at the roadside town of San Javier, about 130 kilometers from Palenque. Bear right there, and again at a second intersection about a kilometer later. Continue for eight kilometers to the village center.

FRONTERA COROZAL

This quiet community along the banks of the Río Usumacinta is the jumping-off point for visiting the Yaxchilán archaeological site, a terrific Maya ruin located about 25 kilometers downriver. It's also a convenient border crossing into Guatemala—just across the river—and you may be asked to show your passport (and pay a small fee) at a checkpoint at the entrance of town, even if you intend to remain in Mexico. The town itself is quite new, founded in 1976 by Ch'ol Maya émigrés from northern Chiapas, along with a small number of Lacandón and Tzeltal families. Relations are far from perfect, but locals take pride in their town's multicultural origins.

Sights

Boats to Yaxchilán archaeological zone

(25 kilometers, 45 mins there/60 mins return) leave from a pier at the end of the main road, where a number of cooperatives and private outfits compete for arriving tourists. The trip is quite enjoyable, zipping down the river in a long colorful *lancha* with Guatemala on one side and Mexico on the other, and the chance to see birds, howler monkeys, and beefy crocodiles sunning themselves on the riverbank. Round-trip prices are fairly uniform and depend on the size of your group: US$65 for 1–3 passengers, US$75 for four, US$95 for 5–7, and US$120 for 8–10. The price includes two hours at the site; you can stay longer, but you'll have to tip the boatman (even better, throw in a Coke and something to eat as well).

If you've got time to kill, the **Museo Comunitario Frontera Corozal** (tel. 55/5329-0995, 8 A.M.–6 P.M. daily, free) is a small well-organized museum with a room about the history of the community, another on local customs, flora, and fauna, and a third on archaeological discoveries, including the museum's pièce de résistance: two 3-meter, 3-ton stelae found in the surrounding forest, carefully restored, and installed here. Signage is in Spanish only.

Accommodations

On the riverfront at the end of the main road, **Escudo Jaguar** (tel. 001-502/5353-5637 or 001-502/5328-6967, www.escudojaguar hotel.com, US$20–60, camping US$7 pp) has comfortable pink thatch-roofed *cabañas,* ranging in size from one to three beds. All have ceiling fans, mosquito nets, and 24-hour electricity; smaller units have shared bathrooms, while larger ones have private bathrooms plus writing desks and private patios with hammocks. Escudo Jaguar has long been Frontera Corozal's preferred hotel, including for tour groups, and as a result is occasionally full. Note that the telephone is a Guatemalan number, although the hotel is in Mexico.

Nueva Alianza (tel. 502/5353-1395, www.ecoturlacandona.com, US$7 pp camping, US$110 pp shared cabins, US$20–60 private cabins) has somewhat simpler accommodations but a more atmospheric location (and generally fewer visitors). Options include camping, large dorm-style cabins, and private units set in a leafy grove.

Food

Escudo Jaguar (tel. 502/5353-5637 or 502/5328-6967, www.escudojaguarhotel.com, 7 A.M.–8 P.M. daily, US$5–10) and **Nueva Alianza** (tel. 502/5353-1395, www.ecoturlacandona.com, 7 A.M.–8 P.M. daily, US$5–10) both have restaurants catering to tour groups, but open to all, serving decent regional fare in large *palapa*-covered dining areas.

Museo Comunitario Frontera Corozal (tel. 55/5329-0995, 8 A.M.–6 P.M. daily) has a small eatery serving simple but reliable meals, including a daily *comida corrida* (lunch special) that includes soup, main dish, and drink.

Information and Services

There is no bank or ATM in town, and no one accepts credit cards; bring enough cash to get you through your stay. **Escudo Jaguar** (tel. 502/5353-5637 or 502/5328-6967, www.escudojaguarhotel.com) has telephone and Internet service for guests; non-guests can usually plead their case.

Getting There and Around

COMBI

From Palenque, **Autotransporte Chamoan** (Av. Miguel Hidalgo btwn. Calles 1a Pte. and Allende) provides *combi* service to Frontera Corozal (US$7, 3.5 hrs) every hour on the hour from 5 A.M. to 5 P.M. daily. The bus stops a short distance from the river dock, where you can catch a boat to Yaxchilán. The same *combis* return to Palenque at 4, 4:30, 5, 5:30, 6, 7, and 8 A.M., and then hourly from 11 A.M. to 4 P.M.

CAR

From Palenque, follow the Carretera Fronteriza for 162 kilometers to *crucero Corozal,* a well-marked turnoff. From there, it's another 22 kilometers to Frontera Corozal. Driving between Palenque and Frontera Corozal used to be unsafe due to armed robberies. The situation has improved immensely, however, and the entire 185-kilometer stretch is considered safe to drive. However, for the sake of caution, it is recommended to drive during daylight hours only.

BOAT

The boat cooperatives that go to Yaxchilán also provide one-way transportation to Betel, Guatemala (US$40 for 1–3 people, US$50 for four, US$60 for 5–7, and US$75 for 7–10; 40 mins), where buses to Flores, outside the archaeological site of Tikal, depart daily at around 11 A.M., 1 P.M., 3 P.M., and 5 P.M. (US$11, 4 hrs). Remember to pass Mexican immigration in Frontera Corozal (8 A.M.–3 P.M. daily) before departing; Guatemalan immigration is in Betel.

Bonampak Archaeological Zone

Bonampak Archaeological Zone (8 A.M.–5 P.M. daily, US$4.50) is a modest site overall, but home to some of the best ancient Maya murals ever discovered. The famous murals adorn the interior walls of a small temple built innocuously on the staircase of the city's main acropolis; painted in brilliant teal, red, and other colors, they depict sacrifices, ritual bloodletting, and violent battle scenes. The images shattered previous assumptions about the Maya, who had been portrayed by many researchers as a peace-loving civilization, in sharp contrast to Central Mexican indigenous groups and, of course, the Spanish colonizers.

HISTORY

Located in a fertile valley, Bonampak is near a small tributary of the Río Lacanjá, with protective hills to one side. The earliest evidence of human occupation at Bonampak are ceramics dated to A.D. 100; it reached its apogee in the Late Classic era (A.D. 600–800). Bonampak has a close and surprisingly amicable relationship with the nearby city of Yaxchilán, just 20 kilometers (12 miles) to the southeast. Bonampak's most notable leader, Chaan-Muan, was married to the sister of Yaxchilán's great king Shield Jaguar. The brothers-in-law joined forces in the 7th century in a war against an unknown third city, possibly Sak Tz'i'. The battle is commemorated in a part of Bonampak's famous murals and lintels. Relatively little else is known about the city, however.

Much more ink has been dedicated to the scandal that arose around the site's discovery in the 1940s. An American conscientious objector—or draft-dodger, depending on the telling—named Karl Frey was part of a team headed by filmmaker Giles Healy to find and document the ruins, which had been reported to archaeologists 40 years prior but never explored. The two had a falling out and the expedition was abandoned; later, in 1946, Frey succeeded in reaching the site, but evidently missed the murals. Healy made the trip several

months later, discovered the murals—even the local Lacandón people seemed not to have known of their existence—and made headlines with his startling find. Frey spent years trying to convince the world he was the true discoverer, to no avail. He formed part of an ill-advised exploration team organized by the Mexican Fine Arts Institute in 1949—a joint Carnegie Institute and INAH exploration had already gone and returned with detailed maps and drawings—during which he drowned in the Río Lacanjá, reportedly trying to save a fellow team member after their canoe capsized.

◀ BONAMPAK MURALS

Bonampak's murals are housed in **Temple I,** which stands on a low level of the **Acropolis,** a large stepped structure that backs onto a jungle-covered hill. In front of the Acropolis is a plaza with low buildings around the other three sides. Researchers believe that the story told through the murals should be read from left to right, from Room 1 to Room 3. The setting of Room 1's mural is the palace, where the child-heir is presented to the court and 336 days later is the focal point of a celebration with actors and musicians. The murals in Room 2 tell the story of a jungle battle, probably in honor of the heir, led by Chaan-Muan. This is considered the greatest battle scene in Maya art.

Next the scene moves to a staircase, where the captives are ritually tortured while Chaan-Muan watches from above. In Room 3 the setting is a pyramid, where costumed lords dance and a captive awaits his death. To the side, noblewomen ritually let their blood, while a pot-bellied dwarf is presented to the court. Anthropologists believe that the child-heir never ruled Bonampak, because there is evidence that the site was abandoned before the murals were even completed. The murals have faded with time and were damaged when the first researchers used kerosene to clean them—the kerosene brought out the colors but weakened the paints' adhesion and hastened the flaking and decay. The Museo

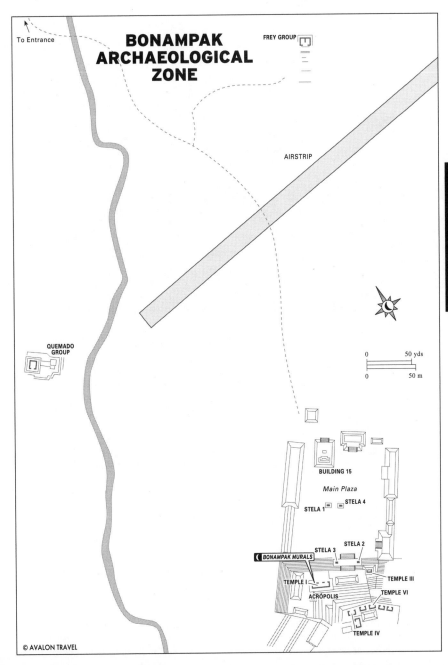

© LIZA PRADO

A small temple on Bonampak's Acrópolis houses some of the best Maya murals discovered to date.

Nacional de Antropología in Mexico City has a reproduction of how the murals likely looked in their full glory, and lesser copies are found in Tuxtla Gutiérrez and Villahermosa. But, though they are old and damaged, you still can't beat the originals.

When visiting Bonampak (and Yaxchilán) be sure to look at the beautifully carved scenes on the underside of the lintels (the slab of stone that forms the top of a doorway). Their location makes them easy to miss, but they are truly some of the best Maya relief carvings you'll see outside of a museum. In Bonampak, Lintel I shows Chaan-Muan holding a captive by the hair; Lintel II shows Itzanaaj B'alam doing the same; and Lintel III shows a figure, possibly Chan-Muan's father, Knot Eye Jaguar, spearing a victim in the chest.

GETTING THERE

Most people visit Bonampak (and Yaxchilán) as part of an all-day round-trip package from Palenque. The "tour" usually includes just transportation—no guide service, though the drivers

are often quite knowledgeable—but it is a very practical option, even for those who eschew packages of any sort. That's because visiting both ruins in a day requires keeping a tight schedule, which is impossible if you're traveling by *combi*. A rental car is quicker, but you still get pinched for things that are included in the tour price (not to mention gas and the rental itself), At Bonampák, a local cooperative controls the 10-kilometer access road, and charges an outrageous US$7 per person for round-trip van service to the ruins. Anyone not arriving by tour must pay, whether arriving by bus or rental car, though small discounts are available for students and seniors. Bikes can be rented a short distance past the control booth and parking area (van operators will try to convince you the stand is closed), but at US$6 for three hours, there's no real savings.

Combi

From Palenque, *combis* operated by **Autotransporte Chamoan** (Av. Miguel Hidalgo btwn. Calles 1a Pte. and Allende) leave for Frontera Corozal hourly 5 A.M. to 5 P.M.

daily; be sure to ask the driver to drop you at *crucero* Bonampak (Bonampak turnoff, US$7, 3.5 hrs), which is a kilometer off the main road and not an automatic stop. From there, you must take a local van (US$7 pp round-trip).

Car

About 130 kilometers from Palenque in the town of San Javier are large signs and a prominent intersection marking the turnoff to Bonampak. Turn right and go a short distance further to a second intersection, known as *crucero* Bonampak (Bonampak turnoff). It's another 10 kilometers to the ruins, but private cars aren't allowed past; instead you must park and take a local van (US$7 pp round-trip).

Yaxchilán Archaeological Zone

The Yaxchilán ruins lie on the Río Usumacinta, Mexico's largest river and the border between Mexico and Guatemala. Archaeologists have found at least 35 stelae, 60 carved lintels, 21 altars, and 5 stairways covered with hieroglyphs here—a treasure trove for epigraphers. Yaxchilán's rulers were obsessed with venerating their dynasty as well as legitimizing their rule and endowed a major monument-carving operation to achieve these goals. In fact, it was Yaxchilán's hieroglyphs that provided much of the raw material that led to the deciphering of the Maya writing system.

HISTORY

Yaxchilán was a powerful city-state during the Classic era, ruled by the Jaguar dynasty, which traced its roots to A.D. 320 and a ruler named Yat B'alam (Jaguar Penis). The earliest recorded date at the site is from A.D. 435, and the first major monuments appeared early in the 6th century.

Yaxchilán's greatest ruler was Izamnaaj B'alam, or Shield Jaguar, who was born in A.D. 647 and ruled for more than six decades (A.D. 681–742), a remarkable feat for a man whose life expectancy would have been less than 40 years. He undertook numerous construction projects, including the construction of Structure 23 on the main plaza. Dedicated to his wife Lady Xoc, it is the only Maya temple known to have been built specifically in honor of a woman. (Palenque's Temple XIII, in which archaeologists recently excavated the so-called Tomb of the Red Queen, may be another,

but that is not confirmed.) But the construction and dedication of Structure 23 may have more to do with politics than enlightenment; Shield Jaguar took a second wife late in life and named the son from that union, Bird Jaguar, heir to the throne. Structure 23, which shows Lady Xoc conducting various noble rituals, may have been a way of appeasing her powerful family.

© LIZA PRADO

It's easy to miss some of Yaxchilán's best engravings, including this one, located on the underside of low doorway lintels.

Bird Jaguar succeeded Shield Jaguar; curiously he was not crowned until A.D. 752, a full 10 years after his father's death. Archaeologists interpret this as a sign of tepid political support for the young monarch; as further evidence they point to Bird Jaguar's obsessive self-aggrandizement once he finally did assume the throne, as if he were desperate to legitimize his position. Bird Jaguar built numerous buildings, most notably Structure 33, and seems to have commissioned a stelae or relief carving to commemorate his every accomplishment, including military victories, bloodletting ceremonies, the sacrifice of important captives, and even winning a ball game match. Bird Jaguar was the beginning of the end for the Jaguar dynasty, which lasted until about A.D. 800. Its last ruler, Ta-Skull, Bird Jaguar's grandson, is credited with just two small rather poorly constructed temples (Structures 3 and 64), which contain the latest known date inscription at Yaxchilán, A.D. 808, commemorating a military victory. Yaxchilán gradually depopulated and by A.D. 900 had been returned to the jungle.

◖ YAXCHILÁN RUINS

A steep path leads up from the boat pier to Yaxchilán's ticket booth. Entering the site, the main path leads to the Main Plaza, with the Great Acropolis a long steep flight of stairs above. But instead of following the main path, consider taking the small path that cuts to your right up the hill to the **Little Acropolis.** It's a steep climb, but once there, the rest of your visit is downhill. The most important structure in this complex is Structure 44, which was built by Shield Jaguar in celebration of his military successes.

Continue on the path to reach the **Great Acropolis** from the backside. It's a pleasant walk, and you may spot howler monkeys in the trees along the way. Around front, you'll be at the top of a long flight of stone stairs and in front of one of Yaxchilán's most notable structures, **Structure 33,** with its intricate facade and soaring roof comb. Built by Bird Jaguar to celebrate himself—who else?—it includes incredibly fine lintels and panels depicting the

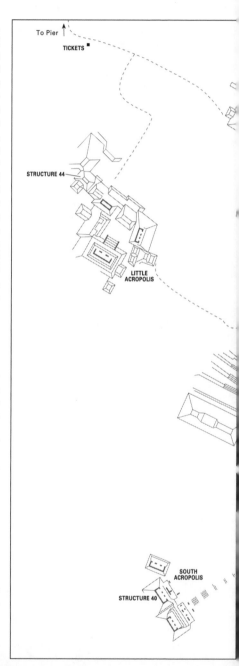

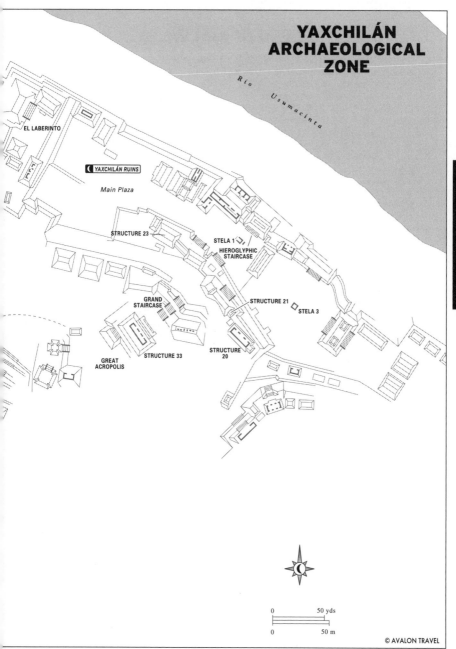

© AVALON TRAVEL

YEAR 2012 – THE END OF AN ERA

On or around December 21, 2012, the ancient Maya calendar known as the Long Count completes its 13th and final *baktun* (a period equal to around 395 years), which in turn will mark the end of the first Great Cycle, a period equivalent to around 5,125 years, when the Long Count calendar will reset. The approaching date has New Agers and doomsayers in a tizzy, and is the subject of countless predictions and prophesies, most of them apocalyptic, described in thousands of websites and a raft of books like *2012: The Return of Quetzalcoatl* by Daniel Pinchbeck (2006) and *Apocalypse 2012: A Scientific Investigation into Civilization's End* by Lawrence Joseph (2007). Predictions range from the end of the world to the dawning of a new age of enlightenment, whether for indigenous rights or honoring the "sacred feminine."

It's unclear what the ancient Maya themselves thought would happen at the end of the Long Count. Although the date is mentioned in various places, no specific prophesies have been uncovered. Without question it would have been considered supremely significant; the Maya were acutely attuned to numerous cycles, including the seasonal solstices and equinoxes, the orbits of the moon and Venus, and periods known as *k'atun* (20 years), *haab'* (52 years), *baktun* (395 years), and others. But unlike dire modern-day predictions

for 2012, the beginning of a new cycle was typically viewed by ancient Maya as auspicious – many pyramids, temples, and stelae were commissioned to mark such dates – and it stands to reason that the end of the Long Count would have been seen and celebrated in a similar light. (Then again, the ancient Maya never crossed a threshold quite like 2012, which they clearly considered, in a certain sense, the end of time, or at least *this* time.) For their part, most mainstream archaeologists discount 2012 doomsday predictions as baseless at best, and potentially damaging to legitimate research into Maya mysticism and cosmology.

Still, some intriguing coincidences do exist, like the fact that the earth, sun, and Milky Way will be aligned in 2012 in a way that occurs only once every 26,000 years, and that solar activity, already more intense now than any time in the last 11,000 years, is expected to peak in 2012, with flares that may be powerful enough to disable satellites and power grids.

For many, the most compelling omen as 2012 approaches is the gathering storm of environmental, health, population, and economic crises facing our planet. Did the ancient Maya peer into the future and see our collective demise, or will 2012, like Y2K a dozen years before, come and go without incident? Only time will tell.

ruler's accomplishments, including summoning his deceased ancestors in the midst of a ball game.

Descending the stairs you'll reach the **Main Plaza,** a long rectangular plaza built alongside the river bank, framed by numerous structures and dotted with large stelae. **Structure 20** and **Structure 21** are to the right of the staircase as you reach the bottom; built by Shield Jaguar and Bird Jaguar respectively, both have lintels portraying rituals related to the birth of heirs. On the other side of the staircase, **Structure 23** is the famous temple built by Shield Jaguar and dedicated to Lady Xoc. This is where archaeologists discovered exquisitely carved

panels portraying the noblewoman performing rituals, including drawing a thorny twine through her tongue.

At the west end of the main plaza is a complex called **El Laberinto** (The Labyrinth), so named for its maze of vaulted passageways and chambers; it likely served as residential quarters. On the other side, the main path leads back through the trees to the boat landing.

The archaeological zone is open 8 A.M.–5 P.M. daily; admission is US$4.50.

GETTING THERE

Yaxchilán is located 25 kilometers down the Río Usumacinta from the town of Frontera Corozal, and can only be reached by *lancha* (long colorful canoe-like boat with a sun cover and powerful outboard motor). The 45-to-60-minute ride (US$65 for 1–3 passengers, US$75 for four, US$95 for 5–7, and US$120 for 8–10) is definitely part of the fun of visiting this remote site—keep an eye out for huge river crocodiles sunning themselves on the banks, their mouths standing open.

THE RÍO USUMACINTA VALLEY

SAN CRISTÓBAL DE LAS CASAS

San Cristóbal de las Casas is a city of many layers, a place to delve into, not merely admire. It is first and foremost a wonderful old colonial town, easily one of Mexico's finest. Low colorful buildings with tile roofs and wrought-iron details line the narrow streets, their wooden doorways sometimes framed by exuberant bougainvillea vines. The shady central plaza is flanked by an elegant mustard-yellow cathedral that seems to glow in the setting sun, often to the sound of a live marimba band.

But San Cristóbal is more than just a pretty face. The indigenous presence is stronger and more visible here than in any other Mexican city. You'll hear Tzotzil and Tzeltal on a daily basis, and share the streets, markets, and public plazas with indigenous people, a great many wearing traditional garb. Beyond San Cristóbal are numerous outlying villages that can be visited by tour or on your own—from the fiercely independent San Juan Chamula to the little-visited communities of Chenalhó and Oxchuc. A highlight for many visitors, these towns are a reminder of the rich ethnic and cultural diversity of modern Maya society.

San Cristóbal's non-indigenous population tends to be progressive and bohemian, as are the majority of foreign travelers and expats. The city boasts numerous art-house theaters, coffee houses, and hipster bars, as well as myriad NGO and research organizations; together they form a unique social milieu that is both thoughtful and a lot of fun.

With so many facets to explore, fascinating sights to take in, and welcoming places to

© LIZA PRADO

HIGHLIGHTS

((El Zócalo: Most Mexican cities have attractive *zócalos* (central plazas), but San Cristóbal's is particularly lovely, with tree-shaded benches and a two-story bandstand with a café and live marimba music most evenings. It's adjacent to the cathedral and city hall, each with plazas of their own, as well as the main pedestrian walkways (page 83).

((La Catedral de San Cristóbal: The city's main cathedral is especially impressive in the late afternoon, when its mustard-yellow facade seems to glow in the setting sun. Inside is an impressive *retablo* altar, and the church steps and plaza are a favorite gathering place for families, tourists, shoe-shiners, and folk-art vendors (page 83).

((Templo y Ex-Convento de Santo Domingo de Guzmán: This grand church is a colonial masterpiece, with an impressively ornate facade and a gorgeous gold-painted altar and wing chapels inside. The former convent houses a museum and award-winning indigenous textile shop, and the city's best *artesanía* market can be found in the adjacent courtyards (page 86).

((San Juan Chamula: The most visited indigenous village outside San Cristóbal, and with good reason: This staunchly independent town has fascinating customs and history and a beautiful church with no pews – and no priest – that is used instead for healing ceremonies conducted by shamans (page 111).

((El Romerillo: This tiny roadside hamlet is home to one of the largest and most important

Chamulan cemeteries, guarded by towering Maya crosses. Its mounded graves are covered by wood "doors" through which family members talk to the dead on All Saints Day (Día de Todos Santos) in November (page 115).

LOOK FOR ((TO FIND RECOMMENDED SIGHTS, ACTIVITIES, DINING, AND LODGING.

© AVALON TRAVEL

spend the night, you'll find it easy—almost too easy—to extend your stay.

HISTORY

San Cristóbal de las Casas was founded in 1528 by Spanish captain Diego de Mazariegos following a bloody four-year conquest of the region's dominant indigenous groups, the Zoques and the Chiapas. Mazariegos originally selected a spot along the steamy Río Grijalva in order to keep an eye on the largest Chiapa settlement a few kilometers distant, but within a month rampant disease forced him to relocate to higher ground and the present location.

The new city was originally called Villareal de Chiapa de los Españoles, the first of many names it would sport over the centuries. In 1535, it was renamed San Cristóbal de los Llanos, after the city's patron saint, then Ciudad Real de Chiapa just a year later. That name stuck for almost three centuries, until 1829, when city leaders adopted the name Ciudad de San Cristóbal, and finally today's San Cristóbal de las Casas, in honor of the crusading anti-slavery bishop Bartolomé de las Casas. And so it remained, save a short period in the 1930s and '40s when it was called Ciudad las Casas (but who's counting?). Of course, indigenous people had names for this highland valley long before the Spanish did, variations of which are still used today, including Jovel and Hueyzacatlán.

San Cristóbal served as the colonial capital of the Chiapanecan highlands—and the entire region, effectively—through most of the 17th and 18th centuries. But in 1768 Chiapas was divided into two mayoralties, to be governed by San Cristóbal and its lowland rival, San Marcos Tuxtla. San Cristóbal remained the political center, but power was clearly draining to the lowlands, where land that was once ruled by disease-carrying insects was being converted into massive ranches and agricultural estates. The Mexican war of independence further elevated San Marcos, and in 1892 the upstart city—by then known as Tuxtla Gutiérrez—was declared the state capital.

If Chiapas was remote when it was ruled from Guatemala (seat of the Spanish Royal Audience), it was doubly so when incorporated into the new Mexican republic, with its capital in far-off Mexico City. Yet Chiapas is a state rich in natural resources, and for nearly a century the state saw its forests cut and its rivers dammed, while roads, schools, utilities, and other public infrastructure lagged far behind the rest of the nation. Of course, being ignored suited Chiapas's vast indigenous population quite well, at least to a point—they went on living as they had for centuries. But eventually native communities saw too much land expropriated and lost too much autonomy; the balance was tipped and discontent boiled over in the form of masked Zapatista rebels storming San Cristóbal's city hall in 1994.

The Zapatista uprising has since faded in memory and San Cristóbal has settled back into a familiar second-city status, with a rich ethnic and cultural mix and a strong anti-establishment streak. Sure, there's a Burger King across the street from Revolución Café, but San Cristóbal still manages to feel like an off-the-beaten-path destination, a place that exudes beauty and intelligence in equal measure.

PLANNING YOUR TIME

You're sure to want at least three days in San Cristóbal, and most travelers would have no trouble staying twice that long, or more. Take a day or two to hit the city's "obvious" sights, including museums, churches, plazas, and markets, which are numerous and fascinating. Spend another day or two visiting the outlying indigenous villages; San Juan Chamula and Zinacantán are must-sees, but a visit to one or more of the lesser-known communities has its own, often more sublime, reward. And be sure to budget some time to simply soak up San Cristóbal's atmosphere, whether lounging in the central plaza, writing postcards at a coffee house, catching a documentary at an art-house theater, or enjoying live music and a drink at a local bar.

ORIENTATION

San Cristóbal's main pedestrian walkway, known as *el andador*, runs though the heart

SAN CRISTÓBAL DE LAS CASAS DETAIL

Moxviquil Reserve/ Orchid Garden

To Huitepec Reserve, **SAN JUAN CHAMULA**, Zinacantán, San Andrés Larrainzar, and Chenalhó

To El Arcotete, Templo Carmen Arcotete, **EL ROMERILLO**, and Tenejapa

PERIFÉRICO NORTE

MUSEO DE LA MEDICINA MAYA ★

AV GENERAL UTRILLA

GUADALUPE VICTORIA

REAL DE GUADALUPE

★ TEMPLO DE GUADALUPE

DIAGONAL HERMANOS PANIAGUA

CINÉPOLIS

AV INSURGENTES

SEE "DOWNTOWN SAN CRISTÓBAL DE LAS CASAS" MAP

AGUASCALIENTES

■ CHEDRAUI

■ TEATRO DE LAS CIUDAD HERMANOS DOMÍNGUEZ

IMMIGRATION OFFICE

COMBIS TO AMATENANGO ■

■ COMBIS TO TUXTLA GUTIÉRREZ

EJE DOS

BLVD JUAN SABINES GUTIÉRREZ (CARRETERA PANAMERICANA)

COMBIS TO GRUTAS DE RANCHO NUEVO AND OXCHUC

CEMETERY

JOSÉ MARÍA MORELOS

★ PLAZA DE TOROS

To Chiapa de Corzo, Cañon del Sumidero, International Airport, and Tuxtla Gutiérrez (Old Highway)

EJE UNO

• BUNGALOWS DEL SOL

To Chiapa de Corzo, Cañon del Sumidero, International Airport, and Tuxtla Gutiérrez (Toll Road)

PERIFÉRICO SUR

© AVALON TRAVEL   SCALE NOT AVAILABLE

To Grutas de Rancho Nuevo, Oxchuc, Amatenango del Valle, Comitán, and Palenque

of downtown, with the *zócalo* and cathedral in the middle, and Santo Domingo church and the Templo Carmen archway on its northern and southern ends. Almost 10 blocks long, the walkway is lined with shops and restaurants, and is always pleasantly busy. (Note: The northern section is technically Avenida 20 de Noviembre, and the southern section is Av Miguel Hidalgo, though few people refer to either as such.) The first three blocks of Real de Guadalupe (extending east from the *zócalo*) are also a pedestrian walkway, though *el andador* always refers to the original.

Sights

You won't run out of things to see and visit in San Cristóbal. There are literally dozens of historic churches and buildings, large and small, nearly all dating to the colonial era, and a seemingly equal number of museums and galleries dedicated to everything from amber to coffee to modern art. On the outskirts of town are a slew of natural attractions, including caves and forest reserves, and beyond that are a vast array of indigenous communities, each quite different from the next.

If you're traveling with a cell phone that has Telcel coverage, you can use it to receive text messages with in-depth information on San Cristóbal's historical sites. Text messages cost US$0.35 and are sent in Spanish, English, French, Italian, and German. (Tzotzil and Tzeltal too, if you happen to be fluent.) Look for the burgundy markers in front of each site for codes.

LANDMARKS
◖ El Zócalo
The official name of San Cristóbal's leafy central plaza is Plaza de 31 de Marzo, but most people refer to it as either El Zócalo or the *parque central* (central park). During the colonial era the plaza served several functions: a public market, a water-gathering spot (a large fountain supplied most of the town's water), a place to collect taxes, and a place of punishment during the years of the conquest. Hundreds of years later, in 1994, Zapatista rebels stormed the plaza and adjoining Palacio Municipal (City Hall).

Today, the plaza serves mostly as a tranquil refuge, with wide walkways, green iron benches, large shade trees, and a two-story central bandstand where you can enjoy coffee and light fare along with nightly live marimba band. Rallies and demonstrations are still held here sometimes, but unruly gatherings are extremely rare. In the plaza and in front of the cathedral, expect to be approached by Chamulan women and children selling hand-woven bracelets, belts, and shawls. Their prices are unbelievably low, and even a small purchase seems greatly appreciated.

Palacio Municipal
On the west side of the central park sits the Palacio Municipal (City Hall). It was built in 1885 after rebel troops led by Juan Ortega burned the original building to the ground during a skirmish between Royalists and Republicans in 1863. When construction of the present building began, San Cristóbal was still the capital of the state and the plan included an edifice that was to take up an entire city block. But the capital was moved to Tuxtla Gutiérrez, and the building was limited to a quarter size of the planned construction. Nevertheless, the final product is still attractive, with neoclassical columns, arches, and a large plaza in the rear where civic ceremonies and demonstrations are held. Notably, the Palacio Municipal suffered major damage during the 1994 Zapatista uprising, though that damage is no longer evident today.

Casa de Mazariegos
One of the oldest buildings in San Cristóbal, Casa de Mazariegos (Av. Insurgentes at Diego de Mazariegos) sits on the southeast corner of the central plaza. Constructed in 1529, it is often referred to as Casa Sirena (Mermaid House) because of the three mermaids or serpent women (take your pick) that are visible on its eastern wall—two bordering a window, one on the corner. Time has destroyed the insignia on the coat of arms over the front door, so although the building often is claimed to have been the home of Diego de Mazariegos, many believe it to be that of the conquistador Andrés de la Tovilla.

CHURCHES
◖ La Catedral de San Cristóbal
Constructed in 1528, San Cristóbal's cathedral (pedestrian walkway, Av. 20 de Noviembre at

SAN CRISTÓBAL DE LAS CASAS

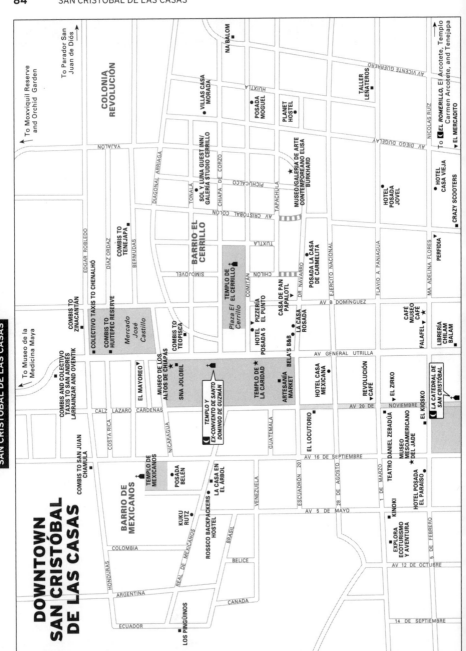

DOWNTOWN SAN CRISTÓBAL DE LAS CASAS

To Moxviquil Reserve and Orchid Garden →

To Parador San Juan de Diós →

To Museo de la Medicina Maya

To **EL ROMERILLO**, El Arcotete, Templo Carmen Arcotete, and Tenejapa →

COLONIA REVOLUCIÓN

BARRIO EL CERRILLO

BARRIO DE MEXICANOS

COMBIS TO SAN JUAN CHAMULA

COMBIS AND COLECTIVO TAXIS TO SAN ANDRÉS LARRAÍNZAR AND OVENTIK

COLECTIVO TAXIS TO CHENALHÓ

COMBIS TO ZINACANTAN

COMBIS TO HUITEPEC RESERVE

COMBIS TO TENEJAPA

COMBIS TO TEOPISCA

NA BALOM

VILLAS CASA MORADA

POSADA MOGUEL

PLANET HOSTEL

HUITLA

TALLER LEÑATEROS

SOL Y LUNA GUEST INN/ GALERÍA STUDIO CERRILLO

MUSEO/GALERÍA DE ARTE CONTEMPORÁNEO ELISA BURKHARD

HOTEL POSADA JOVEL

HOTEL CASA VIEJA

CRAZY SCOOTERS

PERFIDIA

POSADA LA CASA DE CARMELITA

TEMPLO DE EL CERRILLO

Plaza El Cerrillo

HOTEL POSADA 5

PIZZERÍA EL PUNTO

CASA DE PAN PAPALOTL

LA CASA ROSADA

BELA'S B&B

CAFÉ MUSEO CAFÉ

FALAFEL

LIBRERÍA CHILAM BALAM

Mercado José Castillo

EL MAYOREO

MUSEO DE LOS ALTOS DE CHIAPAS

SNA JOLOBIL

TEMPLO Y EX-CONVENTO DE SANTO DOMINGO DE GUZMÁN

TEMPLO DE LA CARIDAD

ARTESANÍA MARKET

HOTEL CASA MEXICANA

REVOLUCIÓN CAFÉ

EL ZIRKO

LA CATEDRAL DE SAN CRISTÓBAL

EL KIOSKO

EL LOCUTORIO

TEATRO DANIEL ZEBADÚA

MUSEO MESOAMERICANO DEL JADE

HOTEL POSADA EL PARAÍSO

KINOKI

EXPLORA ECOTURISMO Y AVENTURA

TEMPLO DE MEXICANOS

POSADA BELÉN

LA CASA EN EL ÁRBOL

KUKU RUTZ

ROSSCO BACKPACKERS HOSTEL

LOS PINGÜINOS

Streets
YALALON, DIAGONAL ARRIAGA, EDGAR ROBLEDO, DÍAZ ORDAZ, BERMUDAS, TONALÁ, CHIAPA DE CORZO, PICHUCALCO, TAPACHULA, AV CRISTÓBAL COLÓN, TUXTLA, CHILÓN, DR NAVARRO, COMITÁN, EJÉRCITO NACIONAL, AV 8 DOMÍNGUEZ, FLAVIO A PANIAGUA, MA ADELINA FLORES, AV VICENTE GUERRERO, AV DIEGO DUGELAY, NICOLÁS RUIZ

CALZ LÁZARO CÁRDENAS, NICARAGUA, COSTA RICA, GUATEMALA, AV GENERAL UTRILLA, AV 20 DE NOVIEMBRE, AV 16 DE SEPTIEMBRE, AV 5 DE MAYO, HONDURAS, COLOMBIA, REAL DE MEXICANOS, BRASIL, BELICE, ARGENTINA, CANADA, ECUADOR, VENEZUELA, ESCUADRÓN 201, 28 DE AGOSTO, 1 DE MARZO, 5 DE FEBRERO, AV 12 DE OCTUBRE, 14 DE SEPTIEMBRE

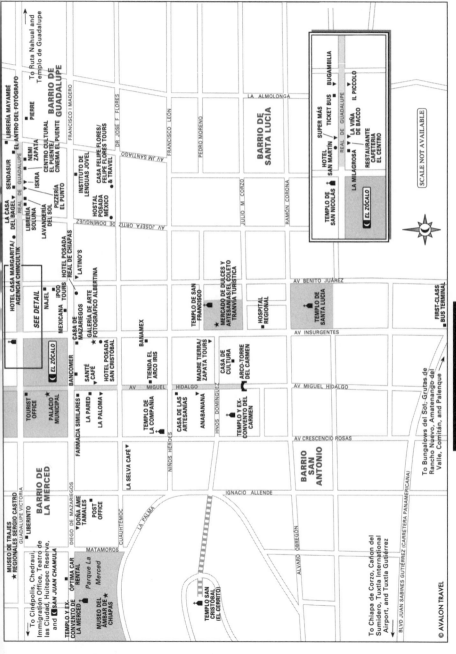

SAN CRISTÓBAL DE LAS CASAS

© AVALON TRAVEL

© LIZA PRADO

San Cristóbal's main cathedral dates to 1528 and is one of the city's most recognizable landmarks.

Real de Guadalupe) sits on the north side of the central square and opens onto the adjoining plaza. The facade is gorgeous, its bright-yellow ocher contrasting with the 17th-century white mortared niches and geometric designs painted white, rust, and black that are reminiscent of the Mudejar style. It's most impressive in late afternoon, when the building's colors are ignited by the setting sun. Inside, the nave and altar are decorated with fine religious art—don't miss the elaborately carved wooden pulpit. The cathedral and the plaza in front come to life during festivals and religious holidays, especially those leading up to Easter and December 12 (Saint's Day for the Virgin of Guadalupe). And every day you can catch a glimpse of the cathedral's bells being rung. Unlike most bells, which are attached to a long rope, these have fin-like counterweights and are rung by a bellman spinning them over and over by hand, like a huge bicycle wheel.

Templo de San Nicolás

Facing the *parque central* behind San Cristóbal's cathedral, the 17th-century Templo de San Nicolás (Real de Guadalupe at Av. General Utrilla) was originally built for the exclusive use of the indigenous population. As such it is simple in style, with only two round towers providing decorative elements to its exterior. Interestingly, San Nicolás is the only church in San Cristóbal to retain its original form.

◖ Templo y Ex-Convento de Santo Domingo de Guzmán

Built in 1547 by the Dominicans, the Templo de Santo Domingo de Guzmán (Av. 20 de Noviembre near Nicaragua) is arguably the most impressive church of the many churches found in the city. It has a gorgeous baroque facade covered with intricately carved mortar, Solomonic columns, and statues tucked into ornate niches—much of it carved by indigenous workers. The interior is equally impressive, its pulpit covered in gold carvings and backed by countless *retablos* (religious paintings) that are offered in gratitude for answered

© LIZA PRADO

the amazingly ornate facade of Templo Santo Domingo, one of San Cristóbal's oldest and most striking churches

prayers. Don't miss visiting El Rosario chapel, which has gorgeous baroque altarpieces as well as the Holy Trinity of Santo Domingo, considered a masterpiece of Central American colonial sculpture.

In the church's courtyard, there's a daily outdoor *artesanía* market; in the attached ex-convent there's also the award-winning weavers co-op **Sna Jolobil** (Ex-Convento del Templo de Santo Domingo, Av. 20 de Noviembre near Nicaragua, 9 A.M.–2 P.M. and 4–7 P.M. Mon.–Sat.) and the **Museo de los Altos de Chiapas** (Ex-Convento del Templo Santo Domingo de Guzmán, Av. 20 de Noviembre near Nicaragua, tel. 967/678-1609, 9 A.M.–6 P.M. daily, US$4).

Templo de la Caridad

Near the Templo de Santo Domingo is the Templo de Caridad (Av. General Utrilla near Comitán), which was founded in 1712. It was once part of the San Juan de Dios convent

and hospital (the latter, the first hospital in San Cristóbal dedicated to treating indigenous people). Today only the church remains; it is forever linked to the Zendal rebellion of 1712, which was sparked when church leaders demanded excessive contributions from the indigenous population to fund the temple's construction. The building itself is reminiscent of its counterpart in Antigua, Guatemala, save for the use of columns on the towers. The highlight of the church, however, is the spectacular Solomonic altarpiece. It is dedicated to the Virgin of Charity and is considered the special protector of the city.

Templo y Ex-Convento de la Merced

Built by Mercedarian friars in the 18th century, the Templo y Ex-Convento de la Merced was used primarily by Spanish residents. The original church was rebuilt extensively over time; today the building that stands in its place is almost entirely a 20th-century creation—in fact, the sacristy remains one of the only colonial vestiges. Next door, the former convent has been renovated—more extensively in some areas than others—and houses the Museo del Ámbar de Chiapas.

Templo y Ex-Convento and Arco-Torre del Carmen

Located at the southern end of the pedestrian walkway, the 17th-century El Carmen complex once housed the only nunnery between Guatemala and Oaxaca. Today, while little remains of the original convent, the imposing church and deep-red bell-tower arch are prominent landmarks in San Cristóbal. The bell tower was built in 1677 to replace the original one, which was destroyed by a flood 25 years earlier.

The building next to the church is what remains of the convent; today it houses the **Casa de Cultura** (tel. 967/678-2349, 9 A.M.–1 P.M. and 4–7 P.M. Mon.–Fri.), which in addition to offering artistic workshops for kids has a beautiful garden and orchid nursery—perfect spots to spend a quiet afternoon writing postcards.

SAN CRISTÓBAL DE LAS CASAS

Templo de San Cristóbal

Every July 17, Catholic worshippers flock to the 18th-century Templo de San Cristóbal (El Cerrito) to honor its patron saint, Saint Christopher. And that's no easy task—the church is on a *cerrito* (small hill) and is reached by a steep set of about 240 steps. It's a nice place to visit at any time of the year, affording a panoramic view of town. If you're not up for the climb, there is a road on the other side of the hill; a cab to the top costs US$2.

Templo de Guadalupe

On a hilltop across town from Templo de San Cristóbal sits Templo de Guadalupe. Built in the 19th century, it is the final destination of thousands of *peregrinos* (literally, pilgrims) who walk or run dozens, and sometimes hundreds, of miles to honor Mexico's patron saint, the Virgen de Guadalupe. Most arrive on or around December 12, amid a colorful celebration of the saint that is held mostly on the road leading up to the church.

MUSEUMS
Museo Na Bolom

Located in the former home of archaeologist Frans Blom and photographer Gertrude Duby Blom, the Museo Na Bolom (Av. Vicente Guerrero 33, tel. 967/678-1418, www.na bolom.org, 10 A.M.–7 P.M. daily, US$3.50 general, US$2 student) showcases the couples' pioneering work in protecting the rain forest of eastern Chiapas and the reclusive Lacandón (Hach Winic) indigenous peoples who live there. Exhibits are displayed in the home's numerous rooms, ranging from descriptions of Lacandón life and customs, to presentations of studies conducted by visiting researchers, to a large collection of colonial-era religious art. There's an impressive research library and innumerable black-and-white photographs taken by Duby Blom. Guided tours (4:30 P.M. Tues.–Sun., US$4.50) of the museum and home are offered in English and Spanish, and include a film on the Bloms' work with the Lacandón. There is also an excellent gift shop across the street.

Museo de Trajes Regionales Sergio Castro

Anyone who is entranced with Chiapas's indigenous culture will enjoy a visit to the Museum of Regional Dress (Calle Guadalupe Victoria at Av. 12 de Octubre, tel. 967/678-4289, by appointment only, US$3), a private collection of local resident Sergio Castro Martínez. Well-versed in the cultural history of Chiapas, Sr. Castro explains the cohesive role that clothes play in each village, adding a few anecdotes and legends along the way. English and French are spoken.

Museo de Los Altos de Chiapas

The Museo de Los Altos de Chiapas (Ex-Convento del Templo de Santo Domingo de Guzmán, Av. 20 de Noviembre near Nicaragua, tel. 967/678-1609, 9 A.M.–6 P.M. daily, US$4) has interesting, if somewhat dated, exhibits on pre-Hispanic cultures, the arrival of the Spanish to San Cristóbal, and historic buildings in San Cristóbal. Signage is in Spanish, though there are English-language guidebooks at the entrance. Upstairs is a temporary exhibit area that often shows impressive art collections. The building itself, the former convent of the Templo de Santo Domingo, has been beautifully restored with its high archways, polished wood floors, and thick stone and adobe walls.

Museo de la Medicina Maya

The Maya Medicine Museum (Av. Salomón González Blanco 10, Col. Morelos, tel. 967/678-5438, 10 A.M.–6 P.M. Mon.–Fri., 10 A.M.–4 P.M. Sat.–Sun., US$2) has exhibits on ancient and contemporary Maya medical practices, including sections on childbirth and the five different types of healers: pulse reader, mountaintop prayer healer, bone healer, herbalist, and midwife. Written guides are available in several languages, and there's a small pharmacy that sells products derived from the on-site medicinal plant garden. And if you have an ailment, you can request a *limpieza* (cleansing, 9 A.M.–2 P.M. Mon.–Fri., US$5). The museum is a project of OMIECH, an

CHIAPANECAN AMBER

Amber is the fossilized sap of coniferous and leguminous trees that existed 25-40 million years ago. Earthquakes and other natural catastrophes buried these trees in several layers of sediment resulting in their petrification, which in turn transformed their sap into amber.

Relatively brittle, amber typically is golden or reddish in hue, although it can be blue, purple, or even pink — its color depends on the makeup of the original sap as well as the minerals found in the surrounding soil and rocks that it was buried under. It can vary in clarity from opaque to translucent.

Prehistoric insects and plants occasionally are found in amber pieces à la *Jurassic Park;* called "inclusions," such pieces have proven vital to entomologists and other scientists in classifying several dozen prehistoric insect and plant species.

Amber is found in relatively few places in the world — Chiapas is one of them, and the only place in Mexico where it has been discovered. The principal Chiapanecan mines are in Simojovel, Huitiupán, and Totolapa, hard to reach towns that aren't geared towards visitors. Touring through the state, however, you'll see amber pieces of all calibers for sale;

if anything, avoid buying amber from street vendors who often cannot authenticate their objects. Also don't bother buying amber pieces with large inclusions like scorpions or spiders — these are very rare and, more often than not, fake. To determine the authenticity of an amber piece, try the following:

Hold it. Amber is never cold to the touch.

Put it in water; if it floats, it's the real deal. (Note: If the piece is in a setting, or has added decorations, it'll alter the amber's buoyancy.)

Put a flame to it. Amber doesn't melt, but instead emits an incense-type smoke.

Shine an ultraviolet light on it; if it glows it's amber. (Jewelers and other reputable vendors should have one of these lights.)

To learn more about amber, as well as to see some fantastic examples of it, visit San Cristóbal's **Museo del Ámbar de Chiapas** (Ex-Convento de la Merced, Diego de Mazariegos near Matamoros, tel. 967/678-9716, www.museodelambar.com.mx, 10 A.M.-2 P.M. and 4-7 P.M. Tues.-Sun., US$2) or Tuxtla's modern **Museo de Paleontología** (Parque Madero, Calzada de los Hombres Ilustres s/n, Prolongación 5a Nte., tel. 961/602-0254, 10 A.M.-5 P.M. Tues.-Fri., 11 A.M.-5 P.M. Sat.-Sun., US$1).

association of indigenous doctors in Chiapas, and can also provide information on local organizations working in indigenous communities. A cab to the museum costs US$2, or walk north on Avenida General Utrilla, over the hill and past the market (about 30 minutes). Consider combining this with a visit to Moxviquil Reserve, which is a short distance further, along the *periférico.*

Museo del Ámbar de Chiapas

The Chiapas Amber Museum (Ex-Convento de la Merced, Parque La Merced, Diego de Mazariegos near Matamoros, tel. 967/678-9716, www.museodelambar.com.mx, 10 A.M.–2 P.M. and 4–7 P.M. Tues.–Sun., US$2) has an extensive, beautiful collection of raw and sculpted amber of various colors and qualities.

There are displays on its sources, its use in pre-Hispanic societies, and how to distinguish it from glass and plastic imitations. There's also a Spanish-language video at the end that, although somewhat garbled, provides a fascinating look into how amber is mined and sculpted. Signage is in Spanish only but guidebooks to the exhibit are available in English, Italian, German, French, and Japanese—ask for one at the ticket booth.

Café Museo Café

The Coffee Museum Café (Calle María Adelina Flores 10, tel. 967/678-7876, 8 A.M.–9 P.M. Mon.–Fri., 8 A.M.–8 P.M. Sat.–Sun., US$2.50) tells the history of coffee in Mexico—from its introduction in the late 17th century to its boom in Chiapas under the dictatorship of

Porfirio Díaz (1877–1911), to present-day co-ops of small coffee producers. There's Spanish signage only, with an English-language translation in the second exhibit room. At the end of the exhibits, visitors are gently prodded into a spacious café in the front; to its credit, it serves excellent coffee. The museum and café are run by Tuxtla-based COOPCAFE, an organization of small coffee producers.

Museo Mesoamericano del Jade

Located inside a large jewelry shop, the Mesoamerican Museum of Jade (Av. 16 de Septiembre at Calle 5 de Febrero, tel. 967/678-1121, www.eljade.com, noon–8 P.M. Mon.–Sat., noon–6 P.M. Sun., US$3) consists of a timeline of the major indigenous cultures of Mexico and their use of jade. The highlights are the replicas of Maya masks and artifacts, including ones from Tikal, Copán, and the famous funerary mask of K'inich Janaab Pakal found in the Temple of the Inscriptions at Palenque. At the end is a large, rather underwhelming reproduction of Pakal's tomb. Signage is in Spanish only.

Museo/Galería de Arte Contemporaneo Elisa Burkhard

Housed in a beautifully renovated colonial home, the Elisa Burkhard Contemporary Art Museum-Gallery (Calle Yajalón 2, no phone, www.museoelisa.wordpress.com, 3–6 P.M. Tues.–Sun., free) is a welcome addition to San Cristóbal's nascent modern-art scene. Three large exhibition rooms feature photography, sculptures, and paintings, most by local and expatriate artists. The gallery also has open-air sculpture and garden areas, a small café, workshop, and a projection room in the works.

Galería Studio Cerrillo

Galería Studio Cerrillo (Calle Tonalá 19-A, 11 A.M.–6 P.M. Tues.–Sun., best to call ahead) is a one-room modern-art gallery at Sol y Luna Guest Inn (Calle Tonalá 27 at Calle Pichicalco, tel. 967/678-5727, www.solylunainn.com). It hosts an oft-changing lineup of installation and performance pieces, many by international artists.

Galería de Arte Fotográfico Albertina

Located just steps from the central plaza, the Galería de Arte Fotográfico Albertina (Av. Insurgentes 1-A, 11 A.M.–2 P.M. and 4–8 P.M. Mon.–Sat., free) is a one-room affair with regularly changing photo exhibits. It has a great little gift shop with Chiapanecan *artesanía,* paintings, and framed photos of local scenery and people. A sculpture garden in the adjoining courtyard is planned for 2010.

NATURAL ATTRACTIONS

Reserva de Huitepec

Just 4.5 kilometers (2.7 miles) from San Cristóbal on the road to San Juan Chamula, the Huitepec Reserve (9 A.M.–4 P.M. Tues.–Sun., US$1.50) is a 135-hectare (334-acre) cloud forest on the slopes of an extinct volcano, where more than 80 species of birds have been identified. Several well-marked trails climb from the main trailhead, and make for a pleasant, if somewhat strenuous, hike. There are guides on-site who can lead tours of the park (US$6 pp, 1 hr) or, with a day's notice, an early-morning bird-watching tour (US$12.50 pp, 2.5–3 hrs). For additional information, and to reserve a bird-watching tour, contact **Pronatura** (Pedro Moreno 1, tel. 967/678-5000, www.pronatura -chiapas.org, 9 A.M.–5 P.M. Mon.–Fri.).

To get to the reserve, take any *combi* headed to San Juan Chamula; the stop in San Cristóbal is on Avenida General Utrilla, on the far side of the market. Tell the driver you'd like to be dropped at Huitepec (US$0.70, 20 mins). You can catch the same *combis* headed back into San Cristóbal.

Reserva y Orquídeas Moxviquil

Smaller but even closer to the center is Moxviquil Reserve (Periférico Norte at Calle Yajalón, tel. 967/678-0542, 9 A.M.–4 P.M. Tues.–Sun., US$1.50), an 85-hectare reserve located just outside San Cristóbal's *periférico*

© GARY CHANDLER

The orchid garden at Moxviquil reserve houses hundreds of orchids and other unique plants.

(beltway). An easy-to-follow trail starts at the park office and makes a pleasant 2.2-kilometer (1.25-mile) loop through shady pine and oak forest; budget 40–60 minutes with moderate climbing. There's a small cave along the way, and an unexcavated Maya ruin; call ahead for a guide to locate the latter. (*Moxviquil* literally means intestines in Tzotzil, but also refers to crossroads, and this area may have served just that purpose for ancient traders.) Back at the entrance, you can't miss the **Orchid Garden** (tel. 967/678-5727, 9 A.M.–6 P.M. Wed.–Sun., longer hours in summer), whose intriguing custom-built greenhouse houses hundreds of orchids and other epiphytes (and was nicknamed the "whale bones" by locals—you'll quickly see why). It's the centerpiece of an ambitious long-term project, with plans for a museum, several more greenhouses, outdoor event and picnic areas, even a playground and gift shop. It's about a mile walk from downtown San Cristóbal, passing through the busy market area, or you can take a cab for about US$2.

Arcotete

On the outskirts of town, in an area called Arcotete, are two very different but equally memorable sights, which together make for a nice outdoor excursion. El Arcotete is an impressive natural archway or tunnel, the last remaining segment of an ancient cave system that has otherwise eroded away. Stalactites hang from the soaring roof, and a river spreads into a gentle little pool along the bottom. (The water, oh-so-tempting especially if you walk or ride here, is clean but wickedly cold.) The arch allegedly got its name from a French soldier named Jean Francois d'Arcotete, who leapt to his death here in despair over a love affair with a woman in San Cristóbal.

Templo Carmen Arcotete, also known as La Quinta or simply La Casita del Obispo (The Bishop's House), is a lovely chapel perched in a picturesque river valley. The chapel, and the nearby remains of a small mansion and sawmill, date to the 1700s when they served as a private retreat for San Cristóbal's sitting bishop. The church's twin bell towers have narrow spiral staircases and are connected by an unusual wooden patio. Inside, the tiny nave has a distinctive teal-blue floor. The church and home are being restored by the INAH, the national historical institute, so access may be limited until their work is completed, but it remains a charming place to visit.

The turnoff to Arcotete is about four kilometers from the San Cristóbal city center, on the road to Tenejapa. From there it's a half kilometer to a second turnoff; here you can follow a dirt road to the right to reach the arch (1.5 kilometers) or continue straight on the paved road to reach the temple (1.5 kilometers). It's an ideal trip for biking, either solo or on a tour, but also quite nice by car or public transportation.

Grutas de Rancho Nuevo

Rancho Nuevo (9 A.M.–4:30 P.M. daily, US$1) is one of many cave systems, or *grutas,* piercing the mountains of Chiapas, and certainly one of the easiest to visit, with electric lighting and a cement pathway wide enough to drive a small car on. That's not to say it's unimpressive—the path winds more than a half mile underground, with a roof that's over 22 meters (75 feet) high in places, and covered in dangling stalactites. Outside are a dozen open-air eateries, a playground, even horseback riding, and weekends can get quite busy with local families. In 1994, Zapatista rebels used the caves to launch attacks against an adjoining military base; as a result, Rancho Nuevo is controlled by the army—those blasts you hear are from target practice—and exploring beyond the designated areas is strictly forbidden. Ocosingo-bound *combis* or pickups can drop you at the Rancho Nuevo turnoff (US$1, 20 mins); from there it's a 500-meter walk to the visitor area.

TOURS
City Tours

Get your bearings on a short city tour operated by **El Coleto Tranvía Turística** (Mercado de Dulces y Artesanías, Av. Insurgentes at Calle Hermanos Domínguez, tel. 967/678-0525), a motorized trolley that makes a one-hour loop of San Cristóbal's key sights; a recorded explanation serves as the guide (Spanish only, English and French in the works). Tours leave from the office (hourly 10 A.M.–1 P.M. and 4–7 P.M. daily, US$5 adult, US$3 child); a minimum of four passengers is required.

As the name suggests, **iPod tours** (Belisario Domínguez 2-B, tel. 967/631-6367, www.ipod tours.com.mx, 8 A.M.–8 P.M. daily, US$18 half-day rental, US$23 one-day rental, US$40 two-day rental, plus US$275 fully refundable deposit) rents iPods that have been uploaded with eight in-depth tours of some of the most important historical sights in San Cristóbal. Each tour lasts between 25 and 45 minutes but, since you control the, er, guide, you can set your own pace. The content includes maps, photos, and videos and is available in four languages—English, French, Italian, and Spanish. There also is information on activities, hotels, restaurants, and shops around town. Sounds kind of familiar...should we be worried?

Regional Tours

There's a lot to see and do beyond San Cristóbal's city limits, and it's definitely worth budgeting time to visit the surrounding villages, Maya ruins, and the many lakes, reserves, and more. The city has many tour operators, so it's worth considering the style of tour you'd like, not merely the destination. Most agencies specialize, be it budget or custom, by car or by bike, day trips or overnighters.

Alex y Raul (tel. 967/678-9141, alexyraul@ yahoo.com) has long offered the most highly recommended tours of San Juan Chamula and Zinacantán. What started as a two-person operation has since grown to nearly a dozen guides, but hasn't lost the balance, insight, and personalized feel that make the tours so good. Chamula-Zinacantán trips leave daily at 9:30 A.M. and return at 2 P.M. (US$17.50 pp) and include bilingual guide, transport, and entrance fees; no reservations are required, just wait at the large wooden cross in front of the cathedral (Av. 20 de Noviembre at Calle Guadalupe Victoria). Tours to other villages can be arranged, including Amatenango and Acuatenango, Tenejapa and Romerillo, even Nahá and Metzabok in the Lacandón rainforest.

Felipe Flores Tours & Travel (Calle Felipe Flores 36, tel. 967/678-3996, www.felipeflores .com) is operated out of the B&B of the same name, and offers personalized tours in and around San Cristóbal and to destinations further afield. Multilingual guides and prompt professional service are the reward for slightly higher prices; choose from short city tours and horseback trips, tours of indigenous villages, or all-day and multiday trips to Toniná, Laguna Miramar, and others.

For mountain bikers, **Los Pingüinos** (Av. Ecuador 4-B at Real de Mexicanos, tel. 967/678-0202, www.bikemexico.com/ pinguinos, 10 A.M.–2:30 P.M. and 3:30–7 P.M. daily) has a number of appealing tours, ranging from a couple hours to several days. Prices are a bit high—US$40–150 per person per day—but include experienced guides, high-quality gear, and (for longer trips) a support vehicle and hotel accommodations. Destinations include some usual suspects—Zinacantán, Chiflón Waterfall, Sumidero Canyon, and others—but getting there by bike, on forgotten roads and narrow forest trails, proves it's the journey that really matters. (A few tours go to lesser-known places, as well.) There are options for bikers of all levels, including downhill cruises and customized private tours.

Another option for bikers is **Ruta Nahual** (Real de Guadalupe 123, cell tel. 044-967/124-2100, rutanahual@hotmail.com, 10 A.M.–1 P.M. and 4–6 P.M. Tues.–Sat.), a local environmentally minded organization that offers reasonably priced biking and hiking tours near San Cristóbal. Outings include four-hour excursions to Huitepec or Moxviquil Reserves, and to little-visited villages and forest regions (US$22–24 per person, including equipment and entrance fees). Ruta Nahual also offers walking tours, including a nighttime city walk delving into the myths and mysteries of various neighborhoods (US$17.50 pp, 2 hrs). English is spoken.

Explora Ecoturismo y Aventura (Calle 1 de Marzo 30 btwn. Avs. 5 de Mayo and 12 de Octubre, tel. 967/678-4295, www .ecochiapas.com, 9 A.M.–2 P.M. and 4–8 P.M. Mon.–Fri., 9:30 A.M.–2 P.M. Sat.) specializes in multiday kayaking and rafting tours on three area rivers: Río Lacanjá, Río La Venta, and Río Usumacinta, which forms the Mexico-Guatemala border. Trips are all-inclusive, often with side trips like hiking in the rainforest and visiting archaeological sites. Detailed itineraries are available on the website (Spanish only), and rates average US$100 per person per day.

For those on a budget, **Zapata Tours** (Av. Insurgentes 19-A at Calle Hermanos Domínguez, tel. 967/674-5152, www.zapata tours.com, 8:30 A.M.–8:30 P.M. daily) has a number of reasonably priced options, including a horseback tour to San Juan Chamula (US$15 pp, 3.5 hrs) and a combo trip to Lagos de Montebello, Chiflón waterfall, and Rancho Nuevo caves (US$25 pp, 4–5 hrs). The "guides" typically speak Spanish only and offer very limited information or explanations. The office is located upstairs from Madre Tierra restaurant.

Agencia Chincultik (Real de Guadalupe 34, tel. 967/678-0957, 8 A.M.–9 P.M. daily) is a longtime do-it-all tour agency, offering all the standard one-day and multiday trips for essentially the same prices. Many hotels arrange tours for guests using Chincultik, and their fleet of vans tends to be newer and more comfortable than others.

Entertainment and Events

San Cristóbal has a vibrant nightlife, mostly in the form of small bars and cafés where you can knock back a beer or mixed drink while listening to live acoustic, rock, or reggae music. More and more spots are staying open into the wee hours, but the majority still close at midnight—to be safe, plan on getting your groove going early. For an even mellower outing, try catching a play, documentary, or Hollywood movie at one of the local theaters.

NIGHTLIFE
Bars and Live Music

A microbrewery and bar, **Iskra** (Real de Guadalupe 53, www.iskracafe.blogspot.com, 2 P.M.–midnight daily) has the relaxed feel of a dive bar without the graffiti on the walls. It's a good spot for just about anyone, offering a drink menu that ranges from homemade brews and stiff drinks to spiked coffee concoctions. Live bands play every night at 9 P.M.—there's a small dance floor but most people just groove between the tables.

A cozy wine bar in the heart of the Real de Guadalupe strip, **La Viña de Bacco** (Real de Guadalupe 7, 2 P.M.–midnight Mon.–Sat.) offers an impressive wine menu featuring labels from Mexico, Italy, France, Chile, and the United States. There are local faves too, including Chamulan *posh* (cane sugar liquor) and warm red wine, which both work wonders to warm you up fast on chilly nights. Tasty tapas are served with each round of drinks—they range from cheese plates to small finger sandwiches—a great deal considering drinks cost US$1–4.50.

Perfidia (Calle María Adelina Flores at Cristóbal Colón, tel. 967/678-1209, www.perfidia.com.mx, noon–midnight Mon.–Sat.) is an artsy bar-gallery-café set in a leafy courtyard in the colonial center. It hosts live bands Thursday through Saturday and has drink specials almost every night of the week from 7 to 9 P.M. (with the exception of Thursday, when there is a one-minute tequila special from 9:59 P.M. to 10 P.M.—move fast!).

A longtime go-to, **Revolución Café** (Av. 20 de Noviembre at 1 de Marzo, tel. 967/678-6664, www.myspace.com/cafebarrevolucion, noon–midnight Mon.–Sat.) still pulls in crowds, mostly for the live rock music that plays in a windowsill-turned-bandstand every night around 9:30 P.M. Mixed drinks tend to be weak—order beer or shots—and if you're hungry, stick to the baguettes. To get a table on weekends, arrive around 8:30 P.M., otherwise enjoy the revelry from the bar or the 2nd floor.

After most of the other nightclubs have closed, stagger to **El Zirko** (Av. 20 de Noviembre at 1 de Marzo, 8 P.M.–3 A.M. Tues.–Sat., free–US$3), where live music, drum and dance shows, and general late-night partying don't pick up until 11 P.M. Drink specials are offered almost nightly—guys hand out coupons in front of the bar or you can pick one up at the tourist office (a coupon, not a guy).

Dance Clubs

With a good-sized dance floor and live music most nights, **Latino's** (Francisco Madero at Av. Juárez, 8 P.M.–3 A.M. Mon.–Sat., free–US$5) is an excellent spot to bust out your merengue and salsa moves. If you don't have any moves—or need to brush up on them—free salsa lessons are offered at 8 P.M. Monday through Thursday.

THE ARTS
Theater

The olive-green **Teatro Daniel Zebadúa** (pedestrian walkway, Av. 20 de Noviembre and Calle 5 de Febrero, tel. 967/678-1357) regularly presents dramatic performances and cultural expositions in its modern space. Tickets vary depending on the show but typically run US$10–20.

Located on the outskirts of San Cristóbal's city center, the cavernous **Teatro de las Ciudad Hermanos Domínguez** (Diagonal Hermanos Paniagua s/n, tel. 967/678-3637, free–US$50) is the town's main theater, hosting dramatic productions, music concerts, dance performances, and town-hall meetings. Stop by the tourist office to find out what's playing while you're in town.

Cinema

An artsy meeting place with subtle Asian decor, **Kinoki** (Calle 1 de Marzo at 5 de Mayo, tel. 967/678-0495, 3:30–11 P.M. daily, US$2–3) has three screening rooms, each smaller than the next but all with comfy couches and reclining chairs. The main theater screens films at 4, 6, and 8 P.M. daily (US$2–3), while the remaining two are private rooms where visitors can watch films "à la carte" from Kinoki's extensive library (US$3 pp, minimum 2–3 people depending on the room). In the center of it all is a small café, which offers gourmet teas and coffee drinks, homemade baked goods, and light meals; snacks can also be brought to you while you're watching your favorite movie.

Cinema El Puente (Calle Real de Guadalupe 55, tel. 967/678-3723, US$2.50) is a good option for artsy flicks and documentaries, screening two films every night but Sunday at 6 and 8 P.M.

If you're hankering to catch the latest blockbuster, **Cinépolis** (Diagonal Hermanos Paniagua 50, www.cinepolis.com.mx, US$5 adult, US$2.50–3.50 before 6 P.M., US$2.50 all day Wed.) is your place. Most Hollywood films—except for animated ones—are subtitled in Spanish, though it doesn't hurt to ask if it's *doblada* (dubbed).

FESTIVALS AND EVENTS

San Cristóbal is a colorful city year-round, but it really comes to life during festivals and holidays. Travelers are always welcome to join the celebrations, if you're lucky enough (or have the requisite planning skills!) to be here on those days. The brilliant colors and effusive celebrations are a photographer's dream, and taking pictures in town is generally okay. However, indigenous people tend to be circumspect about having their picture taken, and in most outlying villages taking photos of religious processions and celebrants is strictly forbidden. Be respectful, and don't attempt it. No matter what the holiday, expect firecrackers, paper streamers, marimba music, and lots of street food.

Carnaval

You may think of Carnaval as a Caribbean and South American obsession, but it's celebrated with unbridled vigor in Chiapanecan indigenous villages, especially San Juan Chamula. (Carnaval roughly coincides with the five "lost days" of the ancient Maya calendar, when chaos and evil spirits reign.)

Festivities last nearly a week, culminating on Fat Tuesday (before Ash Wednesday) when tens of thousands turn out to watch processions marching around the main plaza, and village leaders perform a ceremony that includes dashing back and forth across a long carpet of burning straw. Don't bother bringing a camera—photos are banned during Carnaval.

Semana Santa

Semana Santa (Holy Week, leading up to Easter) is not only an important religious holiday but a big travel and vacation week for all Mexicans, and San Cristóbal gets packed with indigenous faithful, local merchants, and visitors from Mexico City, Veracruz, and elsewhere. On Good Friday, head to Barrio Los Mexicanos, where a live reenactment of the 12 stations of the cross proceeds through the streets and culminates at the barrio's namesake church.

Feria de la Primavera y de la Paz

Easter Sunday kicks off the weeklong Spring and Peace Fair, sometimes called *La Feria Grande* (the Big Fair). Parades, carnival games, mechanical rides, music concerts, art exhibits, sporting events, even bullfights, are held throughout the city. Stop by the tourist office for a schedule of events.

Festival Internacional Cervantino Barroco

Celebrated in mid-October or early November, the Festival Internacional Cervantino Barroco is a weeklong cultural celebration where artists from around the world come to dance, act, give concerts, and display their works of art. The closing ceremony, typically a big ticket number, is held in front of La Catedral de San Cristóbal.

Día de Todos Santos

Día de Todos Santos (All Saints Day, November 1) and **Día de Los Muertos** (Day of the Dead, November 2) are celebrated throughout Latin America, and San Cristóbal is no exception. Families gather at local cemeteries to honor loved ones who have died; in town, November 2 tends to be the main day, while many indigenous communities, especially Chamula, celebrate on November 1.

Día de la Virgen de Guadalupe

December 12th is Saint's Day for the Virgin of Guadalupe, which is celebrated with *peregrinaciones* (pilgrimages)—groups of churchgoers who run or walk for several days from surrounding towns to San Cristóbal's hilltop Church of Guadalupe. Though the Virgen is celebrated citywide, the road leading up to the church is the focal point of the partying.

Shopping

Teeming with shops and markets, San Cristóbal is a place where the genius and beauty of Mexican art is on full display—handmade clothing, toys, textiles, amber jewelry—you'll be hard-pressed to leave without buying something. Bargaining is accepted, but be fair. Many artisans simply charge for the cost of the materials; their time often is given for free.

MARKETS

Every day the plaza surrounding the Templo y Ex-Convento de Santo Domingo hosts an *artesanía* market (Av. 20 de Noviembre near Nicaragua, 8 A.M.–sunset) where you'll see row upon row of colorful *huipiles* and dresses, thick wool sweaters, woven belts, embroidered placemats, Zapatista dolls, stuffed animals, and any number of handmade creations. Be sure to take a walk around the market before you buy—each step likely will reveal something unexpected.

Advertised as the place to buy local sweets,

Mercado de Dulces y Artesanías (Av. Insurgentes at Calle Hermanos Domínguez, 7 A.M.–10 P.M. daily) only has a small section dedicated to sugary Chiapanecan products. There's also a large variety of handwoven clothing, woodwork, leather goods, and jewelry. It's a great place to head if it's raining (it's located indoors) or for last-minute shopping (it's open late).

CHIAPANECAN ARTESANÍA AND TEXTILES

First-prize recipient of UNESCO's Crafts Award for Latin America and the Caribbean in 2002, **Sna Jolobil** (Ex-Convento del Templo de Santo Domingo, Av. 20 de Noviembre near Nicaragua, 9 A.M.–2 P.M. and 4–7 P.M. Mon.–Sat.) is the place to head for the finest textiles around. Meaning The "Weavers' House" in Tzotzil, Sna Jolobil is a profit-sharing co-op made up of 800 weavers from 20 Tzotzil- and

Peruse the hand-woven textiles and colorful *artesanía* at the large craft market held daily in front of Santo Domingo church.

© H.W. PRADO

You don't always have to go to a crafts market to find interesting *artesanía* – sometimes it walks right by.

Tzeltal-speaking villages in the highlands of Chiapas. It's definitely worth a visit; you'll find these outstanding works of textile art hard to resist. Prices are non-negotiable.

Selling products made exclusively in autonomous communities, **Nemi Zapata** (Calle Real de Guadalupe 57-A, tel. 967/678-7487, 9:30 A.M.–8:30 P.M. Mon.–Sat.) has one of the best selections of Zapatista items in town—hand-stitched wall hangings, oil paintings, dolls, hip T-shirts, postcards, and calendars—all with messages in support of The Cause. This is a great place to get premium coffee beans and local honey which also supports Zapatista communities.

For high-end Lacondón *artesanía* and books, head to the gift shop at **Na Bolom** (Av. Vicente Guerrero 33, tel. 967/678-1418, 11 A.M.–7 P.M. daily). A bit off the beaten track, it's well worth a stop. The affiliated museum across the street is a treat in itself.

The state-run **Casa de las Artesanías** (Av. Miguel Hidalgo at Niños Héroes, tel. 967/678-1180, 9 A.M.–9 P.M. Tues.–Fri., 9 A.M.–8 P.M. Sat.–Sun.) sells first-rate items from every corner of Chiapas—from amber jewelry to hand-painted wood toys. Salespeople are particularly helpful and often will share their knowledge about an item—the region it comes from, the process of creating it, and in some cases, even about the artist herself.

An indigenous women's co-op, **Najel** (Belisario Domínguez 6-A, tel. 967/674-0347, 11 A.M.–3 P.M. and 5–9 P.M. Mon.–Sat.) sells high-end handcrafted textiles from neighboring villages. Designs often are one-of-a-kind, making the work that much more special. All items sold are fair trade.

Located on the pedestrian walkway, **Tienda El Arco Iris** (Av. Miguel Hidalgo 6-C, tel. 967/680-8622, 10 A.M.–10 P.M. daily) sells Chiapanecan *artesanías* that have been created in indigenous communities. Items are priced a bit higher than those sold elsewhere, but that's because all proceeds go to supporting projects that feed and educate street kids.

OTHER BOUTIQUES

Gifted photographer Michel Vial sells his artwork on limited-edition postcards and T-shirts as well as straight-up prints at **El Antro del Fotógrafo** (Real de Guadalupe 64, 9:30 A.M.–2:30 P.M. and 5–8 P.M. daily). Most images sold are set in San Cristóbal—many juxtaposing the indigenous population against the graffiti art found around town. Prices are reasonable, similar to the mass-produced items you'll see in other gift shops. You'll leave feeling like you've seen a different side of the city.

La Milagrosa (Real de Guadalupe near Insurgentes, 9 A.M.–9 P.M. daily) specializes in boho-hip *artesanía* and clothing from central Mexico locales like San Miguel de Allende, Mexico City, and Guanajuato. Whimsical and eye-catching, the store's items showcase the skill and versatility of Mexican folk artists. This is a great place to window shop or to get something a little different to take home with you.

BOOKSTORES

La Pared (Av. Miguel Hidalgo 2, tel. 967/678-6367, 11 A.M.–2 P.M. and 4–8 P.M. Tues.–Sat., 3–7 P.M. Sun.) is San Cristóbal's best source of English-language books, offering an excellent selection of new and used novels, Maya history and art books, textbooks for learning Spanish, and current travel guides and maps. You'll find both used and new books, and trades are accepted.

Specializing in used books, **Liberinto** (Guadalupe Victoria 30-C, 10 A.M.–3 P.M. and 4–9 P.M. Mon.–Sat.) not only sells, but also rents its inventory (US$0.50 per book per day). Coffee drinks, sandwiches, wireless Internet, and chess boards make this a relaxing place to hang out too. Literary events are hosted most weekends.

For a great selection of left-leaning Spanish-language books—including children's books—check out **Librería Mayambé** (Av. Diego Dugelay at Real de Guadalupe, tel. 967/678-

6967, 11 A.M.–3 P.M. and 5–9 P.M. Mon.–Sat.). There's a good variety of music CDs and art books too.

Librería Soluna (Real de Guadalupe 13-B, tel. 967/678-6805, 9 A.M.–9 P.M. Mon.–Sat., 10 A.M.–9 P.M. Sun.) has a decent selection of guidebooks and maps plus Maya and Mexican history books. A number of titles are available in English, French, Italian, and German.

El Kiosko (5 de Febrero near Av. 20 de Noviembre, 8 A.M.–9 P.M. Mon.–Sat., 9 A.M.–9 P.M. Sun.) has a good selection of international news magazines, including *Newsweek* and *The Economist*. For international fashion and gossip mags, head to **Librería Chilam Balam** (General Utrilla 3, 10 A.M.–8 P.M. daily), which also has a smattering of guidebooks near the cash register.

WORKSHOPS

Taller Leñateros (Calle Flavio A. Paniagua 54 at Calle Huixtla, tel. 967/678-5174, www.tallerlenateros.com. 9 A.M.–8 P.M. Mon.–Fri., 9 A.M.–2 P.M. Sat.; gift shop at Real de Guadalupe 13, 10 A.M.–6 P.M. Mon.–Fri., 10 A.M.–2 P.M. Sat.) is an award-winning collective of Maya artisans who create remarkable handmade paper products out of everything from flower petals and moss to rags and recycled paper. (The collective's name is Spanish for Woodlanders' Workshop.) Their creations include cards, journals, and beautiful handbound art and poetry books; all make great gifts and keepsakes, and can be purchased at the workshop itself or at a new gift shop near the *zócalo*. Visitors can take a short tour of the workshop (9 A.M.–5 P.M. Mon.–Fri., 9 A.M.–2 P.M. Sat.) to see the various processes—many experimental—used by the artists there. The collective was founded in 1975 by American book-maker Ambar Past, who continues to help guide its work.

Accommodations

Travelers of every taste and budget can find a place to call home in San Cristóbal. The city has some lovely B&Bs, though not as many as you might expect in such a charming and historic city. Hotels are more numerous, both midrange and high-end, and we've listed those that offer the best value for their respective price. There is no shortage whatsoever of budget options, including some great hostels and small hotels. But backpackers beware, as San Cristóbal also has a slew of slapdash "posadas" offering little atmosphere, and even less service or security. You're sure to be approached at the bus station by flyer-toting touts—some are from recommendable places, others are not.

HOSTELS
Under US$25

San Cristóbal's largest and most popular hostel is still **Posada México Hostel** (Av. Josefa Ortíz de Domínguez at Dr. Felipe Flores, tel. 967/678-0014, www.hostellingmexico.com, US$8 dorm, US$12 s/d with shared bathroom, US$14 s/d with private bathroom) with a relaxed ambience, well-kept sleeping areas, and plenty of indoor and outdoor common space. Dorms (mixed and single-sex) and private rooms (some more secluded than others) all have comfy beds and regular cleaning, and guests can make use of lockers, TV and Internet areas, a fully equipped kitchen, even a bar complete with bean bags. An annex down the street has its own kitchen, and tends to be quieter than the main area.

A block and a half from Santo Domingo church, **Rossco Backpackers Hostel** (Calle Real de Mexicanos 16, tel. 967/674-0525, www.backpackershostel.com.mx, US$8.25–10.25 dorm, US$21.25 s, US$25.50 d) is also quite spacious, with large rooms and a long central garden. Standard dorms have 10–14 beds apiece (except the women-only dorm, with eight spots) and shared toilets and showers across the garden, or pay two bucks more for a four-person dorm with in-room bathroom.

Upstairs private rooms are far superior to the downstairs ones, with private bathrooms and skylights in the high ceilings. Breakfast, Internet and kitchen access, and salsa classes are all included. Nightly bonfires draw guests together, and the hostel is known for its party-loving atmosphere.

The friendly **Hotel Posada 5** (Calle Comitán 13, tel. 967/674-7660, www.posada5.com, US$6 dorm, US$7.50 pp shared bathroom, $10 pp private room) has a long airy dorm area with oversize windows looking onto a grassy yard, which is itself big enough for sunbathing or even an impromptu soccer game. Most private rooms get nice light too, and the shared bathrooms are reasonably clean; ditto for the kitchen. There's no indoor hangout space, unfortunately—the kitchen or rear patio suffice for morning coffee or afternoon tea. The park in front is a bit drab, but the neighborhood is pleasant and quiet, and the center's a short walk away. The hotel will cover taxi fare from the bus station.

Once a down-and-out posada called La Casa di Gladys, **Planet Hostel** (Calle Cintalapa 6 btwn. Av. Diego Dugelay and Calle Huixtla, tel. 967/678-5775, www.planethostel.com.mx, US$8 dorm, US$12/16 s/d with shared bathroom, US$15–20 s/d with private bathroom) is now a cool little hostel and a nice alternative to the bigger places. Dorms are small—just six beds apiece—and all rooms have newish mattresses and bright interior paint. A TV room, small rear garden/lounge, and rooftop hammock/barbecue area are all great for chilling out. Wi-Fi, breakfast, kitchen access, and salsa classes are included.

HOTELS
Under US$25

Posada La Casa de Carmelita (Calle Dr. Navarro 15, tel. 967/678-9975, posadacarmelita@yahoo.com.mx, US$10 pp shared bathroom, US$12 pp private bathroom) is a friendly family-run place with spic-and-span rooms and a great location. Rooms with shared bath are pretty dark, but the others open onto a corridor with terrific views of the city and surrounding hills. Meals are available for US$4 apiece. A handful of groups use Carmelita's regularly, so try calling ahead to be sure there's room.

Rooms at **Hotel San Martín** (Calle Real de Guadalupe 16, tel. 967/678-0533, www.travelbymexico.com/chis/sanmartin, US$20 s, US$25 d) are very simple and spare, with twin beds, tile floors, and clean private bathrooms, all looking onto a narrow interior patio. It's far from charming, but not unpleasant, and the location couldn't be more central—just a half block from the *zócalo*. Cable TV and free Internet access are an added bonus.

US$25-50

The colonial ((**Hotel Casa Margarita** (Calle Real de Guadalupe 34, tel. 967/678-0957, www.mundomaya.com.mx/casamargarita, US$35 s, US$40 d) has 30 modern, attractive rooms—all with hot water, in-room safe, cable TV, wireless Internet, and electric heaters. Most open onto the hotel's sunny central courtyard, with its whitewashed arches and tile walkways. Rooms in back and upstairs get less light but are more private, and there's a nice terrace for hanging out. Just over a block from the central plaza, this is a good, reliable option. The same owners run Chincultik tour agency, whose office is attached.

Posada Belén (Plazuela de Mexicanos, tel. 967/678-7486, US$28 s/d, US$45 suite) is a cute little hotel facing a quiet church square just a block from Santo Domingo. The suites (or *especiales*) are worth the extra cost, not least for the small patios overlooking the plaza and church. They also feature wood floors, king-size beds, even small sofas and artsy floor lamps. Standards don't have exterior windows or patios, and lack for natural light as a result, but are perfectly comfortable otherwise.

Hotel Posada Jovel (Flavio Paniagua 28, tel. 967/674-1734, www.mundochiapas.com/hotelposadajovel, US$25–35 d) has long been a solid budget option. The older "posada" section is on the north side of the street, while

the newer "hotel" (and reception desk) is across the street. The latter surrounds a sunny central area, and rooms there are larger and more modern (and therefore more expensive). Posada-side rooms are also clean and cheerful, but some are quite cramped. Call ahead if possible, especially for the cheaper rooms, as the hotel is popular with tour groups. There's free Wi-Fi in the common areas.

Hotel Posada San Cristóbal (Av. Insurgentes 3, tel. 967/678-6881, US$38 s, US$46 d) is an old-fashioned colonial hotel with pleasingly creaky wood floors and a sunny central courtyard, conveniently located between the *zócalo* and the bus station. Rooms are quite large, with patios looking onto the street—ask for one facing Calle Cuauhtémoc rather than busy Avenida Insurgentes. The beds are old and springy—perhaps the biggest drawback here. Newer rooms in back have better amenities but lack the light and charm of the originals.

US$50-100

((**Hotel Casa Vieja** (Calle María Adelina Flores 27, tel. 967/678-6868, www.casavieja.com.mx, US$85 s, US$90 d, US$110 junior suite, US$140 master suite) has the look and stature of a large colonial hotel, but the homey ambience of a small bed-and-breakfast. Rooms have wood-beam ceilings, hand-carved furniture, and views of two enclosed gardens. Rooms are a bit small, especially the bathrooms—our main critique—but overall are quite cozy and attractive. The master suite is gorgeous, with a king bed, peaked ceiling, and terrific views over the terra-cotta rooftops. The restaurant here is well recommended, especially for Sunday brunch.

The childhood home of one of the owners, **Hotel Posada El Paraíso** (Calle 5 de Febrero 19 at Av. 16 de Septiembre, tel. 967/678-0085, www.hotelposadaparaiso.com, US$55 s, US$75 d) is a charming little hotel just steps from the central plaza. Rooms have textured ocher and blue walls, heavy wood-beam ceilings, skylights, and colorful bedspreads—some have cozy lofts reached by handmade ladders. Light sleepers may be less impressed, though—the walls are rather thin, and rooms near the entrance are particularly susceptible to the comings and goings at the front desk. Ask for a room facing the street, or at the back of the building.

A San Cristóbal institution, **Na Bolom** (Av. Vicente Guerrero 33, tel. 967/678-1418, www.nabolom.org, US$66 s, US$88 d, US$120 junior suite, including breakfast) is a hotel, museum, and research center in one, housed in the former colonial home of a distinguished photographer-archaeologist couple. Standard rooms are aging but cozy, with working fireplaces and indigenous artwork; bathrooms could use a face-lift, however. Junior suites are a step above, with king-size beds, whirlpool bathtubs, and great views of the gardens. Guests include visiting researchers and Lacandón villagers, who often come together for Na Bolom's nightly five-course family-style dinner (US$15 pp). The only drawback is the isolated location, about a 20-minute walk from the center.

Hotel Casa Mexicana (28 de Agosto 1 at Av. Utrilla, tel. 967/678-0698, www.hotelcasamexicana.com, US$80 s, US$90 d, US$140-170 suite) is an upscale hotel in the heart of downtown. The main building is a renovated colonial-era mansion, with original artwork hanging on burnished terra-cotta walls and an atrium replete with tropical plants, even a stone-edged pond. But those in the know ask for a room in the annex across the street, which is newer and quieter, with a grassy courtyard in the middle. Rooms on both sides are smallish but nicely appointed, with hand-carved headboards and bright Chiapanecan bedspreads, plus modern touches like flat-screen TVs and wireless Internet. Service is prompt and professional.

Over US$100

Located on the edge of town, the 17th- and 18th-century buildings of **Parador San Juan de Díos** (Calzada Roberta 16, tel. 967/678-4290, www.sanjuandios.com, US$140 s/d, US$200-370 suite) are home to one of the finest hotels in San Cristóbal. The good-size rooms have an eclectic art collector's feel to them: antique Mexican furnishings, original oil paintings, and Persian rugs. Each different from the other, no room disappoints. Service is impeccable.

Hotel Posada Real de Chiapas (Francisco Madero 19, tel. 967/678-0928, www.hotelchiapas.com.mx, US$125 s/d, US$140/160 junior/master suite) is a new addition to San Cristóbal's small collection of upscale hotels. Overall it's a lovely place, with large carpeted rooms and modern amenities, including comfortable beds, coffee makers, and in-room safes. The decor is intended to celebrate indigenous women, with photos and examples of regional textiles and clothing, complete with informational placards. The main complaint here is noise, whether from the street or the hotel's spacious interior courtyard (especially on Saturdays, when there's live music). A handful of rooms, including the suites, face a rear garden and are quieter and worth asking for.

BED-AND-BREAKFASTS US$50-100

Bela's B&B (Calle Dr. Navarro 2, tel. 967/678-9292, www.belasbandb.com, US$30-60 s, US$45-75 d) has just five rooms: two smallish garden units with shared bath—good for singles, a bit cozy for two—and three spacious suites, including a top-floor unit with a balcony overlooking the verdant garden and red-roofed city beyond. All rooms have flannel sheets, electric blankets, space heaters, and luxurious pillow-top mattresses—in a word, Ahhhh! The American owner lives on-site and is an attentive and forthright host. Her three kinetic dogs (small, smaller, and smallest) have free reign in the B&B—great if you like dogs, but not everyone's thing. There's no kitchen access, but a full breakfast and all-day coffee, tea, water, and Wi-Fi access are included.

Sol y Luna Guest Inn (Calle Tonalá 27 at Calle Pichicalco, tel. 967/678-5727, www.mexonline.com/solyluna.htm, US$50/70 s/d) brims with books, photos, and artwork from around Mexico and the world, for an eclectic—some might say cluttered—decor befitting the varied pursuits of its American host. The look extends to the two large guest rooms, which have fireplaces and electric blankets, though you have to go around the corner to use the bathroom (at least for now). Common areas include a large courtyard, lush garden, and cozy sitting area complete with fireplace, armchairs, and dozing housecats. The owner is a California transplant with 15-plus years of information and advice about the city and region, and offers private tours and photo workshops. He also runs a modern-art gallery and orchid collection out of the B&B, and makes a mean breakfast to boot. It's a quiet location; Internet and kitchen access are available.

Over US$100

One of San Cristóbal's loveliest places, **《 Casa Felipe Flores** (Calle Dr. Felipe Flores 36, tel. 967/678-3996, www.felipe-flores.com, US$95–125 s/d) shines in every way, from its architectural nuances and superb artwork to the lush garden and shady patios. Four ground-floor guest rooms have high wood-beamed ceilings, *talavera*-tiled bathrooms, and working fireplaces; a fifth room is reached by way of a spiral staircase and, while much smaller, has terrific views from its rooftop perch. The common living room is no less appealing, with comfy couches, an honor bar tucked into an antique chest, and—on cold nights—a raging fire in the fireplace. American owners Nancy and David Orr live on-site and often join guests for drinks or meals. A hearty breakfast is included in the rate. Cash or travelers checks are accepted.

《 La Bamba Guesthouse (Calle Ejercito Nacional 46, tel. 967/678-7455, U.S. tel. 864/278-0508, www.labambaguesthouse.com, US$150 s/d) has just one unit, but it's certainly among San Cristóbal's finest lodgings, and a terrific deal to boot. This cozy one-bedroom home has a full-size kitchen, comfy living room with fireplace, and tasteful colonial-style decor, with a private entrance and wireless Internet. The coup de grace is the garden—a long, gorgeous plot of trees and lush flowering plants

that connects the guesthouse to the home of La Bamba's friendly and discreet American owner. Two covered garden patios—one with an outdoor fireplace, and both exclusive to the guesthouse—are perfect for morning coffee and an evening glass of wine, while a large rooftop terrace has panoramic views of the city and surrounding mountains. A full breakfast is included; low season and weekly rates are also available.

SHORT-TERM RENTALS

San Cristóbal has a way of beguiling visitors into staying just one more day, one more week, one more year...yet there are surprisingly few furnished houses and apart-hotels available for weekly or monthly rental. The websites **www.sancrisrentals.com** and **www.vacationrentals.com** have decent selections, and you may have luck perusing the bulletin boards at Casa de Pan restaurant, Super Más grocery store, and Kinoki theater.

Over US$50

A great value whether you're staying for a couple days or a couple weeks, **《 Villas Casa Morada** (Av. Diego Dugelay 45 at Chiapa de Corzo, tel. 967/678-4440, www.casamorada.com.mx, US$80 1 br, US$130 2 br) has eight comfortable and charming apartments, each featuring ironwork furniture, wood-burning fireplaces, and fully equipped *talavera*-tiled kitchens. Framed textiles and hand-painted hearths lend a homey Chiapanecan feel, while in-room telephone and Internet access (wired and wireless) keep you connected. Add daily maid service and a 24-hour reception desk and you really get the best of the hotel and apartment worlds. A restaurant serving modern Mexican cuisine is planned for the adjoining building. Weekly rates are available.

Just a block from the Santo Domingo church, **La Casa Rosada** (Dr. Navarro 4, tel. 967/683-8659, lcasarosada@gmail.com, US$60–80/day, US$300–370/wk, US$780–900/mo) has two large colonial style 1-bedroom/1-bath apartments, each with high ceilings, stone floors, fireplace, and a fully furnished kitchen. The rear unit has a private entrance, larger bathroom (including a grand old-fashioned tub), and best of all, a private patio and sunny, flower-filled garden. Its indoor space is smaller than the front unit's, but warmer and cozier for it—the thick walls keep both units cool, even chilly. Gas, electricity, drinking water, wireless Internet, and once-weekly maid service are all included for both apartments; kids and dogs are welcome. The monthly rate is a bit steep, and the units are showing their age, but it's an agreeable option nonetheless.

Posada Moguel (Calle Comitán 41 btwn. Av. Diego Dugelay and Calle Huixtla, tel. 967/116-0957, posadamoguel@hotmail.com, US$350 per week) is an appealing option for writers, researchers, or anyone looking for a home base, not just a hotel. Seven modern apartments surround a stone-paved courtyard with shaded tables and chairs; all have furnished kitchens,

living rooms with fireplace and TV, and bedrooms with two full beds. Decor is tasteful, if a bit plain, and some of the rules are a bit annoying, like charging for extra firewood and toilet paper. The owners live on-site, but are hands-off, even somewhat reclusive—this place is best for those who prefer seclusion and privacy to a B&B-type experience. Same goes for the location—a quiet residential street a moderate walk from the center. There's free Internet access; a one-week minimum stay is required and payment is in cash only.

Other recommended establishments include the colonial-style **Kuku Rutz** (Real de Mexicanos 21/25, tel. 967/631-5532, www.kukurutz.com, US$67 1 br), and **Bungalows del Sol** (Periférico Oriente 100, Fracc. Real del Monte, tel. 967/678-2294, www.bungalowsdelsol.com, US$112.50 2 br), which is located on the outskirts of town.

Food

Chiapas has a number of homegrown culinary specialties, which, together with San Cristóbal's international flair, can make for a rich dining experience. A few upscale restaurants are worth splurging on, but most of the city's best meals, including plenty of vegetarian options, are served at simple restaurants and hole-in-the-wall eateries, whether for falafel, tamales, fresh sandwiches, or homemade pasta.

CHIAPANECAN AND MEXICAN

◖ El Mercadito (Diego Dugelay 11, tel. 967/678-0210, 11 A.M.–5 P.M. daily, US$4–8) has gotta be good: Locals not only line up for its daily lunch offerings, they bring gallon soup pots and oversize plastic containers to tote it away. The menu rotates daily, but includes home-cooked Chiapanecan classics like *sopa de pan* (bread soup, with hunks of bread and melted cheese swimming in veggie stew with a hint of nutmeg) and an amazing chicken mole. The throngs mostly order to go,

but El Mercadito does have a handful of tables for eating in.

Doña Áme Tamales (Calle Diego Mazariegos 28, 9 A.M.–3 P.M. and 4–10 P.M. Mon.–Sat., 6–10 P.M. Sun., US$1 apiece) serves only one thing, but few in town do it better. Tamales—corn dough stuffed with goodies of some sort and steamed in banana leaves or corn husks—are southern Mexico's classic comfort food, and this tidy little eatery typically has 10-plus varieties to choose from, including Chiapanecan specialties like the *chamula* (spicy pork), *cambray* (chicken, olives, and raisins), and *yerbasanta* (a fragrant spice that's something of an acquired taste). The Doña could be a bit more generous with the filling—everyone's an expert, right?—but the flavors are spot-on.

Right on the pedestrian walkway but strangely easy to miss, **Bugambilia** (Real de Guadalupe near Av. Insurgentes, 7 A.M.–10 P.M. daily) is a cozy little place with just a handful of tables and colorful *papel picado* hanging above. Though serving reliable Mexican fare all day, it's tops for breakfast, with several hearty combos including crunchy *chilaquiles,* huevos rancheros, and sizzling *arrachera* steak (US$2.50–4.50). All come with a plate of fruit and a strong cup of freshly made coffee (or sometimes, hot cocoa).

Though relying more on its reputation than its chef, the upscale **La Paloma** (pedestrian walkway, Av. Hidalgo 3 at Calle Cuauhtémoc, tel. 967/678-1547, 9 A.M.–midnight daily, US$5–14) still serves reliable and well-priced Mexican dishes, most with creative flair. Try the squash flowers filled with cheese mousse and served with *huitlacoche* (black corn fungus, a Mexican delicacy—really), the cilantro soup, or the meatballs in thick chipotle sauce. If anything avoid the beef medallions in chocolate sauce—the sauce is tasty enough, but the beef tough.

VEGETARIAN

A hole-in-the-wall with urban flair, **❰ Falafel** (Calle María Adelina Flores 4, 1:30–9 P.M. Mon.–Thurs., 1:30–6 P.M. Fri. and Sun., US$2.80–4.80) serves up delicious Israeli vegetarian meals—sandwiches, egg dishes, hummus plates, and, of course, falafel. Food is made to order, including baking the to-die-for pita bread. Drinks are a treat too—sip a chai latte, Turkish coffee, or a cinnamon-laced hot cocoa while you wait for your meal.

While sometimes hit or miss, **Casa de Pan Papalotl** (Calle Dr. Navarro 10, tel. 967/678-5895, 8 A.M.–10 P.M. Tues.–Sun., US$3–7) offers a wide range of meatless dishes; good bets for lunch include the vegetable-filled empanadas, homemade soups, and quesadillas; for breakfast try the homemade granola and yogurt. For a sure thing, stick with the irresistible baked goods, which are sold at the front of the café. There is another Casa de Pan (Real de Guadalupe 55, tel. 967/678-7215, 8:30 A.M.–10 P.M. Mon.–Sat.) near the *zócalo* in the Centro Cultural El Puente.

LIGHT FARE

❰ Anabanana (Av. Miguel Hidalgo btwn. Calles Niños Héroes and Hermanos Domínguez, 9 A.M.–6 P.M. Mon.–Sat., US$2–5) is a longtime favorite on the pedestrian walkway, and for good reason—they serve up hefty baguette sandwiches, delicious hamburgers and soy burgers, plus traditional Mexican soups and tacos. Dishes are made to order in the tiny kitchen in the center. It's especially popular for lunch, but you can avoid the rush by stopping by before 2 P.M.

La Casa del Bagel (Real de Guadalupe 44-A, tel. 967/631-6187, 7 A.M.–11 P.M. daily, US$2.50–5) offers nine types of bagels with seven types of cream cheese, bagel sandwiches, bagel pizzas…pretty much any bagel creation you can think of plus a tempting list of smoothies, coffee drinks, and gourmet teas. But on top of being a place to satisfy your hunger, it's a total hangout spot with lots of couches in a huge TV room (movie screenings every day at 6:30 P.M.), a billiards room to shoot some pool (US$2/hr), and a garden where you can relax in a hammock awhile. All that or just sit back at one of the tree-trunk tables while you surf the 'net for free.

Occupying a renovated colonial mansion, **❰ La Selva Café** (Av. Crescencio Rosas at Calle Cuauhtémoc, tel. 967/678-7244, 8:30 A.M.–11 P.M. daily) is San Cristóbal's finest café, with a bright spacious indoor seating area and a comfortable cobblestone courtyard in back. The menu includes a dozen different organic coffees, served as rich drip, frothy cappuccinos, and more. Tasty breakfast specials include yogurt, fruit, biscuit, and coffee for US$4.50; there's even free wireless Internet (though electrical outlets are oddly lacking). La Selva also sells ground or whole-bean coffee by the kilo, including decaf, which is virtually impossible to find elsewhere.

Santé Caffé (Miguel Hidalgo 4, tel. 967/631-6351, 8 A.M.–10 P.M. daily, US$3–8) has umbrella-shaded tables facing the pedestrian walkway, and hip leather armchairs and low tables inside. (There's also a small but excellent kids' play area in back.) The coffee is unremarkable, but tea-based "infusions" go well with baguette and panini sandwiches. Beer, wine, and hot dishes are also available.

Few restaurants in San Cristóbal are as serene as **Casa Luz** (Calle Niños Héroes 2, tel. 967/631-6609, 8 A.M.–9 P.M. daily, US$4–10), a café-bookstore-yoga center that serves tasty sandwiches and egg dishes in a bright spacious locale a block from the pedestrian walkway. Meals are well prepared (especially breakfast), but Casa Luz really shines in the details—from the sleek flatware to the homemade papaya jam. The decor is modern and not particularly 'Chiapanecan', but it can be a refreshing alternative to the colonial look found everywhere else. Service is first-rate, and there's free wireless Internet. Massage and yoga are offered on the second floor and get high marks.

OTHER SPECIALTIES

If you're hankering for a slice of pizza, **Pizzería El Punto** (Real de Guadalupe btwn. Avs. Cristóbal Colón and Diego Dugelay, tel. 967/678-0047, 1–11 P.M. Tues.–Sun., US$6.50–13) is where it's at. Thin-crust pies come loaded with toppings—ham figures prominently, though there are plenty of veggie options—and are baked in a wood-burning stove just feet from the entrance. Crisp and creative salads also make a great side if you're sharing, or an entire meal if you're not. El Punto's original site, now its **satellite restaurant** (Plaza El Cerrillo, Calle Comitán 13-A, tel. 967/678-7979, 2–11 P.M. Tues.–Sun.), is a true hole-in-the-wall that's just as good.

Il Piccolo (Real de Guadalupe near Belisario Domínguez, no phone, 2–10:30 P.M. Tues.–Sun., US$7–11) may not be the warmest and fuzziest place—it can feel like a New York deli at lunch hour—but the homemade pastas and to-die-for sauces can't be beat. Just be sure to keep your party to four people or less; the place is so tiny (and the staff so unaccommodating), you'll be shooed away.

Pierre (Real de Guadalupe 73, tel. 967/678-7211, 1–10:30 P.M. Wed.–Mon., 7–10:30 P.M. Sun., US$8–20) offers quality French cuisine, freshly prepared and served in a quirky yellow dining room. Some of the specials are, well, not so special (skip the duck), but the standard chicken and pasta dishes are outstanding; you can taste the time and care spent on them. Be sure to order a bottle of wine with dinner—the list is short but excellent.

GROCERIES

Mercado José Castillo (Av. General Utrilla at Nicaragua, 7 A.M.–6 P.M. daily) is a sprawling public market with just about anything you could want, from great fresh fruit and vegetables to bootleg CDs and flip-flops. It's worth a visit, even just to look.

Across from the market is **El Mayoreo** (Av. General Utrilla s/n, 7:30 A.M.–8:30 P.M. Mon.–Sat., 8 A.M.–6 P.M. Sun.), a large supermarket with decent prices and selection.

The centrally located **Super Más** (Real de Guadalupe near Av. General Utrilla, 8 A.M.–9:30 P.M. daily) has a deli, bakery, and one of the best wine selections in town. Prices are a little higher than average but the location can't be beat.

Many locals derive no small pride from the fact that their modest little city has a **Chedraui** megastore (Diagonal Hermanos Paniagua 50, 8 A.M.–11 P.M. daily), in a small mall that also has retail shops, a movie theater, and a food court.

Information and Services

TOURIST INFORMATION

The city tourist office (Palacio Municipal, tel. 967/678-0665, 8 A.M.–8 P.M. daily) is staffed by enthusiastic if not particularly knowledgeable workers. It's worth stopping to get a city map or a fistful of brochures.

EMERGENCY SERVICES

Hospital Regional (Av. Insurgentes 26, tel. 967/678-0770, 24 hours) is San Cristóbal's best hospital. For meds, **Farmacia Similares** (Av. Miguel Hidalgo at Calle Diego de Mazariegos, tel. 967/674-5961) is conveniently located on the pedestrian walkway and is open 24 hours. The **police station** (Barrio de San Antonio, tel. 967/678-0554, toll-free Mex. tel. 066, 24 hours) is on the Carretera Panamericana at Kilometer 1170.

MONEY

Bancomer (Calle Diego de Mazariegos, 8:30 A.M.–4 P.M. Mon.–Fri., 9 A.M–4 P.M. Sat.) is right on the central plaza while **Banamex** (Av. Insurgentes btw. Calles Cuauhtémoc and Niños Héroes, 8:30 A.M.–4 P.M. Mon.–Fri., 9 A.M–4 P.M. Sat.) is a block and a half away; both have 24-hour ATMs.

MEDIA AND COMMUNICATIONS

The **post office** (8 A.M.–7:30 P.M. Mon.–Fri., 8 A.M.–4 P.M. Sat.) is on Avenida Ignacio Allende between Calles Cuauhtémoc and Diego de Mazariegos.

You can hardly throw a Frisbee in San Cristóbal without hitting an Internet cafe, and most hotels and hostels offer free wireless and desktop Internet service to guests. A good option is **Restaurante Cafeteria El Centro** (7 A.M.–11 P.M. daily, US$1.25/hr), which is centrally located with modern computers and a fast connection, plus Skype, printing, scanning, and international phone and fax service.

For calls, **El Locutorio** (Av. 20 de Noviembre 20-A, 9 A.M.–9 P.M. daily) offers cheap reliable phone service, starting at US$0.20 per minute to the United States, Europe, and around Mexico.

IMMIGRATION

The immigration office (Diagonal Hermanos Paniagua 2, tel. 967/678-0292, 9 A.M.–2 P.M. Mon.–Sat.) is located west of the city center, near the Chedraui supermarket. The office does not officially handle visa extensions, but some travelers have gotten lucky by just stopping by and asking nicely.

LAUNDRY AND STORAGE

One of many launderettes around town, **Lavandería del Sol** (Real de Guadalupe 45, 8 A.M.–7 P.M. Mon.–Sat.) charges US$1 per kilogram (2.2 pounds), with a 2-kilo minimum. They offer same-day service if you drop your clothes off before 10 A.M.

You can store your bags at the **ADO bus terminal** (Av. Insurgentes at Carr. Panamericana, tel. 967/678-0291, 24 hours, US$0.50/hr).

LANGUAGE AND INSTRUCTION

The highly regarded **Instituto de Lenguas Jovel** (Francisco Madero 45, tel. 967/678-4069, www.institutojovel.com) offers private and group Spanish courses, all taught by professionally trained native-Spanish-speaking instructors. Courses include 15, 20, or 30 hours of instruction per week, and can be taken privately or in groups of up to five students (US$195–390 per week private, US$120–240 per week group, depending on hours). Specialized classes for doctors, teachers, social workers, and other professionals are also offered (US$320 per week) and include 15 hours of private weekly instruction, plus visits to local hospitals, schools, or NGOs, depending on your field. Room and board also can be arranged, including home-stays, hotel rooms, or furnished apartments (either shared or private) at very reasonable rates. The school organizes a number of interesting workshops as well, from Mexican cooking to jewelry making.

Operated out of the Centro Cultural El Puente, **El Puente Spanish Language School** (Calle Real de Guadalupe 55, tel. 967/678-3723, www.elpuenteweb.com) offers one-on-one and group Spanish lessons; a week of classes includes 15 hours of instruction for US$120–140. Home-stay packages, which include seven nights' lodging and three meals per day, increase the weekly rate to US$190–230. There is also a small restaurant, gallery, Internet café, and movie house on-site.

La Casa en el Árbol (Calle Real de Mexicanos 10, tel. 967/674-5272, www.lacasa enelarbol.org) offers language classes in the Maya languages of Tzotzil and Tzeltal, which are used throughout the region—a useful skill if you plan to stay in Chiapas awhile! Classes cost US$6.75–3.50 per hour (1–5 students); monthly rates are US$32.50 (4 hours per week, minimum 6 students). Spanish-language courses and home stays are also offered at competitive rates.

© GARY CHANDLER

San Cristóbal is especially scenic in the early morning, when the streets are quiet and mist still lingers in the surrounding hills.

SAN CRISTÓBAL DE LAS CASAS

Getting There and Around

GETTING THERE
Air

The nearest major airport is Tuxtla Gutiérrez's Ángel Albino Corzo International Airport (TGZ); it's a gleaming, modern airport, and its location well east of Tuxtla makes it equally convenient to San Cristóbal. San Cristóbal does have a small airport of its own, but no commercial flights land there.

Taxis charge US$50 from Tuxtla's International Airport to San Cristóbal, and around US$37.50 from San Cristóbal to the airport. **Agencia Chincultik** (Real de Guadalupe 34, tel. 967/678-0957, 8 A.M.–9 P.M. daily) also offers airport drop-off service for US$45 for 1–3 people; reservations are required. Alternately, take a bus to Tuxla, where cabs to the airport are US$17 (45 min).

There is also limited **first-class bus** service (US$10.50, 1 hr). From the airport to San Cristóbal, buses leave at 11:30 A.M., 12:30 P.M., 4 P.M., and 5:30 P.M.; from San Cristóbal back to the airport, there are only two departures at 5:30 A.M. and 3:30 P.M.

Bus

The **first-class bus terminal** (Av. Insurgentes at the Carr. Panamericana, tel. 967/678-0291) is seven blocks from the central plaza. You can avoid the hike down to the bus station to buy tickets by going to **Ticket Bus** (Calle Real de Guadalupe, tel. 967/678-8503, www.ticketbus .com.mx, 7 A.M.–10 P.M. daily), a half block from the *zócalo*; they take cash only.

The new highway between Tuxtla Gutiérrez and San Cristóbal opened in 2006 amid much fanfare, including a visit by then president Vicente Fox. The highway cuts travel time

SAN CRISTÓBAL BUS SCHEDULE

Departures from the **first-class bus terminal** (Av. Insurgentes s/n, tel. 967/678-0291) include:

DESTINATION	PRICE	DURATION	SCHEDULE
Campeche City	US$32	10 hrs	6:20 P.M.
Cancún	US$60-72	17.5-18.5 hrs	12:15 P.M., 2:30 P.M., 3:45 P.M., 4 P.M.
Ciudad Cuauhtémoc	US$9	3.25 hrs	7:45 A.M., 11:30 A.M., 2:35 P.M., 5:30 P.M., 12:45 A.M.
Comitán	US$3	1.5-2 hrs	every 20-60 mins 6:10-11:30 A.M. and every 1-2 hrs 2:35-11:20 P.M.
Mérida	US$44	13 hrs	6:20 P.M.
Mexico City	US$75-95	13-14 hrs	5 departures 4:10-10:30 P.M.
Ocosingo	US$3.50	2.5 hrs	take Palenque bus
Palenque	US$10-12	5-6 hrs	9 departures 7:15 A.M.-11 P.M.
Tapachula	US$18	8 hrs	7 departures 7:45 A.M.-12:05 A.M.
Tuxtla Gutiérrez	US$3	70 mins	every 15-60 mins 3:55 A.M.-10:45 P.M.
Tuxtla Gutiérrez International Airport	US$10	1.25 hrs	5 A.M. and 3:30 P.M.
Villahermosa	US$20	7 hrs	11:20 A.M. and 11 P.M.

between the two cities to just over an hour, and eliminated most of the stomach-lurching curves and precipices that made the old highway so notorious.

There's a new highway being built between Palenque and San Cristóbal, too, but it's yet to be completed. Until it is, figure on 5–6 hours on an extremely winding road, with just one stop in Ocosingo; travelers prone to car-sickness should consider taking Dramamine beforehand.

Combi

Combis (shared vans) come and go to some of San Cristóbal's outlying towns and villages. Their depots are located all around town.

Car

Driving at night is definitely not recommended in Chiapas, due to the possibility of roadside robberies; this is especially a concern on the Palenque–San Cristóbal road, and most rural

SAN CRISTÓBAL *COMBI* SCHEDULE

Combis (shared vans) come and go to some of San Cristóbal's outlying towns and attractions, including:

DESTINATION	ADDRESS	PRICE	DURATION	SCHEDULE
Amatenango	Carr. Panamericana near Av Júarez	US$3	1.5 hrs	every 15-60 minutes 4 A.M.-8 P.M.
Chenalhó	Av General Utrilla near Calle Edgar Robledo minutes	US$2	50 min	every 10-30 5 A.M.-7 P.M.
Chiapa de Corzo*	Carr. Panamericana near Av Júarez	US$2.50	45-60 min	take a Tuxtla Gutièrrez *combi*
Huitepec**	Av General Utrilla near Calle Costa Rica	US$0.65	15-20 min	every 30 minutes 5 A.M.-5 P.M.
Oventik	Av General Utrilla near Calle Edgar Robledo	US$1.65-2	1 hr	every 15-60 minutes 5 A.M.-5 P.M.
Oxchuc	Carr. Panamericana near Av Júarez	US$1.75-3.50	1 hr	every 15-60 minutes 3 A.M.-9 P.M.
San Andrés Larrainzar	Av. Salomón González Blanco s/n	US$1.40-1.65	40 min	every 15-60 minutes 4 A.M.-7 P.M.
San Juan Chamula	Calle Honduras near Av 16 de Septiembre	US$0.75	30 min	every 5-30 minutes 5 A.M.-7 P.M.
Tenejapa	Calle Bermudas near Cristóbal Colón	US$2	30 min	every 5-30 minutes 6 A.M.-8 P.M.
Tuxtla Gutiérrez	Carr. Panamericana near Av Júarez	US$3.35	70 min	every 15-60 minutes 4 A.M.-9 P.M.
Zinacatán	Calle Edgar Robledo near Belisario Domìnguez	US$1.15	25 min	every 5-30 minutes 5 A.M.-6 P.M.

*There are no *combis* that go directly to Chiapa de Corzo. Instead, catch a Tuxtla-bound *colectivo* on the Carretera Panamericana and get off at the first *puente peatonal* (footbridge) shortly past the toll booth. Cross the bridge and catch a *combi* (US$0.40) or taxi (US$2) into town.

**Combis* headed to San Juan Chamula and Zinacantán also can drop off passengers at the entrance to Huitepec; full fare to the final destination, however, must be paid.

roadways. (Even late-night buses should be avoided, as they are occasionally targeted as well.) Driving during the daytime is safe, however, and usually quite beautiful.

The new toll road between Tuxtla and San Cristóbal makes that stretch safer and quicker, albeit with a US$3.50-per-car price tag. You can still take the old highway, too—it takes twice as long and should not be traveled at night, but there's no toll and the views are incredible.

GETTING AROUND

San Cristóbal is a very walkable city, and most sights are easily reached on foot. For outlying destinations, or if you're just tuckered out, taxis are cheap and convenient. A car or scooter can be handy for visiting outlying areas, but bear in mind that tour agencies offer reasonably priced, guided tours to most of the places you're likely to visit with a car.

Taxi

Scores of cabs ply the streets day and night, and you can always find one parked at the central plaza. Prices are fixed, and it's a good idea to confirm the going rate with your hotel receptionist. At the time of research, a ride anywhere around town was US$2, or US$2.50 after midnight.

Car

Driving and parking on the narrow, crowded one-way streets of San Cristóbal is an adventure, to say the least. Outside of town, be very alert for pedestrians, bicycles, and animals along the road. And again, never drive at night.

Óptima Car Rental (Calle Diego de Mazariegos 39 across from Parque La Merced, tel. 967/674-5409, 9 A.M.–2 P.M. and 4–7 P.M. Mon.–Sat., 9 A.M.–1 P.M. Sun.) is San

Cristóbal's one and only rent-a-car shop. An aging VW bug runs US$40 a day, or you can pay US$60 and up per day for something a bit more modern. Prices include taxes and insurance; the latter cannot be deducted, even if you have insurance through your credit card. Discounts are available if you pay in cash, or rent for a week or more. You may find better deals through the international agencies, which have offices at the airport and in Tuxtla.

Scooter

Scooters are cheaper and more maneuverable than cars, but far less forgiving in case of an accident—think twice about renting one if you aren't an experienced rider. Never ride at night or in bad weather, and remember that most local drivers will not be accustomed to sharing the road with you.

Crazy Scooters (Av. Belisario Domínguez 7 at Real de Guadalupe, tel. 967/631-4329, 9 A.M.–2:30 P.M. and 4:30–7 P.M. daily) rents scooters for US$19 for two hours and US$4 per additional hour, or US$35 for the day, including helmet and map.

Bicycle

A number of sights and villages can be reached by bike, and at least two agencies in town specialize in pedaling tours. The same agencies also rent bikes: **Los Pingüinos** (Av. Ecuador 4-B at Real de Mexicanos, tel. 967/678-0202, www.bikemexico.com/pinguinos, 10 A.M.–2:30 P.M. and 3:30–7 P.M. daily, US$14 per day) and **Ruta Nahual** (Real de Guadalupe 123, cell tel. 044-967/124-2100, rutanahual@hotmail.com, 10 A.M.–1 P.M. and 4–6 P.M. Tues.–Sat., US$2–3 per hour). Or try **Crazy Scooters** (Av. Belisario Domínguez 7 at Real de Guadalupe, tel. 967/631-4329, 9 A.M.–2:30 P.M. and 4:30–7 P.M. daily, US$5 first two hours, US$2 per additional hour).

Villages Around San Cristóbal

Surrounding San Cristóbal are numerous indigenous *municipios* (municipalities), each comprised of large and small villages and often encompassing huge swaths of rural territory. Municipalities are ethnically defined—Chamulans not only live in Chamula but share ancient ethnic bonds, distinct from Zinacatecans, Tenejapans, and so on. Some share a common language (Tzotzil and Tzeltal are the most widely spoken) but just as many do not. Virtually all are "Maya" (as are the language groups) but the term belies the highland's tremendous ethnic diversity. *Municipios* exercise considerable autonomy from the state and federal governments; religion, land ownership, conflict resolution, policing, and punishment are all handled by traditional methods, completely independent of "Mexican" institutions.

Getting There and Around

Every village is different, and options for visiting them vary accordingly. It's possible to simply drive, bike, or take public transport to most villages and wander around for a few hours. (Plan to leave by mid-afternoon, as staying overnight, or even after dark, is not permitted.) Tours are an excellent option, too, as you learn much more and tours often include visiting local families, something you're unlikely to experience going solo. Guides also can fill you in on the various do's and don'ts to be sure your visit is as respectful and unobtrusive as possible.

Taking Photographs

Rules about photography are taken very seriously in highland indigenous villages. It is absolutely forbidden to take pictures inside a church, of a religious procession or ceremony, or of any town official. In some towns, you are simply not allowed to take pictures at all. In others, landscapes and location shots are okay, but you should still be discreet. Always ask permission before taking a picture of an individual person, such as in the market; if it's a child, ask their parents as well. Be prepared to be shushed away, or asked for money in exchange. Refrain from attempting any clever photography, as locals are well aware of zoom lenses, cell-phone cameras, tiny point-and-shoots, etc. If you do get caught taking a picture when you shouldn't, officials may confiscate your memory chip (they know about those too) and issue a fine, usually US$50–150. Those who refuse to pay may end up in a village jail cell until they pay—really.

◖ SAN JUAN CHAMULA

With more than 10,000 residents, San Juan Chamula is Chiapas's largest indigenous town, and the Chamula municipality—with some

EL CARGO

At some point in his or her lifetime, every villager of San Juan Chamula – as in other indigenous communities – is expected to assume a religious *cargo*. Literally a "burden," in the case of Chamulans it also means a position of responsibility in the town's complex spiritual practices.

A *cargo*-holder's primary role sounds simple enough: to care for a wooden statue representing one of the many saints honored by Chamulans, usually for a term of one year. But this task is neither easy nor cheap. For starters, the statue has its own home, which the caretaker and his or her family move into for the duration of the term. The caretaker must supply the statue with a constant supply of fresh flowers and pine boughs, which must be cut in the mountains or bought in the market,

along with other offerings. On saints' days and other special occasions, the caretaker must organize and host a huge celebration, providing food, soda, and alcohol for the entire village. Certain saints are more highly revered than others – caring for them earns a villager higher honor, but at greater expense.

All told, a *cargo* can cost the equivalent of thousands or even tens of thousands of dollars, a staggering expense for someone who may earn less than five dollars a day. *Cargo*-holders often borrow the money and can spend years or a lifetime paying off the debt. Still, very few shirk their duty. When asked how he managed it, one *cargo*-holder shrugged and said, "Better to carry a burden for a year than for the rest of eternity."

60,000 residents—is arguably the largest indigenous polity in the New World. San Juan is Chamula's political and religious center, and also the place most visited by outsiders, located just 12 kilometers from San Cristóbal. A trip to San Juan is practically a given for anyone visiting San Cristóbal; it's one of the most unique and fascinating places you may encounter in Chiapas.

Traditional Dress

Chamulan women are easily distinguished by their traditional dress, including white *huipiles* with simple flowers embroidered around the necklines and thick black wool skirts cinched with red belts. Many women also wear sky-blue wool *rebozos* (shawls) that sometimes hide a baby tucked into its folds. These garments are handwoven on a waist loom and generally are made of wool that has been carded by the women from animals raised on the family plot.

Chamulan men wear machine-made hats, western-style pants and shirts, leather boots, and long, woolen tunics; most men wear white tunics and the village leaders wear black tunics. A man also wears a special official dress

of authority during the time he serves on the town council.

Women and little girls are often barefoot—it is partly a question of money, but it also stems from a traditional belief that the earth makes females fertile through their feet. Tourists often are tempted to give indigenous people or children shoes, but some recipients consider such unsolicited charity offensive; it's better to donate shoes—or better yet, money—to organizations with established relationships with indigenous communities (ask about recommended groups at San Cristóbal's state tourism office).

Iglesia de San Juan Bautista

San Juan's colorful blue and white flowered church is a deeply important place for villagers, and a must-see for visitors. Though it appears like any other church on the outside, it's obvious from the moment you enter that it's no ordinary Catholic space. (In fact, the only standard Catholic ceremonies conducted here are baptisms, which are conducted by guest priests since Chamula's leaders won't allow any permanent clergy to be placed here.) A rich aroma greets you as you walk in the door: a mixture of

© H.W. PRADO

The church at San Juan Chamula may be Mexico's most unique house of worship.

pine, flowers, incense, and candles. The floor is covered with pine needles, cut fresh from the forest and carried here every Saturday. The statues of the saints are dressed in many layers of brilliantly flowered clothes with mirrors hung around their necks. Most of the statues are now kept in glass boxes because villagers occasionally sought revenge when a request to the saint was not fulfilled. It wasn't unusual for an angry churchgoer to break a statue's finger off, turn the statue backward to face the wall, or even to take the statue outside and stick its head in the ground.

Hundreds of candles placed on the floor glow reverently in the dim light—red candles burn for someone who is ill, black candles announce death, but most are white and are part of detailed private ceremonies performed with the help of shamans for various daily or family matters. Besides candles, ceremonies utilize chickens, eggs, *posh* (a traditional cane sugar liquor) and—amazingly—Coca-Cola and Pepsi. Belching is considered an effective way to rid the body of bad spirits; *posh* was used originally, but carbonated soft drinks do a far better job and were quickly adopted by Chamulan shamans. Some see this as corrupting, but it can also be viewed as an example of Chiapas's indigenous people choosing certain modern creations to enhance traditional practices. And why not? They are not, after all, blind to the world around them.

Tickets (US$2) are required to enter the church; tour guides typically handle this for their groups, but independent visitors should stop at the tourism office, located in the city hall facing the central plaza, to purchase one.

Festivals

Religious holidays are a unique times to visit San Juan Chamula, with its raucous celebration, solemn processions, and special ceremonies, all set against a backdrop of music, fireworks, and plenty of food and drink. During festivals, *cargo*-holders, town leaders, shamans, and ordinary villagers all wear special ceremonial clothing, all different depending on the wearer's position but none without bright colors and exquisitely woven and embroidered designs.

Carnaval is San Juan's biggest and most notoriously excessive celebration, lasting for a full week and including elaborate costumes, rituals, and role-playing. Whatever the occasion, be prepared to encounter dense crowds and a certain number of supremely drunk men. Remember, too, that taking pictures during festivals is prohibited.

ZINACANTÁN

In nearby Zinacantán, life moves at a far different pace. The town's main industry is growing and exporting flowers, and driving there you'll see large hothouses dispersed in hills and valleys. The Zinacatecans have been merchants since the early 1600s and still travel around the region selling their homegrown vegetables, fruit, and flowers. A growing tourism business also helps explain the town's relative prosperity.

Traditional Dress

The traditional clothing worn by men is the most colorful in the area, and includes straw hats, short white pants, and pinkish tunics decorated with bright embroidered flowers and fuchsia tassels. The women, on the other hand, wear dark skirts and white blouses trimmed with a minimum of color, topped with a beautiful blue *rebozo* (shawl).

Textiles

Zinacatecan textiles are noted for their colorful embroidery in flamboyant reds, pinks, purples, and blues. The work is done outdoors in the family yard with most of the women attached to a waist loom. They create tablecloths, bedspreads, place mats, and of course the men's tunics. Most tours stop in a weaving family's home for a chance to see (and of course buy) their wares.

TENEJAPA

Tenejapa is a tidy, prosperous Tzeltal Maya town known for its master textile weavers and Thursday market (which has spilled over to

Sunday as well). It also has a beautiful church and central plaza, yet you can count on one hand the number of travelers who go there on any given day. Tenejapa is notable for its peaceful and tolerant atmosphere, and not just toward visitors: It's one of only a few highland indigenous communities where both Catholics and Protestants live and worship openly, and where converts are not routinely expelled. However, taking photographs inside the church, or of officials or processions, remains strictly forbidden.

Textiles

Sna Jolobil, the award-winning cooperative with a shop attached to San Crisóbal's Santo Domingo church, was founded in Tenejapa, and the town has long been renowned for the quality and inventiveness of its textiles. The cooperative has a small shop a few doors to the right of the main church, and its founder, María Meza, lives on the road leading into town. Visitors are welcome to knock on her door and ask to see her work; there's no number, but look for a white house three doors uphill from the corner.

Central Plaza and Thursday Market

Tenejapa's well-tended central plaza is bordered on two sides by brightly painted municipal buildings, including the **Casa de Cultura** (tel. 967/674-8139, 9 A.M.–1 P.M. and 4–8 P.M. Mon.–Fri.), where textiles and other local handicrafts are sometimes displayed. There's also a large mural, brimming with highland Maya imagery and symbolism. **Iglesia San Ildefonso** (hours vary), Tenejapa's main church, also faces the plaza, and features rich velvet tapestries draped from the rafters above the nave. The altar is an exuberant display of candles, saints, and a large image of Christ, while along the walls are more statues, many dressed in traditional Tenejapa garb. Remember, no photos!

The Thursday market begins on the road on the far side of the church, and extends several blocks. The atmosphere is noticeably mellow and makes for a pleasant stroll. There's very little aimed at tourists, but fresh fruit or a bag of peanuts (roasted or boiled) is always a nice purchase.

Plaza San Sebastián

From the central plaza, turn left at the road on the far side of the church to reach the smaller Plaza San Sebastián, a broad cement square that's often occupied by high schoolers playing basketball and soccer. At the opposite end is a church in the works, Templo San Sebastián, built on the remains of the 18th-century original that was started but never completed (check out the thick stone walls along the base). According to legend, construction was abandoned on the first one after the statue of San Sebastián, which was to be installed there, kept mysteriously moving itself to the main church on the central plaza. Village leaders took that to mean the saint was unhappy with the location, and the church was never completed.

◖ EL ROMERILLO

This small Chamulan community, located about halfway between San Cristóbal and Tenejapa, is home to Chamula's principal cemetery. A sublime sight, the graveyard occupies a small rise alongside the main road, with a series of high blue-painted crosses at the crest. The graves are also marked with smaller crosses, as well as thick wood boards placed over the earthen mounds. The boards represent doors, and every November 1 (Día de Todos los Santos, or All Saints Day) the living gather in the cemetery to commune with their dead. The grave of a loved one is first cleaned to appear freshly dug, then decorated with flowers, offerings of food and drink, and a thick layer of pine boughs (evergreens represent eternal life). Then, holding a shawl over their heads, family members lift an edge of the board and speak directly, sometimes at length, with the spirit of their deceased relative. Photos are forbidden on that day, but travelers are welcome to attend—it's a remarkable event—and can take

© LIZA PRADO

Maya crosses guard the graves at El Romerillo cemetery, one of the area's most important and unique indigenous burial grounds.

pictures any other day. The boards, flowers, and decorations remain in place until refreshed the following year.

SAN ANDRÉS LARRAINZAR

This somewhat downtrodden Tzotzil Maya community is best known for having hosted peace talks between government and Zapatista forces, and as the namesake of the promising (but poorly implemented) San Andrés Peace Accords. The town is draped over several small steep hills, and exploring here can be something of a workout.

San Andrés Larrainzar is 25 kilometers from San Cristóbal on the highway to (and past) San Juan Chamula. Look for a turnoff after about 18 kilometers, where signs direct you left (uphill) to San Andrés. The town's main entrance is at a sharp left-hand turn in the highway; continue straight to reach the center.

Traditional Dress and Textiles

Weaving is a traditional skill (performed exclusively by women) as well as an important source of income. Larrainzar women are known for incorporating bits of yarn into the warp and weft of their back-strap looms to create special designs. One product is the brocade, an ancient design associated with the Maya of Yaxchilán that incorporates traditional symbols such as the snake, toad, diamond, flower, and monkey. The background color is usually bright red with many colors woven in.

Many women of San Andrés Larrainzar, and some men, continue to dress in traditional garb. Women wear raw white cotton blouses thickly embroidered with intricate geometric designs on a red background, and accompanied by a long blue skirt with a few light-blue lines woven across it.

Sunday Market

The main reason to come to San Andrés Larrainzar is the Sunday market, a colorful display of fruits and vegetables, live chickens (and dead ones too), handwoven textiles, and every sort of household item imaginable. Like most indigenous markets, the crowds and movement

drop off considerably after 10 A.M., and is essentially over by midday.

OVENTIK

Not so much a village as a roadside settlement, Oventik is one of five original Zapatista administrative centers known as *caracoles* (literally snails or shells), though in this context the meaning is more akin to "hub." Located a short distance past San Andrés Larrainzar, Oventik is the most accessible of the *caracoles*—notwithstanding the masked guards at the large entrance gate—and is easily reached by car or *combi* from San Cristóbal. Visitors vary widely in their reviews of Oventik; some find it to be a fascinating peek into the day-to-day working of the Zapatista movement, while others find it exasperatingly bureaucratic and ultimately a bit dull. Few disagree that it's an attractive place, ensconced in pine trees and an ever-present mist, with large colorful murals on virtually every building.

History

The EZLN established Oventik and the other *caracoles* in 2003, after the Mexican Congress adopted a much watered-down version of the 1996 San Andrés Peace Accords, and the Supreme Court rejected hundreds of legal complaints over the law's inadequacy, particularly regarding indigenous autonomy. Each *caracol* has a *Junta de Buen Gobierno* (Good Government Council), which is made up of non-military representatives from its affiliated communities and whose work includes maintaining communal schools and clinics, gathering information and issuing reports on the Mexican army's movements in their area, collecting taxes, and mediating local conflicts. The Juntas tend to be excruciatingly inefficient due to the frequent rotation of their members and an affinity for paperwork, but the Zapatistas deserve credit for realizing, at least in part, one of their central goals: autonomous self-government for (some of) Chiapas's rural and indigenous communities.

Visiting the Village

A visit to Oventik begins at the gate, where

you have to present photo identification to the masked guard; they'll ask for a passport, but a driver's license suffices. (You should never hand over your passport unless absolutely necessary, here or anywhere.) You'll be escorted to a series of colorful clapboard buildings manned by masked representatives; each time you'll be asked your name, profession, and reason for visiting and your answers painstakingly noted in large registers. Eventually you will meet with a member of the Junta, who approves (or disapproves) your visit. The whole process can take hours, most of which is spent waiting around. Needless to say, it's best to arrive early.

Once approved, you can wander Oventik's lone road, talking pictures of the murals (but not of people), eating at the small restaurant, or shopping in the *artesanía* shops. Foreign volunteers and local residents come to Oventik for administrative matters, and they are interesting to chat with (if open to talking). Staying a few days can make for a much richer experience—bunking in the community school or with local families, and visiting outlying villages. However, it must be arranged with the Junta over a series of visits, and isn't always possible—don't show up planning to stay the night.

CHENALHÓ

Chenalhó is a quiet Tzotzil Maya town located at the bottom of a narrow valley, with a lively Sunday market and striking textiles and weaving. Chenalhó women continue to wear the town's traditional clothing, including *huipiles* with bright-red embroidered panels around the neck, and indigo skirts.

Chenalhó is located 33 kilometers past San Juan Chamula, on the same highway. At about 18 kilometers is a Y-intersection; bear right (going left takes you to San Andrés Larrainzar) and in another 15 kilometers the road descends in a series of steep hairpin turns before bumping right into Chenalhó's central plaza.

Iglesia San Pedro and Chenalhó Cemetery

Maya crosses stand in front of Chenalhó's attractive main church, Iglesia San Pedro, while

green valley walls rise dramatically behind. On the opposite side of the plaza, and a block back, a path leads over a short bridge and up a steep slope to the town cemetery, whose bright colors and rich offerings are well worth a quick look. It is okay to take pictures of the graves, but not anyone praying or performing a ceremony there. Likewise, pictures of the church facade are permitted, but not the interior.

OXCHUC

Only a handful of the thousands of travelers who pass this vibrant Tzeltal Maya ever stop. Located right along the highway between San Cristóbal and Palenque, it's one of the easiest indigenous villages to reach from San Cristóbal, yet when you visit you may well be the only foreigner in town—a striking difference from well-traveled villages like San Juan Chamula and Amatenango.

Saturday Market

An especially good time to visit Oxchuc is Saturday—market day—when the streets and central plaza are packed with people. Keep your eye out for rats—not scurrying through the gutter, but sold at stands, either freshly killed or grilled on a stick. Oxchuc is known for its *sopa de rata* (rat soup), a traditional Tzeltal dish made from rats that feed on medicinal plants, and thought to be curative.

Iglesia Santo Tomás

Set slightly back from Oxchuc's central square, Iglesia Santo Tomás has a rich mustard exterior and a gaping interior—in fact, its nave is one of most voluminous in the state. White-washed walls rise to wooden cross beams incised with ornate floral patterns, while long wide colorful bolts of fabric hang nearly to the floor, a feature of many indigenous Chiapanecan churches. A striking double arch frames the church's fine *retablo* altar.

Santo Tomás is also notable for two modest domed structures adjoined to the outside courtyard walls. Known as *posas,* from the Spanish word *posar* (to pose or sit), these miniature chapels served as worship and baptismal stations

SAN CRISTÓBAL DE LAS CASAS

before the church itself was constructed. Although *posas* were common in early missions, Oxchuc's are the only ones in Chiapas remaining in their original form, with faded Dominican paintings still visible inside.

El Corralito

Just off the highway about 15 kilometers past Oxchuc, the Río Jataté tumbles down a long rocky slope to form El Corralito waterfall (7 A.M.–5 P.M. daily, US$0.50 pp or US$3 per car). Until recently, most people caught only a glimpse of the falls as they whizzed past in the car or bus. Now, there are picnic areas at top and bottom, a parking area, bathrooms, even a restaurant (though it's frequently closed). A paved trail climbs about 200 meters alongside the falls, and at the top the river widens into several appealing swimming holes. All in all, it's a pleasant stop on the way between San Cristóbal and Palenque, or as an add-on to a visit to Oxchuc.

Clear cool water tumbles down a leafy hillside at El Corralito.

To get to El Corralito, catch any Ocosingo-bound *combi* from San Cristóbal (US$3, 1.5 hrs) or Oxchuc (US$0.50, 20 mins).

AMATENANGO DEL VALLE

The Carretera Panamericana (Hwy. 190) rolls past the small pottery-making village of Amatenango del Valle, where passersby are treated to an incredible display of classic Tzeltal Maya artisanship; most notable are the rustic clay doves, some tiny, some measuring over one meter (3.3 feet) in height.

Traditional Dress

Though the men of Amatenango del Valle tend to wear western clothes—jeans, boots, and cowboy hats—the women still wear traditional clothing. Changed little over the centuries, the clothing includes a loose red and yellow raw cotton shirt that has been embroidered with wool yarn and a dark-blue checked skirt, often a length of cloth that has been wrapped around the body. Women also typically wind a bright-red ribbon in their hair.

Pottery

All of the pottery made in Amatenango del Valle is created without a wheel. Pieces made from natural gray clay are sun-dried and then fired in an aboveground open fire rather than in a kiln—a technique dating to pre-Hispanic times. Unfortunately, the pottery is not as durable as some, but the pieces are a wonderful souvenir if you can get them home.

A number of San Cristóbal–based tour operators stop here on the way to or from the Lagunas de Montebello, but if you are driving it is easy to visit on your own. Driving past town, you'll see jars, doves, and other pieces set up right on the highway's shoulder. If you stop, the owner of the particular collection of pieces typically will come running out of her home. You can try asking to see the artist's workshop—not all artisans are open to this (or are working at the moment you pull up)—but it makes for an interesting few minutes. As elsewhere, ask permission before taking pictures.

THE LAKES REGION

This region's namesake lakes—the Lagunas de Montebello—are a remarkable cluster of over 50 lakes and ponds, each unique in size, shape, and seemingly even in color, ranging from emerald green to cobalt blue. The lakes are nestled in the nooks and crannies of a hilly pine forest, boasting dramatic overlooks and a cool temperate climate. About a dozen of the lakes are accessible by road, and tour groups from San Cristóbal commonly visit 10 or more in a day, some to enjoy the view and snap a picture, others to swim or canoe.

But Lagunas de Montebello are not the only lakes, or water, that this region has to offer—far from it. Laguna Miramar, a huge pristine lake deep in the Lacandón rainforest, is one of Chiapas's most stunning natural treasures. Getting there is no less memorable: Normally reached by bus from Ocosingo, there's a back-door approach from the Lakes Region, including a two-hour boat ride through Zapatista-controlled territory.

Las Guacamayas, an excellent eco-center, is built along the wide Río Lacantún, with hikes and boat rides in the lush Montes Azules biosphere reserve on the opposite bank. Las Nubes, another eco-center, is all about water, located where the Río Santo Domingo rages and tumbles through a series of waterfalls and narrow channels. And then there are the waterfalls of Cascada El Chiflón, one of the state's biggest, with mist-swept trails climbing both banks.

Amid the many natural and watery wonders of this area is the incredibly underrated city of Comitán, not only a convenient base for exploring the area, but a charming and peaceful destination in itself.

© H.W. PRADO

HIGHLIGHTS

◖ El Zócalo: Shady benches, a gurgling fountain, and live music in the central bandstand make this a classic colonial plaza. But the modern-art sculptures, welcoming red-suited tourism officers, and amiable atmosphere, day and night, make it *cien por ciento* (100 percent) Comitán (page 122).

◖ Cascada El Chiflón: Extending more than a kilometer, this impressive series of waterfalls has radiant turquoise water and includes a 120-meter tumbler that's one of the tallest in Mexico. Trails lead up both sides, with mist-drenched observation points and a zip line across the main cascade (page 129).

◖ Parque Nacional Lagunas de Montebello: Nearly 60 lakes, each seemingly a different hue, all ensconced in a cool pine forest, have long made this a favorite destina-tion. Spend a day hopping from lake to lake – a photo-op here, a spin in a kayak there – either on your own or with a tour (page 134).

◖ Laguna Miramar: Said to be the purest body of water in Mexico, Laguna Miramar is postcard gorgeous, with warm crystalline water that's ideal for swimming, kayaking, even snorkeling. It's all the more lovely for its remote, hard-to-reach location, deep in the Lacandón rainforest (page 138).

◖ Las Guacamayas: A relaxing and beauti-ful ecocenter on the edge of the Montes Azules biosphere reserve, Las Guacamayas has hiking and boat tours through the rainforest, and is a nesting ground for hundreds of endangered *guacamayas* (scarlet macaws). It's a great stopover on the roundabout route between Comitán and Palenque (page 140).

LOOK FOR ◖ TO FIND RECOMMENDED SIGHTS, ACTIVITIES, DINING, AND LODGING.

PLANNING YOUR TIME

Parts of the Lakes Region can be visited on a day trip from San Cristóbal, and that is still the most common option. Tour agencies offer all-day outings that include stops in Lagunas de Montebello and El Chiflón waterfall (and sometimes the pottery village of Amatenango del Valle on the way back). Although it makes for a long day, it's a logical option if your time is short.

You'll enjoy the area much more, however, by basing yourself in Comitán, two hours east of San Cristóbal. A friendly and oft-overlooked city, Comitán has excellent museums, plazas, and architecture, and great value in lodging and restaurants. In fact, plan on arriving early

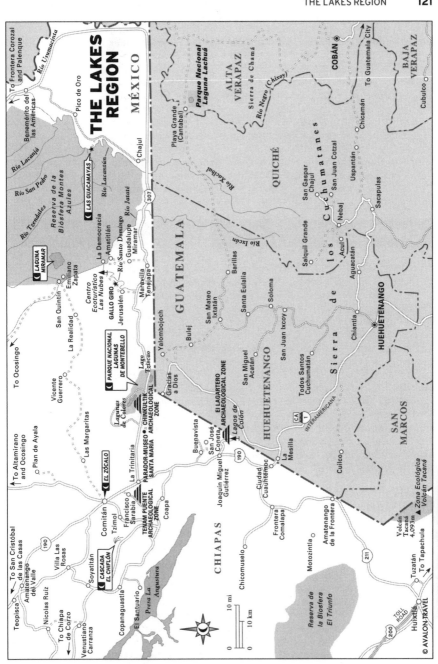

© AVALON TRAVEL

so you'll have a full day to enjoy this "mini San Cristóbal" (just don't call it that to locals!). From there, you can still visit Lagunas de Montebello and El Chiflón as a day trip, or two days if you include the Maya ruins of Tenam Puente and Chinkultik, with far less driving time than from San Cristóbal.

Staying in Comitán also gives you a jump on getting to more remote attractions east of Lagunas de Montebello, namely Las Guacamayas and Las Nubes eco-centers, and the isolated and gorgeous Laguna Miramar. The first and last are especially lovely, and worth budgeting at least two nights apiece. All can be reached fairly easily by public transportation, though having a car certainly makes getting around quicker and more efficient.

Beyond Las Guacamayas, you can continue from the Lakes Region up and around to the Río Usumacinta Valley (including Yaxchilán and Bonampak archaeological sites) and eventually to Palenque. The roads are quite good, but *combi* service can be a bit spotty— you may have to leap-frog a bit leaving Las Guacamayas. Still, it's a great way to reach Palenque without backtracking.

Comitán

Two hours east of San Cristóbal, Comitán is an engaging and well-located city that's often overshadowed by its better-known neighbor. The city bursts with art, from its outstanding modern-art museum to whimsical sculptures dotting the central plaza, and its tidy streets and bright colonial architecture invite you to wander and explore. (All those steep hills are another matter!) Comitán is ideally located for day trips to Lagunas de Montebello, Cascada El Chiflón, and Chinkultik and Tenam Puente archaeological sites—all within an hour, compared to three-plus hours from San Cristóbal—or for getting an early start to places further afield, like Las Guacamayas and Laguna Miramar.

SIGHTS
(El Zócalo
The central plazas of some Mexican cities— like Tuxtla Gutiérrez and Mexico City—are big wide-open squares, with little to obscure the view from end to end. Comitán takes the opposite approach, filling its split-level central plaza, or *zócalo*, with benches, planters, a fountain, a bandstand, and numerous intriguing modern sculptures. Most importantly, it's a living, breathing plaza, enjoyed by locals and tourists alike, whether to relax under a shade tree during the day or to listen to live marimba music at night. And you can always find one of Comitán's red-uniformed information officers in the central plaza, happy to dispense directions and suggestions.

Templo Santo Domingo de Guzmán
Dating from 1556, the Templo Santo Domingo de Guzmán (Av. Rosario Castellanos at Calle Central Ote., 10 A.M.–7 P.M. daily) is the most imposing building on the central plaza. It was the last Dominican church built in Chiapas and is unique for its severity—other than the mustard-yellow paint job, the octagonal choir window is the only decoration on its facade. Be sure to take a good look at the bell tower; the Mudejar-style arcading was only recently discovered under its stucco surface, a major discovery for early colonial architecture buffs. The convent, unfortunately, was demolished; the brick building that stands in its place houses the **Centro Cultural Rosario Castellanos** (central plaza, Av. Rosario Castellanos at 1a Calle Sur Ote., tel. 963/632-0624, 9 A.M.–8 P.M. Mon.–Fri., 10 A.M.–5 P.M. Sat.–Sun., free).

Palacio Municipal
Built in the 19th century, the neoclassic Palacio Municipal (central plaza, Av. Central near

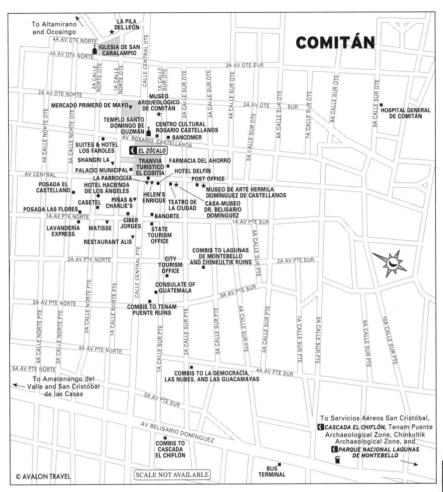

Calle Central Ote.) houses the city's government offices. Step inside and check out the spectacular mural that runs along the stairway, a work created by Manuel Suasnávar depicting Comitán's long history.

Museo Arqueológico de Comitán

The Comitán Archaeological Museum (1a Calle Sur Ote. btwn. Av. Rosario Castellanos and 2a Av. Ote. Sur, tel. 963/632-5760, 9 A.M.–6 P.M. Tues.–Sun., free) traces the history of the Maya in Chiapas and has an impressive collection of artifacts from nearby archaeological zones, especially those found in tombs. Don't miss the Sala Tenam Puente, which showcases items from the namesake site—the room is easy to miss as it's located across the courtyard from the rest of the museum. If it's locked, ask the guard; more often than not he'll open it for you. Signage is in Spanish only.

Museo de Arte Hermila Domínguez de Castellanos

Housing an exceptional modern-art collection,

Mudejar-style arcading was discovered on the bell tower of Comitán's Templo Santo Domingo de Guzmán.

the Museo de Arte Hermila Domínguez de Castellanos (Av. Central 51, tel. 963/632-2082, 10 A.M.–6 P.M. Mon.–Sat., 10 A.M.–2 P.M. Sun., US$0.50) is a welcome surprise. The artwork is showcased on two floors—temporary exhibits are on the 1st floor—and features mostly distinguished Oaxacan and Chiapanecan painters and sculptors. Near the entrance is a small room with three paintings by Rufino Tamayo, one of Mexico's most accomplished artists. The museum is named after the daughter of Dr. Belisario Domínguez, whose own museum is just a few doors down.

Casa-Museo Dr. Belisario Domínguez

Dr. Belisario Domínguez House Museum (Av. Central 35, tel. 963/632-1300, 10 A.M.–6:45 P.M. Mon.–Sat., 9 A.M.–12:45 P.M. Sun., US$0.50) showcases the life of Dr. Belisario Domínguez, one of Chiapas's most important politicians, whose primary causes were the improvement of public services to Chiapas as well

as promoting freedom of speech. A Mexican senator during the early 1900s, Dr. Domínguez was assassinated in 1913 after he publically called for the resignation of the president of Mexico, Victoriano Huerta. The museum is in his family home and contains a replica of his pharmacy, a sitting room and bedroom, his medical tools, and document upon document about his life as well as his own writings. Signage is in Spanish only.

Iglesia de San Caralampio and Barrio La Pila

The neo-rococo Iglesia de San Caralampio (4a Av. Ote. Nte. at 2a Calle Nte. Ote., hours vary) is a striking rust and mustard-yellow church that sits on a leafy plaza. It's named after an obscure Russian Orthodox saint whose image is said to have stopped an outbreak of smallpox and cholera from a nearby ranch during the 19th century.

The church is in one of the oldest and prettiest neighborhoods in the city—Barrio La Pila. It is

© H.W. PRADO

a colorful colonial place, one worth wandering about in. Look for the neighborhood's namesake, **La Pila del León** (4a Av. Ote. Nte. at 1a Calle Nte. Ote.), Comitán's first public water source.

ENTERTAINMENT AND EVENTS

Centro Cultural Rosario Castellanos

Named after an early feminist writer from Comitán who advocated for the rights of indigenous populations, the Rosario Castellanos Cultural Center (central plaza, Av. Rosario Castellanos at 1a Calle Sur Ote., tel. 963/632-0624, 9 A.M.–8 P.M. Mon.–Fri., 10 A.M.–5 P.M. Sat.–Sun., free) is a bustling place with artistic performances and exhibits displayed year-round. If you'll be here a while, consider signing up for one of their workshops.

Teatro de la Ciudad Junchavín

Located inside a renovated 19th-century mansion, the neoclassical Teatro de la Ciudad Junchavín (central plaza, 1a Calle Sur Pte. 2, tel. 963/632-0946) has a wide range of artistic programming: drama, music, dance, film screenings…even children's theater. Ticket prices vary with the performance but typically range from free to US$20.

Nightlife

Comitán doesn't exactly have a hopping nightlife scene, but there are a few decent bars and clubs. Good ones to check out are **Shangri La** (1a Calle Ote. 6, tel. 963/110-6682, 6 P.M.–3 A.M. Tues.–Sat.), an upscale club with live salsa and merengue bands on weekends, and **Piñas & Charlie's** (Calle Central Pte. 31, tel. 963/113-2459, 9 P.M.–3 A.M. Tues.–Sat.), a casual bar with 3-for-1 beers on Thursday.

Festivals and Events

The **Festival Internacional de las Culturas y las Artes Rosario Castellanos** is a week-long cultural festival featuring live music, art expositions, and lectures, many of them free. It is typically held in mid-July in a variety of venues around town.

Celebrating one of Comitán's most venerated saints, **Día de San Caralampio** is the biggest and most colorful of many saint's-day festivals held during the month of February. The festivities are held every February 10 on the steps and plaza of his namesake church, San Caralampio (4a Av. Ote. Nte. at 2a Calle Nte. Ote).

Tours

Leaving from the southwest corner of the central plaza, the **Tranvía Turístico El Cositía** (Av. Central at Calle Central Pte., tel. 963/632-1426, 9 A.M.–2 P.M. and 4–8 P.M. daily, US$4.25) is a trolley tour of Comitán's key sites; the tour lasts 45–60 minutes and includes historical information and local anecdotes. It's a good way to get an overview of Comitán's offerings without having to tackle the steep hills on foot. Tours leave hourly as long as there are five passengers aboard.

Servicios Aéreos San Cristóbal (Aéródromo Miguel Alemán, Carr. Comitán–Trinitaria Km. 1262, tel. 963/632-4662, toll-free Mex. tel. 800/523-4954, www.servicios aereossancristobal.com) offers aerial tours of the region, including flyovers of Lagunas de Montebello (US$200, 30 mins); Lagunas de Montebello, Las Nubes, and Laguna Miramar (US$500, 90 mins); drop-off and pickup at Laguna Miramar (US$230 each way); or round-trip outings to Yaxchilán and Bonampak (US$785, 5.5 hrs including time at both ruins). Flights are in single-propeller Cessna planes with room for up to four passengers.

ACCOMMODATIONS

Under US$25

Posada las Flores (1a Av. Pte. Nte. 17, tel. 963/632-3334, US$7/11 s/d with shared bathroom, US$15 s, US$20 d) offers basic but clean rooms situated around a sunny courtyard. Most have wood-beam ceilings and twin beds. Only three have private bathrooms; these have cable TV too. The others share spic-and-span bathrooms located near the reception area. All in all, this is a great deal, especially if you're traveling solo.

Hotel Delfín (Av. Central Sur 21, tel.

963/632-0013, US$20 s, US$25 d) has wood-paneled rooms with private hot-water bathrooms and cable TV. Rooms are dark and somewhat charmless—bright bedspreads enliven them a bit—but they're clean and the location on the central plaza can't be beat. If you've got a car, there's parking too.

US$25-50

The colonial ◖ **Posada El Castellano** (3a Calle Nte. Pte. btwn. Avs. Central and 1a Nte. Pte., tel. 963/632-3347, www.posadaelcastellano.com.mx, US$34 s, US$37 d) is one of the nicest hotels in town. All 22 rooms open onto a bright courtyard complete with potted plants and a gurgling fountain. Rooms are comfortable and appealing, with firm beds, cable TV, and in-room phones. There's also free Internet access in a private computer room. The onsite restaurant serves reliable and well-priced Mexican dishes.

If you can overlook the garish colors and the strangely lumpy walls (are those marshmallows?), **Suites & Hotel Los Faroles** (1a Av. Ote. Nte. 16, tel. 963/632-0220, luecama@hotmail.com, US$25 s, US$30 d, US$30–34 studio s/d) is a great option. Accommodations are spotless with gleaming tile floors, comfy beds, hot-water bathrooms, and wireless Internet too. Studios are a bit bigger than the hotel rooms and can sleep four (US$46 t/q); they come with fully equipped kitchenettes tucked into a corner of the room (ask for kitchen accoutrements at the front desk). It's worth requesting a room on the 2nd floor, as they get more light than those on the ground floor. That, and the colors are toned down just a bit.

Over US$50

The fanciest place in town, the ◖ **Hotel Hacienda de los Ángeles** (2a Calle Nte. Pte. 6, tel. 963/632-0074, www.hotelhaciendalosangeles.com.mx, US$75 s/d, US$100–125 s/d suites) is a nouveau-colonial place with 25 elegant rooms and suites. It has all the amenities you'd expect at this rate: cable TV, in-room telephone, safe, coffee maker, and wireless Internet. There's also air-conditioning and heating—both

rarities in this part of the state. Other pluses include an indoor pool with a mosaic-tile floor and an upscale restaurant. Rates include full breakfast—American-style or buffet, depending on the day—and a welcome cocktail.

FOOD

Sitting in a row of Mexican eateries, ◖ **La Parroquia** (Av. Central at Calle Central Pte., 8 A.M.–11 P.M. Mon.–Sat., 9 A.M.–11 P.M. Sun., US$3–6) is a cut above the rest. Food is prepared to order, portions are hearty, and the service is attentive. Best of all, there are outdoor tables, all with great views of the central plaza.

If all the tables at La Parroquia are full, try **Helen's Enrique** (Av. Central 19, tel. 963/632-1730, 8 A.M.–midnight daily, US$6–10) at the far end of the same block. It offers a good variety of international and Mexican dishes that are reliable, if not particularly notable.

Restaurant Alis (Calle Central Pte. near 2a Av. Nte. Pte., no phone, 8 A.M.–6 P.M. daily, US$3–5) is a locals' favorite, offering tasty Chiapanecan meals at good prices. Best of all is the daily *comida corrida,* lunch specials that include soup, choice of main dish, dessert, and drink (US$4.25).

◖ **Matisse** (1a Av. Pte. Nte. 14, tel. 963/632-5172, 2 P.M.–midnight Tues.–Sat., 2–6 P.M. Sun., US$8–16) is a chic restaurant with streamlined furnishings, billowing fabrics, and Matisse-inspired artwork on the walls. The class extends to the food—Italian gourmet all the way—with a number of creative pasta and meat dishes to choose from. It's a particularly bright spot on Comitán's restaurant scene.

Mercado Primero de Mayo (2a Av. Ote. Nte. at Calle Central Ote., 6 A.M.–5 P.M. daily) is a classic Mexican market selling all sorts of fresh vegetables and fruits, meats, and breads. It makes a good place to stock up on snacks or meals if you're heading to the Lagunas de Montebello (or beyond) for a while.

INFORMATION AND SERVICES
Tourist Information
Dressed like Canadian Mounties sans horses,

the tourist police are men who patrol the central plaza to welcome tourists to the city. Offering any assistance needed, they are the best source of information on Comitán—from *combi* schedules and recommended tours to hotel information. Their jackets are stuffed full of brochures and maps that they readily hand out. If you don't do maps, they'll gladly escort you to, well, just about anywhere in town.

There are two tourist information offices in town: The state tourism office (1a Av. Sur Pte. near Calle Central Pte., 8 A.M.–8 P.M. Mon.–Fri., 9 A.M.–2 P.M. Sat.–Sun.) is the better of them, with plenty of brochures, maps, and staffers with ready advice on Comitán and its surrounding areas. In case they're busy, it's worth a shot to head to the city tourism office (1a Calle Sur Pte. at 2a Av. Sur Pte., tel. 963/632-0491, 9 A.M.–2 P.M. and 4:30–7:30 P.M. Mon.–Fri., 9 A.M.–2 P.M. Sat.–Sun.), which offers friendly, if limited, advice on the region.

Emergency Services

The **Hospital General de Comitán** (9a Calle Sur Ote. 11, tel. 963/632-3314, www.hospital comitan.com.mx, 24 hours) is the place to head in a medical emergency. For meds, **Farmacia del Ahorro** (1a Calle Sur Ote. at Av. Central Sur, tel. 963/632-7777, 7 A.M.–11 P.M. daily) is on the central plaza. To reach the **police,** dial toll-free 066.

Money

Just off the central plaza, **Bancomer** (Av. Rosario Castellanos at 1a Calle Sur Pte., 8:30 A.M.–4 P.M. Mon.–Fri., 9 A.M.–4 P.M. Sat.) has two ATMs. There is a **Banorte** (1a Av. Sur Pte. near Calle Central Pte., 9 A.M.–5 P.M. Mon.–Fri.) across the street from the state tourism office.

Media and Communications

The **post office** (Av. Central near 2a Calle Sur Ote.) is open 8:30 A.M.–4:30 P.M. Monday–Friday, 8:30 A.M.–2 P.M. Saturday. For Internet, **Cíber Jorges** (1a Av. Pte. Nte. near Calle Central Pte., 9 A.M.–9 P.M. Mon.–Fri.,

noon–8 P.M. Sat.) charges US$0.50 per hour. If you want to make a long-distance call, head to **Casetel** (2a Calle Nte. Pte. near 1a Av. Nte. Pte., 9:30 A.M.–2:30 P.M. and 4:30–8:30 P.M. Mon.–Sat., US$0.21 per minute to U.S., Canada, and Europe); they also have Internet access for US$0.50 per hour.

Consulates

The **Consulate of Guatemala** (tel. 963/632-2669, 9 A.M.–1 P.M. and 2–5 P.M. Mon.–Fri.) is located at 1a Calle Sur Poniente (near 3a Av. Sur Pte.). As of 2009, citizens of the United States, Canada, and European countries do not need a visa to enter Guatemala.

Laundry and Storage

Lavandería Express (1a Av. Nte. Pte. at 3a Calle Nte. Pte., 9 A.M.–2 P.M. and 4:30–8 P.M. Mon.–Sat., US$1 per 1 kg/2.2 lbs) offers next-day laundry service only. For storage, the bus terminal (tel. 963/632-0980, 24 hours) charges US$0.50 per bag per day.

GETTING THERE
Bus

Comitán's modern bus terminal (Av. Belisario Domínguez near 4a Calle Sur Pte., tel. 963/632-0980) is 11 blocks from the central plaza. Departures include:

- Ciudad Cuauhtémoc: (US$5, 1.5 hrs) 9 A.M., 9:35 A.M., 1:20 P.M., and 7:20 P.M.

- Ocosingo: (US$9, 4.5 hrs) take any Palenque-bound bus

- Palenque: (US$16, 6.5–7 hrs) 1:40 P.M. and 9:15 P.M., or travel via San Cristóbal

- San Cristóbal: (US$3–3.50, 1.75 hrs) take any Tuxtla Gutiérrez–bound bus.

- Tapachula: (US$13, 6 hrs) 9:35 A.M., 1:20 P.M., 7:20 P.M., 10:35 P.M., 12:10 A.M., and 1:55 A.M.

- Tuxtla Gutiérrez: (US$6.50–7.50, 3 hrs) every 30–60 mins 7 A.M.–4:40 P.M., then 6 P.M., 7:55 P.M., 8:40 P.M., 11:20 P.M., and 3:25 A.M.

Combi

Comitán is a popular jumping-off point for several area sights.

- Cascada El Chiflón, Rápidos de la Angostura Comitán–Tuxtla (Blvd. Belisario Domínguez near 1a Calle Sur Poniente), US$2, 1 hr, every 30 mins, 5 A.M.–6 P.M.

- Chinkultik Archaeological Zone, Líneas de Pasajeros Comitán-Lagos de Montebello (2a Av Sur Pte near 2a Calle Sur Pte, tel. 963/632-0875), US$1.50, 45 mins, 3 A.M.–6 P.M.

- La Democracía (Amatitlán), Transportador Tzobol (4a Ave Pte Sur 139, tel. 963/632-7739), US$5.50, 3.5 hrs, 4 A.M., 5 A.M., 8 A.M., noon, and 1 P.M.

- Lagunas de Montebello, Líneas de Pasajeros Comitán–Lagos de Montebello (2a Av. Sur Pte. near 2a Calle Sur Pte., tel. 963/632-0875), US$1.50–2.50, 45–60 mins, 3 A.M.–6 P.M.; private tours of the lakes also can be arranged here (US$67–84, 6–8 hrs)

- Las Nubes, Transportador Tzobol (4a Ave Pte Sur 139, tel. 963/632-7739), US$3.75, 4 hrs, four departures between 8 A.M.–2 P.M.

- Tenam Puente Archaeological Zone, Transporte Ejidal Tenam Puente (3a Av. Sur Pte. near 1a Calle Sur Pte.), US$1, 30–45 mins, every 30 minutes 7 A.M.–6 P.M.

ROADBLOCKS AND POTHOLES

Although buses and *combis* will take you just about anywhere you want to go in Chiapas, having a rental car lends you quite a bit more freedom and flexibility. And there are many more places travelers can safely visit by private car, thanks to recent improvements in road conditions and roadside security. Some general tips if you plan to get your own wheels:

As a precaution, **do not drive at night,** especially between San Cristóbal and Palenque, and along the Carretera Fronteriza (Border Highway) between Palenque and Comitán. Security has been much improved, but roadside robberies do occasionally occur after dark.

There are numerous **military and police checkpoints** along the state's main highways, especially along the long Carretera Fronteriza. Drug smugglers and illegal immigrants are the main target, and most tourists are waved through. If you are stopped, you may be asked for your driver's license and vehicle registration, and your trunk and bags may be searched. Friendly cooperation – and not having anything illegal – is the best approach.

You may encounter **Zapatista checkpoints,** where typically a group of people wait with a rope across the road and charge a passage fee, usually around US$5 per car. These aren't the armed masked men you might be imagining: In fact most aren't even Zapatistas, per se, but members of local *ejidos* who use EZLN affiliation (real or otherwise) for political leverage in local disputes. The police and military usually turn a blind eye to such checkpoints – they're relatively benign, and challenging them only creates more problems – and the best thing for travelers is, again, to simply cooperate.

Avoid the far eastern corner of Chiapas, which remains a fairly isolated and lawless place, mostly due to drug trafficking. It's perfectly fine to drive the Carretera Fronteriza, but plan on using the cutoff between Chanjul and Pico de Oro – which is how you to get to Las Guacamayas anyway – to avoid the far eastern border area. Even if you don't plan to stop at Las Guacamayas, it's recommended you follow that route.

There are **no gas stations** on the Carretera Fronteriza between Comitán and Palenque. Instead, look for roadside stands selling gas in 5-, 10-, and 20-liter jugs (at surprisingly reasonable prices). Make a habit of stopping frequently, to keep your tank above half-full. Note, too, that there is no Ángeles Verdes (Green Angels) roadside service on much of this stretch of highway.

- Las Guacamayas, Transportador Tzobol (4a Ave Pte Sur 139, tel. 963/632-7739), US$9, 4–5 hrs, 3:30 A.M., 4:30 A.M., 6:40 A.M., 10 A.M., 11:20 A.M., 12:30 P.M., and 3 P.M.

Car

Just 76 kilometers (47.2 miles) from San Cristóbal, Comitán is an easy drive on Highway 190. Be sure to fill your gas tank before you leave town, though—gas stations are far and few between east of Comitán. In a pinch, some people sell gas from their front door—look for jugs filled with petrol along the highway.

GETTING AROUND
Taxi and *Combi*

You'll have no trouble hailing a cab in Comitán, especially around the central plaza and near the bus station. The in-town rate is US$2.

Combis ply the streets in this town, going every which way; rides cost just US$0.45.

Car

A rental car is the easiest way to explore the Lakes Region—you'll have the freedom to stop where you want and you'll never have to wait by the side of the road for a *combi* to pass. The nearest car rental agencies are in San Cristóbal de las Casas and Tuxtla Gutiérrez.

Around Comitán

A number of sights are within easy reach of Comitán, making for a fun day-trip or a series of stop-offs on your way deeper into the Lakes Region. The most popular attraction, Cascada El Chiflón, boasts a series of impressive waterfalls—including its 120-meter main cascade—and even a zip line. Two modest but interesting Maya ruins—Tenam Puente and Chinkultik—are just off the highway between Comitán and Lagunas de Montebello, as is the historic hotel-restaurant Parador-Museo Santa María, boasting beautiful grounds and a fine religious art museum. For something a bit off the beaten path, a number of small towns outside Comitán have superb colonial era churches

◖ CASCADA EL CHIFLÓN

One of the highest and most powerful waterfalls in Chiapas and all of Mexico, Cascada El Chiflón tumbles 120 meters down a nearly vertical limestone cliff, sending waves of mist wafting across the hot dry landscape. Almost as impressive is the water's bright teal color (reminiscent of Agua Azul falls near Ocosingo) and the series of not-too-shabby secondary cascades above and below the main one, extending for over a kilometer. Just an hour from Comitán,

El Chiflón is popular with locals and travelers alike, and one of the area's most impressive sights.

The waterfall happens to be the dividing line between two municipalities, and the two sides can't agree on how to manage the falls jointly. As a result, Cascada El Chiflón has two completely separate and independent entrances, one on each side of the river. **Cadena de Cascades El Chiflón** (tel. 963/703-6584, chiflont@gmail.com, www.chiflon.com. mx) is on the east side of the river, nearest Comitán, while **Cascadas Velo de Novia** (tel. 045-963/703-4534, www.chiflon.com.mx, chiflont@gmail.com) is on the west side, nearer San Cristóbal and Tuxtla.

Both sides have parking areas, a restaurant, cabins, and well-maintained trails leading alongside the river to the main cascade, with lookout points along the way; both are also open 7 A.M. to 6 P.M. daily, and charge US$1 admission. Overall, Cadena de Cascadas El Chiflón has nicer installations, especially the cabins, plus a small museum and a platform on a rock outcrop right at the foot of the main falls. However, the trail at Velo de Novia has better panoramic views, and tends to be somewhat less crowded.

© LIZA PRADO

A stomach-lurching zip line and mist-drenched platform are the best ways to soak up the impressive main falls at Cascada El Chiflón.

The only joint operation is a two-part **zip line** (US$4 each leg) just below the primary falls. Not only is it a lot of fun, it allows you to zip across, enjoy the view from the other side, and then zip back.

Accommodations and Food

Centro Ecoturístico Cadena de Cascadas Chiflón (US$25 s, US$25–34 d) offers a set of comfortable wood-paneled rooms just feet from the east side of the river. All have private bathrooms and good beds. The walls don't reach the *palapa*-roof ceiling, though, so hope for quiet neighbors.

Cascadas Velo de Novia (US$8.50 s/d camping, US$18 s/d with shared bathroom) offers the more rustic accommodations of the two establishments, with just two small rooms in a thatch-roofed hut; the bathroom facilities are the ones used by restaurant patrons. Five new *cabañas,* each with private bathroom, were in the works at the time of research. Camping, with gear included, also is available—a nice option if you're on a tight budget.

Both centers have small open-air **restaurants** (7 A.M.–5:30 P.M., US$3–7) offering basic Mexican eats. If you stay the night, eat early or plan to have dinner at an outdoor restaurant on the highway.

Getting There

In Comitán, **Rápidos de la Angostura Comitán-Tuxtla** (Blvd. Belisario Domínguez near 1a Calle Sur Pte., every 30 mins 5 A.M.–6 P.M., US$2) provides *combi* service to El Chiflón; the trip takes about an hour. *Combis* drop visitors along the highway about a kilometer (0.6 mile) from the park entrance. If you don't feel like hoofing it, you won't have to wait long for a three-wheel *tuk-tuk*–style taxi to pass by (US$0.50).

TENAM PUENTE ARCHAEOLOGICAL ZONE

Built on a series of tree-covered hills and ever-climbing terraces, Tenam Puente (8 A.M.–5 P.M. daily, US$3) is larger than it may first appear, and is the sort of site whose appeal lies as much in exploring and discovering its many facets as in the structures themselves. Fifteen kilometers (9.3 miles) south of Comitán, it's a popular stop for tour groups from San Cristóbal, though it rarely feels crowded. Budget about 1.5–2 hours to visit the entire site and the small museum.

History

Like nearby Chinkultik, Tenam Puente was a modest power on the western highland fringe of the Maya world, peaking around A.D. 600–900. The notorious collapse of Maya centers in the 9th century was far more damaging to large lowland powers like Palenque and Yaxchilán than smaller highland centers like Tenam Puente. In fact, highland cities that survived the collapse's initial shock may have even benefited from the abrupt humbling of their lowland competitors. Tenam Puente, like nearby Chinkultik, appears to have survived until around A.D. 1200 before finally being abandoned. Like many highland sites, Tenam Puente is notable for the lack of ornamental embellishments found elsewhere, such

THE LAKES REGION

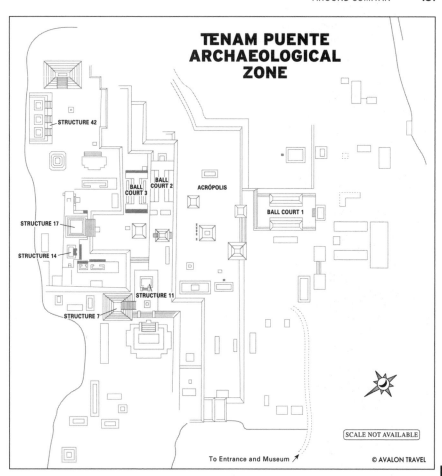

TENAM PUENTE
ARCHAEOLOGICAL
ZONE

STRUCTURE 42

BALL COURT 3

BALL COURT 2

ACRÓPOLIS

BALL COURT 1

STRUCTURE 17

STRUCTURE 14

STRUCTURE 11

STRUCTURE 7

SCALE NOT AVAILABLE

To Entrance and Museum ↗

© AVALON TRAVEL

as corbelled arches and roof combs. Likewise, only one dated stela has been found here (from A.D. 790), now housed in the archaeological museum in Tuxtla Gutiérrez.

Today, Tenam Puente is the focus of a yearly pilgrimage to celebrate the Day of the Holy Cross (May 3).

Visiting the Ruins

Entering the site, you first encounter a large grassy plaza with a **ball court** on one side— one of three ball courts found here. From the long northeast side of the plaza, the **Acrópolis** rises in a series of broad consecutive terraces, its impressive upper pyramids all but invisible from below, but affording dramatic views of the surrounding countryside from their summits. A carving of a decapitated captive can be seen at the base of **Structure 17.** The Acrópolis covers some four hectares in all, and most of its notable structures were originally covered in plaster and painted in rich colors.

Museum

Across from the ticket booth is a one-room museum (8 A.M.–5 P.M. daily) with detailed information on the history of the ruins as well as descriptions of the excavated structures. It's worth a stop, even a quick one, to get an overview of the archaeological site. Signage is in English and Spanish.

Getting There

From Comitán, **Transporte Ejidal Tenam Puente** (3a Av. Sur Pte. near 1a Calle Sur Pte.) runs *combis* to and from the ruins every 30 minutes from 7 A.M. to 6 P.M. daily (45 mins, US$1). Be sure to let the driver know that you're headed to the ruins, otherwise he'll let you off at the last stop, two kilometers below the entrance. The last *combi* heads back to town at 4:30 P.M.

CHINKULTIK ARCHAEOLOGICAL ZONE

This small but intriguing ruin (8 A.M.–5 P.M. daily, US$3.50 admission plus toll of US$0.50 pp and US$2 per vehicle) is built atop a bluff with great views, and makes for a nice stop headed to or from nearby Lagunas de Montebello National Park. In theory, that is: The site is closed more often than not, owing to a long-running dispute between the local community and government archaeological officials. Ask in Comitán for the latest, or at the control booth near the highway turnoff.

History

Though never a major power, the ancient city of Chinkultik thrived between the 3rd and 9th centuries A.D., with the bulk of its major structures built after A.D. 590. The city declined in the 9th century, but not nearly as dramatically as lowland powers like Palenque and Yaxchilán did; in fact, modest highland sites like this one, and nearby Tenam Puente, survived well into the second millennium. The city was abandoned for good in the 13th century for unknown reasons; the first organized archaeological study of Chinkultik was conducted in the 1960s.

Visiting the Ruins

Many of the 200-plus structures here remain unexcavated, but the site's dramatic location makes it worthwhile all the same. The main structure, the **Acrópolis**, is built atop a prominent bluff, with panoramic views of the lake-dotted countryside. On one side, a steep embankment drops some 50 meters to a cenote below, where archaeologists recovered numerous jade, ceramic, and obsidian artifacts in its deep clear waters, probably thrown there as part of religious ceremonies.

Near the entrance and across a small stream is the **Plaza Hundida** (Sunken Plaza), a spacious plaza enclosed on all four sides by low stone stairways. Several large pyramids face the plaza, but remain cloaked in brush and low trees, awaiting excavation. A ball court and second plaza are located down a side path, left of the entrance.

Chinkultik is often closed, unfortunately, due to a longstanding dispute between local residents and state and federal agencies over its operation. Despite years of on and off negotiations, the conflict has only gotten worse: In September 2008, local residents occupied the ruins, arguing that admission fees should better benefit the communities there, which are among the state's poorest. When police came to evict them, the protesters managed to detain and disarm nearly 80 officers. That provoked swift reaction from the state, and on October 3, police with riot gear and automatic weapons stormed the ruins and nearby village in trucks and on horseback. Six protesters were killed in the ensuing melee, and many more wounded or arrested. Prosecutors opened an investigation into the incident, including allegations of execution-style killings, but as this book went to print a report had yet to be issued, and the site remained closed indefinitely to visitors.

Accommodations

By far the fanciest place to stay in the Lakes Region is the **Parador-Museo Santa María** (Carr. Trinitaria–Lagunas de Montebello Km. 22, tel. 963/632-5116, www.parador santamaria.com.mx, US$167 s/d), a beautifully renovated 19th-century hacienda. The

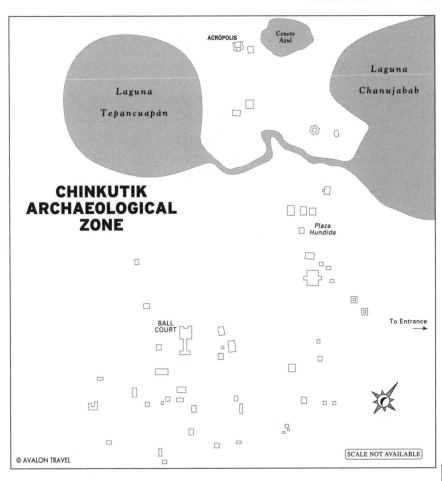

ACRÓPOLIS

Cenote
Azul

Laguna
Tepancuapán

Laguna
Chanujabab

CHINKUTIK
ARCHAEOLOGICAL
ZONE

Plaza
Hundida

BALL
COURT

To Entrance

© AVALON TRAVEL

SCALE NOT AVAILABLE

lush and well-maintained grounds include a small religious-art gallery (US$2, free for hotel guests or diners), a pleasant outdoor restaurant (8 A.M.–7 P.M. daily, US$7–14), and a welcoming pool. Rooms themselves are comfortable and well appointed with period antiques and oil paintings; however, they're somewhat sparse and feel more like museum exhibits than hotel rooms. Leave the door to your room open—the green fields and mountain view give the place some much-needed life.

The only way to get to the Parador-Museo Santa María without breaking a sweat is to drive yourself or to hire a cab. That said, if you don't mind walking 1.5 kilometers (0.9 mile) down a county road, jump on any *combi* from Comitán that's headed to the Lagunas de Montebello; ask the driver to drop you at the turnoff.

Getting There

Chinkultik is located about 45 kilometers east of Comitán and just a few kilometers west of the entrance to Lagunas de Montebello National Park. The ruins are north of the highway, two kilometers down a paved access road.

From Comitán, *combis* headed to Lagunas de Montebello can drop you at the turnoff, where it's a hot but not unpleasant walk through agricultural fields to the site entrance. *Combis* leave from 2a Avenida Sur Poniente near 2a Calle Sur Poniente in Comitán, every 10 minutes 3 A.M.–6 P.M. (US$1.75, 40 mins). Taxi service here is almost nonexistent.

Eastern Chiapas

Chiapas's beautiful and ecologically rich eastern corner is slowly opening to ordinary travelers, with improved roads and new attractions that help shake off a reputation for isolation and frontier-style lawlessness. Lagunas de Montebello National Park has long been a highlight of the state, with dozens of picturesque lakes nestled in a hilly pine forest. But rather than marking a turn-around point for travelers, Lagunas de Montebello now serves as gateway to a handful of new (or newly accessible) natural attractions. Don't miss Las Nubes, a small ecocenter perched alongside an impressive series of river rapids and waterfalls with nearby hiking and rafting; or Las Guacamayas, where you can hike or boat through the lush Montes Azules biosphere reserve, spotting monkeys, toucans, macaws, and lush rainforest flora. The region also offers access to Laguna Miramar, a stunning forest lake and another longtime state highlight.

◖ PARQUE NACIONAL LAGUNAS DE MONTEBELLO
About an hour's drive east of Comitán is Lagunas de Montebello national park (8 A.M.–sunset daily, US$1.75 pp), a striking array of lakes, lagoons, and ponds whose colors famously range from emerald green to pale blue, from deep purple to reddish black. The nearly

Traditional wooden rafts are one of many ways to explore the beautiful lakes at Parque Nacional Lagunas de Montebello.

© H.W. PRADO

THE LAKES REGION

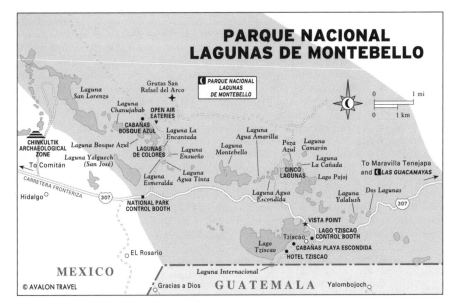

PARQUE NACIONAL LAGUNAS DE MONTEBELLO

60 lakes are nestled in a cool pine forest, and around 15 are accessible and easy to reach by car or foot; a visit here typically includes driving from lake to lake, stopping at some for just a quick look and photo, and at others to swim or explore by canoe or kayak, available for rent along the shore. There are caves and even cenotes that can be visited, as well, either on foot or horseback.

Visiting the Park

The **Lagunas de Colores** group of lakes is straight ahead as you pass through the control booth. There are five in all, including Laguna de Encantada, Laguna Ensueño, Laguna Esmeralda, Laguna Agua Tinta, and Laguna Bosque Azul, their colors ranging from emerald to indigo. The road dead-ends in a parking area overlooking Laguna Bosque Azul, the largest and most accessible lake, where there are simple open-air eateries plus cabins where you can rent boats to explore the lake.

From the far end of the parking area, a mild 1.5-kilometer (1-mile) trail leads mostly downhill to **Grutas San Rafael del Arco,** several limestone caves and an intriguing natural archway with a river running through it. It's fairly well signed, though you might pay one of the local kids a dollar or two to be sure you see everything.

Horseback riding (US$5–8 per hour) is available from the parking area, too. The *grutas* are a popular destination, but not recommended as it's perfectly easy to walk there yourself. A better option is riding to Dos Cenotes (twin limestone sinkholes), a trip of about 90 minutes.

Bearing right after the control booth, the road leads past turnoffs for several more lakes. The first is **Laguna Montebello,** a large beautiful lake at the end of a 250-meter dirt access road. This is a good lake for swimming and horseback riding, including to Dos Cenotes. There's a US$0.50 admission fee, which is good for admission to the rest of the lakes along this road as well.

Down the main road, the next turnoff after Laguna Montebello is for **Cinco Lagunas,** or Five Lakes (not to be confused with the five Lagunas de Colores). All but one are visible from the road; the second, **Laguna La Cañada,** is the most impressive, an hourglass-shaped lake that's considered to be one of the park's most picturesque. It's an especially good place to paddle a kayak, available for rent (US$10 pp) near the roadway.

Yet another turnoff leads to **Lago Pojoj,** with a vibrant blue hue and an island in the middle that can be reached by kayak.

Lago Tziscao, the largest of Montebello's lakes, is an expansive elbow of water with an observation point at one end and a somewhat dreary village built up nearby. Two hotels—one not bad, the other not so good—are right along the shore, where at least the views are attractive. Kayaks can be rented at both hotels. The better of the two hotels also offers boat tours (US$30, up to four people, Playa Escondida, tel. 963/634-9238), typically lasting around three hours including stops at a few small islands and a little-visited Maya ruin. Admission to the lake is US$0.50, charged right as you enter the village, and is also good for the other lakes along the main road.

Accommodations and Food

There are simple accommodations along Lago Tziscao and Lagunas de Colores. There's not much atmosphere, but staying here does allow you to enjoy the lakes in the early morning and at dusk, free of day trippers from Comitán and San Cristóbal.

Right on Lago Tziscao, **Restaurant y Cabañas Playa Escondida** (tel. 963/634-9238, US$2.50 pp camping, US$6.75 pp room with shared bathroom, US$8.50 pp room with private bathroom) is by far the best place to stay in town. Renovated in 2007—and in some cases, constructed—most accommodations are in A-frame cabins that have gorgeous views of the lake. Rooms are clean, if spare, and have hot-water bathrooms and 24-hour electricity. The grounds are well tended, inviting guests to lounge about, with a rowboat or two at the ready (and free) for guests to explore the lake. There also is a decent **restaurant** (6 A.M.–9 P.M., US$2–5) on-site, serving classic Mexican meals, so no worries about finding good, affordable eats. Boat tours of the lake can be arranged.

A short distance further, **Hotel Tziscao** (tel. 963/633-5244, US$35 up to four people)

has spectacularly bad service but the cabins are reasonably comfortable, making it an acceptable alternative if Playa Escondida is full. Tiny A-frame wood cabins have two queen beds and a plain bathroom; the little porch in front would be a lot nicer if the huge cinder-block restaurant weren't plunked down right in front, blocking the view. (Somehow it's not surprising though.)

A kilometer (0.6 mile) from the Lagunas de Colores parking lot, **Cabañas Bosque Azul** (aka Cabañas de Doña Josefa, tel. 963/632-5971, US$20 s/d with shared bathroom, US$29–37.50 s/d) has 20 wood-plank cabins, most with lofts and private bathrooms (hot water until 8 P.M. only). Beds are on the saggy side, and the bare bulbs and cement floors don't help the matter, but the rooms are reasonably clean and the lake is just steps away. Pedal boats are available for guests to rent (US$12.50/hr).

The lakes' best grub is at a cluster of **open-air eateries** (8 A.M.–sunset daily, US$1.25–3) facing the Lagunas de Colores parking lot, each with a handful of plastic tables set up under a low shelter. Service varies from friendly to rough-and-tumble, but the offerings are virtually identical—empanadas and quesadillas with bean, squash flower, and other fillings—prepared on a *comal* (griddle) over an open flame.

Getting There

A vehicle is all but essential for visiting the lakes. Most people come in a van as part of a package tour, but you can also hire a taxi or *combi* in Comitán, or hire a truck and driver in the park itself.

If you're driving a rental or private car, consider hiring one of the freelance guides who stand along the highway as you approach the national park (they can also be hired at Lagunas de Colores). Guides come along in your car, directing you to the various lakes and lookout points, and indicating which are best for swimming, kayaking, horseback riding, etc. There's no fixed fee or route, but US$8–10 for a 2–2.5 tour seems average.

From Comitán, public transportation to the Lagunas de Montebello is provided by **Lineas de Pasajeros Comitán-Lagos de Montebello** (2a Av. Sur Pte. near 2a Calle Sur Pte., tel. 963/632-0875, every 10 mins 3 A.M.–6 P.M., 45–60 mins, US$2.50). *Combis* are required to take passengers to the Lagunas de Colores parking lot, not just drop them at the control booth; you can pick them up at the same place to return. The same company offers private tours by *combi* (US$67, 6 hrs), stopping at nine different lakes. If you want to tag on a visit to the Chincultik ruins, the tour costs an additional US$17. Prices are per van.

Once at the Lagunas de Colores parking lot, you can hire a truck and driver (US$35 per day) to take you to the lakes; if you hire a freelance guide, they can help arrange the truck.

A one-way cab ride from Comitán to the Lagunas costs around US$20, while a six-hour tour, including stops at nine lakes, costs around US$75 per carload.

CENTRO ECOTURÍSTICO LAS NUBES

The Río Santo Domingo is a major tributary of the mighty Río Jataté, both essential arteries in eastern Chiapas and the Lacandón rainforest, supporting numerous communities and *ejidos* along their banks. Centro Ecoturístico Causas Verdes Las Nubes (tel. 963/565-4710, ecoturismo_nubes@hotmail.com, US$1 pp)—better known simply as Las Nubes (The Clouds)—is a popular water park located along a particularly turbulent stretch of the Río Santo Domingo. The river, which grows to 50 meters across in some places, narrows considerably here as the water roars past in a series of stout waterfalls and churning rapids. In the dry season the water is a striking turquoise hue similar to Agua Azul near Ocosingo (when it's not a frothing white, that is). During heavy rain, sediment turns the water a turbid brown, but the added volume makes the rapids that much more dramatic.

Sights

Not surprisingly, a visit to Las Nubes is all about the water. The eco-center maintains an **observation tower** and **hanging footbridge**, both affording dramatic views of the riotous rapids. There's also a 50-meter-high **zip line** (US$4.25 per descent) set up to whisk guests across the river in a heartbeat (or two, if the first one skipped).

There are also several **hiking trails** near and along the river; the trails are easy enough to navigate on your own, though you may see and learn more with the help of a guide (US$8.50/hr, up to 8 people).

Believe it or not, there are also some lovely and safe areas for swimming. **Playa Las Iguanas** is an attractive sandy beach fronting a stretch of river, and an easy walk from Las Nubes. It's part of a new and separate ecotourism project, with plans to construct cabins and a restaurant as well; a nominal admission fee may be charged to use the beach once the buildings are completed.

White-water rafting is a popular and natural activity here, as well. **Gallo Giro** (Montes Azules Trópico Gallo Giro Centro Ecoturístico, tel. 963/633-4284) offers kayak and rafting trips from its riverside base a short distance upstream. Trips typically end at Las Nubes, and start either at Gallo Giro itself (US$50, 1 hr, 2–7 people) or upstream at the town of Jerusalén (US$85–110, 2.5 hrs); the latter includes more challenging white water (up to Class III) and a short nature walk along the way. Kayak rentals (US$8.50/hr) and eerie nighttime rafting and walking tours (US$18–25, 2–4 hrs) also are available. Ask the Las Nubes receptionist to call for reservations and arrange a pick-up. Or you can walk—it's a pleasant 4.5 kilometers (2.75 miles) from Las Nubes along the main access road.

Accommodations and Food

Las Nubes offers fifteen simple *cabañas* (US$42–50 s/d), each with a private hot-water bathroom and a porch. All are within earshot of the Río Santo Domingo and back into a large grassy area that just begs for a game of Ultimate Frisbee. The fifty-buck price tag is a bit steep—consider camping for US$2 per person if you've got your own gear—but it's undeniably a beautiful spot.

There is a restaurant—well, more like a **mess hall**—located alongside the river, across from the *cabañas*. It is a simple affair, with a makeshift roof, long communal tables, and a basic kitchen. Options are limited to what the cook decides to prepare that day and prices are set (i.e., breakfast and dinner cost US$3.75, lunch US$5). Beware that meals are not made to order—massive quantities of scrambled eggs, for instance, are made first thing in the morning then served cold (or slightly reheated, if you're lucky) until they're finished—so come early to get the fresh stuff.

You also can stay at **Gallo Giro** (Montes Azules Trópico Gallo Giro Centro Ecoturístico, tel. 963/633-4284); rooms have brick-tiled floors, peaked ceilings, and a fan, but are rather dark and musty, with cold-water shower only. A small *comedor* serves standard meals.

Getting There
Combi service to Las Nubes is provided by **Transportador Tzobol** (Comitán, 4a Av. Pte. Sur, near market, tel. 963/632-7739, US$3.75, 4 hrs) 8 a.m.–2 p.m. every day. Las Nubes is located 12 kilometers (7 miles) off of the Carretera Fronteriza; the road is dirt but easily passable in a front-wheel-drive vehicle.

◖ LAGUNA MIRAMAR
The largest lake in the Lacandón rainforest (16 square kilometers), and one of the cleanest and purest bodies of water anywhere in Mexico, Laguna Miramar (Reserva Integral de la Biósfera Montes Azules) truly is a jewel of Chiapas and the whole country. In fact, from the air, that's exactly that it looks like: a radiant blue gemstone in a vast blanket of green forest, its deep indigo center fading to a lovely aquamarine at the edges. Its name, Spanish for "view of the sea," is surprisingly apt for a lake that's hundreds of kilometers from the nearest ocean.

Laguna Miramar owes its pristine state to an agreement among the surrounding communities to ban virtually all development within a

kilometer of the lake, and to prohibit the use of motorboats. With no chemicals or waste from roads, hotels, farmland, or leaky boat engines, Miramar's water is crystal clear, and you can see the bottom a dozen meters or more down. It also happens to be bathtub warm, perfect for swimming.

Visiting the Reserve
Emiliano Zapata is the only community (of four around the lake) that has any sort of tourism infrastructure, including food, lodging and guide service, and is the place to head whether arriving by bus or boat. On arriving there, you should seek out the *presidente de turismo* (tourism president), a local officer whose job is to arrange lodging and guides for visitors, and to collect applicable fees, including a US$2.50 daily visitors fee.

The lake itself is a full seven kilometers (4.2 miles) from Emiliano Zapata and accessible only on foot (about 90 minutes, longer in rainy season when the trail is muddy). Along the way,

TROPICAL MONKEYS

Chiapanecan jungles are home to two species of monkeys: spider and howler. Intelligent and endearing, these creatures are prime targets for the pet trade. They have been so hunted, in fact, that today they are in danger of extinction. Experts estimate that for every monkey sold, three die during transportation and distribution. In an effort to protect these creatures, the Mexican government has prohibited their capture or trade. There are a number of places in Chiapas where you're likely to see tropical monkeys – or at least hear them, in the case of howlers – including Yaxchilán archaeological zone, Las Guacamayas eco-center, and Laguna Miramar. Spider and howler monkeys are most active at sunrise and sundown; consider waking early or staying late to increase your chances of spotting a few.

you're likely to see, or at least hear, *saraguatos* (howler monkeys) whose other-worldly roar belies their relatively small size.

The trail ends at a long narrow beach, which serves as a jumping-off point for visiting the lake. The best and most popular way to explore Laguna Miramar is by **kayak** or **cayuco** (traditional dugout canoe), both available for rent at the beach (US$10/day). The tourism president also can arrange for a guide (US$8/day) to take you to various sights around the lake, including caves and prehistoric paintings. It's worth asking about exploring one of the lake's islands (some of which have ancient Maya ruins) or hiking in the rainforest on a far side of the lake—unfortunately, those areas are part of neighboring *ejidos* and may be off-limits to tourists. For the same reason, if you'd like to simply paddle around on your own—a sublime experience, especially once you're oriented—be sure to confirm where you are and are not permitted to go ashore.

Be aware that from June to October can be quite rainy, which sullies the lake water somewhat, and can turn the dirt trails into a slippery, muddy mess.

Accommodations and Food

There are a half dozen simple cement **cabañas** (US$9 pp) in Emiliano Zapata, each with a fan and two beds, and so-so shared bathrooms. Or you can **camp** or sling a **hammock** (US$2.50 pp, plus US$2.50 to rent hammock and mosquito net) in a sturdy *palapa*-covered cement platform either in town or by the lake. (Both areas have compost toilets available to visitors.) Be alert for tarantulas and scorpions, which may hide in clothes or shoes left in the open.

Emiliano Zapata has a few simple family-run eateries, and a small bodega for non-perishables; you can also hire local women to prepare home-cooked meals. If you sleep at the lake, you'll need to bring everything with you, including water. A camp stove definitely comes in handy, but you also are permitted to build small fires on the beach, and can sometimes share the one lit by the lake's permanent *vigilante* (guard).

Getting There

The traditional way to get to Laguna Miramar is by bus, a bone-jarring six-to-seven-hour journey from Ocosingo to the small town of San Quintín (US$6, 4 departures daily). From there, it's a 15-minute walk to Emiliano Zapata, past an imposing Mexican military base established here following the Zapatista uprising in 1994.

A more scenic and far less punishing route is by boat, approaching from the south along the Río Jataté. *Lanchas* (motorboats) leave from the community of La Democracia, winding two hours through increasingly pristine rainforest to arrive right at Emiliano Zapata (US$70 each way, up to six people); any number of local boatmen can take you, though boat operator Hipólito Vásquez is recommended for having life vests aboard. Be sure to arrange for a pickup, unless you plan to leave by bus. Be aware that partway up the river you will be required to pay a passage fee to Zapatista militants who control that section of the forest, around US$10 per boat.

From Comitán, **Transportador Tzobol** (4a Av. Pte. Sur, tel. 963/632-7739) has direct service to the town of Amatitlán (US$5.50, 3.5 hrs, 4 A.M., 5 A.M., 8 A.M., noon and 1 P.M.), located just across the river from La Democracía and connected by a bridge. Otherwise take any *combi* to the town of Maravilla Tenejapa, and transfer to an Amatitlán *combi* there (US$2, 40 mins).

If you're driving, look for a turnoff marked Guadalupe Miramar, a few kilometers east of Maravilla Tenejapa on the Carretera Fronteriza. From there, a dirt road winds through a number of small communities to Amatitlán, with La Democracía just across the bridge.

Chiapas has few vistas more stunning than Laguna Miramar from the air. **Servicios Aéreos San Cristóbal** (Aérodromo Miguel Alemán, Carr. Comitán–Trinitaria Km. 1262, tel. 963/632-4662, toll-free Mex. tel. 800/523-4954, www.serviciosaereossancristobal.com) offers scenic flyovers of Laguna Miramar (US$500, 90 mins, including Lagunas de Montebello and Las Nubes), as well as

THE LAKES REGION

drop-off/pickup service (US$250 per leg), using four-passenger Cessna single-engine planes, departing from its base in Comitán.

LAS GUACAMAYAS

Named after the scarlet macaws that nest here in large numbers, Las Guacamayas Centro Ecoturístico (tel. 555/151-1869, www.lasguacamayas.com.mx) is a rewarding and highly successful community ecotourism project on the edge of the lush Montes Azules biosphere reserve. Visitors can take guided hikes or boat trips in the reserve, where you're likely to see monkeys and numerous birds, even a tapir or jaguar if you're extremely lucky. Most importantly, this is the only place in Mexico to see large numbers of scarlet macaws, which have all but disappeared from traditional nesting zones in Oaxaca, Veracruz, Campeche, and Tabasco. While a small number are present year-round, you'll see the greatest number from March to August, when scores of mating pairs occupy natural and artificial nests around the property and village. Lodging is in spacious and comfortable wood cabins, ranging from suites to dorm-style units, and an on-site restaurant serves reasonably good food.

History

Opposite the reception desk is a multilingual explanation of the formation of Las Guacamayas. The host community, Reforma Agraria, was founded in its present location in 1980 by several dozen ethnic Chinanteco families who fled Oaxaca (or left voluntarily, or were relocated, depending on the telling). After limited success with a variety of crops, the community found a niche growing export-quality chili peppers, which it continues to pursue today. In 1991, the community got state and federal funding to protect the scarlet macaw that nested there, and later to launch the eco-center.

Sights

Las Guacamayas offers guided excursions by foot and boat, most priced by the group (up to eight people; ask at reception about joining other guests to share costs). Hour-long ***guacamaya* tours** (US$25 per group)—leisurely walks around the center's grounds and surrounding areas, sometimes including the village itself, to spot nesting macaws—are available most mornings and evenings. A bit more rigorous, **Reserve tours** (US$40 per group) are two-hour guided hikes through protected rainforest areas belonging to the Montes Azules biosphere reserve.

You'll get deeper into the reserve on a **boat tour,** though the price—US$100 for two hours, US$115 for three—can be prohibitive unless you can share the trip with other guests. Tours leave in the early morning, heading a short distance down the Río Lacuntún (which forms the border of the biosphere reserve) before cutting up a small tributary that winds through a dense canyon of trees where it's common to spot howler and spider monkeys, toucans, egrets, herons, king fishers, and other birds. There is usually an opportunity to get off the boat and walk a short distance in the forest.

Between trips—which take place in the morning and evening—you can enjoy a nice river-stone beach and swimming area, plus an observation tower and a small enclosure with a few deer walking about. You might also spot a family of howler monkeys that hangs out in the trees here. That said, if there's a critique to be made of Las Guacamayas, it's that there's not enough to do, especially if you stay more than just a night or two. Bring a good book and a deck of cards.

Accommodations

Las Guacamayas has a wide variety of lodging, making it accessible for visitors of all budgets. At the top end are suites (US$85–95 d) with king-size bed, mini-fridge, and indoor and outdoor sitting areas, including a hammock and views of the river. Standard units (US$55–90) are either double or triple occupancy, with or without a river view. All have fans, private hot-water bathrooms, and covered patios, some with hammocks, great for chilling out between trips. For travelers on a budget, there are two small but comfortable shared *cabañas*

Comfortable cabins overlook the Río Lacuntún at Las Guacamayas, with the pristine Montes Azules biosphere reserve on the opposite bank.

(US$15–18 pp) with common hot-water bathrooms. Camping is also permitted (US$5 pp with own gear, US$7 pp without) with access to toilets and cold-water showers.

Getting There

Public transport in this area is improving, but still quite variable; whenever possible double-check departure times, whether at the *combi* terminals in Comitán or Palenque, or at the reception desk in Las Guacamayas. Likewise, build a certain amount of flexibility into your plans to account for any travel hiccups.

From Comitán: **Transportador Tzobol** (tel. 963/632-7739, 4a Av. Pte. Sur) has departures for Las Guacamayas at 3:30 A.M., 4:30 A.M., 6:40 A.M., 10 A.M., 11:20 A.M., 12:30 P.M., and 3 P.M. (US$9, 4–5 hrs). There's return service at 3 A.M., 5 A.M., 7 A.M., 10 A.M., noon, and 12:45 P.M.; times are variable, however, so it's a good idea to double-check with the receptionist. Another *combi* line, **Lineas Montebello** (tel. 963/632-0875), also has service here, but only to the Reforma Agraria turnoff, about a kilometer from Las Guacamayas center.

Driving east on the Carretera Fronteriza, there's a well-signed turnoff for Las Guacamayas just outside the community of Chajul (about 200 kilometers from Comitán, or 15 kilometers past the Ixcán turnoff on the same highway). From there it's another 16 kilometers to Reforma Agraria, with the road alternating from paved to dirt. Be alert for potholes and washouts, which plague this stretch of roadway and can be huge, especially during or after the rainy season.

From Palenque: **Lineas Montebello** (Av. Manuel Velasco Suárez near Coppel department store, tel. 916/345-1260) has service to/past the Reforma Agraria turnoff every 60–90 minutes 3:30 A.M.–1:30 P.M. daily. Note that some departures only go as far as Benemérito de las Américas (US$7.50, 4 hrs), where you can catch a connecting *combi*.

Going from Las Guacamayas to Frontera Corozal or Palenque typically requires you to transfer at Pico de Oro (US$1, 20 mins) and sometimes again in Benemérito de las Américas (US$1.50, 40 mins past Pico de Oro). Tzobol *combis* arriving from Comitán typically continue to Pico de Oro—catch the earliest one to be sure to have time to make it all the way to your destination, or ask the Guacamayas receptionist to arrange a taxi (US$7 to Pico de Oro, US$18 to Benemérito de las Américas).

THE LAKES REGION

TUXTLA GUTIÉRREZ

Let's be honest: You didn't come all the way to Chiapas to hang out in a big busy city like Tuxtla Gutiérrez. Home to a half million people, Tuxtla is a world apart from the lush forests, colonial cities, and indigenous villages most travelers associate with Mexico's most rural state. Tuxtla's hotels, museums, and architecture are of mostly 20th-century extraction—even the main cathedral, though quite impressive, is a modern revision of the colonial-era original.

But don't write off Tuxtla altogether! Some of Chiapas's top sights are just outside the city. They include Cañón del Sumidero, a long winding canyon with jaw-dropping thousand-meter walls; Sima de las Cotorras, a massive sinkhole that's home to squawking multitudes of green parrots; and beautiful wind-wisped Aguacero waterfall. The small town of Chiapa de Corzo has several architectural gems, including a gorgeous 16th-century fountain, and a two-week-long festival that draws crowds of visitors. Northwest of Tuxtla is the Ruta Zoque (Zoque Route), a little-traveled loop in the Chiapanecan hinterland that includes low-key towns and terrific colonial churches.

And the city itself is not without its attractions. If you've got kids, they'll love Tuxtla's great zoo and the huge *convivencia infantil*, or children's park. A science museum opened in 2006 and there's an excellent archaeological museum, albeit rather dated in style. And every night of the week you'll find a friendly crowd and live marimba music at Parque Marimba, the city's loveliest spot.

If your jaunt through southern Mexico has left you in need of a big-city fix, whether that

© GARY CHANDLER

HIGHLIGHTS

◖ Parque Marimba: Shake a leg and enjoy live marimba music every night of the week at this small but exceptionally lovely city park, just a few blocks from Tuxtla Gutiérrez's central square. By day it's shady and peaceful, with plenty of quiet corners for relaxing with a book (page 146).

◖ ZOOMAT: Considered by many to be Latin America's best zoo, Tuxtla's ZOOMAT has large leafy enclosures and only houses animals found in Chiapas. Every mammal species in the state is represented here, including jaguars, tapirs, otters, and armadillos, plus numerous birds, reptiles, and other creatures (page 148).

◖ Parque Nacional Cañón del Sumidero: Take a boat ride from Chiapa de Corzo through this winding river gorge, whose walls are a whopping thousand meters (0.6 mile) high in places, with wispy waterfalls forming mossy patterns on the steep face. It's an easy day trip from San Cristóbal or Tuxtla Gutiérrez (page 156).

◖ Sima de las Cotorras: Almost perfectly circular and deep enough to hide a 45-story building, this massive *sima*, or sinkhole, is all the more impressive for the prehistoric paintings on a ledge halfway up its sheer stone walls, not to mention the thousands of parrots that nest in trees on the sunken floor (page 158).

◖ El Aguacero: At the end of a long dirt road, at the bottom of a steep canyon walkway, and down a tangled riverside path, El Aguacero is worth the effort: a picturesque waterfall falling in dozens of rivulets from a long ledge, blown into a misty cloud by the wind (page 159).

◖ La Pila: Built in the 16th century using specially designed bricks, this huge public fountain in Chiapa de Corzo has flying buttresses and ornate designs, and is considered one of the finest examples of Mudejar colonial architecture in the state (page 161).

LOOK FOR **◖** TO FIND RECOMMENDED SIGHTS, ACTIVITIES, DINING, AND LODGING.

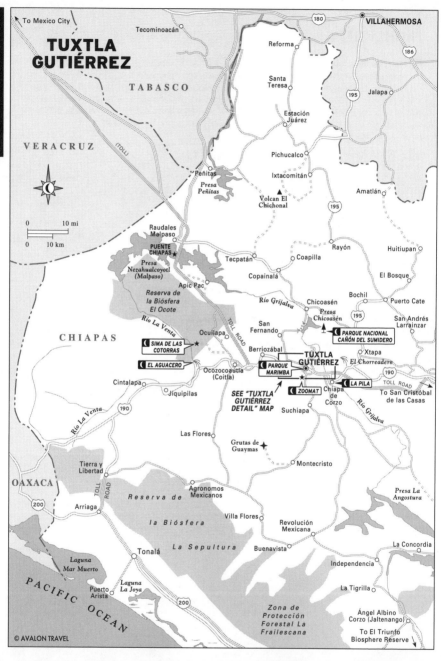

TUXTLA GUTIÉRREZ

To Mexico City

Tecominoacán

VILLAHERMOSA

180

Reforma

186

Santa
Teresa

195

Jalapa

TABASCO

Estación
Juárez

VERACRUZ

(TOLL)

Pichucalco

Ixtacomitán

Amatlán

Peñitas

*Presa
Peñitas*

Volcan El
Chichonal

195

0   10 mi

0   10 km

Raudales
Malpaso

Rayón

Huitiupan

**PUENTE
CHIAPAS** ★

*Presa
Nezahualcoyotl
(Malpaso)*

Tecpatán

Coapilla

El Bosque

Copainalá

Apic Pac

Río Grijalva

Chicoasén

Bochil

Puerto Cate

*Reserva de
la Biósfera
El Ocote*

San
Fernando

*Presa
Chicoasén*

195

San Andrés
Larrainzar

Río La Venta

Ocuilapa

☾ **SIMA DE LAS
COTORRAS** ★

Berriozábal

**PARQUE NACIONAL
CAÑON DEL SUMIDERO**

CHIAPAS

TOLL ROAD

**TUXTLA
GUTIÉRREZ**

Xtapa

El Chorreadero

☾ **EL AGUACERO**

Ocozocoautla
(Coitla)

☾ **PARQUE
MARIMBA** ★

190

Cintalapa

Jiquipilas

☾ **LA PILA**

TOLL ROAD

☾ **ZOOMAT**

Chiapa
de
Corzo

To San Cristóbal
de las Casas

*SEE "TUXTLA
GUTIÉRREZ
DETAIL" MAP*

Suchiapa

Río Grijalva

Las Flores

Grutas de
Guaymas ★

Río La Venta

190

Montecristo

Tierra y
Libertad

OAXACA

TOLL ROAD

Reserva de

Agronomos
Mexicanos

*Presa La
Angostura*

200

Arriaga

la Biósfera

Villa Flores

Revolución
Mexicana

La Concordia

La Sepultura

Buenavista

Tonalá

Independencia

*Laguna
Mar Muerto*

Puerto
Arista

*Laguna
La Joya*

200

La Tigrilla

PACIFIC OCEAN

*Zona de
Protección
Forestal La
Frailescana*

Ángel Albino
Corzo (Jaltenango)

To El Triunfo
Biosphere Reserve

© AVALON TRAVEL

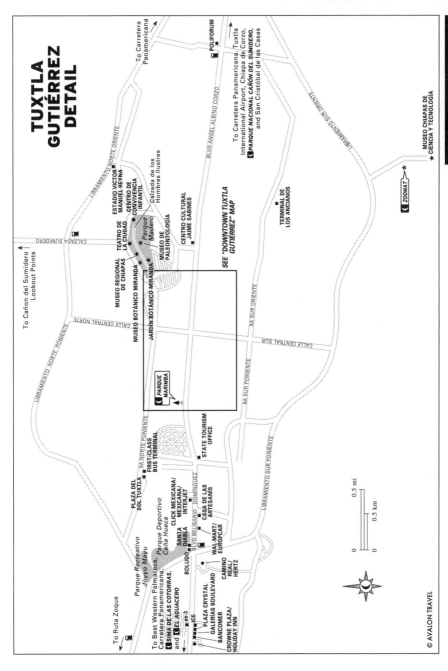

TUXTLA GUTIÉRREZ DETAIL

To Carretera Panamericana

POLIFORUM

LIBRAMIENTO NORTE ORIENTE

To Cañon del Sumidero
Lookout Points

CALZADA SUMIDERO

ESTADIO VICTOR
MANUEL REYNA

CENTRO DE
CONVIVENCIA
INFANTIL

Calzada de los
Hombres Ilustres

TEATRO DE
LA CIUDAD

Parque
Madero

CENTRO CULTURAL
JAIME SABINES

MUSEO REGIONAL
DE CHIAPAS

MUSEO DE
PALEONTOLOGÍA

MUSEO BOTÁNICO MIRANDA

JARDÍN BOTÁNICO MIRANDA

BLVD ANGEL ALBINO CORZO

To Carretera Panamericana, Tuxtla
International Airport, Chiapa de Corzo,
PARQUE NACIONAL CAÑON DEL SUMIDERO,
and San Cristóbal de las Casas

LIBRAMIENTO SUR ORIENTE

MUSEO CHIAPAS DE
CIENCIA Y TECNOLOGÍA

ZOOMAT

TERMINAL DE
LOS ANCIANOS

9A SUR ORIENTE

CALLE CENTRAL SUR

*SEE "DOWNTOWN TUXTLA
GUTIÉRREZ" MAP*

CALLE CENTRAL NORTE

LIBRAMIENTO NORTE PONIENTE

To Cañon del Sumidero
Lookout Points

To Ruta Zoque

*Parque Recreativo
Joyyo Mayu*

*Parque Deportivo
Caña Hueca*

To Best Western Palmareca,
Carretera Panamericana,
SIMA DE LAS COTORRAS,
and *EL AGUACERO*

ICE

PLAZA CRYSTAL
GALERÍAS BOULEVARD
BANCOMER

CROWNE PLAZA/
HOLIDAY INN

CAMINO
REAL/
HERTZ

WAL-MART/
EUROPCAR

BOLUDO

SANTA
DIABLA

BLVD BELISARIO DOMÍNGUEZ

CASA DE LAS
ARTESANÍS

CLICK MEXICANA/
MEXICANA/
INTERJET

PLAZA DEL
SOL TUXTLA

FIRST-CLASS
BUS TERMINAL

5A NORTE PONIENTE

STATE TOURISM
OFFICE

PARQUE
MARIMBA

9A SUR PONIENTE

LIBRAMIENTO SUR PONIENTE

0   0.5 mi

0   0.5 km

© AVALON TRAVEL

means Wal-Mart or a hot shower and HBO at the Camino Real, Tuxtla Gutiérrez is your guilty pleasure. (Don't worry, no one back home has to know.)

PLANNING YOUR TIME

Tuxtla Gutiérrez itself it worth a day—time enough to visit the zoo and a museum or two, then while away the evening at Parque Marimba or a bar. Chiapa de Corzo and Cañón del Sumidero warrant a full day too, but can be done as a day trip from San Cristóbal if you're based there. Sima de las Cotorras, El Aguacero, and the Ruta Zoque are all on the far side of Tuxtla away from San Cristóbal (and best visited with a rental car) so an overnight trip makes more sense. Of the group, Sima de las Cotorras has the best accommodations, and if you stay the night you'll be there when the parrots come and go, in the evening and early morning.

Sights

PLAZA CÍVICA

Plaza Cívica is Tuxtla's large central square, bordered by busy streets on two sides and fronted by San Marcos cathedral and various local, state, and federal government buildings. The broad stone-paved plaza has relatively few shade trees, and in that way is more like the *zócalo* in Mexico City than the shady central square in San Cristóbal. (For that, head to Parque Marimba, nine blocks west of the center.) The Plaza Cívica sometimes serves as a gathering place for protests and demonstrations, and the traffic is a constant reminder that you're in a big city, but overall it's a placid place, both day and night. There's a tourist information kiosk on the plaza's southwest corner.

CATEDRAL DE SAN MARCOS

Across Avenida Central from the Plaza Cívica is San Marcos cathedral, a stark white structure that extends more than a city block. The long narrow nave is flanked by gold-painted relief arches, in which oversize paintings (in equally oversize frames) portray dramatic religious scenes. The altar has large-scale paintings as well, and there's a small shady plaza outside the main doors. The cathedral's German-made 48-bell carillon chimes hourly, with a large repertoire of international tunes, while carved figures of the 12 apostles trolley around a short track in the bell tower. San Marcos was originally built in the second half of the 16th century as a Dominican convent. Today only the central section of the front arch remains.

◖ PARQUE MARIMBA

Just 15 minutes by foot from the central plaza, Parque Marimba (Av. Central Pte. btwn. 8 and 9 Calle Pte.) is cool and quiet

Tuxtla's Catedral de San Marcos dates to the 1500s, but has undergone extensive renovation and redesign.

© LIZA PRADO

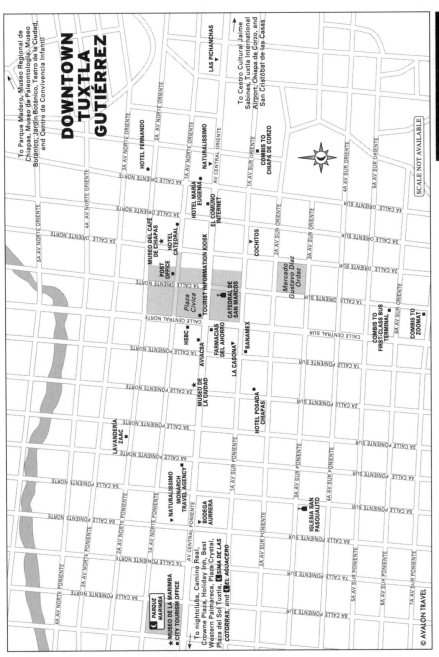

DOWNTOWN TUXTLA GUTIÉRREZ

To Parque Madero, Museo Regional de Chiapas, Museo de Paleontología, Museo Botánico, Jardín Botánico, Teatro de la Ciudad, and Centro de Convivencia Infantil

To Centro Cultural Jaime Sabines, Tuxtla International Airport, Chiapa de Corzo, and San Cristóbal de las Casas

LAS PICHANCHAS

COMBIS TO CHIAPA DE CORZO

SCALE NOT AVAILABLE

HOTEL FERNANDO

NATURALISSIMO

HOTEL MARÍA EUGENIA

MUSEO DEL CAFÉ DE CHIAPAS

HOTEL CATEDRAL

EL CAMINO INTERNET

POST OFFICE

TOURIST INFORMATION KIOSK

Plaza Cívica

COCHITOS

CATEDRAL DE SAN MARCOS

Mercado Gustavo Díaz Ordaz

HSBC

AVIACSA

FARMACIAS DEL AHORRO

BANAMEX

COMBIS TO FIRST-CLASS BUS TERMINAL

COMBIS TO ZOOMAT

LA CASONA

MUSEO DE LA CIUDAD

HOTEL POSADA CHIAPAS

LAVANDERÍA ZAAC

NATURALISSIMO

MONARCH TRAVEL AGENCY

BODEGA AURRERA

IGLESIA SAN PASQUALITO

PARQUE MARIMBA

MUSEO DE LA MARIMBA
CITY TOURISM OFFICE

To nightclubs, Camino Real, Crowne Plaza, Holiday Inn, Best Western Palmareca, Plaza Crystal, Plaza del Sol Tuxtla, SIMA DE LAS COTORRAS, and EL AGUACERO

AVALON TRAVEL

© AVALON TRAVEL

4A AV NORTE ORIENTE
3A AV NORTE ORIENTE
2A AV NORTE ORIENTE
1A AV NORTE ORIENTE
AV CENTRAL ORIENTE
1A AV SUR ORIENTE
2A AV SUR ORIENTE
3A AV SUR ORIENTE
4A AV SUR ORIENTE
5A AV SUR ORIENTE

5A CALLE ORIENTE NORTE
4A CALLE ORIENTE NORTE
3A CALLE ORIENTE NORTE
2A CALLE ORIENTE NORTE
1A CALLE ORIENTE NORTE
CALLE CENTRAL NORTE
1A CALLE PONIENTE NORTE
2A CALLE PONIENTE NORTE
3A CALLE PONIENTE NORTE
4A CALLE PONIENTE NORTE
5A CALLE PONIENTE NORTE
6A CALLE PONIENTE NORTE
7A CALLE PONIENTE NORTE
8A CALLE PONIENTE NORTE

8A AV NORTE PONIENTE
7A AV NORTE PONIENTE
6A AV NORTE PONIENTE
5A AV NORTE PONIENTE
4A AV NORTE PONIENTE
3A AV NORTE PONIENTE
2A AV NORTE PONIENTE
1A AV NORTE PONIENTE
AV CENTRAL PONIENTE
1A AV SUR PONIENTE
2A AV SUR PONIENTE
3A AV SUR PONIENTE
4A AV SUR PONIENTE
5A AV SUR PONIENTE
6A AV SUR PONIENTE
7A AV SUR PONIENTE
8A AV SUR PONIENTE

4A CALLE ORIENTE SUR
3A CALLE ORIENTE SUR
2A CALLE ORIENTE SUR
1A CALLE ORIENTE SUR
CALLE CENTRAL SUR
1A CALLE PONIENTE SUR
2A CALLE PONIENTE SUR
3A CALLE PONIENTE SUR
4A CALLE PONIENTE SUR
5A CALLE PONIENTE SUR
6A CALLE PONIENTE SUR
7A CALLE PONIENTE SUR

during the day, and is a great place to enjoy live music (marimba mostly, of course) at night. Shade trees and walkways encircle the park's ornate kiosk, which has a small snack shop in one corner. The kiosk doubles as a bandstand in the evenings, and the park's benches—several deep in places—fill up with locals of all ages, from old-timers to families with young kids. It's a lively, cheerful atmosphere, and tourists are always welcome. The music typically starts at 6 P.M. and continues until 9 P.M. on weekdays, and until 10 P.M. on Saturday and Sunday.

◖ ZOOMAT

Tuxtla's city zoo, the Zoológico Regional Miguel Álvarez del Toro (tel. 961/614-4700, 8:30 A.M.–5 P.M. Tues.–Sun., US$3) is better known by its acronym, ZOOMAT. It occupies a 100-hectare (247-acre) swath of forest with large enclosures containing only—and virtually every—species of animal found in Chiapas. Following a meandering 2.5-kilometer trail, you'll spot jaguars, pumas, and little *tigrillos;* beautiful macaws, birds of prey, and the elusive and much-revered quetzal; and unusual creatures such as tapirs, otters, and anteaters. An interesting innovation of the zoo is the Casa Nocturna, where artificial lighting has led various nocturnal creatures to think day is night and night is day. Once your eyes adjust, you can watch them going about their business—a lot more interesting than seeing them sleep. The museum also offers nighttime visits in the crocodile and reptile section (8 P.M. Tues. and Thurs., US$8).

To get to ZOOMAT, take the R-60 minibus (US$0.45, 30 mins, every 10 mins 5:30 A.M.–6 P.M.) from the corner of 7 Avenida Sur Oriente and 1 Calle Oriente Sur; from the central plaza, a cab costs around US$5.

PARQUE MADERO

Located in the northeast corner of the city, Parque Madero holds three museums, a lovely botanical garden, the city's theater…even a children's amusement park. There's lots to do here, though just sitting under a shade tree is nice on a hot day (and makes for great people-watching too). On your way through the park, check out the busts of some of the country's most notable leaders, known as the **Calzada de Los Hombres Ilustres.**

Museo Regional de Chiapas

The Chiapas Regional Museum (Calzada de los Hombres Ilustres s/n, Prolongación 5a Nte., tel. 961/613-4479, 9 A.M.–6 P.M. Tues.–Sun., US$4) has fascinating exhibits that walk visitors through Chiapanecan history, from the Protoclassic era to the present. The ground floor—which has an unfortunate resemblance to an airplane hangar—has a superb collection of Maya artifacts, arguably the finest in the state. A separate wing houses an exhibit on the colonial and republican era and boasts a collection of Chiapanecan fine art. Signage is mostly in Spanish, with intermittent English translations.

© LIZA PRADO

Tuxtla's regional museum boasts some truly extraordinary pieces, especially from Chiapas's top archaeological sites.

Museo de Paleontología Eliseo Palacios Aguilera

The Paleontology Museum (Calzada de los Hombres Ilustres s/n, Prolongación 5a Nte., tel. 961/602-0254, 10 A.M.–5 P.M. Tues.–Fri., 11 A.M.–5 P.M. Sat.–Sun., US$1) is a modern and welcoming natural-history museum. It focuses on findings in Chiapas, from dinosaur bones and fossilized vegetables to amber deposits. There is an area where visitors can watch paleontologists at work as well as various hands-on exhibits and screening rooms. It's an interesting stop, especially if you are traveling with kids. Signage is in Spanish only.

Museo Botánico Dr. Faustino Miranda

Down the Calzada de los Hombres Ilustres sits the Botanical Museum (Calzada de los Hombres Ilustres s/n, Prolongación 5a Nte., tel. 961/612-3622, 9 A.M.–3 P.M. Mon.–Sat., 9 A.M.–1 P.M. Sat., free), a small museum with four permanent exhibits on Chiapas's plant life. Exhibits include ones on trees, medicinal plants, and flowers. A temporary exhibit changes every three months.

Jardín Botánico Dr. Faustino Miranda

Across the walkway from the museum, take a break from the heat with a stroll through the well-kept botanical garden (Calzada de los Hombres Ilustres s/n, Prolongación 5a Nte., tel. 961/612-3622, 9 A.M.–6 P.M. Tues.–Sun., free), specializing in regional flora—from tiny orchids to towering trees. A meandering path leads visitors through the lush garden, with signage indicating the scientific and common names of the plant life.

Centro de Convivencia Infantil

An amusement park for small children, the Centro de Convivencia Infantil (Calzada de los Hombres Ilustres s/n, Prolongación 5a Nte., no phone, 9:30 A.M.–8 P.M. Tues.–Sun., free) has a host of kiddie rides plus miniature golf, ponies, boat and train rides, and fun extras like face

painting and carnival games. Most rides cost US$0.75–1.50 but entrance to the grounds, including the playgrounds, is free. Not remotely high tech or manicured, this is a good place to take your little ones, especially if they're still in primary school.

MUSEO CHIAPAS DE CIENCIA Y TECNOLOGÍA

The Museo Chiapas de Ciencia y Tecnología (Calzada Cerro Hueco 3000, tel. 961/639-2564, 9 A.M.–5 P.M. Tues.–Fri., 10 A.M.–5 P.M. Sat.–Sun., US$1.75 adult, US$0.85 child) is a hands-on science and technology museum. Geared at kids and teens, it has modern exhibition halls that describe the universe, life, and the human body, nano- and bio-technology, and artificial intelligence. There is also a recreational zone complete with games and experiments that teach the basics of physics, biology, chemistry...even math. It's a fun stop, especially on a rainy day.

MUSEO DE LA CIUDAD

The City Museum (Av. Central Poniente and 2 Calle Pte. Nte., no phone, 9:30 A.M.–8 P.M. Mon.–Fri., until 1 P.M. Sat., free) has a handful of rooms exhibiting mostly antiques and domestic memorabilia from Tuxtla's early days. Signage is in Spanish only, and not terribly engaging at that, but some of the old photos and curios—most loaned or donated to the museum by longtime local families—lend a certain humanity to times past. There are also documents and artifacts from periods of upheaval, including the Mexican Revolution (in which the Hijos de Tuxtla, or Sons of Tuxtla, played a small but notable role) and the 16th- and 17th-century tug-of-war between colonial powers in present-day Mexico and Central America for control over Chiapas. Upstairs is a large but unremodeled gallery used for temporary exhibits.

MUSEO DE LA MARIMBA

Facing Parque Marimba, Museo de la Marimba (9 Calle Pte. Nte. at Av Central Pte, 9 A.M.–2 P.M. and 4–6 P.M. Tues.–Fri.,

9 A.M.–noon Sat., US$2) is a small but well-organized museum with interesting displays on the origin, evolution, and cultural significance of marimbas, including touch-screen exhibits where you can see and hear recordings of famous musicians and performances. It also has a large collection of instruments, from simple to spectacular marimbas, and you can peek in on students taking marimba lessons in the attached classroom. The admission price is a bit high for the size of the museum, but it's a worthwhile stop nonetheless.

Entertainment and Events

Tuxtla is no Cancún or Mexico City, but like any big city it's got plenty to see and do at night, from movies to music and dance performances to all-night clubs.

NIGHTLIFE

Tuxtla's nightclub scene is very much a locals one, where people dress to impress. Thursday to Saturday are the best nights, with things getting started around 10 P.M. and really boiling over after midnight.

Spanish for Holy Devil, **Santa Diabla** (Blvd. Belisario Domínguez, one block east of Hotel Camino Real, tel. 961/602-6862, 8 P.M.–2 A.M. Wed.–Sat.) has two distinct parts: the mellow Santa side where you can sip drinks and chat with friends, and the red-lit Diabla part, with live music and dancing.

Right next door, **Boludo** (Blvd. Belisario Domínguez, one block east of Hotel Camino Real, 9 P.M.–3 A.M. Thurs.–Sat.) is pretty much all *diabla,* a raucous club where dancing on the bar is a foregone conclusion most nights.

For a Freddie Mercury fix, head to **es-3** (Blvd. Belisario Domínguez, opposite Plaza Crystal, 8 P.M.–3 A.M. Wed.–Sat.), ground zero for classic rock in Tuxtla. It's a small-ish 2nd-floor bar, with a sunken main floor and black walls scrawled with the names of the gods of '70s rock: Pink Floyd, Led Zep, and of course, Queen. If you're wondering, the name is a play on the Spanish pronunciation of "stress," though why you'd name a bar that remains a mystery.

Ice (Blvd. Belisario Domínguez at Plaza Crystal, 8 P.M.–3 A.M. Tues.–Sat.) exudes a hip lounge vibe, with dim lighting, mood music, and every drink under the sun. Ice is located across from es-3, next to the entrance to the mall parking garage.

MUSIC AND DANCE

Parque Marimba (Av. Central Pte. btwn. 8 and 9 Calle Pte., daily 6 P.M.–close) is one of the best places to go for live marimba and other traditional music, and a bit of low-key dancing and people-watching.

The famous **Las Pichanchas** restaurant (Av. Central Ote. at 7 Calle Ote.) has *ballet folklórico* nightly at 9 P.M.; call to reserve a table with a good view. Another restaurant, **La Casona** (1 Av. Sur Pte. 134 at Calle Central Sur), has live marimba afternoons starting at 2 P.M. and at 11 A.M. Sunday.

CULTURAL CENTERS

A beautiful building set on lush grounds, the **Centro Cultural Jaime Sabines** (12 Ote. Nte. at Av. Central, tel. 961/612-5198, www.conecultachiapas.gob.mx/jaimesabines, 9 A.M.–9 P.M. Mon.–Sat.) often hosts dance and dramatic performances, as well as concerts and art exhibits. Call or stop by for a schedule of events.

THEATER

Teatro de la Ciudad Emilio Rabasa (Parque Madero, Prolongación 5a Nte., tel. 916/613-1349, 9 A.M.–4 P.M. Tues.–Sun.) presents dramatic, dance, and musical performances throughout the year; independent films are occasionally screened here too. Ticket prices vary depending on the show but typically range US$5–30.

CINEMA

Tuxtla's main movie theaters are located in malls. **Cinemark** (Galerías Boulevard, tel. 961/615-2969) is on Bulevar Belisario Domínguez at Calle Oro Ferraro, while **Cinépolis** (Plaza del Sol Tuxtla, 5a Av. Nte. Pte. s/n, tel. 961/615-2969) is next to the ADO bus station. (Cinépolis has theaters at the Poliforum and Plaza Mirador malls as well.) Both chains charge around US$4.75 for adults, US$4 for children and seniors, and US$3 before 3 P.M. and all day Wednesday.

FESTIVALS AND EVENTS

Tuxtla Gutiérrez is the traditional starting point for an annual **Carrera Panamericana,** or Pan Am road rally (www.panamrace.com), the last open road race of its kind in the world. Using vintage race cars, two-person teams cover some 3,000 kilometers (1,864 miles) from Tuxtla to the Texas border. The race is typically held the third week of October and draws close to 100 teams and their support squads, from professional roadsters to amateur stock-car junkies. The start of the race is sometimes moved to Veracruz or Oaxaca, but if you happen to be in Tuxtla when the race is starting you can join locals in admiring scores of racing cars lined up on Avenida Central Poniente awaiting the big start.

Whenever Tuxtla's professional soccer team, the **Jaguares de Chiapas** (www.conexionjaguar .com), plays at home, *fútbol* aficionados and casual fans alike flock to the Estadio Victor Manuel Reyna (20 Calle Ote. at Libramiento Nte. Ote.) to cheer them on. If you want to join the crowd, head to the stadium during the soccer season, which runs from August to May. Tickets cost US$4.25–25 and can be purchased in advance at the soccer club's headquarters (Blvd. Belisario Domínguez 3777) or at Tienda Jaguarmanía (Blvd. Belisario Domínguez at Calle Oro Ferraro) in the Galerías Boulevard mall.

SHOPPING

Tuxtla is an excellent place to shop if you are looking for car parts, a washing machine, or tight disco clothes. It definitely is not a mecca of Chiapanecan handicrafts, but rather a place to get last-minute T-shirts or machine-made knockoffs of indigenous products.

If you're set on buying quality Chiapanecan folk art, **Casa de las Artesanías** (Blvd. Belisario Domínguez 2035, tel. 961/602-9800, 8 A.M.–8 P.M. Mon.–Fri. and 9 A.M.–8 P.M. Sat.) is where it's at. It's got a little of everything: handwoven textiles, wood carvings, pottery, leather products, amber jewelry, *laca,* and coffee.

If the mall is more your style, head to **Plaza Crystal** (Blvd. Belisario Domínguez at Calle Oro Ferraro, 10 A.M.–9 P.M. daily), where there are plenty of department stores, upscale boutiques, and a decent food court. **Plaza del Sol Tuxtla** (5a Av. Nte. Pte. at Blvd. Antonio Pariente Algarín, 8 A.M.–midnight daily) is another option, with a huge Soriana (like Wal-Mart), various specialty stores, an arcade, bowling alley, and a movie theater. Other malls in Tuxtla include **Poliforum** (Blvd. Angel Albino Corzo) and **Plaza Mirador** (Libramiento Nte. Pte. 2851).

Accommodations

UNDER US$50

In the thick of downtown, **Hotel Posada Chiapas** (2 Calle Pte. Sur btwn. 1 and 2 Calles Sur Pte., tel. 961/612-3354, US$17 s/d, US$25 s/d with a/c and cable TV) is a motel set around a sunny courtyard. Rooms themselves are boxy and curiously dark but they're clean and have decent beds. If you opt for air-conditioning, ask for a room with a mini-split air-conditioner—they're quiet and effective.

The rooms at **Hotel Fernando** (2 Calle Nte. Ote. at 4 Calle Ote. Nte., tel. 961/613-1740, www.hotelfernando.com, US$25 s, US$30 d, US$34 s with a/c, US$37.50 d with a/c) have gleaming tile floors, spotless bathrooms, cable TV, and even wireless Internet. Those on the top floor have great views of the city and a nice breeze to boot. The only downer about the place is the location—a somewhat drab neighborhood—though it's walking distance from both Parque Madero and Plaza Cívica.

Just a block from the central plaza, **Hotel Catedral** (1a Calle Nte. Ote. 367, tel. 961/613-0824, US$21 s, US$25 d) offers well-maintained rooms with fans and cable TV, though the beds are a little springy. Be sure to ask for a room in the back—they're closet-like dark but don't suffer from street noise like those in the front do, especially in the mornings.

US$50-100

Best Western Palmareca (Blvd. Belisario Domínguez 4120, tel. 961/617-0000, toll-free Mex. tel. 800/500-0102, www.palmareca.com, US$66 s with a/c, US$71 d with a/c, US$79–83 suite) is a surprisingly comfortable hotel on the far end of town. Set back from the road, rooms come in two categories: sleek with muted colors, chocolate wood furnishings, and modern fixtures; or traditionally Mexican with bright colors and *talavera* tiles. Most front a lush garden with an inviting lap pool and kiddie pool; all have cable TV, in-room phones, and wireless Internet. There's also a small gym on-site. Rates include an excellent breakfast buffet.

Hotel María Eugenia (Av. Central Ote. at 4a Calle Ote. Nte., tel. 961/613-3767, toll-free Mex. tel. 800/716-0149, www.mariaeugenia.com.mx, US$58 s with a/c, US$67 d with a/c) is considered the best hotel in the center of town. In fact, it's decidedly humdrum with plywood furnishings, plastic walls for a showering area, and old-school decor; the pool, a nice thought, is sadly neglected. What the hotel does have is a perfect location if you want to be near the action. That, and good city

views from the rooms on the upper floors (be sure to ask for one of those).

OVER US$100

Perched on a hill overlooking Tuxtla, the **Camino Real** (Blvd. Belisario Domínguez 1195, tel. 961/617-7777, toll-free Mex. tel. 800/901-2300, www.caminoreal.com/tuxtla, US$160–250 s/d with a/c) is the city's top luxury chain hotel. Rooms are modern and well appointed, with subtle Mexican decor and sweeping city views. All open onto a multitiered lobby with an enormous Plexiglass ceiling. Below is a rock-inlaid pool with a waterfall (à la Agua Azul—use your imagination) and a 24-hour restaurant that overlooks it (the buffet breakfast is pricey, but the best in town). Additional services included a luxurious spa, a fully equipped gym, and a business center.

Sitting next to each other and opening onto a shared pool are the business-oriented **Crowne Plaza** (Blvd. Belisario Domínguez 1081, tel. 961/617-2200, toll-free Mex. tel. 800/000-0404, www.hotelesfarrera.com, US$107–255 s/d with a/c) and the family-friendly **Holiday Inn** (tel. 961/617-1000, toll-free Mex. tel. 800/507-7935, www.hoteles farrera.com, US$103–167 s/d with a/c, two children stay for free). The Crowne Plaza is unquestionably the better of the two, with rooms that are sleek though comfy with deep beds, fine linens, carpeted floors, and earth tone decor. The ambience is subdued—almost library quiet—though there are lots of casual meeting areas. The Holiday Inn's rooms are nice enough but lack the elegance of the Crowne Plaza. Rooms have dated furnishings, tile floors, and checkerboard bedspreads; add cable TV, in-room phones, and air-conditioning and you've got a standard room. In addition to the pool, the hotels share two restaurants and a gym.

Food

MEXICAN

Tuxtla's best-known restaurant is 【 **Las Pichanchas** (Av. Central Ote. at 7a Calle Ote., tel. 961/612-5351, noon–midnight daily, US$6–15), with a large lively dining area decorated with an eclectic array of folk art, paper streamers, and random doodads. The menu includes a long list of local and regional dishes; try an assortment of tamales and an appetizer plate with local cheeses and sausages. The restaurant's signature drink is *el pumpo,* made with fresh pineapple juice and vodka, served in a bulbous dried gourd. For the complete experience, come during a dinner performance: live marimba music and a series of skits and traditional dances, starting at 9 P.M. nightly. If possible, call ahead to reserve a good table.

Closer to the central plaza, **La Casona** (1 Av. Sur Pte. 134 at Calle Central Sur, tel. 961/612-7534, 7 A.M.–11 P.M. Mon.–Sat., until 10 P.M. Sun., US$4–8) has a similar concept, with colorful Mexican tablecloths and wrought-iron chairs. The menu is predominantly Mexican, but a few international options mean you can order chicken mole one day, and chicken cordon bleu the next. Enjoy live marimba music 2–6 P.M. Monday–Saturday and 11 A.M.–6 P.M. Sunday.

【 **Cochitos** (1 Ave Sur Ote. btwn. 2 and 3 Calle Ote. Sur, no phone, 9:30 A.M.–7 P.M. Mon.–Fri., 9:30 A.M.–3 P.M. Sat.) serves just two things—tacos and gorditas—with just one filling—pork. It comes in two forms, however: *maciza* (prime leg meat) and *surtido* (ear, cheek, tongue, etc.). Portions are as hefty as they are tasty, and there's no better place to fill up cheap. The small sweaty dining area is packed at mealtimes, and just as many order their grub to go.

OTHER SPECIALTIES

Naturalissimo (tel. 916/613-9648, 7 A.M.–10 P.M. daily, US$3–7) is a combination store-restaurant specializing in organic products and vegetarian food. There are two locations: Avenida Central Oriente at 4 Calle Oriente, and 6 Calle Poniente Norte at Avenida Central Poniente. The menu is identical at both and includes mostly faux-meat dishes like hamburgers and tacos *al pastor* made of soy. Also look for good *comida corrida* (lunch specials, US$7) and deluxe shakes (US$3) made with various fruit and veggie juices—everything from beets to papaya. The setting is a bit sterile, but the food is a nice change of pace.

The restaurant at **Hotel María Eugenia** (Av. Central Ote. 507, tel. 961/613-3767, 7 A.M.–11 P.M. daily, US$4–12) won't win any charm awards, but it has long hours and serves a variety of reliable meals, from pasta and quesadillas to grilled meat and fish fillets. The breakfast buffet (US$10) includes made-to-order eggs, pancakes, sausage, yogurt, and cereal.

GROCERIES

Near Parque Marimba, **Bodega Aurrera** (Av. Central Pte. at 6 Calle Pte., 8 A.M.–10 P.M. daily) is an aging but serviceable supermarket with produce, canned food, and more. For a much larger selection, hop a cab or *combi* to megastores **Wal-Mart** (Blvd. Belisario Domínguez 2058, 8 A.M.–10 P.M. daily) or **Soriana** (Plaza del Sol Tuxtla, 5a Av. Nte. Pte. at Blvd. Antonio Pariente Algarín, 8 A.M.–midnight daily).

In the center of town, the **Mercado Gustavo Díaz Ordaz** (1 Calle Ote. Sur at 3 Calle Sur Ote., 6 A.M.–6 P.M. Mon.–Sat., 6 A.M.–3:30 P.M. Sun.) has mountains of bright fruits and vegetables, rows of live chickens, and scores of flower stands, shoemakers, bicycle repair shops—you name it, it's here. When you visit, be sure to try a cold glass of *tazcalate,* a sweet drink made from local chocolate, cinnamon, and *pinole* (roasted corn).

Information and Services

TOURIST INFORMATION

There's a city tourism office at Parque Marimba and a smaller kiosk on the southwest corner of the Plaza Cívica; both are open 10 A.M.–2 P.M. and 4–8 P.M. daily. Service can be quite thorough and helpful—or not—depending on who's on duty when you pass by.

Try your best to pry any useful information from the staffers at the state tourism office (Blvd. Belisario Domínguez at 15 Calle Pte. Nte., tel. 961/617-0550, ext. 35012, www.turismo chiapas.gob.mx, 8 A.M.–4 P.M. Mon.–Fri.); better yet, just stick to requesting maps and brochures. The state tourism office also maintains a tourist information kiosk (9 A.M.–3 P.M. Tues.–Sun.) at the zoo.

EMERGENCY SERVICES

Hospital Sanatorio Rojas (2 Av. Sur Pte. 1487, tel. 961/602-5138) is a private hospital with 24-hour emergency services. For meds, **Farmacias del Ahorro** (Av. Central, no phone, 24 hours) is conveniently located across from the cathedral.

There is no police station near the center, but officers usually patrol the area on foot. For emergency assistance, call toll-free 066.

MONEY

HSBC (Calle Central Nte., 9 A.M.–7 P.M. Mon.–Fri., 9 A.M.–3 P.M. Sat.) faces the central plaza and has a reliable ATM.

Bancomer (9 A.M.–5 P.M. Mon.–Fri., 10 A.M.–2 P.M. Sat.) is near the outlying hotels, and across from Plaza Crystal mall. All the malls have ATM machines from various banks, and some have walk-in branches as well.

MEDIA AND COMMUNICATIONS

The **post office** (8 A.M.–4:30 P.M. Mon.–Fri., 8 A.M.–noon Sat.), is inside the large gated federal complex on the east side of the central plaza.

Tuxtla's center area has a zillion Internet cafés, some large and high tech, others holes-in-the-wall with just a handful of computers. **El Comuno Internet** (Av Central Ote. btwn. 3a and 4a Calles Central, 9 A.M.–11 P.M. daily, US$0.50/hr) is an agreeable spot, with a fast connection, air-conditioning on hot days, and Skype, scanning, printing, and other services.

IMMIGRATION

The immigration office (Libramiento Nte. Ote. s/n, tel. 961/614-3288, 9 A.M.–1 P.M. Mon.–Fri.) is located on the outskirts of town, next to the Universidad Pablo Guardado Chávez.

LAUNDRY AND STORAGE

Lavandería Zaac (2a Av. Nte. Pte. near 3a Calle Pte. Nte., 8 A.M.–2 P.M. and 4–8 P.M. Mon.–Fri., 9 A.M.–4 P.M. Sat.) charges US$2.50 per three kilos of laundry.

The **ADO bus station** (5a Av. Nte. Pte. at Blvd. Antonio Pariente Algarín, tel. 961/125-1580) has a 24-hour *guarda equipaje,* or luggage storage. Rates are US$0.50–1.20 per hour, or US$5–12 per day, depending on the size of the bag.

Getting There and Around

GETTING THERE

Air

Tuxtla's gleaming **Aeropuerto Internacional Ángel Albino Corzo** (TGZ, tel. 961/615-0537) is located 35 kilometers (21 miles) east of town. Airlines serving it include: **Aviacsa** (Av. Central Pte. 160, tel. 961/611-2000, toll-free Mex. tel. 800/006-2200, www.aviacsa.com); **Click Mexicana** (Blvd. Belisario Domínguez 1748, tel. 961/612-5771, toll-free Mex. tel. 800/112-5425, www.mexicana.com); **Interjet** (Plaza Veranda, Blvd. Belisario Domínguez 1748, tel. 961/121-5725, toll-free Mex. tel. 800/011-2345, www.interjet.com.mx); and **Mexicana** (Blvd. Belisario Domínguez 1748, tel. 961/612-5771, toll-free Mex. tel. 800/502-2000, www.mexicana.com).

To get to the airport, ADO offers twice daily service from the first-class bus terminal (US$7, 50 mins, 9 A.M. and 3 P.M.). Closer to the center, **Monarch Travel Agency** (tel. 961/600-0236, cell tel. 044-961/132-8191, 4a Calle Pte. Nte. 145) operates an airport shuttle with departures scheduled at 5:30 A.M., 9 A.M., 11 A.M., 1 P.M., 2:30 P.M., 4:30 P.M., and 6 P.M. (US$9 pp, minimum two people, reservations required).

A taxi to the airport costs US$17 (45 mins), and the same to return. There is no return bus service from the airport to Tuxtla, strangely enough.

Bus

Tuxtla's first-class bus terminal (5a Av. Nte. Pte. at Blvd. Antonio Pariente Algarín, tel. 961/125-1580) opened in 2007 and is newer than the airport, with all levels of ADO and OCC service, plus a minimart, luggage storage, and HSBC cash machine. It's connected to the Plaza del Sol Tuxtla mall, which has a large food court, even a bowling alley and movie theater, in case you've got a long wait.

Colectivos to Chiapa de Corzo (US$0.90, 30 mins) leave every 10–15 minutes 5 A.M.–10 P.M. daily from 1 Avenida Sur Poniente at 4 Calle Oriente Sur.

Car

Most rental car companies here (and elsewhere in Chiapas) require you to purchase expensive supplemental insurance, even if your credit card offers it for free. One exception is **Europcar** (TGZ airport, tel. 961/153-6098, www.europcar.com, or downtown at Blvd. Belisario Domínguez 2075, tel. 961/121-4922, 9 A.M.–9 P.M. daily), which has base rates as low as US$9/day and only requires third-party coverage (US$10/day). Other options include **Budget** (at airport and at Blvd. Belisario Domínguez 2510, tel. 961/615-0672) and **Hertz** (at airport and Hotel Camino Real, Blvd. Belisario Domínguez 1195, tel. 961/615-5348).

GETTING AROUND

Tuxtla's downtown area is large, but still manageable on foot; the walk from the Plaza Cívica to Parque Marimba takes about 15 minutes. You'll want to catch a cab or *colectivo* to places beyond the center, like ZOOMAT, the bus station, and the larger hotels and malls.

Bus

Colectivos (public minibuses, also known as *combis*) charge US$0.45 and cover virtually the entire city, plus many outlying destinations. Route 1 is very handy, running the length of Avenida Central (which becomes Blvd. Belisario Domínguez) and passing Wal-Mart, the state tourism office, a couple of malls, and most of the large hotels along the way. Catch Route 3 to get from the bus station into town, getting off at Parque Marimba or Mercado Gustavo Díaz Ordaz. *Combis* to ZOOMAT leave from the corner of 1 Calle Oriente Sur and 7 Avenida Sur Oriente.

Taxi

Taxis do not use meters, instead charging a fixed rate of US$2.50 anywhere inside the surrounding beltway, aka the *libramento*. It's a good idea to ask at your hotel for the current fare and to reconfirm it with the driver before setting off.

TUXTLA GUTIÉRREZ BUS SCHEDULE

DESTINATION	PRICE	DURATION	SCHEDULE
Campeche City	US$40-52	12.5 hrs	5 P.M., 10:30 P.M., and 11:30 P.M.
Mérida	US$50-70	14 hrs	5 P.M., 6 P.M., 10:30 P.M., and 11:30 P.M.
Mexico City	US$70-85	12-13 hrs	11 departures 5:30 P.M.-11:30 P.M.
Oaxaca City	US$30-35	10 hrs	11:30 A.M., 7:20 P.M., 8:30 P.M., 9:30 P.M., and 11:55 P.M.
Palenque	US$13-18	6 hrs	11 departures 6 A.M.-11:55 P.M.
Pijijiapán	US$8-14	4.5-5 hrs	take Tapachula bus
San Cristóbal	US$3	70 mins	every 30-60 mins 5:25 A.M.-11:55 P.M.
Tapachula	US$14-25	5.5-8 hrs	every 30-60 mins 3:30 A.M.-12:30 A.M.
Tonalá	US$6-11	2.5-4 hrs	take Tapachula bus
Villahermosa (via Puente Chiapas)	US$20-25	4-5 hrs	hourly 5-7 A.M. and every 1-2 hrs 11:15 A.M.-11:50 P.M.

Around Tuxtla Gutiérrez

The long broad valley surrounding Tuxtla Gutiérrez has a number of terrific attractions, especially of the outdoor variety. By far, the best known is Cañón del Sumidero, a winding river canyon whose sheer stone walls climb 1,000-meters high in places—a true must-see. Two-hour boat trips from the town of Chiapa de Corzo, just east of Tuxtla, are the most common way to visit the canyon, but a road along the rim also offers impressive vistas. West of Tuxtla are two excellent and less-visited sites: Sima de las Cotorras, a gargantuan sinkhole that's the summer nesting ground of more than 1,000 green parrots, and El Aguacero, an isolated and picturesque waterfall at the bottom of a lush canyon. Cañón del Sumidero is easy to visit via public transportation—either from Tuxtla or San Cristóbal—while the latter two are best reached by car.

◖ PARQUE NACIONAL CAÑÓN DEL SUMIDERO

The sheer stone walls of Sumidero Canyon rise hundreds of meters—and in one spot a full kilometer—above the tranquil river below, an awe-inspiring channel that's one of Chiapas's most recognizable and impressive natural wonders. Two-hour boat tours of the canyon leave from Chiapa de Corzo, winding 40 kilometers downriver to the Chicoasén Dam. It's a spectacular neck-cramping journey, and highly recommended as a day trip from either Tuxtla Gutiérrez or San Cristóbal. Agencies in both cities offer package tours, but it's perfectly easy to do it yourself, by car or *combi*, especially if you leave the afternoon to enjoy Chiapa de Corzo's museums and architecture.

The canyon was tens, even hundreds, of meters deeper before 1981 and the construction of the Chicoasén Dam, one of three *presas* on the mighty Río Grijalva. In Chiapa de Corzo, a painting in the Ex-Convento de Santo Domingo portrays an infamous story associated with the canyon: Early in the conquest, an indigenous community was invaded by Spanish troops. They fought fiercely, but could not defeat their better-armed opponents.

Facing defeat, the indigenous men and women—many holding their children—leapt from the canyon walls to their deaths, rather than be captured.

Cañón del Sumidero

Chiapa de Corzo is the main starting point for boat trips through Cañón del Sumidero. **Boat tours** (US$10 pp, 9 A.M.–4 P.M. daily) depart from the embarcadero at the end of Calle 5 de Febrero, downhill from the central plaza. Boats leave when they are full (12–16 people); afternoon trips are especially beautiful, but you'll have less waiting time if you arrive between 9 A.M. and noon, especially in the low season.

The boat takes a little over an hour to reach the dam, with stops and explanations along the way, including at the canyon wall's highest spot (1,000 m/0.6 mi) and various cave and rock formations, plus a beautiful mist-blown waterfall known as *árbol de navidad* (Christmas tree) for the lush triangle of moss and vegetation clinging to the wall beneath it.

© GARY CHANDLER

The Río Grijalva winds through Chiapas's iconic Cañón del Sumidero, whose sheer limestone walls are up to a thousand meters high and are graced by numerous wispy waterfalls.

You can also visit Cañón del Sumidero from above. Catch a **trolley** (US$7.50 pp, 9 A.M. and 1 P.M. Sat.–Sun., daily during holidays) from Parque Marimba in Tuxtla Gutiérrez for a three-hour trip along the western rim of the canyon, stopping at five *miradores* (lookout points) for stomach-lurching views of the canyon and river below. You can also drive the route yourself; it's part of the national park, so there's an entrance fee of US$2 per car.

Parque Ecoturístico Cañón del Sumidero (tel. 961/602-8500, www.sumidero.com, US$25–29 adult/child) is another of those "eco-parks" where visitors have a series of brief eco-ish encounters and spend the rest of the day reliving it by the pool and over seconds at the $12 buffet. Admission includes the standard boat trip through the canyon (the park is located just before the dam), but there are no return boats until 4:30 P.M.—you're literally trapped there until then. Most activities, like kayaking, rappelling, and a five-station zip line, cost an additional fee (US$5–15); there are also hiking and biking trails and a small zoo.

Getting There

Combis from Tuxtla Gutiérrez (US$1, 40 mins, 5 Calle Ote. Sur and 1 Av. Sur Pte.) leave every 10 minutes from 6 A.M. to 10 P.M. and drop you on the north side of Chiapa de Corzo's central plaza. Catch return buses in the same place, on the opposite side of the street.

From San Cristóbal, take any Tuxtla-bound *combi* (US$3, 45 mins) from their stop on Carretera Panamericana at Avenida Insurgentes, near the ADO bus terminal. *Combis* from San Cristóbal don't enter Chiapa de Corzo proper, so ask to be dropped at the first *puente peatonal* (foot bridge, a short distance after the toll booth); there, cross to the other side and catch a taxi (US$2.50) or *colectivo* into town (US$0.45). If you get dropped at the second foot bridge—some drivers seem to prefer stopping there—you can still cross and get a ride into town, it's just a bit further. To return to San Cristóbal, catch a bus or taxi to the same spot, where San Cristóbal–bound *colectivos* pass frequently. However, they tend to be

pretty full; if you're a group of three or more, you may have better luck getting onto the same *combi* by backtracking to Tuxtla (just 15 minutes) and boarding a San Cristóbal *combi* at their point of origin.

◖ SIMA DE LAS COTORRAS

Chiapas is full of caves and sinkholes (known as *simas*), but none compare to the gargantuan Sima de las Cotorras (Centro Ecoturístico Tzamanguimo, tel. 968/689-0289 or 968/105-6480, 7 A.M.–7 P.M. daily, US$2), about a 90-minute drive west of Tuxtla. Almost perfectly circular, the sinkhole is 160 meters across and a stomach-lurching 140 meters straight down—like a giant posthole cut into the limestone crust. At the bottom is a small forest, a naturally protected summer nesting area for the sinkhole's namesake residents: thousands of *cotorras,* or green parrots. In the morning and evening, the birds enter and leave the sinkhole in an awesome cacophonous hurricane, flying in broad wheeling spirals and squawking incessantly. It's a marvel to witness, and staying the night lets you see both the evening and morning shows.

While Sima de las Cotorras is impressive any time, the best time to visit is March to October, when the parrots are most numerous. (They spend the rest of the year in the warm lowlands nearer the coast.) In season, the parrots typically leave the *sima* at 5:30–6 A.M. and return at 4–5 P.M.

Nearly as impressive are a set of *pinturas rupestres* (ancient paintings) on a narrow ledge right in the middle of the sheer cliff wall. The ledge circles around the *sima*, climbing slowly to the lip; to see the paintings up close, it's a knee-knocking 200-meter walk down the ledge, with 70 meters of sheer cliff above and below you. Local guides will take you there for about US$5; better yet, on Saturdays and (most) Sundays, a rock-climbing club guides visitors to the paintings with the assurance of a fixed safety rope set up for the purpose (US$6). The same team offers rappelling (US$30 to the ledge, US$60 to the *sima* floor). The climb back up is extremely strenuous.

There's a second and smaller *sima* a half-hour

© GARY CHANDLER

It's hard to say what's more impressive about Sima de las Cotorras – the curving 140-meter-deep walls or the squawking whirlwind of a thousand-plus nesting parrots.

walk from the main one, also with ancient paintings in it. If you simply want to admire the view, there's a trail leading around Sima de las Cotorras that takes about 20 minutes to complete, with a number of good vista points along the way.

Accommodations and Food

A cluster of new and very pleasant **cabins** (US$25–55 for 2–4 people) are set a short distance into the trees; each includes one to two bedrooms and large hot-water bathrooms. Sturdy stone exteriors give way to terra-cotta floors, wood beams, and even patios with hammocks.

The **restaurant** (7 A.M.–8 A.M. daily, US$3–7) is built right on the edge of the sinkhole, with excellent views and decent food.

Getting There

Driving from Tuxtla on Highway 190, look for signs for Sima de las Cotorras as you pass through the small town of Ocozocoautla. From the turnoff, it's 3.5 kilometers on a paved road to Crucero San Luis, where a huge sign directs you left onto a dirt road. It's another 12 kilometers from there, passing through the small town of Piedra Parada (home to a huge family restaurant called El Borrego Líder). The road is in decent shape, though it is muddy and slippery after heavy rains.

You can theoretically catch a **round-trip shuttle** (US$10 pp, children 2-for-1, escobar250_9@hotmail.com) from Parque Marimba in Tuxtla on Saturday and Sunday at 11:50 A.M. (and daily during vacation periods). The trip lasts six hours, including a stop at Ocuilapa, a Zoque community known for its pottery. Ten people are required for the shuttle to depart, so low-season departures may be unreliable; ask at the tourist office in Parque Marimba for the latest.

◖ EL AGUACERO

Aguacero waterfall (7 A.M.–5 P.M. daily, US$2) is one of Chiapas's most picturesque *cascadas,* with countless rivulets falling from a long moss-covered ledge, the wind drawing them out in a graceful mist. El Aguacero is located at the bottom of a deep canyon, its water emerging from the mouth of a cave, and there's a sheer cliff, shooting hundreds of meters high, on the opposite bank. The Río Venta is swift but tranquil, and a number of sandy spots make for a pleasant lunch break.

The access road dead-ends at a small parking lot, where an amiable family charges admission and operates a simple restaurant (with terrific canyon views, but frequently out of supplies). A pathway—with 724 stairs, the family proudly informs visitors—winds steeply down to the river, where you bear left (upriver) about 250 meters to the falls. You'll have to clamber a bit—crossing overgrown brush and fallen trunks, and hopping rock to rock in places—and eventually remove your

RESERVA DE LA BIOSFERA EL TRIUNFO

Draped over the rugged tree-clad peaks of the Sierra Madre de Chiapas, El Triunfo Biosphere Reserve is a gorgeous and little-visited reserve spanning nearly 120,000 hectares (1,200 square kilometers) and ranging from lush tropical rainforest to cool cloud forest. The wide variety of microclimates and landscape translates into a staggering array of flora and fauna. It's a bird-watcher's paradise, with close to 400 species of birds, including three of the rarest in Latin America – Horned Guan, Azure-rumped Tanager, and the long-tailed Resplendent Quetzal. The park contains over 2,300 varieties of flowers, plants, and trees; hundreds of butterfly and amphibian species; plus spider monkeys, tapir, and five species of wildcat, including the jaguar (though spotting its tracks is much more likely than the cat itself). The best time to visit El Triunfo is during the dry months, from January to May.

VISITING THE RESERVE

Entry to El Triunfo is strictly controlled; all visits must be with an organized tour. Typical excursions begin with transport from Tuxtla Gutiérrez to Jaltenango (aka Ángel Albino Corzo), where travelers stay the night in a basic hotel. The following morning, visitors are transported by four-wheel-drive truck to Finca Prusia, a coffee-producing village on the edge of El Triunfo, where there's usually an opportunity to tour the fields and processing facilities. Later, travelers set off on a tough 14-kilometer (9.3-mile) hike, mostly uphill, to Campamento El Triunfo, a basic lodge with dorm rooms and running water. (Mules carry all the baggage and supplies, fortunately.) Visitors on 3- or 4-night trips remain based here, making hikes and birdwatching trips into the reserve, by day and even at night, always led by expert birders or naturalists. (There is also a network of well-maintained trails for visitors to explore on their own.) Visitors on longer trips – including 10-day expeditions ending at the Pacific Ocean – continue to the more rustic camps of Cañada Honda and El Limonar.

PRACTICALITIES

El Triunfo's ecotourism program, **Fondo de Conservación El Triunfo** (FONCET, San Cristóbal 8, Fracc. Residencial La Hacienda, Tuxtla Gutiérrez, tel. 961/125-1122, www.fondoeltriunfo.org), is managed by the NGO **Ecobiósfera S.C.** (San Cristóbal 8, Fracc. Residencial La Hacienda, Tuxtla Gutiérrez, tel. 961/125-1177, www.ecobiosfera.org.mx). It offers four-day excursions into the reserve for US$650 per person or US$335 per person for FONCET members (membership is US$99 per year). Trips typically take place in March and April, and include transportation to and from Tuxtla Gutiérrez, mules and porters, and guide services, plus meals and accommodations. See the Ecobiósfera website for scheduled trips; reserve at least two weeks in advance.

The **Mesoamerican Ecotourism Alliance** (MEA, toll-free U.S. tel. 800/682-0584, www.travelwithmea.org) also offers all-inclusive tours of El Triunfo, including a 10-day excursion (US$3,178-3,428 per person, six people minimum) that ends at the Reserva Natural La Encrucijada. Be sure to double-check the details of the trip before you book; at the time of research, MEA's itinerary included a hotel in Tuxtla that is no longer in operation.

© GARY CHANDLER

A sublime waterfall at the bottom of a deep river canyon, El Aguacero is well worth the long hike to reach it.

shoes (or get them wet) to reach the base of the falls. It's definitely worth it, though, especially on hot days when the falls are perfect for cooling off. The path and riverbank are good places to spot herons and collared aracaris, and curious insects like praying mantis and stick-bugs.

Getting There

The well-marked turnoff to Cascada El Aguacero is about 16 kilometers southeast of Ocozocoautla (or 60 km from Tuxtla) on Highway 190. From there, it's three kilometers down a dirt road. The last section is quite steep and slippery; if it has rained recently, consider parking where the road starts to descend sharply and walking the final 750 meters to the entrance. There is no public transportation.

Chiapa de Corzo

This quiet colonial town between Tuxtla and San Cristóbal is best known as the jumping-off point for boat tours through Cañón del Sumidero, a winding must-see canyon whose 1,000-meter (3,281-foot) walls will lodge a crick in your neck in no time. But Chiapa de Corzo has plenty of history and appeal in its own right, and is well worth exploring in conjunction with a trip down the canyon. Not to be missed are the city's architectural treasures, among them an outstanding 16th-century fountain in the main plaza and massive Dominican church and convent, which now houses a fine museum and gallery space. Chiapa de Corzo is also known for its artistic roots, especially in lacquerware (*laca*) and marimba music, and hosts a lively and eclectic festival in January, which lasts for two weeks and draws tens of thousands of visitors.

HISTORY

Chiapa de Corzo was the first official Spanish settlement in present-day Chiapas. Originally called Villa Real, and later Chiapa de Indios, it was founded in 1528 on the banks of the Río

Grijalva by conquistador Diego de Mazariegos, following the bloody subjugation of the dominant Chiapa indigenous people. The Chiapanecs, a warrior people who had themselves conquered the native Zoques around A.D. 1000, held off better-armed Spanish invaders for four years, and many are said to have thrown themselves from the Sumidero Canyon walls rather than be captured. Within a month of the city's founding, however, rampant disease forced Mazariegos to move the new capital upland to present-day San Cristóbal. Some settlers remained, however, and the city slowly grew, establishing vast cacao and sugarcane plantations, and eventually was selected, in 1545, as the site of a major Dominican mission. The city adopted its current name in 1888 in honor of Ángel Albino Corzo, a revered municipal president.

SIGHTS
◖ La Pila

One of the most unique and striking colonial structures in Chiapas, perhaps all of Mexico, La Pila (The Fountain) rises dramatically from the

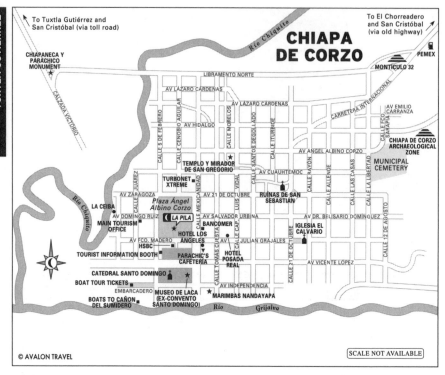

To Tuxtla Gutiérrez and
San Cristóbal (via toll road)

To El Chorreadero
and San Cristóbal
(via old highway)

Río Chiquito

CHIAPA DE CORZO

PEMEX

MONTÍCULO 32

CHIAPANECA Y
PARACHICO
MONUMENT

LIBRAMENTO NORTE

CALZADA VICTORIO

AV LÁZARO CÁRDENAS

AV LÁZARO CÁRDENAS

CARRETERA INTERNACIONAL

AV EMILIO
CARRANZA

CALLE FCO
SARAPIA

CALLE 5 DE FEBRERO

CALLE CENOBIO AGUILAR

AV HIDALGO

CALLE MORELOS

CALLE SANTOS DEGOLLADO

CALLE ITURBIDE

AV ÁNGEL ALBINO CORZO

CHIAPA DE CORZO
ARCHAEOLOGICAL
ZONE

CALLE LA LIBERTAD

★ TEMPLO Y MIRADOR
DE SAN GREGORIO

MUNICIPAL
CEMETERY

AV CUAUHTÉMOC

CALLE RAYÓN

CALLE ALLENDE

CALLE LAS CASAS

TURBONET
XTREME

CALLE MEXICANIDAD

AV 21 DE OCTUBRE

CALLE VIDAL

CALLE LUIS

RUINAS DE SAN
SEBASTIÁN ★

CALLE JUÁREZ

AV ZARAGOZA

Plaza Ángel
Albino Corzo

LA CEIBA

AV DOMINGO RUIZ

LA PILA 🌙

AV SALVADOR URBINA

AV DR. BELISARIO DOMÍNGUEZ

CALLE 12 DE AGOSTO

Río Chiquito

MAIN TOURISM
OFFICE

BANCOMER ■

CALLE TOMÁS CUESTA

AV

HOTEL LOS
ÁNGELES ★

CALLE 21 DE OCTUBRE

IGLESIA EL
CALVARIO ■

AV FCO. MADERO

HSBC ■

CALLE JULIÁN GRAJALES

TOURIST INFORMATION BOOTH ■

PARACHIC'S
CAFETERÍA

HOTEL
POSADA
REAL ▼

AV VICENTE LÓPEZ

CATEDRAL SANTO DOMINGO ★

BOAT TOUR TICKETS ■

EMBARCADERO

MUSEO DE LACA
(EX-CONVENTO
SANTO DOMINGO)

AV INDEPENDENCIA

BOATS TO CAÑÓN
DEL SUMIDERO ■

★ MARIMBAS NANDAYAPA

Río   Grijalva

© AVALON TRAVEL

SCALE NOT AVAILABLE

southern end of Chiapa de Corzo's large central plaza. Built in 1562, it features classic Mudejar and Gothic features, including an octagonal shape (some say intended to resemble the Spanish crown), numerous arches, and flying buttresses extending from each of the corners. It's made entirely of red-orange brick, yet remains in remarkably good condition thanks to extensive restoration. A system of pipes once drew river water into the fountain's central basin (also octagonal), supplying the town with water and townswomen a place to socialize and do laundry. A gorgeous central dome is braced by Gothic arches and decorated inside and out with intricate brickwork. Today, informational plaques provide a thumbnail history of the city.

Catedral Santo Domingo

Santo Domingo cathedral (daily except 3–4 P.M.) doesn't face Chiapa de Corzo's main square, so its size and prominence aren't immediately obvious. Yet this is one *big* church, and even larger if you count the adjacent ex-convent of the same name (now a museum and exhibition space). The cathedral stretches nearly a city block, with thick white walls and high wood-beam ceilings. The altar originally featured ornate *retablos* (large finely carved wood panels), though they've all disappeared, save a fragment on view at El Calvario church, east of the center. The current altar is quite pretty all the same, made of warm unpolished wood that's incised with delicate flower patterns. The church's gargantuan main bell, which dates to 1576, was cast from copper, silver, and reportedly a dash of gold, and weighs upwards of 4,500 kilograms (10,000 lbs); its tolling can be heard for miles.

Ex-Convento Santo Domingo

The Ex-Convento Santo Domingo was built in

© GARY CHANDLER

Built in 1562 out of specially designed bricks, La Pila is considered one of Chiapas's best preserved Mudejar-style colonial structures.

1554, in the usual design of Dominican friars, with tile floors, thick walls, and broad archways edging serene patios. The original structure was destroyed by an earthquake in the 1800s, then painstakingly reconstructed. Today its spacious courtyards and numerous *salas* (rooms) are put to excellent use as an exhibition space, with temporary and revolving exhibits ranging from ceremonial masks and indigenous textiles from around Chiapas and Mexico, to profiles of local and renowned artists and cultural figures. The convent is home to the Museo de Laca (Lacquerware Museum).

Museo de Laca

Housed on the 2nd floor of the Ex-Convento Santo Domingo, the impressive Lacquerware Museum (10 A.M.–5 P.M. Tues.–Sun., free) exhibits Chiapa de Corzo's stand-out *laca,* or lacquerware. Examples include tiny jewelry boxes, bulbous gourds, and enormous wood chests, all covered with bright colors and incredibly intricate designs on a jet-black background. The painting is done by hand—literally, in some cases, as early artists often used their fingernails instead of paintbrushes to create the finest details; feathers and cat hair were also utilized. Lacquerware (of sorts) has long been produced by native communities in Michoacán, but was introduced in Chiapas and elsewhere by Spanish colonizers. Mexican artisans applied their own style and materials to European techniques, and were also greatly influenced by Asian ceramics, which arrived by way of Spanish galleons en route from the Philippines.

Marimbas Nandayapa

For nearly a century, the Nandayapa family of Chiapa de Corzo has designed and built some of the finest and most sought-after marimba instruments in the world. The marimbas come in all sizes, including 8-foot, 6.5-octave concert masters, and their intricate adornment makes each one as much a piece of art as a musical instrument. The family home doubles as its **workshop** (Av. Independencia 36, tel. 961/616-0012, cnandayapa@yahoo.com) and visitors are offered hour-long presentations on marimba history,

MARIMBA

The marimba is the sound of Chiapas, an instrument whose bright upbeat tones accompanies virtually every important event and celebration.

Adapted from xylophone-like instruments brought to the Americas by enslaved West Africans, marimbas have two rows of wooden bars arranged somewhat like the keys on a piano that are struck with mallets. Up to five musicians can play a single instrument, and the finest marimbas have intricate wood inlays that make them pieces of art as much as musical instruments. The marimba is revered throughout southern Mexico and Central America, but especially in Chiapas and neighboring Guatemala (where it is the national instrument).

Today, Chiapas produces some of the world's finest marimbas. In Chiapa de Corzo – considered the birthplace of the modern marimba – the instruments are constructed from *hormiguillo*, or "singing wood," which gives the marimba a brilliant ringing sound; mallets made from the strong but flexible *guisisil* wood are wrapped at one end with natural rubber to help them fly across the keys. And the marimba is no longer the lesser stepsister of concert instruments – it lacks only two octaves to equal the range of a concert piano, and more and more scores are being written for the marimba by classical and popular musicians around the world.

construction, and music, including a short concert. Unfortunately, the workshop is open only to groups with advance appointments; there are plans for drop-in hours, but nothing definite. Carlos Nandayapa Vargas is the current point person; he speaks Spanish, English, and Italian, and may be able to include independent travelers (US$2.50 pp) in an already-scheduled group.

Ruínas de San Sebastián and San Gregorio

Perched atop twin hills in the city's northeastern corner are the remains of two 17th-century churches, today known as Templo y Mirador de San Gregorio (San Gregorio Church and Vista Point) and Ruínas de San Sebastián (San Sebastián Ruins). Both evoke the one-time wealth and import of Chiapa de Corzo, with highlights of the original Mudejar, Renaissance, and baroque architecture still detectable, albeit faintly. Nowadays the two sites are better known for their impressive views of town and Río Grijalva; San Sebastián has a quaint open-air temple beside the ruin, dedicated to the Virgin of Guadalupe.

El Chorreadero

The mountains behind Chiapa de Corzo, and throughout Chiapas for that matter, are perforated by countless channels formed by underground rivers. That water eventually reemerges, as at El Chorreadero (literally The Spout). Located about 10 kilometers from Chiapa de Corzo, El Chorreadero (Carretera Libre a San Cristóbal, 8 A.M.–6 P.M. daily, US$1) is a 25-meter waterfall pouring out the mouth of a cave, partway up a soaring stone cliff. A slippery pathway climbs up into the *gruta* (cave), where you can walk about 50 meters to the edge of a dark interior lagoon fed by another waterfall. It's no Victoria Falls, but an interesting sight nonetheless, and a popular local getaway on hot days, with several swimming holes and a small restaurant and bathrooms (albeit pretty grubby). El Chorreadero is the end of a nearly 3-kilometer underground journey of the Río Escopetzo; there's a surprisingly good map, with explanations in Spanish and English, near the entrance.

To get there by car from Chiapa de Corzo, take the *carretera libre* (free highway) toward San Cristóbal to the well-marked turnoff. Otherwise, *combis* marked Chorreadero, Bochil, or Ixtapa will drop you at the turnoff (US$1, 15 mins); from there, it's another kilometer downhill to the entrance.

The *combis* can be caught in Chiapa de Corzo near the Pemex gas station or the Monumento Chiapaneca y Parachico (statues of two traditional costumed dancers), both several blocks from the central plaza.

Chiapa de Corzo Archaeological Zone

Archaeologically speaking, the Chiapa de Corzo ruins are one of the most significant sites in central Chiapas, but you'd never know it from looking at its various sections. Clustered in the northeast corner of town, the site receives little attention or priority; one major structure is literally the median of a major intersection.

According to studies, the site was occupied from 1400 B.C. to around A.D. 700, a remarkably long period. It was the region's most influential settlement in the early Pre-Classic era (800–450 B.C.), controlling trade routes along Río Grijalva and into the highlands. Archaeologists have found artifacts here from Guatemala, El Salvador, Oaxaca, Campeche, Yucatán, Tabasco, and Veracruz.

The site is composed of mostly low platforms and foundations, around 200 in all, scattered over two square kilometers; many homes in this area have unexcavated structures in their backyards. The main visitation area includes **Montículo 1** (a six-meter-high pyramidlike structure with remains of a temple on top) and **Montículo 5** (a large residential complex); another structure, Montículo 32, is enclosed in a traffic circle at the northeast exit of town, and probably served a ceremonial purpose. The site was undergoing extensive renovation at the time of research, which hopefully will improve its presentation and accessibility.

CHIAPA DE CORZO ARCHAEOLOGICAL ZONE

To El Chorreadero and San Cristóbal (via old highway)

To Tuxtla Gutiérrez and San Cristóbal (via toll road)

MONTÍCULO 26

LIBRAMENTO NORTE

MONTÍCULO 32

CARRETERA INTERNACIONAL

AV LÁZARO CÁRDENAS

To Chiapa de Corzo center

AV EMILIO CARRANZA

CALLE LA LIBERTAD

CALLE FCO. SARABIA

AV HIDALGO

MONTÍCULO 73

MUNICIPAL CEMETERY

ENTRANCE TO RUINS

MONTÍCULO 5

MONTÍCULO 1

© AVALON TRAVEL

SCALE NOT AVAILABLE

ENTERTAINMENT AND EVENTS

Chiapa de Corzo's biggest celebration, the **Festival de San Sebastián**, takes place January 8–23 every year. The festival has many facets, but the highlight are the *parachicos:* boys and men swathed in colorful blankets and colonial Spanish garb, carrying tin rattles and wearing wood pink-skinned masks and a huge dome of yellow "hair." Accompanied by women in extravagant flowered dresses carrying lacquered gourds, the *parachicos* dance and cavort in rowdy processions around the city center, especially on January 15, 17, 18, 20 (the biggest day), and 22. Legend has it that the festival arose after an ailing Spanish boy was cured by Saint Sebastian, and his mother threw a huge celebration *para el chico* ("for the boy"), from which today's term is derived.

The San Sebastián festival is a special—and popular—time to be in Chiapa de Corzo; some visitors stay for the entire two weeks. No matter how long you plan to stay, definitely reserve your hotel well in advance; for those who don't get a hotel room (most don't), *colectivos* to and from Tuxtla run even later than usual.

ACCOMMODATIONS

Chiapa de Corzo sees few overnight visitors, as most of the attractions can be taken in on a day trip. The exception is during the San Sebastián festivities in January, for which hotels are booked a month or more in advance.

A long way from California, but right on the plaza, **Hotel Los Ángeles** (Calle Mexicanidad and Av. Julian Grajáles, tel. 961/616-0048, US$28 s/d with fan, US$33 s/d with a/c) offers spotless rooms, albeit somewhat small and plain, all with cable TV and hot-water bathrooms, in a pleasant colonial-style building. There's free Wi-Fi in the lobby and 1st-floor rooms, and the hotel's small restaurant is recommended. Potted plants help spruce up the common areas, and upper-floor rooms face a bright open-air corridor.

A block from the plaza, **Hotel Posada Real** (Av. Julian Grajáles 192, tel. 961/616-1015, hotelposadareal@hotmail.com.mx, US$34/40 s/d, US$46 d/q) has large, welcoming rooms with gleaming tile floors, air-conditioning, wireless Internet, and cable TV. Less well known than other hotels in town, it nevertheless strikes a good balance between comfort and value, with friendly service to boot.

La Ceiba (Av. Domingo Ruiz 300, tel. 961/616-0389, US$58/64/70 s/d/t) is considered the best hotel in town, but may be resting a bit too much on its laurels. The grounds are certainly lovely, with palms, banana trees, and other tropical plants. And it's the only hotel with a pool—located a bit too close to reception, but heaven on a hot day. Rooms are spacious and clean, but in need of a serious face-lift, especially the springy beds and plain bathrooms. La Ceiba is located two long blocks from the central park.

FOOD

A phalanx of overpriced look-alike restaurants at the embarcadero employ aggressive waiters and competing marimba bands, all in an attempt to corral tourists going to or from boat trips down the canyon. Eateries in town are mellower, and offer a better value.

Part of the Hotel Los Ángeles, **Parachic's Cafetería** (Calle Mexicanidad and Av. Julian Grajáles, 7 A.M.–10:30 P.M. Wed.–Mon., 7 A.M.–3 P.M. Tues., US$3.50–6) has a bright appealing dining area, with cantaloupe-colored walls and pretty iron-and-wood settings. An open-air corridor with tables in the back looks onto the hotel's parking lot, but gets nice air and light nonetheless. It serves simple tasty meals, like beef stuffed chiles rellenos, mole enchiladas, and spicy pork tacos, and has a good lunch deal: soup, main dish, and a drink for US$4.50.

Facing the central plaza, **Los Corredores** (Calle Francisco Madero 35, tel. 961/616-0760, 9 A.M.–7 P.M. daily) has reasonably good food and a pleasant setting, especially in the rear garden area. The restaurant is best known for beef and pork dishes prepared with *pepita*, a thick spicy sauce made from pumpkin seeds.

INFORMATION AND SERVICES

Tourist Information

Just off the central plaza is the state tourism office (Av. Domingo Ruiz at 5 de Febrero, tel. 961/616-1013, 8 A.M.–4 P.M. Mon.–Fri.); the eager-to-please staff also have an **information desk** (9 A.M.–3 P.M. Tues.–Fri.) inside an *artesanía* shop on Calle 5 de Febrero, the road leading down to the embarcadero.

Emergency Services

The **Centro de Salud** (Calle 21 de Octubre at Calle Iturbide, tel. 961/616-0205, 24 hours) is your best option in a medical emergency. **Farmacia Esperanza** (Calle 21 de Octubre btwn. Calles Mexicanidad and Tomás Cuesta, tel. 961/616-0454, 7 A.M.–11 P.M. daily) is one of several pharmacies near the central plaza.

Money

There's no shortage of banks in Chiapa de Corzo. **Bancomer** (Calle Mexicanidad, 8:30 A.M.–4 P.M. Mon.–Fri.) is right on the central plaza and has reliable ATMs, while HSBC and Banamex are nearby and open similar hours.

Media and Communications

For Internet try **Turbonet Xtreme** (Calle Mexicanidad 11-A, 8 A.M.–10 P.M. daily, US$0.75/hr), a block north of the central plaza. For international calls, you're best off using a Ladatel card at a public pay phone; cards can be purchased at corner stores and pharmacies.

GETTING THERE AND AROUND

Long-distance buses from Tuxtla and San Cristóbal do not enter or even stop at Chiapa de Corzo, leaving *colectivos* to provide service there.

From Tuxtla Gutiérrez: *Colectivos* to Chiapa de Corzo leave every 10 minutes 6 A.M.–10 P.M. from the corner of 5 Calle Oriente Sur and 1 Avenida Sur Poniente (US$1, 40 mins), and drop passengers on the north side of Chiapa de Corzo's central plaza. The same buses return to Tuxtla, picking up passengers on the opposite side of the street.

From San Cristóbal: Take any Tuxtla-bound *colectivo* (US$3, 45 mins) from the stop on the Carretera Panamericana near the ADO bus terminal. They follow roughly the same schedule as the *colectivos* but don't enter Chiapa de Corzo; instead you'll be dropped on the highway near a pedestrian bridge—cross the bridge and catch a local *colectivo* into town (US$0.45). To return, catch a bus or taxi to the same spot, where San Cristóbal–bound *colectivos* pass frequently.

Around town, taxis typically charge US$2, or US$3 to the highway bus stop.

Ruta Zoque

Northwest of Tuxtla is the state's hinterland, a hot, dry region long defined by the meanderings of the mighty Río Grijalva. This little-traveled area is best known for the impressive colonial churches and convents built by Dominican missionaries in the early (and most optimistic) years of the conquest. Their host towns are decidedly modest—quaint, slow-moving communities with precious little in the way of hotels and other services, though charming in their own right. Although called the Ruta Zoque (Zoque Route), little survives of Chiapas's earliest culture, which grew to prominence in this same river valley.

HISTORY

The Zoque indigenous group emerged as a distinct entity around 1000 B.C.; descendants of the Olmecs, Mesoamerica's first civilization, they occupied the rich river valleys of the Río Grijalva, in present-day western and northwestern Chiapas. Today's cities of Chiapa de Corzo, Ocozocoautla, Jiquipilas, and Tonalá all grew from what were once Zoque strongholds. The

Río Grijalva was a vital trade corridor between central Mexico and Central America, and the Zoques naturally formed strong commercial ties—and sometimes fierce rivalries—with neighboring groups. The Zoques were invaded several times, notably by the Chiapas, arriving from the north around A.D. 1000, then by the Aztecs several centuries later, and finally by the Spanish in the mid-1500s.

In modern times, this stretch of the Río Grijalva has drawn the focus of government planners and civil engineers, who constructed not one but two massive hydroelectric dams—and a third further upriver in the center of the state—plus the graceful Puente Chiapas, which connects Chiapas to Veracruz, Mexico City, and beyond.

CHICOASÉN

The town of Chicoasén is less well known than is the nearby hydroelectric dam that borrowed its name and helped to create the popular Cañón del Sumidero waterway (not to mention a large part of Mexico's energy supply). A scenic view of the canyon and a small 17th-century church are the main attractions here, but really only worth a stop if you have a car and extra time. Boat trips along the canyon are possible from the neighboring town of Usumacinta, but are more convenient from Chiapa de Corzo. The dam is an engineering marvel—at 260 meters high, it's one of Mexico's largest—but is under military guard and off-limits to visitors.

Mirador Manos Que Imploran

On the other side of the dam from Chicoasén, a narrow road descends 2.5 kilometers from the highway to Mirador Manos Que Imploran (Imploring Hands Overlook). The vista is impressive, especially southward into the mouth of the canyon, where you can see passenger boats plying the water far below. Unfortunately it's also a favorite haunt of ornery *zopilotes* (black vultures), which have to be shooed off the platform before you can enjoy the view.

The turnoff is unmarked, but not hard to spot. Coming from Tuxtla, it's about 1.5 kilometers after the tunnel, before you reach the dam, and about 10 kilometers south of Chicoasén proper. The road is paved, but steep and winding in places.

Templo del Señor del Pozo

This tiny church, located at the end of Chicoasén's curiously narrow central plaza, was built at the end of the 17th century as a temporary residence for visiting friars. The facade was reconstructed in 1962, but the interior walls and arches are original, having been rescued from collapse in 2005 as part of a campaign to restore historic structures in the Zoque region.

COPAINALÁ

Copainalá is a tidy little town built on opposing banks of a steep *barranca*, or river gully. It's backed by squat hills and high west-facing cliffs that glow red at sunset. Its central plaza is long and narrow—to make it any wider would require tiers—with a basketball court, tree-shaded benches, and small shops and eateries around the edges. The town is home to a beautiful colonial church—the main reason to stop—and a short drive from a small lake with swimming and boating. Copainalá celebrates its patron saint, San Miguel del Archangel, September 26–29.

Templo San Miguel del Archangel

Construction of Copainalá's distinctive San Miguel del Archangel church and convent (Calle Central, 9 A.M.–2 P.M. and 5–8 P.M. Mon.–Fri., 9 A.M.–8 P.M. Sat.–Sun.) began in the 1570s and took nearly a century to complete. The church later fell into such disrepair that locals began calling it *la ruína* (the ruin), a name still used today despite extensive restoration in 2001. The church's bell tower is a classic example of Mudejar (Arab-Iberian) architecture, with its imposing square design and intricate brickwork. A spiral staircase is enclosed in a curious brick column on the tower's south face (alongside an unusually dramatic false archway), though visitors are rarely permitted to climb to the top. The nave's high stone walls are original, save the fresh coat of stucco, and have minimal adornment; the altar is also rather austere, featuring a simple—albeit huge—wooden cross.

Museo Comunitario

Though fairly amateurish, Copainalá's small community museum (opposite Templo San Miguel, tel. 968/661-0174, 10 A.M.–5:30 P.M. Mon.–Fri., free) has a handful of noteworthy archaeological pieces, including clay masks related to Zoque jaguar cults, and costumes and photos from Copainalá's numerous festivals. For Spanish speakers, the museum's soft-spoken attendant can explain the stories woven into many local events, like the unique *weya weya* dance marking the beginning of Carnaval.

Accommodations

Hotel Levi (Calle Central 31, tel. 968/131-4075, US$12 d with fan, US$18 d with fan and TV, US$30 with a/c and TV) is the better of Copainalá's two hotels, but that's not saying much. The location is great—a half block from San Miguel church—and the lobby is warm and appealing; the rooms, however, have worn beds and dreary cement walls, and get incredibly stuffy, making air-conditioning all but essential.

TECPATÁN

In 1564, Dominican missionaries chose present-day Tecpatán, then a small Zoque village with a rudimentary church, to serve as the region's primary mission and convent. Construction of the massive church and convent lasted nearly 50 years and required the work of thousands of Zoque laborers, drawn from all over the region. Many settled here permanently along with their families, turning the modest village into a veritable indigenous city; even today Tecpatán dubs itself the Capital of the Zoque Empire. As in Copainalá, the church and convent fell into disrepair during the liberal reform period of the late 1800s, and reopened in 1951. The church is a highlight of the Ruta Zoque, and

Tecpatán itself is a friendly and mellow place, built in the foothills connecting the hot Río Grijalva valley and the mountains of northwest Chiapas.

Templo y Ex-Convento Santo Domingo de Guzmán

Santo Domingo de Guzmán Church and Convent (Calle Central at 1a Calle Nte., 9 A.M.–2 P.M. and 4–7 P.M. Mon.–Fri., 9 A.M.–noon Sun., free) is one of Chiapas's finest colonial structures, combining elements of Mudejar, medieval, and Renaissance design. It is a huge complex, including the ruined church, a lovely convent, and ornate facade and bell tower facing a large grassy esplanade used by local schools for soccer practice.

A low arched passageway serves as the complex's main entrance; it leads into the courtyard of the former convent—the only colonial-era cloister in Chiapas whose original structure is still standing. (In fact, it's in much better shape than the church, thanks to extensive restoration.) The atrium is encircled by two floors of open-air corridors, with colonnades and ornate vaulted ceilings, and connected by a distinctive spiral staircase.

A doorway in the convent's south arcade leads into the remains of the once-grandiose main church. The roof has long since collapsed, but a series of brick arches span the deep gaping nave, including a double arch at the west end that would have supported a choir loft, and are covered in moss and leafy vines. A large pretty archway and partial dome cover the remains of the curiously modest altar space.

Santo Domingo's facade and bell tower must have been truly arresting in their heyday—even now, much deteriorated, they remain an impressive sight. The facade is fairly austere—sturdy Tuscan pilasters frame the arched main and upper doorways, with relatively little adornment—but rises imperiously from its raised esplanade, and was originally covered in stucco. The bell tower climbs even higher, with cylindrical and polygonal towers at its corners and a vaulted medieval-style belfry on top. A spiral staircase in the center of the main tower is typically locked, but the *padre* has the key and might be convinced to let you up for a peek.

Accommodations

Hospedaje Helachos (Calle 1a Nte. at Calle Central, tel. 968/653-3191, US$12 s/d with shared bathroom, US$15 s/d) has extremely simple rooms and furnishings, including cold-water bathrooms and not much natural light. Small TVs, friendly service, and a good location—just a half block from Santo Domingo—are some consolation.

GETTING THERE AND AROUND

A rental car makes touring the Ruta Zoque significantly easier and faster. The road is fairly well maintained, although narrow and windy in places, and armed with countless *topes* (speed bumps), many unmarked. Otherwise, *combis* and small buses leave from Tuxtla's Terminal de los Ancianos (9 Av. Sur Ote. at 13 Calle Ote. Sur) bound for Chicoasén, Copainalá, and Tecpatán. Tecpatán buses stop at all the preceding towns, but at the highway turnoff only.

THE PACIFIC COAST

Pacific coast? What Pacific coast? Between exploring the cool highlands of San Cristóbal, the dry plateau around Tuxtla Gutiérrez, and the sweaty rainforest outside Palenque, it's easy to forget that Chiapas even *has* a coastal region, let alone hundreds of miles of sparkling grey-black sand and tangled mangrove forests. There are even Maya ruins and a cruise ship port—whodathunkit?

Of course, beach towns like Puerto Arista and Boca del Cielo are very well known to local residents of Tuxtla, who flock there on weekends and holidays to escape the inland heat. Some foreign travelers do the same, especially midweek which tends to be much less hectic. You can also beat weekend crowds by heading to lesser-known beach spots, like Costa Azul outside Pijijiapán, just an hour further down the coast.

But even lifelong Chiapanecans are surprised to learn just how much the coastal region has to offer. The mangrove forests near Barra de Zacapulco, part of a massive biosphere reserve, are the tallest in Latin America, soaring to over 25 meters (80 feet) and forming tangled waterways that make for memorable tours. Chiapas's coast is also a major nesting zone for sea turtles, with several centers where travelers can join nighttime beach patrols or help release hatchlings back into the sea. And there are myriad opportunities for fishing, bird-watching, kayaking, and more.

Venturing inland, the coastal region has even more surprises—and rewards. It's one of Mexico's top coffee-producing areas, and travelers can visit working organic coffee *fincas* (plantations), with cozy guest rooms and fascinating tours. For something more adventuresome, the

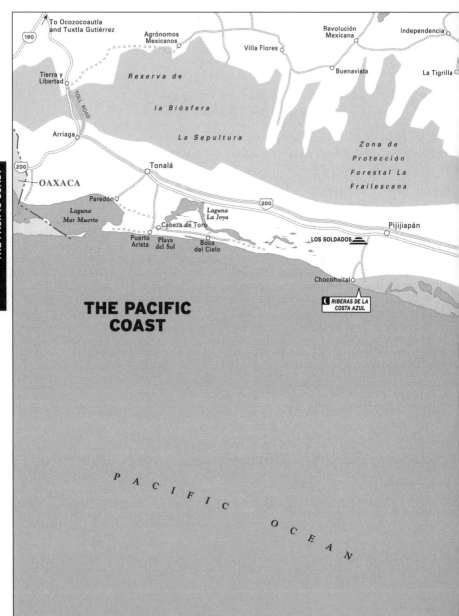

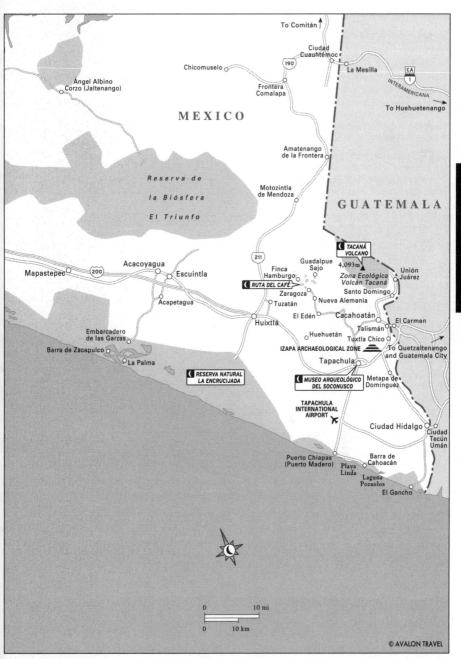

THE PACIFIC COAST

HIGHLIGHTS

◖ **Riberas de la Costa Azul:** Beat the crowds at Puerto Arista by heading just down the coast to the Costa Azul, with broad gray-black sand, calmer water, and beachside *palapas* serving the freshest of seafood. Camp on the beach or stay in the bustling town of Pijijiapán, about 20 kilometers inland (page 180).

◖ **Reserva Natural La Encrucijada:** Barra de Zacapulco is the jumping-off point for boat tours into this impressive nature reserve, home to birds, crocs, and the tallest mangrove trees in Latin America – 25 meters (80 feet) or more. Join nighttime sea turtle patrols or just relax on the wide windswept beach (page 182).

◖ **Museo Arqueológico del Soconusco:** An excellent collection of artifacts, from pottery to musical instruments to stone monu-

ments, helps showcase the rich culture and history of Izapa and other ancient Pacific-coast cities. Kids will get a kick out of the stelae rubbings and vocabulary games too (page 185).

◖ **Tacaná Volcano:** Nearly 4,100 meters (13,120 feet) and still classified as active, Tacaná makes for a challenging three-day climb, with stunning views of the Pacific and the distant peaks in both Mexico and Guatemala as a reward for reaching the cool, bare summit (page 194).

◖ **Ruta del Café:** Journey into the heart of Chiapanecan coffee country – and one of the state's most scenic areas – where you can spend the night at centuries-old coffee plantations, see how the beans are harvested and processed, and of course sample some of the world-famous end product (page 196).

LOOK FOR ◖ TO FIND RECOMMENDED SIGHTS, ACTIVITIES, DINING, AND LODGING.

three-day ascent of Volcán Tacaná is one of Chiapas's best—and least known—hikes. Even the bustling border city of Tapachula has some unexpected charm, from the lively central plaza to a startlingly good restaurant scene.

PLANNING YOUR TIME

Most people spend just a few days or a weekend on the Pacific coast, though there's plenty to see and do to fill a week or more.

For a quick beach break, Puerto Arista and Boca del Cielo are logical choices. Costa Azul is another possibility—more isolated and scenic, but lacking lodging on the beach; unless you're camping, the nearest bed is in Pijijiapán.

With more time, consider basing yourself in Tapachula for two to three days; one day to explore the city itself, including the archaeological museum and excellent restaurants, and another day or two to visit nearby sights like the Maya ruins of Izapa and the beach at Barra de Cahoacán.

From Tapachula, several overnight trips are possible, including to Barra de Zacapulco, where you can take a boat tour through the impressive mangrove forests and enjoy the wide clean beach, or to La Ruta del Café, where you could spend up to three days touring various working coffee *fincas*.

Climbing Tacaná Volcano is a goal for many who come to this area; it's typically a three-day outing, starting from the small town of Union Juárez.

Tonalá

Hot and busy, though not unpleasant, Tonalá is the hub of the coastal region's ranching and agricultural activity, and known in particular as the mango capital of Chiapas for the extensive mango orchards nearby. For travelers, Tonalá is probably better known as a gateway—or at least a turnoff—to the beach towns of Puerto Arista and Boca del Cielo. It's also a practical and agreeable place to break up a trip, with reliable hotels, restaurants, and bus service, and an attractive central plaza.

SIGHTS
Parque La Esperanza
Tonalá's central square is spacious and lively, shaded by palm and mango trees, and a hub for school kids, businesspeople, and travelers alike. Look for a tall stone monolith; it's a stela depicting Tlaloc, the Aztec god of rain and fertility, found at the nearby Horcones archaeological site.

Casa de Cultura
Halfway between Parque La Esperanza and the bus station, Tonalá's Casa de Cultura (Av. Hidalgo btwn. Calles 15 de Mayo and Miguel López Negrete, 10 A.M.–4 P.M. Mon.–Fri., free) houses a modest archeological museum, with a small number of artifacts from Iglesia Vieja and other archaeological sites in the area, plus a collection of work by the noted Chiapanecan ceramicist Rodolfo Disner.

ACCOMMODATIONS
Tonalá is a frequent and logical stop for business travelers, and as a result the hotels in town tend to be long on services and short on charm. Bear in mind that these hotels (and most others on or near the coast) can double in price during vacation season.

Hotel Grajandra (Av. Hidalgo 204, tel. 966/663-0148, US$45 s/d with a/c) has large rooms with red tile floors and attractive bathrooms, complemented by friendly professional service and a load of amenities, including in-room Wi-Fi and telephones, cable TV, air-conditioning, a swimming pool, restaurant, and parking. Just a half block from the ADO terminal, it's super convenient for those traveling by bus, but five long blocks from the central square.

Hotel Galilea (Av. Hidalgo 111, tel. 966/663-0239, US$30/40 s/d with a/c) is as centrally located as you can get, occupying a historic building right on Tonalá's lively main square. Rooms are a bit dated—old-school TVs, air-conditioning, etc.—but beds are comfy and the service friendly. Parking, wireless Internet, and a reliable restaurant are additional pluses.

FOOD
The restaurant at **Hotel Galilea** (Av. Hidalgo 111, tel. 966/663-0239, 7 A.M.–10 P.M. daily, US$4–8) has indoor seating, plus a handful of tables beneath an open-air patio overlooking the main plaza. Dishes are simple and straightforward, including eggs, roast chicken, and fish fillets, all well prepared.

Taquería el Gallito (Av. Hidalgo at Calle 30 de Julio, 6 P.M.–3 A.M. daily, US$0.50 apiece) is a classic after-hours taco joint, serving up cheap tasty tacos at plastic tables, with a TV tuned to a soccer match and ceiling fans pushing around the hot air.

INFORMATION AND SERVICES

Most services can be found on or near the central plaza. **Banamex** (Av. Hidalgo at Calle Oriente) has a reliable ATM machine, and **Caseta Cristy** (Av. Rayon at Calle Francisco Madero, 9 A.M.–10 P.M. daily) is a good place to check email (US$1/hr) and make inexpensive long-distance phone calls (US$0.20–0.40/min to U.S., Canada, and Europe).

GETTING THERE AND AROUND
Bus

Tonalá's main bus terminal (Av. Hidalgo at Calle 12 de Octubre, tel. 966/663-0540) is six blocks west of the center of town, and has service to:

- Arriaga: (US$2, 30 mins) take any Tuxtla bus

- Cintalapa: (US$6.25, 1.5 hrs) take any Tuxtla bus

- Pijijiapán: (US$5.50, 1 hr) take any Tapachula bus

- Tapachula: (US$14.50–17.50, 3.5 hrs) 5 A.M., 5:40 A.M., 6:20 A.M., and every 1–3 hours 9:15 A.M.–7:45 P.M.

- Tuxtla Gutiérrez: (US$11–13, 3 hrs) 5 A.M., 6 A.M., 9:05 A.M., and every 1–2 hours noon–8:50 P.M.

Combi

Combis provide service to the beach. Those to Puerto Arista (US$1.20, 30 mins) leave every 15 minutes from a stop on Avenida Matamoros between Calles 5 de Mayo and 20 de Marzo, about five blocks southeast of the center. For Boca del Cielo (US$2, 1 hr) the stop is one block down, on Avenida Juárez between the same cross streets. Both run roughly every 15–30 minutes from 5:30 A.M. to 6 P.M.

Puerto Arista

Though it's a popular getaway for Chiapanecans from Tonalá and Tuxtla, the beaches and facilities at Puerto Arista aren't exactly glorious. This one-street town has a handful of basic hotels and simple *palapa* restaurants. The beach itself is ashy volcanic sand and the surf can be quite heavy, but it makes a mellow place to kick back for a day or two. Puerto Arista is one of those vacation towns that's either packed— say, during Semana Santa or Christmas—or utterly dead.

SIGHTS
Campamento Tortuguero Nuevo Puerto Arista

This state-sponsored turtle protection and preservation program (no phone, 8 A.M.–5 P.M. daily) is one of four installations in the area (the others are in Boca del Cielo, Costa Azul, and Barra de Zacapulco). It's essentially operated by one person, whose main activities are

patrolling the beach by foot and ATV in search of fresh turtle nests (whose eggs are relocated to protected enclosures) and *liberación* (releasing) of hatchlings back into the sea. Travelers are welcome to participate; beach patrols are about three hours long and depart between 7 and 11 P.M., while hatchling releases take place at low tide, usually between 6 and 11 P.M. Both take place year-round, but July to November is peak nesting season, and hatchlings are most numerous May to October. The *campamento* is located 2.5 kilometers (1.5 miles) west of town, just before Villa Murano hotel; stop by beforehand for the night's schedule.

Playa del Sol

Playa del Sol sees surprisingly few visitors, especially considering it's just two kilometers (1.2 miles) east of Puerto Arista, and easier to get to than Boca del Cielo. A broad scenic beach, Playa del Sol is ideal for beachcombing and

SEA TURTLES

Four of the world's eight sea turtle species nest on Chiapanecan shores – olive Ridley, hawksbill, Pacific green, and leatherback. All eight species are endangered in Mexico, due mostly to a combination of antiquated fishing practices, beachfront development that has destroyed nesting grounds, and a taste for turtle meat and eggs. Until recently their meat, fat, and eggs were a common supplement to the regional diet. In Mexico, killing sea turtles for food has waned considerably – just a generation ago, turtle soup was popular from Baja to Chiapas – but poaching remains a serious problem thanks to a widespread belief that raw sea turtle eggs, eaten with lime and pinch of salt, are a natural aphrodisiac.

Chiapas's state government has set up four centers to help protect sea turtles and their habitats. At the centers in Puerto Arista, Boca del Cielo, Riberas de la Costa Azul, and Barra de Zacapulco, biologists maintain close surveillance of known nesting grounds to find eggs and relocate them to protected enclosures; once hatched, the turtles are released back into the sea. Volunteers are welcome to participate in either of these tasks. Beyond this, travelers can help protect sea turtles simply by refusing to purchase items like tortoise-shell jewelry or foods made with their meat.

long lazy walks, or just relaxing on the sand watching fishermen pull their boats ashore to unload the day's catch. Like everywhere along this coast, the surf can be quite rough here; take care wading or swimming.

A clutch of beachfront *palapa* restaurants serve fresh seafood for virtually identical prices, around US$5–10 for a large plate. **Mary Mar,** on the right-hand side where the access road hits the beach, has hammocks and a small clean wading pool—great for kids when the surf is high. A few sandy lots to the left, **El Navigante** is another good choice, with a friendly proprietor. **Camping** is allowed (and free) at most of the *palapas* here, provided you eat there, and includes use of the bathrooms and showers, if they've got them.

To drive to Playa del Sol from Puerto Arista, head back toward Tonalá about two kilometers (1 mile) to the Boca del Cielo turnoff; turn right and continue about 2.5 kilometers (1.5 miles) to the village of Cabeza de Toro, where there's a sign and turn-off to Playa del Sol about halfway through town. A well-marked turnoff leads another 1.5 kilometers (1 mile) to the beach. You can also catch one of the **ATV taxis** that trundle up and down the beach between Puerto Arista and Playa del Sol (US$3 pp), or rent one yourself in either place (US$10/hr).

Laguna La Joya

You might never know it from just driving around, but the coast here is backed by a massive crescent-shaped lagoon known as Laguna La Joya, extending well inland from Puerto Arista to past Boca del Cielo. Fringed by low trees and tangled wetlands, it's home to countless water birds, not to mention a significant amount of the fish caught and sold here. There are no official tours of the lagoon, but local fishermen occasionally take visitors on fishing or bird-watching tours, and the lagoon itself, a rippling expanse of blue with the jagged spine of the Sierra Madre rising abruptly in the distance, has a striking beauty. You should be able to find a willing guide along the waterfront in the village of Cabeza de Toro, on the road toward Boca del Cielo. (Coming from Puerto Arista, turn in at the large water tower.) A two-or-three-hour outing should cost around US$45; try to pass by in the morning to arrange an afternoon tour.

ACCOMMODATIONS AND FOOD

Prices fluctuate considerably between weekend and midweek, and rainy and dry season, and especially during holidays. The prices listed below are weekend rates during the dry season; midweek and rainy season rates are around

40 percent lower, while peak periods, especially Semana Santa and around Christmas, can be considerably higher.

By far the best value in Puerto Arista is ◖ **Hotel Lucero** (El Boulevard, tel. 994/600-9042, www.hotel-lucero.com, US$40 s/d with a/c), located about 800 meters east of the main intersection. Straddling the boulevard, the hotel's guest rooms, reception, and two gleaming swimming pools are on the inland side, while the sand-floor restaurant and two more pools—that's four in all!—face the beach. Rooms are a bit plain, but spacious and extremely clean, with TV and air-conditioning; upstairs units have partial ocean views. The hotel offers friendly service and secure parking.

Hotel Arista Bugambilias (El Boulevard, tel. 994/600-9044, US$60 d with a/c) is Puerto Arista's best known and most upscale hotel, but with some peculiar flaws, like tiny rooms and foam pads on the beds instead of regular mattresses. Air-conditioning and TVs are pluses, and the grounds are lovely, with a small appealing pool and a restaurant overlooking the ocean. Then again, you expect those things—and a bit more—for this price.

Run by a friendly Canadian ex-pat, **José's Camping y Cabañas** (El Boulevard, left of main intersection, tel. 994/600-9048, US$3 pp camping, US$7 pp dorm, US$20 s/d with shared bath, US$29 s/d with private bath) has a mellow atmosphere and Puerto Arista's cheapest digs, including camping, a dorm-style cabaña, and simple private cabins with shared bathroom. (Units with private bathroom are also available, but aren't much cheaper than staying on the beach in town.) *Cabañas* are tidy, though a bit dark, all with fan, screened windows, and a *palapa*-covered sitting area. There's a small pool, and good fresh meals are prepared on request. The large leafy grounds are a block inland from the beach and about one kilometer from the center of town. To reach José's Camping y Cabañas from the main intersection, turn left at the Hotel Lucero.

Hotel Aguamarina (El Boulevard at 2 Calle Pte, right of the main intersection, tel. 994/600-9018, US$25–50 s/d with fan, US$35–58 s/d with a/c) is one of numerous look-alike two-star hotels facing the beach along Puerto Arista's main drag. While far from deluxe, the Aguamarina is marginally better than the others, with reasonably clean rooms, reliable fans, and air-conditioning. There's also a small pool and a restaurant serving decent meals under a beachfront *palapa*. Parking is available, though the hotel's location—just a block west of the main intersection—makes it convenient for those arriving by *combi* as well.

For eats, walk down the main drag and see what looks appealing—fresh seafood is the specialty everywhere.

INFORMATION AND SERVICES

If it's actually open during its posted business hours, **Plaza Puerto Arista** (El Boulevard, 9 A.M.–4 P.M. daily) has an ATM and an Internet café (US$1/hr). It is located to the right of the main intersection, opposite Hotel Arista Bugambilias. Beyond that, there aren't any other traveler services in town.

GETTING THERE AND AROUND

Puerta Arista is essentially a one-road town, so it's nearly impossible to get lost. The main road runs along the beachfront and goes by various names, including Boulevard Zapotal or Avenida Mariano Matamoros, but most people refer to it as simply El Boulevard. Street numbers are equally variable—for simplicity, addresses are listed here as either east or west of the main intersection, where the road from Tonalá hits the boulevard.

Car

Coming from Tuxtla Gutiérrez on Highway 200, the Puerto Arista exit is just past Tonalá, and well marked. From there it's another 16 kilometers to town and the beach.

Bus

Combis and collective taxis to and from Tonalá (US$1.25, 45 mins) pick up and drop off near the main intersection in Puerto Arista, departing every 15–30 minutes from 5:30 A.M. to 7 P.M. daily. There is no direct service from Puerto Arista to Boca del Cielo; instead, you have to wait at the Boca del Cielo turnoff (about 2 kilometers from Puerto Arista) for a *combi* or taxi from Tonalá.

BOCA DEL CIELO

About 15 kilometers (9 miles) down the coast is Boca del Cielo, set on a narrow spit of sand separated from the mainland by a shallow inlet. It is far less developed than Puerto Arista, with sand-floor restaurant-*posadas*, (known as *palapas*) instead of modern hotels, and a quieter, more laid-back scene. Still, Boca del Cielo's proximity to Tuxtla means it gets crowded on many weekends and holidays, and prices are higher than one might expect.

Sights
BEACH
Boca del Cielo's main draw is its beach—a broad expanse of grey-black sand that extends for what seems like forever in either direction. Like much of Chiapas's coastline, the beach appears desolate at first, but has a sparkling scenic beauty that grows on you. The beach has fewer visitors and less boat traffic than at Puerto Arista, not to mention fewer vendors and less litter. Although the ocean here can be equally rough, the inlet offers safer swimming and wading, especially for kids. (Just be alert for boats and strong currents, mainly near the mouth of the inlet.)

CAMPAMENTO TORTUGUERO BOCA DEL CIELO
Another of the four sea turtle protection installations along this coast (no phone, 8 A.M.–5 P.M. daily) (others are in Puerto Arista, Costa Azul, and Barra de Zacapulco), this one's run by a friendly two-person team. The program does nightly beach patrols in search of fresh nests (around 7–11 P.M.) and frequent hatchling releases (around 5–7 P.M.). Tourists are welcome to take part in either; drop by during the day to sign up, and the staffers will swing by your *palapa* that evening. The most active months

are July to November for beach patrols, and May to October for hatchling releases.

Accommodations and Food
There's no shortage of *cabañas*—or *palapas* as they are called—in Boca del Cielo, lined up shoulder to shoulder on the sandy spit facing the open ocean. Most are quite dreary, unfortunately, but a handful seem to make an extra effort to keep their rooms clean and pleasant. If you've got camping gear, virtually all *palapas* allow you to pitch a tent and use their restrooms, as long as you agree to also eat your meals there during your stay.

Palapa y Cabañas Érika (tel. 966/664-7230, US$23 s/d with shared bathroom, US$33 s/d with private bathroom, US$45 s/d with private bathroom and a/c) is one of Boca del Cielo's nicest options, especially with the addition of a handful of new cement air-conditioned rooms in 2009. Standard *cabañas* are far from luxurious, but are comfortable and tidy, with electric fans, palm walls, and mosquito nets. Expect friendly service too.

Next door, **Palapa Los Demetrio** (tel. 966/106-9471, US$23 s/d) also has new cement-constructed units, with clean shared bathrooms and a long covered patio with hammocks. Older rooms have private bathrooms, but are worn out and less appealing.

Palapa El Delfín (tel. 966/664-7012 or 966/664-5898, US$25 s/d) has just four *cabañas,* all with private bathrooms and two queen beds. The mattresses are a bit springy, but en suite bathrooms are something of a rarity in these parts.

Cabañas La Luna (tel. 966/100-9509, lunachiapaneca@gmail.com, US$15 d) is located at the far end of the beach, with very simple wood cabins with shared bath, *palapa* roofs, and bright exterior paint. Pedal boats are available for rent to explore the mangroves on the lagoon side.

Getting There and Around
Boca del Cielo is 15 kilometers east of Puerto Arista; there's a well-marked turnoff about two kilometers north of Puerto Arista (and 14

kilometers south from Highway 200). From there it's 16 kilometers to a second turnoff, which leads a kilometer more to Boca del Cielo's main embarcadero.

Combis and collective taxis come and go from the embarcadero parking lot (aka *el caracol*) every 30–60 minutes from 5:30 A.M. to 6 P.M. daily. It's US$1.25 to the Puerto Arista turnoff (20 mins), and US$1.75 (1 hr) to Tonalá.

Motorboats, or *lanchas,* shuttle passengers across the narrow lagoon separating the mainland from the beach and oceanfront *palapas.* The fixed rate is a ridiculous US$7—it's all of 90 meters—but the return trip is customarily paid for by the *palapa* where you eat or stay.

Pijijiapán

Somehow Pijijiapán (pronounced pee-hee-hee-a-PAN) got the reputation for being the Pacific coast's most charming town, a quiet and whimsical place with crayon-colored homes topped by red tile roofs. In reality, this small city is rather less enchanting than that; while not unpleasant, it's a bustling knot of homes and businesses with architecture that owes more to the '50s and '70s than the colonial era. The town's primary church and plaza have been nicely renovated, but are strangely isolated in a corner of town at the top of a hill—few people, tourists or otherwise, hang out there, and the core of Pijijiapán lacks an open common area.

What Pijijiapán does have is proximity to a scenic and little-visited beach known as Riberas de la Costa Azul. The 19-kilometer access road is now paved, but you're still likely to have the place virtually to yourself anytime other than holidays. With an excellent hotel a short distance from the highway, Pijijiapán is a decent option if you need a place to stop for the night.

◖ RIBERAS DE LA COSTA AZUL

Riberas de la Costa Azul, usually shortened to just Costa Azul (or Playa Azul), is a long wide expanse of glittering grey-black sand, interrupted here and there by fishing boats secured by long mooring ropes and waterlogged tree trunks half-buried in the sand. An hour further from Tuxtla Gutiérrez than Puerto Arista, Costa Azul sees only a fraction of the tourist and weekend-warrior traffic that Puerto Arista, and is more friendly and serene than Boca del Cielo.

Beach

The beach at Costa Azul is one of Chiapas's best—broad and flat, backed by high palm trees and a smattering of tidy wooden structures. The beach is rarely crowded, and those who do come tend to be locals from Pijijiapán looking for a relaxing afternoon. Even fewer people stay the night—camping is the only option—so evenings are especially peaceful. And while the surf remains very strong, most waves break well offshore, making it safer to swim and wade here than many other parts of the Pacific coast. (However, the dark sand can be shockingly hot—take your flip-flops with you if you go walking down the beach!)

Campamento Tortuguero Costa Azul

An isolated outpost of the state sea turtle protection program is located on the beach about three kilometers (1.8 miles) west of Costa Azul's main cluster of palapas. Like its sister installations in Puerto Arista and Boca del Cielo, Campamento Tortuguero Costa Azul (no phone) conducts nighttime beach patrols and releases hatchlings into the sea. Visitors are welcome to join, but rarely do since the activities take place at night and there are no beach accommodations here. It's a pleasant enough walk during the daytime (or a US$15 boat ride

© GARY CHANDLER

THE PACIFIC COAST

Soaring palm trees, thatched huts, and a wide clean beach make Riberas de la Costa Azul one of Chiapas's best ocean getaways.

from the embarcadero) and you might be able to see a tank of *tortuguitas,* recently hatched and awaiting release.

Los Soldados

A short distance off the road to Costa Azul, near where it hits the highway, are three large granite rocks bearing ancient carvings. Officially called La Retumbadora, they are more commonly referred to as Los Soldados (The Soldiers), as the largest and best preserved of the group depicts three men wearing what appear to be protective uniforms and headdresses. Archaeologists believe the stones date to 1200–900 B.C. and were carved by Olmecs, Mesoamerica's first major civilization and predecessors of the Maya. Ask at the top of the Costa Azul road for directions, as there are no signs.

ACCOMMODATIONS AND FOOD

Hands down the best place in town, **Hotel San José** (3a Calle Nte. Pte. at 2a Av. Ote. Nte., tel. 918/645-0011, US$30/35 s/d) makes you wish there was some reason to stay longer in Pijijiapán. Midsize rooms have comfortable mattresses, cable TV, and air-conditioning. Rooms near the reception desk get a Wi-Fi signal, or else you can connect in the large welcoming central foyer. It's a friendly family-run place—Mom makes tasty breakfast and other light fare in the hotel's small café-restaurant. There's also secure parking and easy highway access.

Hotel Esteros (Calle Central btwn. 1 and 2 Av. Nte. Pte., tel. 918/645-0264, US$22 s/d with fan, US$35 s/d with a/c) is the hotel most locals think of as the best in town, which it may well have been a decade ago. While still reasonably comfortable, the rooms are definitely showing their age.

In Riberas de la Costa Azul, a cluster of *palapas* serve fresh seafood (US$6–9) at tables overlooking the ocean, while a tidy central clearing has public bathrooms and changing areas. There are no *cabañas* like in Boca del Cielo—one reason there are far fewer tourists here—but camping is permitted.

INFORMATION AND SERVICES

Bancomer (8:30 A.M.–4:30 P.M. Mon.–Fri.) and **Banamex** (8:30 A.M.–4:30 P.M. Mon.–Fri.) both have reliable cash machines and are kitty-corner from each other at the intersection of 2 Avenida Norte Poniente and 1 Calle Poniente Norte.

Next to Banamex, **Cyber M@nzur** (2 Av. Nte. Pte. and 1 Calle Pte. Nte., 9 A.M.–9 P.M. Mon.–Sat.) charges US$1 per hour to use the Internet.

GETTING THERE AND AROUND

Bus

Pijijiapán's bus station (tel. 918/645-0207) is just off the eastbound lane on Highway 200, at the top of the main road into town. First-class service on OCC (an affiliate of ADO) includes:

- Tapachula: (US$9, 2.5 hrs) every 2 hours 10:20 A.M.–11:20 P.M.

- Tonalá: (US$4.50, 1 hr) take any Tuxtla bus

- Tuxtla Gutiérrez: (US$15, 4.5 hrs) hourly 8:40 A.M.–7:40 P.M.

Combi

Combis and collective taxis park across the street from the bus terminal in Pijijiapán, with service as far as Tonalá (US$2.50, 50 mins) and Tapachula (US$7, 2 hrs).

Combis to Costa Azul (sometimes marked Chocohuital, for the town near there) make the trip from downtown Pijijiapán, leaving every hour 5 A.M.–6 P.M. from a stop at 1 Avenida Norte Poniente between 1 and 2 Calles Poniente Norte (US$1.50, 30 mins).

Boat

Like many places along this coast, Costa Azul occupies a long narrow spit that's separated from the mainland (and main village area) by an equally long and narrow inlet. Boats zip beachgoers across the inlet for just US$0.60 per person; to return, agree on a pickup time with the boatman, or simply stand on the pier and wave until someone at the embarcadero sees you.

Car

Highway 200 splits just outside of Pijijiapán, with town on the southern (ocean) side. Getting on and off the eastbound lanes is easy enough, but getting from town to the westbound side requires crossing a hard-to-find bridge in the corner of town; ask for directions.

There's a well-marked exit for Riberas de la Costa Azul off Highway 200 a short distance west of Pijijiapán. From there, it's 19 kilometers to the coast along a paved access road.

Barra de Zacapulco

Barra de Zacapulco is a quiet thatch-roofed hamlet perched on a low strip of sand, or *barra,* between the ocean and a long inland lagoon. It has a gorgeous and expansive ocean beach, plus a tourist center that's the jumping-off point for trips into Reserva Natural La Encrucijada, a massive 144,868-hectare (559-square-mile) reserve that's home to a wide variety of wildlife and Latin America's tallest mangrove trees, over 25 meters (80 feet) high. Most people come to visit the reserve, but Barra de Zacapulco also makes for a relaxing seaside getaway—a scenic and little-visited spot where you can enjoy simple pleasures like long walks on the beach, accompanied by flocks of tiny water birds scuttling along the shore.

SIGHTS

◖ Reserva Natural La Encrucijada

A sprawling swath of deserted shoreline, coastal wetlands, seasonal flood zones, and towering mangrove forests, La Encrucijada supports a vast array of plants and animals, including nearly 300 types of birds, for the simple reason

© LIZA PRADO

THE PACIFIC COAST

A boat ride through Reserva Natural La Encrucijada takes you past the tallest mangrove trees in Latin America.

that there are so many different ecosystems for them to thrive in. Numerous unique and endangered animals live in the reserve as well, including jaguars, ocelots, giant Mexican anteaters, river crocodiles, roseate spoonbills, and giant wrens (endemic to Chiapas). It's also an important winter nesting ground for dozens of migratory birds, arriving from as far away as Canada. La Encrucijada boasts the tallest mangroves in Latin America, their tangled masses climbing more than 25 meters (80 feet) high, forming a spectacular canopy over the reserve's many waterways. Seasonal flooding supports the region's only major *zapatón* forest—better known to many as 'money trees'. Threats to La Encruijada's vibrant ecology include disruptions in its water supply—mostly by agricultural and human consumption—and increased sediment deposits caused by deforestation, including in the mountains of El Triunfo, where much of the reserve's fresh water originates.

Boat tours of La Encrucijada can be arranged at the **Centro Turístico de Barra de Zacapulco** (tel.918/596-2500, US$35 per boat, 2–3 hours), or at the **Embarcadero de las Garzas** (no phone, US$50 per boat, 2–3 hours). The price difference represents the cost of taking a private boat ride to Barra de Zacapulco, which is closer to the area tours typically take place. *Lanchas* (motorboats) go deep into the tall mangrove forests, past thatch-roofed villages and down small tributaries, perfect for wildlife-watching especially at sunrise and sunset. Tours last about three hours and can be booked at any hour. Most tours do not include getting off the boat, though a number of small islands have trails; if interested, ask your guide about exploring these.

Beach

Most of Chiapas's beaches are long and wide, but the one at Barra de Zacapulco is especially so—its grey-black sand stretching dozens of meters from the ocean breakers to a band of stocky palm trees, and disappearing into the distance in either direction. It's all the more appealing for being virtually litter-free, thanks to its isolation and lack of development. Most of the time it's nearly people-free too, making it an idyllic destination for travelers looking for low-key beach time. Holidays are a notable exception, especially Semana Santa (the week before Easter) and the week following Christmas, when the beach at Barra de Zacapulco can be packed with vacationers and loose trash makes its ugly appearance. The surf here is somewhat mellower than other beaches along this part of the Pacific, though care should still be taken when swimming and wading, and children probably should not enter the water alone.

Campamento Tortuguero Barra de Zacapulco

Located about 200 meters (600 feet) south of Barra Zacapulco's town beach, Campamento Tortuguero de Barra de Zacapulco is the southernmost of the four state-sponsored sea turtle protection and preservation programs. Two marine biologists live and work on-site, often patrolling the beach at night in search of sea turtle nests, typically of olive Ridley turtles; the eggs are relocated to a large protected coral on the beach for their incubation period, and once hatched are released into the sea.

Travelers are very welcome to volunteer with either task; both take place year-round, with the most number of eggs found between July and December, and the highest release of hatchlings between September and November. Even if there are no night patrols when you visit, the Campamento Tortuguero is still an interesting place to stop by, with turtle and crocodile tanks, incubation corals, and even a small outdoor museum featuring turtle shells, whale bones, and dolphin skeletons, most found on these shores.

ACCOMMODATIONS AND FOOD

Centro Turístico de Barra de Zacapulco (tel. 918/596-2500, US$2.50 hammock, US$17 s/d) offers six *palapa*-roofed *cabañas,* all opening onto the expansive well-kept town beach. Rundown is the term that comes to mind when you enter—sagging mattresses, bed sheets that double as curtains, mosquito screens with holes, toilets without seats…but, if you spend most of your time on the beach, the few hours you spend in the room every night won't feel so oppressive. Better yet, skip the *cabañas* altogether and rent a hammock, sleeping in the open air just a few dozen feet from the surf. Or if you've got camping gear, bring it and stay for free. Just be sure to eat a meal or two at the center's restaurant. Shared bathrooms are clean enough and have showers and flush toilets (with seats, even!).

The only regularly operating restaurant in Barra de Zacapulco is at the Centro Turístico. Meal hours vary depending on the number of guests, but typically run 8 A.M.–10 P.M. in high season. The menu relies heavily on the day's catch, but basic egg dishes, rice, and beans are offered every day (US$2.50–4.50). During the high season—Christmas and Semana Santa, mostly—makeshift *comedores* (eateries) open up on the beach, serving simple meals.

GETTING THERE AND AROUND
Boat

The only way to get to Barra de Zacapulco is by boat. *Colectivo* boats depart from the marina Embarcadero de las Garzas every 30 minutes 7 A.M.–5:30 P.M. (US$2.50, 20 mins). To return, let the driver know what time and/or day you'd like to be picked up (the latest one passes by around 4:30 P.M.); if you don't, you could spend hours on the dock in Barra de Zacapulco waiting for a *colectivo* to pass close enough to see you. In a pinch, ask any passing fisherman to take you to the embarcadero; the rate varies dramatically, but could be as high as US$15.

If you're only interested in taking a mangrove tour of the Encrucijada Reserve, these can be booked right from the embarcadero.

Bus and *Combi*

Embarcadero de las Garzas is the marina that serves as the starting point for boats headed to Barra de Zacapulco. If traveling by public transportation, getting there is a three-step process from any direction. First, take a bus to Escuitla from either Tapachula (US$2–4.75, 1.5 hrs, every 30–60 min 4 A.M.–6 P.M. and every 1–1.5 hrs 7:30–11:30 P.M.) or Tonalá (US$5.25–8.75, 2.5 hrs, every 30–60 min 4:15 A.M.–11:45 P.M.). Once there, jump on a *combi* or take a collective taxi to Acapetahua (US$0.50, 10 mins). Finally, take a *combi* from there to Embarcadero de las Garzas (US$0.85, 30 mins).

Car
A car is the easiest, and most convenient, way to get to the Embarcadero de las Garzas, the jumping-off point for boats to Barra de Zacapulco and tours of the Encrucijada Reserve. To get to Embarcadero de las Garzas, take Highway 200 to either Acacoyagua or Escuintla, and turn southwest towards the ocean. The roads from these towns meet eventually, becoming one paved and well-maintained road that passes through green pastures and small towns until dead-ending at Embarcadero de las Garzas.

If you're only going to spend the day in the area, street parking is safe and plentiful. For overnight trips, leave your car in one of the grassy parking lots near the dock (US$2 per day, 24 hrs).

Tapachula

A sweaty, bustling city, and Mexico's main border town with Guatemala, Tapachula is far from charming, but it's not without its shining stars. The restaurants are among the best and most varied in the state, and the archaeological museum makes a fascinating stop for adults and kids alike. Add to that the many surrounding sights—windswept beaches, an untouched mangrove reserve, upscale coffee *fincas,* and the looming Tacaná Volcano—and together, they all make Tapachula well worth exploring.

SIGHTS
Parque Central Miguel Hidalgo
Tapachula's Parque Central (6a Av. Nte. at 5a Calle Pte.) may be the prettiest place in town, lined with trees and benches, with a soaring fountain, an 18th-century church, and several renovated colonial buildings. It also is a bustling, modern square, with huge discount shops and shoe boutiques, open-air eateries and chain restaurants, and sidewalk vendors peddling everything from balloons to cucumber shampoo.

◖ Museo Arqueológico del Soconusco
A great little museum on Parque Hidalgo, the Soconusco Archaeological Museum (8a Av Nte. near 1a Calle Pte., 9 A.M.–6 P.M. Tues.–Sun., US$3.25) outlines the archaeological history of Tapachula and its surrounding areas. Gorgeous artifacts—stelae, pottery,

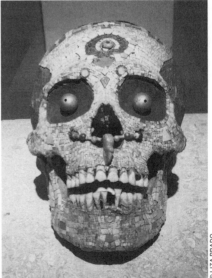

© LIZA PRADO

Tapachula's Museo Arqueológico del Soconusco showcases extraordinary artifacts like this turquoise-encrusted skull.

musical instruments, ball-court vestments—showcase Izapa's former glory as well as the artistic influences of the Olmecs and Aztecs. The exhibits are distributed over two floors with hands-on extras for kids like stelae rubbings, mix-and-match Olmec heads, and Aztec vocabulary games.

ENTERTAINMENT AND EVENTS
Museo Cultural y Turístico de Soconusco

Once Tapachula's city hall, the lovely Museo Cultural y Turístico de Soconusco (Parque Hidalgo, 8a Av. Nte. near 1a Calle Pte., 9 A.M.–6 P.M. Tues.–Sun.) functions more as a

cultural center than a museum. Stop by for a schedule of events; in addition to offering art workshops, it often has art exhibitions and events.

Casa de la Cultura de Guatemala en Tapachula

The Casa de la Cultura de Guatemala en Tapachula (4a Av. Sur 25, tel. 962/625-0356, apuertaabierta@hotmail.com, 2:30–9:30 P.M. Wed.–Thurs., 9 A.M.–11 P.M. Fri.–Sat.) often has live music events and special performances, most highlighting Guatemalan culture (of course). If you'll be in town awhile, consider signing up for one of its popular cooking, music, or writing classes.

SHOPPING

Tapachula is all about shopping—Guatemalans cross the border in droves to partake in the sport. Unfortunately, it's mostly geared at household goods and personal items like clothing and leather shoes; there's precious little in the way of Chiapanecan *artesanía* and mementos to take home.

Artesanía

The **Instituto de las Artesanías** (Avenida Central Ote. near 1a Av. Nte., tel. 962/118-3190, 9 A.M.–8 P.M. daily) is one of the only places in town with a wide selection of folk art. Items from every corner of Chiapas can be found: clay doves, impressive textiles, *laca* crosses, amber jewelry, handcrafted toys.... Quality is incredibly high and prices are reasonable—both reasons to stop and have a look.

Bookstores

One of the best bookstores in the state, **Librería Tapachula** (Parque Hidalgo, 8a Av. Nte. near 1a Calle Pte., tel. 962/626-0727, 10 A.M.–8 P.M. daily) has an excellent selection of books, including good foreign-language offerings in the fiction, history, and guidebook sections. Beautiful folk art from around Mexico and music CDs are also available.

A used bookstore, **Utopia** (1a Calle Ote. near 1a Av. Nte., no phone, 9 A.M.–2 P.M. and 5–8 P.M. Mon.–Fri., 9 A.M.–5 P.M. Sat.) has rows, stacks, and piles of books and magazines crammed into its one-room shop. Cool jazz is piped in, creating a perfect ambience for browsing and poking through the collection. There is a small foreign-language section as well as a decent CD selection.

ACCOMMODATIONS
Under US$50

One of the best deals in town, **([Galerías Hotel & Arts** (4a Av. Nte. 21, tel. 962/642-7596, www.galeriasartshotel.com, US$33–37.50 s with a/c, US$47 d with a/c) is a modern and comfortable hotel with spacious rooms, spotless bathrooms, and extras like cable TV, air-conditioning, in-room phones, and free Internet access. In keeping with its name, each room is named after an artist; beyond a few posters on the walls, though, the homage pretty much stops there. Details, schmetails—this is an excellent option all around.

Casa Grande (8a Av. Sur at 2a Calle Pte., tel. 962/626-6701, US$17 s/d, US$34–42 s/d with a/c) is a rambling old *casona* (mansion) with rooms that open onto a leafy courtyard and a common area filled with Mexican folk art. Rooms themselves are a bit worn but wall stenciling and *talavera* tile floors help some (replacing the electric shower heads would be a plus). Many have cable TV and air-conditioning, the latter a must if you can swing it.

US$50-100

The boutique **([Casa Mexicana** (8a Av. Sur at 2a Calle Pte., tel. 962/626-6605, www.casamexicanachiapas.com, US$56 s with a/c, US$65–73 d with a/c) offers artsy and luxurious rooms in a beautiful 19th-century mansion. The 10 rooms are all slightly different, each dedicated to a notable Mexican woman, and decorated with original art and antique furnishings (check out the Christian altars turned into headboards). All open onto a lush garden courtyard with a mosaic tile pool and part of the hotel's gourmet restaurant, Tapachtlán (7:30 A.M.–noon Mon.–Sat., US$3.50–6), which is open for breakfast. All around, service is impeccable. Wireless Internet and private parking are also available.

One of the only high-rises in town, **Hotel Tapachula** (9a Calle Pte. 17, tel. 962/626-6060, www.hoteltapachula.com, US$57.50 s with a/c, US$66 d with a/c, US$74–87 suite with a/c) is an upscale hotel with cookie-cutter style. Rooms are spacious and comfortable, with marble floors, central air-conditioning, and views of the city below. There also is a well-tended pool and an on-site restaurant, which serves a daily breakfast buffet.

Hotel Don Miguel (1a Calle Pte. 18, tel. 962/626-1143, www.hoteldonmiguel.com.mx, US$45 s with a/c, US$56 d with a/c) is an old-school hotel trying its darnedest to keep up with the crowd. It's not far behind—pillow-top beds, wireless Internet, and rooms with a view help it along. The decor still has a ways to go, but overall this is a solid choice.

FOOD

As a major business traveler hub, Tapachula is, if anything, a place to have a spectacular meal. From gourmet Mexican to hole-in-the-wall Chinese, it's hard to go wrong in this town.

Mexican

The southwest end of Parque Hidalgo has a row of open-air restaurants, each specializing in different Mexican dishes. The most popular is **Los Comales** (tel. 962/626-2405, 24 hours, US$3–8), which offers what many Tapachulans claim are the best tamales in town. If you're a meat lover, head a couple doors down to **Las Tablitas** (11 A.M.–1 A.M. daily, US$5–8.75), where the menu is all about meat—rib eye steaks, lamb chops, and chicken shish kabobs—often accompanied with a steaming baked potato. All the entrées are served on a wood block, or *tablita,* hence the name of the place.

Hostal del Rey (4a Av. Nte. 19, tel. 962/628-9600, 7 A.M.–11 P.M. Mon.–Sat., 7 A.M.–3 P.M. Sun., US$3–7) is a cushy, air-conditioned place, popular with the blue-haired set. Breakfast combos are particularly good here, including a fruit plate and a bottomless cup of coffee (US$3.50–5).

Chinese

A classic Chinese restaurant, at least by American standards, the red and gold **Restaurant Confucio** (5a Calle Pte. 8, tel. 962/626-4449, 10 A.M.–6 P.M. daily, US$5–10) offers an extensive and excellent menu—from chow mein and sesame chicken to Hunan beef and hot wings. Portions are hearty and the air-conditioning strong. Take out is available too.

Jin-Ma (6a Av. Nte. 3, tel. 962/122-3471, 9 A.M.–8 P.M. daily, US$2.50–4) is a tiny family-run restaurant in the city center. Dishes vary daily and are served cafeteria style. It's a popular spot, especially for lunch; get there early to nab a table and to get the freshest of the entrées.

Other Specialties

Considered the best restaurant in town, **Casas Viejas** (4a Av. Sur 30, tel. 962/625-2797, 9 A.M.–11 P.M. Tues.–Sat., 1–5:30 P.M. Sun., US$6–14) is set in a renovated *casona* with a lovely garden patio. The menu changes frequently but meals are gourmet intercontinental, many with Mexican flair. Start with a crisp and refreshing salad, which can be ordered as a half or full serving, the latter big enough to be a meal. Move on to the entrée—if you can't decide on one, try the signature dish, *salmón a la naranja,* salmon cooked to perfection and served on a bed of mashed potatoes, all with a hint of orange. And be sure to save room for dessert—chocolatey delights and creative crepes will keep you wanting more.

The bustling **Tortas Germán** (8a Av. Nte. at Avenida Central Pte., no phone, noon–midnight Mon.–Sat., US$1–2.50) serves up some of the best burgers and *tortas* (Mexican-style sandwiches) in town. *Tortas* come on large rolls, stuffed with any number of meat and chicken combos plus mayo, mustard, onion, jalapeño—the works. Up the ante by adding a fried egg and ham, a classic Tapachulan move.

The cakes in the window are to die for at **Ángeles Alta Reposteria** (4a Av. Nte. 24-B, tel. 962/625-6800, 7 A.M.–11 P.M. daily, US$2.50–5), a stylish café in the heart of downtown. Cappuccinos and other caffeinated drinks aren't too shabby either, all whipped up on a state-of-the-art espresso machine. Come here to catch up on postcards or to take a break from the hubbub outside. Breakfast is also served.

Groceries

Mercado Sebastián Escobar (12a Av. Nte. at 5a Calle Pte., 6 A.M.–5 P.M.) is Tapachula's bustling municipal market. Come here for just about anything—from fresh fruit and live chickens to flip-flops and bootleg CDs.

Supermercado Piticó (7a Calle Pte. near 2a Av. Nte., 8 A.M.–6 P.M. Mon.–Sat., 7 A.M.–3 P.M. Sun.) is a small but well-stocked grocery store; expect basic foodstuffs, snacks, and toiletries.

INFORMATION AND SERVICES
Tourist Information

The tourist office (central plaza, 8a Av. Nte. near 1a Calle Pte., tel. 962/625-5409, 8 A.M.–4 P.M. Mon.–Fri.) has lots of brochures and maps; unfortunately, staffers are a bit reluctant to give much information beyond that. There also is a tourist information kiosk (17 Calle Ote. at 3a Av. Nte., 1–5:30 P.M. Mon.–Sat.) at the OCC bus station, across from the baggage claim area.

Emergency Services

The best hospital in town, **Hospital de Especialidades Ciudad Salud** (Carr. Tapachula–Puerto Chiapas Km. 15, tel. 962/620-1100, 24 hours), is actually *outside* of town. But just barely—located about 15 kilometers (9 miles) south of Tapachula, this state-of-the-art hospital is, hands down, the place to go in an emergency. For meds, try **Farmacia del Ahorro** (6a Av. Nte. at 3a Calle Pte., tel. 962/626-8161, 24 hours), which also delivers.

Money

Accessing your money should be no problem in this bustling border town; around the central plaza alone there are a handful of banks with ATMS. A few convenient ones include: **HSBC** (2a Av. Nte. at 1a Calle Pte., 9 A.M.–4 P.M. Mon.–Fri., 9 A.M.–3 P.M. Sat.); **Scotiabank** (6a Av. Nte. at 5a Calle Pte., 9 A.M.–5 P.M. Mon.–Fri., 10 A.M.–3 P.M. Sat.); and **Santander** (1a Calle Pte. near 4a Av. Nte., 9 A.M.–4 P.M. Mon.–Fri., 10 A.M.–2 P.M. Sat.).

Media and Communications

The **post office** (8 A.M.–4 P.M. Mon.–Fri., 8 A.M.–noon Sat.) is located at 1a Calle Oriente near 7a Avenida Norte. For the size of the city, it's a wonder there's only a handful of Internet cafés. A good one is **Cyber Ocio** (9a Calle Pte. near 2a Av. Nte., no phone, 8 A.M.–9 P.M. Mon.–Fri., US$0.50), with flat screens and lots of fans blowing hot air around. For international calls, go to **Caseta Telefónica** (8a Av. Nte. near 1a Calle Pte., 7 A.M.–8 P.M. daily, US$0.17 per minute to the U.S. and Canada,

US$0.50 per minute to European countries), half a block from Parque Hidalgo.

Laundry and Storage

Lavandería El Jabón (2a Av. Sur near 6a Calle Pte., 8 A.M.–9 P.M. Mon.–Sat., 9 A.M.–2 P.M. Sun.) charges US$1 per three kilograms of clothes and offers same-day service.

Store your bags at the **OCC bus station** (17a Calle Ote. at 3a Av. Nte., tel. 962/626-2881) for just US$0.50 per 24 hours.

Immigration and Consulates

The **immigration office** (4a Av Norte near 33a Calle Pte, tel. 962/626-1263) is open 9 A.M.–1 P.M. Monday–Friday.

The **Consulate of Guatemala** (tel. 962/626-1252, 10 A.M.–3 P.M. and 4–6 P.M. Mon.–Fri.) is located at 5a Avenida Norte near Avenida Central Oriente. As of 2009, citizens of the United States, Canada, and European countries do not need a visa to enter Guatemala.

GETTING THERE
Air

The **Tapachula International Airport** (TAP, Carr. Tapachula–Puerto Chiapas Km. 18.8, tel. 962/626-4189) is located about 18 kilometers (11 miles) south of Tapachula on the road toward Puerto Chiapas. The airport has ATMs, car rental booths, small eateries, and a couple newsstands. Airlines that service it include **Aviacsa** (Av. Central Sur at 1a Calle Pte., toll-free Mex. tel. 800/284-2272, toll-free U.S. tel. 800/967-5263, www.aviacsa.com) and **Aeroméxico** (Avenida Central Ote. near 1a Av. Nte., tel. 962/626-3921, toll-free Mex. tel. 800/021-4000, toll-free U.S. tel. 800/237-6639, www.aeromexico.com).

Sociedad Transportes 149 (2a Av. Sur near 6a Calle Pte., tel. 962/925-1287) provides shuttle service from the airport to Tapachula (US$5.50 pp); there is no shuttle service to the airport, however. A cab ride into town costs US$12.50 for two passengers.

Servicio 12 de Octubre (13a Calle Pte. near 4a Av. Nte.) provides *combi* service between Tapachula and the airport (every 15

mins 7 A.M.–9 P.M., 30 mins, US$0.75)—well, kind of. It'll drop you off at the turnoff to the airport, about 500 meters (0.3 mile) from the front door. To get to Tapachula, go to the opposite (south) side of the highway from the airport and keep your eyes peeled for the *combi* with the seagull and sun painted on it. The last one passes around 6 P.M. daily.

Bus

First-class, deluxe, and international buses service the **OCC bus station** (17a Calle Ote. at 3a Av. Nte., tel. 962/626-2881), located 10 blocks from Parque Hidalgo. It's far enough from most hotels to merit taking a cab (US$1.75). The station has two ATMs in the waiting area as well as a tourist information kiosk (1–5 P.M. Mon.–Sat.) in the baggage claim area.

Combi

Unión y Progreso (5a Calle Pte. near 12a Av. Nte.) runs *combis* every 5–10 minutes

TAPACHULA BUS SCHEDULE

Departures from the **OCC bus terminal** (17a Calle Ote. at 3a Av. Nte., tel. 962/626-2881) include:

DESTINATION	PRICE	DURATION	SCHEDULE
Arriaga	US$13.50	4-4.5 hrs	6 A.M., 9 A.M., 11 A.M., noon, 2 P.M., 5 P.M., 11:50 P.M.
Ciudad Cuahtémoc	US$9.25	4.5 hrs	take San Cristóbal bus
Comitán	US$14	6 hrs	take San Cristóbal bus
Escuintla	US$4.75	1.5 hrs	take Arriaga bus
Guatemala City*	US$15-20	5.5-6 hrs	6 A.M., 7 A.M., 9:30 A.M., 2:30 P.M.
Huixtla	US$2.85-3.50	45 mins	7 departures 6 A.M.–11:45 P.M.
Pijijiapán	US$8.75	2.5-3 hrs	take Arriaga bus
San Cristóbal	US$18.50	7.5 hrs	7:30 A.M., 9:15 A.M., 2:30 P.M., 9:45 P.M., 11:30 P.M.
Tonalá	US$12.50-15	3-4 hrs	13 departures 6 A.M.–11:50 P.M.
Tuxtla Gutiérrez	US$21.50-39	5.5-7.5 hrs	23 departures 6 A.M.–11:59 P.M.

*Direct service to Guatemala City is provided by TICA Bus (tel. 962/626-2880, www.ticabus. com), Linea Dorada (Guatemala tel. 502/232-5506, tikalmayanworld.com), and Trans Galgos Inter (Guatemala tel. 502/2232-3661, www.transgalgosinter.com.gt). All have ticket agents at Tapachula's bus station at intermittent times during the day.

4 A.M.–10:30 P.M. from Tapachula to Izapa Archaeological Zone (30 mins, US$0.85).

To get to Santo Domingo and Unión Juárez, take a Unión y Progreso *combi* to Cacahoatán (US$1.50, 1 hr) and transfer to a *combi* headed to Unión Juárez (US$0.50, 40 mins) that stops at Santo Domingo (US$0.25, 30 mins).

Servicio 12 de Octubre (13a Calle Pte. near 4a Av. Nte.) provides *combi* service to Barra de Cahoacán (every 15 mins 7 A.M.–9 P.M., 1 hr, US$1.25); the last *combi* from Barra de Cahoacán leaves at 5:30 P.M. daily. Servicio 12 de Octubre also drops passengers off near the airport (TAP, Carr. Tapachula–Puerto Chiapas Km. 18.8, tel. 962/626-4189).

GETTING AROUND
Taxi

Taxis abound in Tapachula so hailing one is easy; rides in town cost around US$1.75, a bit more at night. If you need an early-morning or late-night ride, call **Radio Taxis Cristóbal Colón** (tel. 962/626-1112).

Car

Although you won't need a car to visit Tapachula proper, renting one is a great way to visit the surrounding area. At the time of research there were only two car rental agencies in town, both offering similar rates (US$50–80 per day including unlimited mileage and insurance): **Thrifty** (2a Av. Sur 14, tel. 962/626-0982, toll-free Mex. tel. 800/021-2277, www.thrifty.com, 8 A.M.–7 P.M. Mon.–Sat.) and **AVC** (Av. Tapachula 2-A, tel. 962/626-2316, www.avc renteunauto.com, 8 A.M.–2 P.M. and 4–8 P.M. Mon.–Fri., 8 A.M.–6 P.M. Sat.).

Around Tapachula

BARRA DE CAHOACÁN

Just under 40 kilometers (24 miles) from Tapachula sits the beach of Barra de Cahoacán, literally the end of the road with a long stretch of private homes and seaside shacks. It's a wide expanse of beach with soft brown sand and rough surf, a place that's packed on weekends with Tapachulans looking to escape from the heat, and sublimely empty on weekdays. Beachfront umbrellas and *palapas* are available for rent (US$8.50 per day, including four chairs) from any number of beachfront eateries, and there are public restrooms and showers just steps away.

Sights

With five different varieties of mangrove trees, **Laguna Pozuelos** (Barra de Cahoacán, tel. 962/605-1404, 8 A.M.–5 P.M. daily, US$34–50 up to 6 people) is a good place to take a bird-watching tour, especially in the morning when you're more likely to see snowy egrets, kingfishers, and neotropic cormorants. Tours last about 1.5 hours and often include a quick dip where the ocean meets the lagoon.

If you're looking for total R&R, **Playa Linda** is a windswept and almost always empty beach next to Barra de Cahoacán. It's accessible from the main road via *andadores,* small alleys between private homes that lead straight to the ocean, or just by walking north along the beach from Barra de Cahoacán. It's a wonderful place to spend a day, searching for shells or just lying on your towel with a good read.

Note: There are no services on Playa Linda so bring your own food, water, and shade.

Accommodations and Food

The three-story **◖ Playa Linda Hotel** (Barra de Cahoacán, tel. 044-962/692-5234, www .playalindahotel.com, US$8.50 per person camping, US$29–42 s/d, US$50–59 suite, US$67–84 2-br apt.) is, hands-down, the best hotel along this coastline. Opened in 2008, it has spotless rooms with tile floors, good beds, TVs with DVD players, and strong fans (air-conditioning is in the works). All share large porches with hammocks strung here and there, and enjoy nice breezes (oceanside rooms get the best breeze during the day, streetside get the best at night, and the suite is breezy day and night). Camping is also available (bring your own gear), with access to clean, shared bathrooms. A well-maintained pool sits in the center of the property, with a walkway leading straight to the beachfront eateries. Rates are significantly higher on weekends.

Strangely looking like a cross between an M. C. Escher drawing and an abandoned construction sight, the **Hotel Arena de Cuarzo** (Playa Linda, tel. 045-962/625-4078, US$32 s/d) is a behemoth whitewashed building with outdoor stairs seemingly leading nowhere, lookout towers popping out here and there, and windowless window frames just about everywhere. Rooms themselves are very '80s, enormous, and all about marble, but they're surprisingly comfortable and clean; all have fans, TVs, and private bathrooms. The grounds—on a huge swath of oceanfront land—have one deep pool and a kiddie one (both only occasionally filled). There is also a restaurant on-site, serving basic Mexican and seafood dishes.

A string of **open-air eateries** (8 A.M.–8 P.M. Mon.–Fri., 8 A.M.–9 P.M. Sat.–Sun., US$4–7) are set up right on Barra de Cahoacán. All serve fresh seafood dishes, mostly fried fish and shrimp cocktails, at plastic tables overlooking the ocean. Look for those with *palapas* for rent on the beach; though you have to pay a premium to use them, you can get food and drinks delivered all day long.

Getting There

Combi service from Tapachula to Barra de Cahoacán is provided by **Servicio 12 de Octubre** (13a Calle Pte. near 4a Av. Nte., every 15 mins 7 A.M.–9 P.M., 1 hr, US$1.25). If you're not staying the night at the beach, be sure to catch the last *combi* back, which leaves at 5:30 P.M. daily.

IZAPA ARCHAEOLOGICAL ZONE

Izapa Archaeological Zone (8 A.M.–5 P.M. Wed.–Sun., free) is the Pacific coast's most significant Maya ruin, having dominated the region for

nearly a thousand years. Though not as grandiose as ruins elsewhere in the state, it still makes for an interesting day trip from Tapachula.

History

Many archaeologists believe Izapa was settled as early as 1500 B.C., which would have made it a contemporary of the Olmecs, Mesoamerica's first complex society. A number of artifacts found at Izapa seem to mimic common Olmec motifs, leading some, including noted author and scholar Michael Coe, to describe Izapa as a connective link between the Olmec and the Maya cultures. Others say the influence is fleeting, however, and no definitive answer has emerged.

What is clear is that Izapa's artisans were both highly skilled and extremely prolific. Excavations have uncovered scores of stelae, altars, and other monuments, many more than at other ruins from the same period. Frogs, toads, crocodiles, and other reptiles and amphibians, which represent fertility and rebirth in most Maya contexts, figure prominently in Izapa's artwork; it is also notable for depicting large groups of figures rather than just one important personage.

Izapa was occupied for nearly 3,000 years before being abandoned in A.D. 1200.

Visiting the Ruins

The ruins are made up of about 80 structures, divided into three distinct building groups. The main one, **Group F**, is located along the highway, with the massive Tacaná Volcano looming in the distance. Group F covers a relatively small area, consisting mostly of low-lying structures, a ball court, and a handful of weathered stelae and sculptures.

The other two groups, **Group A** and **Group B,** are made up of a number of uncovered mounds, stone sculptures, and stelae. They're located on the opposite side of the highway from Group F, approximately 400 meters (0.25 mile) down a dirt road.

Getting There

From Tapachula, take a **Unión y Progreso** (5a Calle Pte. near 12a Av. Nte., every 5–10

© LIZA PRADO

A modest archaeological site today, Izapa was once the most influential Maya city on the Pacific Coast.

mins 4 A.M.–10:30 P.M.) *combi* that's headed to Cacahoatán. Ask the driver to let you off at the Izapa ruins (30 mins, US$0.85). To return, just wait alongside the highway for a *combi* to pass by.

Heading east from Tapachula, look for Ruínas Izapa Restaurante; from there, Group F is about 200 meters (0.13 mile) further down the highway, while Groups A and B are about 400 meters (0.25 mile) down a dirt road (the turnoff is just before the restaurant). Partway down the dirt road, you'll hit a three-way fork; go down the center road to hit the ruins.

SANTO DOMINGO

Santo Domingo is a pleasant little village that grew out of one of Chiapas's first coffee *fincas*. The main house on the original (and still operating) farm has been converted into the Centro Turístico Casa Grande, which houses a coffee museum and restaurant.

Sights

Located in the creaky attic of the Casa Grande, the **Museo de Café** (tel. 962/627-0055, 10 A.M.–6 P.M. daily, US$0.50) provides an excellent overview of coffee history—from its beginnings in Ethiopia to the present-day Chiapanecan *fincas*. It also has a detailed display on the growth and processing of the coffee bean, a fascinating step-by-step exhibit. Signage is in Spanish only, though the photos and machinery are worth a look even if you don't do *español*.

Tours

Tours of Santo Domingo's **coffee plantations** (*cafetales,* in Spanish) are offered year-round by the Centro Turístico Casa Grande (tel. 962/627-0055, US$12.50 per group, 2.5–3 hrs). Guides lead visitors around the property while describing the process of growing, harvesting, and prepping coffee beans for export; tours are in Spanish only. A fascinating walk, it makes you appreciate your morning cup of joe that much more. Reservations are recommended.

A handful of hikes in Santo Domingo's

verdant hills also can be arranged through the Centro Turístico Casa Grande (tel. 962/627-0055). The most popular hike leads to **Pico de Loro** (Parrot's Peak, US$20 per group), a rock overhang in the shape of a parrot's beak, about six kilometers (3.5 miles) away. If you're not in the mood to break a sweat, Pico de Loro is also reachable by car from a road located between Santo Domingo and Unión Juárez—signage is nonexistent, so confirm you're going the right way as you drive up.

Accommodations and Food

Though part of the Casa Grande complex, **Hotel Santo Domingo** (Carretera Tapachula-Union Juárez, tel. 962/627-0060, www.centro ecoturisticosantodomingo.com, US$17 s, US$25 d) is surprisingly basic, with spacious though musty rooms, aging amenities, and beds that could use replacement. Nevertheless, the rooms are clean, all have private bathrooms, and the location is pleasant. In a pinch, it will do just fine.

With tables on a breezy 2nd-floor balcony, **Casa Grande Restaurant** (tel. 962/627-0055, 8 A.M.–8:30 P.M. daily, US$3.50–6.50) has gorgeous views over its coffee plantations and Tacaná Volcano—probably the best seats in town. The menu is equally impressive, though only for its breadth; the food—Mexican and international—is reliable but not much more. Even if you're not hungry, it's worth ordering a coffee and sitting awhile to enjoy the view.

Getting There

To get to Santo Domingo from Tapachula, take a **Unión y Progreso** *combi* (5a Calle Pte. near 12a Av. Nte.) to Cacahoatán (every 5–10 mins 4 A.M.–10:30 P.M., US$1.50), about an hour away. Once you arrive in Cacahoatán, cross the street to the Cordova depot and take a *combi* headed to Unión Juárez (every 10 mins 5 A.M.–8:30 P.M. daily). Be sure to let the driver know you want to get off at Santo Domingo (US$0.75, 20 mins), otherwise he'll blow right past the little town.

On the return trip, be sure to leave early enough to catch the last *combi* back to Tapachula; the last one to Cacahoatán passes through Santo Domingo around 7:15 P.M., and the last one from Cacahoatán to Tapachula leaves at 8 P.M.

UNIÓN JUÁREZ

Just a 20-minute *combi* ride past Santo Domingo is Unión Juárez, a colorful village built on the slope of a mountain. It's considered the best starting point for an ascent of the Tacaná Volcano, though there's not much reason to come here otherwise. Stroll around the multilevel plaza, enjoy a cup of coffee, and rest up for the challenging hike that lies ahead.

◖ Tacaná Volcano

Towering nearly 4,100 meters (13,120 feet) above the Soconusco region, Tacaná is an active volcano whose name means House of Fire in the local Mam dialect. Sailors used to refer to the volcano as the Lighthouse of the South, for the glowing lava flows that were once visible well out to sea. Tacaná straddles the Mexico-Guatemala border, and is the second-highest peak in Central America (Volcán Tajumulco, in Guatemala, is the highest at 4,220 mts/13,845 ft). Climbing it is a challenging but scenic two- or three-day trek, passing through tropical, pine, and cloud forests, before eventually reaching the windswept summit and its spectacular views. The volcano is part of a protected biosphere reserve, and you're likely to see a variety of birds and animals along the way as well.

THE ASCENT

There are two routes up Tacaná—Chiquihuites and Talquián—both leaving from Unión Juárez, a small town northeast of Tapachula. The Chiquihuites route is the less steep of the two, and is the route guides typically recommend. The trailhead is located about 12 kilometers (7.5 miles) from Unión Juárez and is accessible by private vehicle only; if you've got a guide, the ride typically is included in the rate, otherwise grab a taxi at Unión Juárez's central plaza. From the Chiquihuites trailhead, it is a 3.5-to-4-hour hike to the base camp, Los

Papales, where you can camp or make use of a rustic shelter (US$1 pp); local caretakers can prepare basic meals for US$1–2.

After spending the night at Los Papales hikers head to the top, another 5–6 hours away. The view from the summit is stunning, encompassing the highest peaks in Guatemala and an expansive view of the Pacific Ocean. There's a campsite just 10 minutes below the summit, where most hikers spend a second night to be able to catch the sunrise at the summit—one of the best in Mexico—before heading down the volcano. Strong hikers can do the trip in just two days, usually by reaching the upper campsite the first day, a punishing 8–10-hour haul.

The less-traveled Talquián route starts at its namesake village, about seven kilometers (4 miles) north of Unión Juárez, and is reachable by foot or cab. There, a stone monument marks the beginning of the trail; it's five to six hours of hiking to the small settlement of Trigales, and another six to seven hours of tough climbing to the summit. Camping is permitted along the trail but be sure to ask permission if you are clearly on private property.

The best time to climb Volcán Tacaná is during the dry season, December–April.

PRACTICALITIES

Come prepared! Though Tacaná doesn't require technical climbing, it can get quite cold—at or below freezing at the summit. Bring several layers of clothes, including thermal underwear, hat and gloves, plus hiking boots, camping gear, and basic foodstuffs. There are springs along the way where you can fill your water bottle, but be sure to bring a water filter or purifying tablets. Be mindful of the fact that the altitude may slow you down considerably; give yourself plenty of time to tackle the volcano and carry enough supplies to get you there and back.

A guide is recommended, as there are several settlements on the volcano and numerous paths crisscrossing the Tacaná trail. The one exception to this is during Semana Santa (the week leading up to Easter), when hundreds of people turn out to climb the volcano and you literally can follow a trail of litter to the summit.

Guides can be hired in Unión Juárez; stop by the Palacio Municipal to ask about available guides or contact Fernando Valera Fuentes (tel. 962/647-2015, fernandovalerafuentes@gmail.com), an experienced and recommended guide based out of Hotel Colonial Campestre. Rates vary dramatically—expect to be quoted anywhere from US$50 to US$125 per group (typically four to five people), and figure an additional US$10–20 in the rainy season. Typically those with higher rates include two guides (one at the front, the other at the rear so that every hiker can ascend at his or her own pace), have CB radios, and/or have basic first aid training.

Camping gear can be rented at Hotel Colonial Campestre for US$20, which includes a four-person tent and two sleeping bags. Food and other supplies can be picked up around Unión Juárez.

Accommodations and Food

Half a block from the central plaza, **Posada Aljoad** (tel. 962/647-2025, US$12.50 s, US$17 d) has basic cement-floor rooms with flaking walls and springy beds—but they're clean and have private bathrooms with hot water. In this part of Chiapas, that's about as good as it gets.

Hotel Colonial Campestre (no phone, US$17–30 s/d) is all about the spectacular views of the green hills below. Too bad the sun goes down and all you've got are four walls to look at. Rooms are depressing at best—spacious though crumbling and not remotely appealing. At least there's wireless Internet at the hotel restaurant and the recommended guide for the ascent of Tacaná Volcano basically runs the place. Look for the bridge connecting the two sides of the hotel a couple blocks south of the central plaza.

There are a handful of mom-and-pop **restaurants** lining the terraced central plaza, all offering Chiapanecan and classic Mexican meals. Prices are very affordable (US$2–6) and hours typically run 8 A.M.–9 P.M. daily.

THE PACIFIC COAST

Getting There

From Tapachula, take a **Unión y Progreso** *combi* (5a Calle Pte. near 12a Av. Nte.) to Cacahoatán (every 5–10 mins 4 A.M.– 10:30 P.M., 1 hr, US$1.50). Once in Cacahoatán, cross the street to the Cordova depot and take a *combi* to Unión Juárez (every 10 mins, 5 A.M.–8:30 P.M. daily, US$1), about 40 minutes away.

On the return trip, be sure to leave no later than 7 P.M. so that you're sure to catch the last *combi* to Tapachula from Cacahoatán at 8 P.M.

◖ RUTA DEL CAFÉ

One of the most scenic regions of Chiapas, the Ruta del Café (Coffee Route) includes some of the state's largest coffee plantations, or *fincas,* many of which were started by German immigrants in the late 1800s and are still run by their descendants today. Visitors can tour the fields and processing facilities, and stay the night in comfortable guest rooms. (Worth doing for the morning coffee alone!)

This area is one of the rainiest regions in all of Mexico. Not surprisingly, the best time to visit is during the dry season (Oct.–Feb.), which also coincides with the harvesting and prepping of beans for export—a fascinating sight.

Finca Argovia

Accessible by paved road, Finca Argovia (Carr. Nueva Alemania Km 39, tel. 962/692-3051, www.argovia.com.mx) is a coffee and flower farm that is popular with tour groups. It is a lush, tropical place with updated 19th-century buildings and a river that runs through it.

Three **tours** of the *finca* are offered to visitors: the Tour de Flores (US$12.50 pp), a Jeep and walking excursion of the flower nurseries and fields; the Tour de Café (US$8.50 pp), a walking tour of the *beneficio* (wet mill); and the Tour del Mirador (US$8.50), a 520-meter (0.35-mile) walk through the coffee fields to a lookout tower that has glorious views of the Ruta del Café and Volcán Tacaná (not to mention good bird-watching too).

Finca Argovia's **accommodations** are comfortable enough but lack the amenities and charm expected at these rates. Prices mostly reflect the size of the room, not its sophistication. The four categories offered are: hotel rooms, which open onto the gardens of the main house (US$67 s/d); smallish *cabañas* (wood cabins) with basic bathrooms and pine floors and porches (US$75 s *cabaña,* US$84 d *cabaña*); *casitas* (little houses) that are bigger and more modern than the cabins but lack the porch (US$100 s/d); and a bungalow, a small fully equipped two-bedroom house (US$134). None of the accommodations have TV, radio, or telephones.

Tierra de Café (8 A.M.–10 P.M. daily, US$5–12) is a welcoming 2nd-story restaurant that overlooks a lush, tropical landscape. Specializing in international cuisine, it has pretty much something for everyone. Next door is a breezy *palapa*-roof lounge, which offers all sorts of cool drinks.

Finca Hamburgo

Owned and operated by the Edelmann family

RUTA DEL CAFÉ

Sinai
FINCA HAMBURGO
FINCA IRLANDA
El Naranjo
FINCA SAN FRANCISCO
FINCA LA CHIRIPA
Guadalupe Sajo
FINCA GÉNOVA
FINCA MARAVILLAS
Mexiquito
San Enrique
FINCA ARGOVIA
To Hwy 20 and Huxtila
Zaragoza
FINCA EDUVIGES
Nueva Alemania
Villa Hidalgo
El Edén
To Huixtla
200
Cinco de Mayo
Huehuetán
0   2 mi
0   2 km
To Tapachula
© AVALON TRAVEL

since 1888, Finca Hamburgo (tel. 962/626-7578, www.fincahamburgo.com) is the most stately of the coffee *fincas*. The grounds are picture perfect: rolling hills of coffee plants, red-roofed A-frame buildings that transport you to an 18th-century farm, and views of the surrounding mountains that seem to go on forever.

The *finca* offers several **tours** within its compound and in the surrounding area: a guided tour of the *beneficio de café* (wet mill) where the multistep process of preparing coffee beans for export occurs (US$5 pp); a walk through the *cafetales* (coffee fields) and nurseries to learn how Hamburgo's different coffees are cultivated and harvested (US$10 pp); and a four-to-six-mile tour along the Río Cuilco in Hamburgo's sister property, Finca La Chiripa, including a hair-raising zip line ride over the river (US$12.50 pp).

Near the entrance to the *finca,* in what was once the freight funicular house (the first one in Chiapas), is the **Museo del Café** (8 A.M.–5 P.M. daily, free). A detailed history of the farm is related here, complete with family photographs, farm machinery, and other antique knickknacks. Tours often include a guided stop at the museum, though it's easy enough to walk through it yourself. Signage is in Spanish, English, and German.

Finca Hamburgo's **accommodations** (US$60–75 s/d, US$130 suite) are in three beautiful pine chalets. Modern and spare, the rooms are high-end but subtle. All share a long porch with plenty of rocking chairs for guests to enjoy the views. Lounging, in fact, is encouraged—every morning a thermos of coffee is left at each room's door so that visitors can enjoy a leisurely start to their day.

Even if you're not staying overnight, enjoy a meal at Hamburgo's hilltop **Perleberg Restaurante** (8 A.M.–4 P.M. daily, 7:30 A.M.–10 P.M. if there are hotel guests, US$6–10). The menu is solidly international with a nod to the owners' German and Chiapanecan heritage (how often do you see *bratwurst und bockwurst* and tamales *de chipilín* on the same menu?). Even if it's just over coffee and dessert, the view from the tables is worth a stop.

CHIAPANECAN COFFEE

Whether you enjoy it at a shady outdoor café or in front of the fire at your B&B, coffee is one of the simple but ubiquitous pleasures of traveling in Chiapas. San Cristóbal, in particular, has dozens of coffee shops, most serving rich locally grown organic brew.

Mexico is the world's fifth-largest exporter of coffee – after Brazil, Vietnam, Colombia, and Indonesia – and Chiapas is far and away Mexico's number-one coffee-producing state, with over 227,000 hectares (560,690 acres) of land dedicated to the crop; Oaxaca, by comparison, ranks second with just 68,000 (167,960 acres) hectares. Equally impressive is the fact that over 90 percent of Chiapas's coffee farmers grow their beans on plots under five hectares (12 acres) of land. (Which makes for a lot of coffee farmers, around 121,000 at last count.) The small-time nature of Chiapas's coffee industry provides some buffer against the bean's notorious price fluctuations – few farmers rely solely on coffee – and also avoids the environmental and labor abuses so often associated with large-scale plantations.

Wireless Internet access is also available here (US$4/hr).

Finca Irlanda

Although just a 15-minute drive from Finca Hamburgo, Finca Irlanda (tel. 962/625-5485) is a world away from its manicured neighbor. Trees tower over the estate, plant life is lush and abundant, and a small reserve has been set aside for a diversity of animals to live in (and for visitors to explore). Finca Irlanda is also an entirely ecofriendly coffee *finca*, depending on shade-grown coffee plants, worm composting, water recycling, bio-gas, and other green features for its coffee production and the *finca* lifestyle on the whole. In fact, in 1967 Irlanda was reportedly the first *finca* in the world to export organic coffee.

THE PACIFIC COAST

A 40-hectare (99-acre) reserve within Finca Irlanda, **La Montañita** is home to over 230 types of birds, including the blue crowned motmot, collard aracari, and lineated woodpecker. Several hiking paths run through the reserve for visitors to enjoy; admission ranges US$5–20 depending upon which trail you take.

If you have trouble spotting wildlife in La Montañita, there also are several large aviaries on-site, filled mostly with birds that were found injured or were rescued from the illegal trade of tropical birds. Perhaps the most photographed is a quetzal, glorious tail and all, that has been at the *finca* since.

Tours of the *finca*—the *beneficio* (wet mills), coffee fields, and nurseries—can be arranged; call to schedule a tour.

Irlanda's homey **accommodations** (US$42 s/d, US$67 suite) are set in a large old building across from the main house. Rooms are breezy and bright with spotless bathrooms, beautiful cedar floors, and pillow-top beds. All rooms open onto an inviting porch that is outfitted with hanging chairs—perfect for a good read. Breakfast is included in the rate.

Getting There

You'll need your own transportation to explore the Ruta del Café. Hold on tight—after Finca Argovia the road is mostly unpaved, with huge sections containing large rocks, potholes, and loose dirt. During the rainy season (Apr.–Sept.), a four-wheel-drive vehicle is absolutely necessary; the rest of the year a front-wheel-drive car will make it, but only very slowly (and prepare to be stared at by unbelieving eyes). Regardless of the vehicle, be sure to fill your tank in Tapachula; there are no gas stations on the Ruta del Café, and villages are few and far between.

From the center of Tapachula, budget the following time to get to each finca: Argovia (38 km/23 mi, 1 hr), Hamburgo (54 km/33 mi, 1.75 hrs), Irlanda (60 km/36 mi, 2 hrs).

If you don't have a vehicle, *fincas* occasionally will provide transport to guests. At the time of research, only Finca Hamburgo offered round-trip transport from Tapachula (US$12.50 pp).

Combis (5a Calle Pte. near 12a Av. Nte., 5 A.M.–5 P.M. daily) headed to the town of Zaragoza from Tapachula drive past the turnoffs to Finca Argovia (US$1, 1.5 hrs) and Finca Hamburgo (US$1.25, 2.5 hrs). You'll have to walk the final two kilometers to Argovia, and up a steep hill to Hamburgo, but it's way cheaper than renting a car—just pack light.

BACKGROUND

The Land

GEOLOGY

Chiapas is Mexico's eighth-largest state, covering 75,632 square kilometers (29,200 square miles), and certainly among the most geologically diverse. Geologists generally divide Chiapas into seven zones, five of which form a "stack" of long narrow bands of differing altitudes, all roughly parallel to the state's Pacific coastline.

The Pacific coastal plain, aka the Soconusco or *tierra caliente* (hot lands), is the long hot plain running the length of the coast, averaging just 20–30 kilometers (12–18 miles) across. It was once covered in forest but is now one of the state's most productive agricultural zones.

The imposing Sierra Madre de Chiapas mountain range juts up abruptly from the Pacific plain, with average altitudes of 1,500–3,000 meters (5,000–10,000 feet) plus the state's highest peak, Volcán Tacaná, at nearly 4,100 meters (13,120 feet).

The northern slope of the Sierra Madre descends into Chiapas's central depression, which has an altitude of 420–800 meters (1,400–2,650 feet) and a fairly hot dry climate. Tuxtla Gutiérrez and Cañón del Sumidero are located in this band.

Moving northward, the land leaps up again, this time forming the high cool central plateau, also referred to as Los Altos (the highlands),

© LIZA PRADO

where San Cristóbal is located. It boasts extensive, though fast diminishing, pine and oak forest and altitudes as high as 2,200 meters (7,250 feet).

To the northeast are the eastern highlands, sloping downward from the central plateau into the lush Lacandón jungle and Usumacinta river valley, along the Guatemalan border.

To the northwest are the northern highlands, which are higher and hillier than the eastern highlands and eventually give way to the Gulf coast plain, a hot lowland area in the state's northernmost reaches, bordering the state of Tabasco.

CLIMATE

Chiapas has two seasons, rainy and dry, the former extending from May to October, the latter from November to April. There's far more variation in average temperatures depending on region, altitude and season. The highlands around San Cristóbal tend to have cool agreeable weather, with daytime temperatures ranging from the 50s to 70s, depending on the season, with crisp cold nights, occasionally dropping near freezing—be sure to pack a jacket and knit hat! Highlanders consider the central depression, where Tuxtla and Chiapa de Corzo are located, to be exceedingly hot, though many foreign travelers appreciate the warm arid climate, especially when San Cristóbal is experiencing one of its occasional cold fronts. Hot humid conditions prevail around Palenque, and even more so along the Pacific coast and the northern Gulf plains.

ENVIRONMENTAL ISSUES

Without question, the single most pressing environmental issue in Chiapas—and indeed Mexico as a whole—is deforestation. All of the state's major forest areas show significant human intrusion. Many historically forested areas, including the long narrow Pacific plain, have been utterly denuded of trees to make room for cattle grazing and large-scale agricultural production, from mangos to sesame seeds. The Lacandón jungle—the last large expanse of virgin tropical forest in North America—has been reduced by

50 percent since 1960. Cutting and trimming trees for heating and cooking also accounts for significant and sustained losses, especially in rural highland areas where the average family is estimated to use around 12 kilograms (26 lbs) of firewood every day.

Deforestation is of particular concern in Chiapas, which is one of the world's richest biodiversity zones. Accounting for the rate of habitat loss as well as the amount of biodiversity contained there, Mexico is considered by many observers to be among the top 15 most environmentally threatened places in the world. Scientists also believe the devastating flooding in Tabasco in 2007—at the height of which an incredible 80 percent of the state's surface area was under water—was significantly worsened by clear-cutting along the Río Usumacinta, which forms the Mexico-Guatemala border and drains into Tabasco basin and the Gulf of Mexico.

Traditional methods of controlling deforestation—say, declaring areas off-limits to most or all cutting—are complicated by Mexico's unique history of land use, including a constitutional commitment to provide all farmers with land to cultivate. Under that system, much of Chiapas's remaining forest is currently owned or controlled by *ejidos,* communal landowning entities that historically have exercised considerable autonomy and are often reluctant to accept restrictions on how their land is used. Some have created ecotourism projects as a way of earning money on lands without destroying them, but slash-and-burn methods are still widespread.

Pollution is another environmental issue facing Chiapas, particularly pollution of the state's many waterways, both above- and belowground. Chiapas boasts extensive wetlands along the Pacific coast, much of it abutting the state's most productive agricultural lands. Pesticides and fertilizers used by farmers occasionally leach into adjacent wetlands, damaging fragile ecosystems.

Capturing exotic or endangered animals for sale as pets or food is another concern. Toucans, macaws, quetzals, monkeys, and sea turtles are all protected by Mexican law, but remain favorite targets of poachers.

Flora

Chiapas has approximately 10,000 plant species (including 1,650 considered to be medicinal), more than any other state in Mexico. This is a reflection, in large part, of the state's numerous geologic and vegetation zones, each supporting a distinct collection of flora.

VEGETATION ZONES
Tropical Rainforest

Chiapas is especially notable for its extensive tropical rainforest, none more impressive than the Selva Lacandón (Lacandón jungle). At 1.8 million hectares (18,000 square kilometers, roughly three times the size of Delaware), the Lacandón jungle is Mexico's largest and best-preserved tropical rainforest; combined with the Maya and Calakmul biosphere reserves (in Guatemala and Campeche state, respectively) it forms part of one of the largest contiguous expanse of tropical forest north of the Amazon. Within the Lacandón jungle is the 331,000-hectare Montes Azules biosphere reserve, which contains 20 percent of Mexico's plant species, including the country's tallest tropical trees, 70-meter-tall mahogany behemoths. Other trees typical to the state's tropical rainforest regions include *caoba, chicozapote, mamba,* and ceiba. (The latter were considered sacred by the ancient Maya—a link between the underworld, the material world, and the heavens. Even today, these huge trees are generally not disturbed, including those growing in the middle of crop or cattle fields.) The rainforest is also home to palms, ferns, lianas, and numerous epiphytes, including orchids.

Pine and Cloud Forests

Chiapas's steep mountain slopes make for a quick succession of microclimates and habitats, and an incredibly rich assortment of plant life. This is particularly evident on the Pacific side of the Sierra Madre de Chiapas mountain range, and in El Triunfo Biosphere Reserve. Lower elevations feature common tropical trees like *palo de agua* and *zapotillo,* giving way to pine and evergreen species like *pino moctezuma* and *pino real* (the tallest pine species in Chiapas, growing to 40 m/130 ft), and finally, cool damp cloud-forest conditions along the jagged ridge tops commonly home to species including liquidambar, *encino* (oak), and magnolia, plus a dizzying array of bromeliads, orchids, and cycads.

Pino real and *encino* trees also can be found in the extensive pine and oak forests in the state's central plateau and highlands, around San Cristóbal and surrounding indigenous villages. These forests are heavily impacted, supplying much of the highlands with timber and firewood.

Savanna

Savanna-like habitat can be found in Chiapas's hot arid central depression (where Tuxtla Gutiérrez is located), where low scrub trees like *nanche* and *cacaito* thrive. A different type of savanna covers much of the state's Pacific lowlands, where the hotter, more humid conditions favor trees like the *jícara,* whose large bulbous gourds have been dried and used as containers for millennia.

Mangroves

Mangrove forests spread in tangled knots along much of the Pacific coast, providing vital habitat to myriad birds, amphibians, and aquatic creatures, and supplying nutrients to adjacent estuaries and even ocean ecosystems. Three species of *mangle* (or *manglar*) are most common—white, black, and red—and those in the Reserva Natural La Encrucijada are said to be the tallest in Latin America, growing to an impressive 25 meters (80 feet).

Fauna

Forty percent of Mexico's animal species can be found in Chiapas, three quarters of those in the Montes Azules biosphere reserve alone. Many animals are endemic to Chiapas, or even their immediate surroundings; spotting them can be difficult, though with patience and a skilled guide, not impossible.

MAMMALS
Nine-Banded Armadillos
The size of a small dog and sporting a thick coat of armor, this peculiar creature gets its name from the nine bands (or external "joints") that circle the midsection and give the little tank some flexibility. The armadillo's keen sense of smell can detect insects and grubs—its primary food source—up to 15 centimeters (6 inches) underground, and its sharp claws make digging for them a cinch. An armadillo also digs underground burrows, into which it may carry a full bushel of grass to make its nest, where it will sleep through the hot day and emerge at night. Unlike armadillos that roll up into a tight ball when threatened, this species will race to its burrow, arch its back, and wedge in so that it cannot be pulled out.

Tapirs
South American tapirs are found from the southern part of Mexico to southern Brazil. A stout-bodied animal, it has short legs and a tail, small eyes, and rounded ears. The nose and upper lip extend into a short but very mobile proboscis. Tapirs usually live near streams or rivers, which they use for daily bathing and as an escape from predators, especially jaguars and humans. Shy and placid, these nocturnal animals have a definite home range, wearing a path between the jungle and their feeding area. If attacked, the tapir lowers its head and blindly crashes off through the forest; they've been known to collide with trees and knock themselves out in their chaotic attempt to flee.

Peccaries
Two species of peccaries—hoofed mammals that look like midsize pigs with bristles—are found in Chiapas: the collared peccary and the white-lipped peccary. The feisty collared peccary stands 50 centimeters (20 inches) at the shoulder and can be one meter (3.3 feet) long, weighing as much as 30 kilograms (66 pounds). It is black and white with a narrow semicircular collar of white hair on the shoulders. This is the more common of the two, and is found in woodlands, rainforests, and agricultural areas; it typically travels in groups of 5–15. The white-lipped peccary is reddish brown to black and has an area of white around its mouth. Larger than the collared peccary, it can grow to 105 centimeters (41 inches) long and is found deep in tropical rainforests living in herds of 100 or more.

Primates
Two types of monkeys live in the jungles of Chiapas: spider monkeys and howler monkeys. Both are threatened species, mostly as a result of the destruction of their habitats and poaching for trade and meat. In an effort to protect these creatures, the Mexican government has prohibited their capture or trade.

Spider monkey are agile creatures who swing, climb, and hang from the upper reaches of trees, often using their tails as a fifth limb. They tend to be members of troops that number up to 25 (usually one dominant male plus several females and their offspring); during the day, however, they break off into smaller groups to forage for food, mostly fruit and leaves. Spiders need large tracts of land to survive—typically an area that measure from 2.5 to 4 square kilometers (1 to 2 square miles)—which means they can be seen in nature reserves or areas that are uninhabited by humans.

Howler monkeys are slow-moving primates who tend to stay at the top of trees, where they gather most of their food (leaves, fruit, and flowers). They are mostly black, with a fringe of brown or blonde hair on their sides, and are large, weighing 4–7 kilograms (9–16 lbs). Howlers are known for the males' distinctive call (though females also occasionally vocalize)—it's piercing and eerie, and they can be heard at dawn or dusk up to five kilometers (3 miles) away. Their calls are thought to be a way to communicate with other howler troops, in order to defend their feeding sites, which change regularly. Good places to hear howlers are Yaxchilán Archaeological Zone, Las Guacamayas, and Laguna Miramar.

Felines

Seven species of cats are found in North America, four in the tropics. One of them—the jaguar—is heavy-chested with sturdy, muscled forelegs. It has small, rounded ears and its tail is relatively short. Its color varies from tan and white to pure black. The male can weigh 65–115 kilograms (143–254 lbs), females 45–85 kilograms (99–187 lbs). The largest of the cats in Chiapas, the jaguar is about the same size as a leopard. Other cats found here are the ocelot and puma. In tropical forests of the past, the large cats were the only predators capable of controlling the populations of hoofed game such as deer, peccaries, and tapirs. If hunting is poor and times are tough, the jaguar will go into rivers and scoop up fish with its large paws. The river also is one of the jaguar's favorite spots for hunting tapirs, where the latter comes to drink.

BIRDS

With over 600 species of birds, many of them rarely seen elsewhere, Chiapas is a veritable bird-watcher's paradise. Birds are most easily spotted in Chiapas's nature reserves, like El Triunfo and La Encrucijada, though there is excellent bird-watching at Chiapas's archaeological zones too, when the trees that surround the ancient structures come alive with birdsong at dawn and dusk.

Scarlet Macaw

Measuring up to one meter (3 feet) in length, the scarlet macaw is the largest of the parrot family. A stunning bird, it boasts bright colors and long tail feathers. In Mexico, it is found exclusively in the eastern part of Chiapas, although it once could be found in Veracruz, Tabasco, and Oaxaca—habitat destruction and poachers reduced their numbers considerably. They feed mostly on fruit and seeds, migrating along with ripening fruit. Scarlet macaws are monogamous and pair up for life; together, a couple cares for its nestlings until they are four months old. The birds can live up to 80 years.

Toucan

Two species of toucans live in Chiapas: the collared aracari and emerald toucanet. They typically travel in flocks of 3–12, staying at the upper reaches of the trees. Their distinctive bills and bright colors make them visible when they fly from tree to tree, often searching for fruit. They are important inhabitants of tropical forests, as they disperse tree seedlings that they pass or regurgitate. Toucans also are notable for being monogamous; both genders incubate and feed their nestlings.

Resplendent Quetzal

Though the ancient Maya made abundant use of the dazzling quetzal feathers for ceremonial costumes and headdresses—male quetzal's tail feathers grow at least 18 inches long—they hunted other fowl for food; nevertheless, the quetzal is the only known bird from the pre-Columbian era and is now almost extinct. Today, they are still found (though rarely) in the high cloud forests of Chiapas and Central America, where they thrive on the constant moisture.

Horned Guan

The Sierra Madre de Chiapas is the only area that the elusive horned guan inhabits in Mexico. Living above 3,350 meters (10,990 feet), it is a large turkey-like bird with black glossy feathers, red legs, and a red horn on top of its head. It eats mostly fruits, leaves, and small invertebrates and lays just two eggs during its January–June breeding season. The horned guan is an endangered species; poaching as well as the continued destruction of its habitat make it at risk of extinction.

Waterbirds

Chiapas's coastal wetlands, mangroves, and lagoons play host to hundreds of bird species; a boat ride through one of these areas will give you an opportunity to see the amazing variety of species from wintering osprey and peregrine falcons to neotropic cormorants, giant wrens, limpkins, and mangrove black-hawks. You're also sure to see dozens of wading birds feeding in the shallow waters, including roseate spoonbills and flocks of egrets.

REPTILES

Although reptiles thrive in southern Mexico, humans are their worst enemy. In the past, some species were greatly reduced in number because they were hunted for their unusual skin or meat. Although hunting them is now illegal in most countries, enforcement can be spotty and black marketers still take their toll on the species.

Turtles

Tens of thousands of sea turtles of various species once nested on Mexico's shores. As the coast became populated, turtles were severely over-hunted for their eggs, meat, and shells, and their numbers began to fall. Hotel and resort developments have hastened the decline, as there are fewer and fewer patches of untrammeled sand in which turtles can dig nests and lay eggs. The Mexican government and various ecological organizations are trying hard to save the dwindling turtle population. The government is also enforcing tough penalties for people who take turtle eggs or capture, kill, or sell these creatures and their byproducts.

Four species of turtles nest on the Chiapanecan coast: olive Ridley, hawksbill, Pacific green, and leatherback; a handful of state-funded centers have been set up to monitor and protect them. Located in Puerto Arista, Boca del Cielo, Riberas de la Costa Azul, and Barra de Zacapulco, these centers are staffed by marine biologists who search for turtle eggs and relocate them to protected corrals; when the hatchlings break through their shells, they are brought to the beach and are allowed to rush toward the sea—the hope is that the experience will imprint a sense of belonging there so that they return to the same beach where they are released. In some cases the hatchlings are scooped up and placed in tanks to grow larger before being released into the open sea.

Caymans

The cayman is a part of the crocodilian order. Its habits and appearance are similar to those of crocodiles, with the main difference being its underskin; the cayman's skin is reinforced with bony plates on the belly, making it useless for the leather market. (Alligators and crocodiles, with smooth belly skin and sides, have been hunted almost to extinction in some parts of the world because of the value of their skin.)

Several species of cayman frequent the brackish mangrove waters along the Pacific coast. They are broad-snouted and often look as though they're sporting a pair of glasses. A large cayman can be 2.5 meters (8.2 feet) long and very dark gray-green with eyelids that look swollen and wrinkled. Some cayman species have eyelids that look like a pair of blunt horns. They are quicker than alligators and have longer, sharper teeth. Skilled hunters, cayman are quick in water and on land, and will attack a person if cornered. If you spot a cayman, the best advice is to give it a wide berth.

Green Iguanas

Seen frequently in Chiapanecan rainforests, the dragon-like green iguana is one of the 20-plus species of *Iguanidae* that inhabit southern Mexico. Many grow to be one meter (3.3 feet) long and have a blunt head and long, flat tail. Bands of black and gray circle its body, and a serrated column reaches down the middle of its back almost to the tail. The young iguana is bright emerald green and often supplements its diet by eating insects and larvae.

The lizard's forelimbs hold the front half of

© H.W. PRADO

Caymans and crocodiles are a common sight along the Río Usumacinta, Cañon del Sumidero, and in Chiapas's thick mangrove forests.

its body up off the ground while its two back limbs are kept relaxed and splayed alongside its hindquarters. When the green iguana is frightened, however, its hind legs do everything they're supposed to, and it crashes quickly (though clumsily) into the brush searching for its burrow and safety. This reptile is not aggressive—it mostly enjoys basking in the bright sunshine—but if cornered it will bite and use its tail in self-defense.

From centuries past, recorded references attest to the green iguana's medicinal value, which partly explains the active trade of live iguana in the marketplaces. Iguana stew is believed to cure or relieve various human ailments, such as impotence.

Other Lizards

You'll see a great variety of other lizards in Chiapas; some are brightly striped in various shades of green and yellow, others are earth-toned and blend in with the gray and beige landscape. Skinny as wisps of thread running on hind legs, or chunky and waddling with armorlike skin—the range is seemingly endless and fascinating.

Coral Snakes

Two species of coral snakes, which are related to the cobra, are found in Chiapas. They have prominent rings around their bodies in the same sequence of red, black, and yellow or white and grow to 1–1.5 meters (3.3–4.9 feet). Their bodies are slender, with no pronounced distinction between the head and neck.

Coral snakes spend the day in mossy clumps under rocks or logs, emerging only at night. Though its bite can kill within 24 hours, chances of the average tourist being bitten by a coral (or any other) snake are slim.

Tropical Rattlesnakes

The tropical rattlesnake (*cascabel* in Spanish) is the deadliest and most treacherous species of the rattler. It differs slightly from other species by having vividly contrasting neck-bands. It grows to 1.5 meters (5 feet) long and is found mainly in the higher and drier areas of the tropics. Contrary to popular myth, this serpent doesn't always rattle a warning of its impending strike.

INSECTS

Air-breathing invertebrates are unavoidable in any tropical locale. Some are annoying (gnats and no-see-ums) and some can cause pain when they bite (red ants), but many are beautiful (butterflies and moths) and all are fascinating.

Butterflies and Moths

Chiapas has an incredible abundance of beautiful moths and butterflies, some 80 percent of all the species found in Mexico. Hikers might see the magnificent turquoise emperor, regal greatstreak, bar-celled oleria, orange kite swallowtail, Florida white, tiger eye hairstreak, cassius blue, red-bordered pixie, malachite, and

forest bluevent. The famous monarch also is a visitor during its annual migration from Florida to the Central American mountains where it spends the winter.

Bees

Many Chiapanecan communities raise bees for honey production, a tradition that began with the ancient Maya, who were expert beekeepers. (Honey was one of the most prized—and widely traded—commodities in the Maya world; some researchers say the Descending God figure at several archaeological sites is the god of bees.) The beekeeping tradition that lives on today is much reduced, thanks in part to the availability of cheap standard honey. Nevertheless, Chiapanecan honey, which is harvested using modern methods, is still marketed at organic and health-food stores.

History

ANCIENT CIVILIZATION

The Pacific coast of Chiapas and present-day Guatemala is believed by archaeologists to be the cradle of Maya civilization. It was there that the earliest proto-Maya tribes—from which the great pre-Colombian Maya societies eventually grew, and today's Maya are descended—first formed small fixed settlements, practicing basic agriculture and producing surprisingly sophisticated pottery and tools. They slowly spread south into Central America and north as far as the Gulf coast of the Yucatán Peninsula, splintering into dozens of distinct ethnic and language groups. Present-day Chiapas came to be home to various groups, many of which are still present today: Tzotziles and Tzeltales cultivated the highlands, Choles inhabited the northern jungles, Tojolabales lived in the plains in today's Lakes Region, and the Mam people lived in the coastal regions. The western portion of the state was originally occupied by Zoques (who may be more closely related to Olmecs than

Mayas), who were later conquered by Chiapa war tribes, probably arriving from Central Mexico. The Chiapas were the dominant power at the time of first Spanish contact, and so the state bears their name.

PRECLASSIC PERIOD

As occurred throughout Mesoamerica, Chiapas's early tribal inhabitants evolved increasingly complex social systems, including the widespread adoption of the Long Count calendar. The earliest Long Count date to be found in Chiapas corresponds to B.C. 36, inscribed on a monument at Chiapa de Corzo archaeological site. This same period saw the rise of one of Chiapas's great early city-states, Izapa, near present-day Tapachula. Dominating the coastal lowlands for nearly a thousand years, the Izapans worshipped gods that were precursors of the Classic Maya pantheon and commemorated religious and historical events in bas-relief carvings that emphasized costume and finery.

EARLY CIVILIZATIONS AND MAYA TIMELINE

Period	Year
Paleoindian	before 7000 B.C.
Archaic	7000-2500 B.C.
Early Preclassic	2500-1000 B.C.
Middle Preclassic	1000-400 B.C.
Late Preclassic	400 B.C.-A.D. 250
Early Classic	A.D. 250-600
Late Classic	A.D. 600-800
Terminal Classic	A.D. 800-1000
Early Post-Classic	A.D. 1000-1250
Late Post-Classic	A.D. 1250-1519

CLASSIC ERA

Some of the Maya world's most outstanding so-cieties flourished in and around Chiapas during the Classic era (A.D. 200–900), including Palenque, Yaxchilán, Bonampak, and Toniná, plus Tikal and Piedras Negras in present-day Guatemala, and Calakmul in Campeche state. The Classic period saw the emergence of a new and vigorous breed of rulers and dynasties, bent on deifying themselves and their ancestors, particularly through the construction of grand pyramids, temples, and monuments. All the arts and sciences of the Maya world, from architecture to astronomy, were likewise focused on this goal. In Chiapas, as elsewhere, painting, sculpture, and carving reached their climax during the Late Classic era; objects such as Lord Pakal's sarcophagus lid from Palenque are now recognized as being among the finest pieces of world art.

And yet, by A.D. 925, nearly all of the city-states had collapsed and were left in a state of near-abandonment; the last known Long Count date was recorded in A.D. 909 in the Chiapanecan city-state of Toniná. The Classic Maya decline is one of the great enigmas of Mesoamerican archaeology. There are myriad theories—disease, invasion, peasant revolt—but many researchers now believe the collapse was caused by a combination of factors, including overpopulation, environmental degradation, and a series of devastating droughts. With the abandonment of the cities and the dispersal of specialists (like astronomers, scribes, and religious figures), Maya cultural advances also stopped, and many were lost. Many religious customs and beliefs also were never seen again.

POST-CLASSIC PERIOD

The collapse of great lowland Maya centers shook the entire Maya world, and serves as the marker between the Classic and Post-Classic periods. However, not all city-states were completely abandoned; in Chiapas, smaller entities like Tenam Puente, Chinkultik, and Izapa managed to survive the upheaval, and even blossomed once free of the long shadow—political, economic, and military—of the fallen lowland powers. Nevertheless, the Post-Classic era is marked by the narrowing of Maya influence and the arrival of Central Mexican immigrants and invaders. While Maya communities remained vibrant and fiercely independent—as the first would-be European conquerors soon discovered—the era of grandiose Maya cities, especially in Chiapas, was over.

SPANISH CONQUEST AND COLONIZATION

The first Spanish garrison arrived in present-day Chiapas in 1524 on orders from Hernán Cortés. Making its way up the Río Grijalva, the expedition encountered fierce resistance from Chiapa warriors, whom one soldier-chronicler described as "the most courageous warriors encountered in the New World." The Spanish managed to capture the main

© H.W. PRADO

Toniná's remarkable and rather morbid Mural de las Cuatro Eras depicts the four eras that the world passes through in Maya cosmology.

Chiapa city—many Chiapa are said to have leapt from the Sumidero Canyon rather than be taken prisoner—but soon withdrew in the face of constant insurrection. Three years later, Diego de Mazariegos led a larger, better-armed expedition from Mexico City and captured western Chiapas, founding present-day Chiapa de Corzo, the state's first colonial capital. However, rampant disease prompted him to move the capital to the cooler healthier highlands, founding Ciudad Real (today's San Cristóbal de las Casas) in 1528. Mazariegos himself died a short time later, and control of Chiapas transferred from New Spain (today's Mexico) to the viceroyalty in Guatemala, beginning a long tug-of-war between Mexico and Guatemala for control of the region.

Chiapas was a relative backwater for most of the early colonial period. The coastal and lowland areas were used for cattle ranches and sugar cane plantations, but European diseases decimated the native population and the "necessary" slave labor supply. However, it was during this period that Dominican friar Bartolomé de las Casas launched his remarkable and tireless crusade to abolish slavery in the New World. De las Casas was named bishop of Chiapas in 1544, though his unwavering abolitionism—he refused to absolve slaveholders, even on their deathbeds—meant his tenure was short, just two years.

Chiapas's indigenous communities did not submit passively to Spanish subjugation. The first major indigenous uprising was in 1712, when Tzeltales in the highland area of Canuc rebelled against colonial abuses; the rebellion spread to neighboring Tzotzil communities before being crushed by Spanish troops rushed in from Guatemala.

FROM COLONY TO COUNTRY

After Mexico won independence from Spain in 1820, it reclaimed Chiapas and even annexed Guatemala and the rest of Central America. Three years later eastern Chiapas joined Guatemala in forming the Central American Federation, but it was reincorporated into Mexico when the CAF failed in 1842. (A

BISHOP BARTOLOMÉ DE LAS CASAS: PROTECTOR OF THE INDIANS

San Cristóbal de las Casas is named in part for Bishop Bartolomé de las Casas, the controversial 16th-century bishop of Chiapas and fierce defender of Native American rights. He's particularly known for helping dismantle the Spanish *encomienda*, under which colonists (often military men who helped conquer a particular region) were given royal sanction to enslave the native people, often under brutal conditions.

Born in Seville in 1484, de las Casas first visited the New World at age 18, when he traveled to Hispaniola (now the Dominican Republic) to help oversee land and laborers acquired by his father, a crew member on Columbus's second voyage. Aghast at the mistreatment of the native Taino population, de las Casas renounced his family's holdings and spent the rest of his life advocating for indigenous autonomy, and coercing kings and colonists to abandon slavery and indentured servitude.

De Las Casas worked and traveled widely in the New World, advocating with ever-greater conviction for indigenous rights and autonomy. He was helped in the effort by his family's unusually powerful connections, including to Spain's royal court and elite families like Christopher Columbus's. He managed to extract a series of anti-slavery decrees, including the New Laws of 1542, which effectively outlawed the *encomienda* system. Their enactment by Charles V, after meeting with a contingent led by de las Casas, remains one of the Spanish priest's crowning achievements.

De las Casas was promoted to bishop of present-day Chiapas in 1544, a move his critics hoped would distance him from the royal court, but which in fact earned him greater influence and authority than ever. He returned to the New World committed to enforcing the laws he'd helped create. He instructed his priests – 45 in all, the Church's largest missionary effort at the time – to decline confessions from anyone still holding slaves, and famously refused to absolve a prominent *encomendero*, even on his deathbed. The local elite were outraged, especially in the capital Ciudad Real, now San Cristóbal, where he was initially denied permission to even establish a church. (He founded his first church in present-day Chiapa de Corzo instead.)

Almost as radical as his anti-slavery work was de las Casas' insistence on an egalitarian, non-coercive brand of evangelism. In Chiapas, he instructed priests that conversion was to be free and voluntary, and informed converts that their loyalty was properly to God, the King of Spain, and their own communities – not, that is, to local colonial authorities. For his efforts, de las Casas received death threats and was nearly driven from the city, and his tenure as bishop of Chiapas lasted just two years. Among the indigenous, however, he is revered to this day, referred to as Brother Bartolomé.

The bishop left Mexico for Spain in 1547 – never to return, as it turned out. Instead, de las Casas spent his later years writing prolifically. In 1552, he published *A Brief Account of the Destruction of the Indies* – his most famous (and famously excoriating) work – and continued work on his lengthy treatise *History of the Indies* and numerous other pieces, many still regarded as master texts in anthropology, theology, and canonic law.

Bishop Bartolomé de las Casas, one of the most principled and fearless voices of the colonial era, died in Madrid in 1566 at the age of 82. A powerful symbol of indigenous rights, his name was added to San Cristóbal's in 1943.

final portion was wrested from Guatemala by longtime Mexican dictator Porfirio Díaz in the 1880s.)

The 19th century saw two products—timber and coffee—spark fundamental changes in Chiapas's political, economic, and environmental landscape. Large logging companies, mostly European-owned, began harvesting ancient mahogany and cedar trees in Chiapas's vast eastern rainforest, using the Río Usumacinta to float freshly cut logs to processing plants downstream. The industry was the first step in what has become a steady march of deforestation in Chiapas—which continues to this day. It also created what has become an all too familiar pattern: foreign or out-of-state entities exploiting Chiapas's natural resources, while leaving little or no lasting benefit for the state or its residents.

The steep south-facing slopes of the Sierra Madre de Chiapas mountains are ideal for growing coffee, and huge plantations—also owned primarily by foreigners, in this case Germans—emerged in the late 1800s, especially near Chiapas's border with Guatemala. The plantations were complemented by ranching and agriculture in the coastal lowlands, and the region became Chiapas's first economic success story. A rivalry developed between coffee producers and lowland agro-business interests on one hand, and the political elite concentrated in the highlands, especially in San Cristóbal, at that time the state capital. (It was a microcosm of the division emerging throughout Mexico—between upstart market-oriented liberals and traditional church-backed conservatives—and which eventually led to the Mexican Revolution of 1910.) Liberals prevailed, expropriating huge tracts of Church-owned land for development, and even moving the state capital to present-day Tuxtla Gutiérrez in 1892.

Liberal gains in the latter part of the 19th century were not necessarily good for Chiapas's indigenous population, however. Reforms designed to spur development and encourage foreign investment left "backward" peasant farmers increasingly marginalized, especially through the expropriation of farm lands and the growth of debt labor.

MEXICAN REVOLUTION AND AGRARIAN REFORM

The Mexican Revolution promised fundamental changes in Mexico's covenant with its poor and indigenous farmers. The war broke out in 1910, but came to Chiapas in 1914, when revolutionary forces took control of the state and promptly abolished debt servitude. However the decree served to unite Chiapas's landowners, both lowland liberals and highland conservatives, who saw much of their work force simply walk off the job. They responded by organizing armed gangs that terrorized revolutionary officials and their supporters, and succeeded in undercutting many of the reforms won by the revolution. In remote areas, particularly eastern Chiapas, powerful ranchers and landowners continued to operate virtual fiefdoms well into the 1930s.

Beginning in 1934, the Mexican government, under the inspired guidance of president Lázaro Cárdenas, finally took up the task of truly enforcing land and agrarian reforms envisioned in the 1917 constitution. Cárdenas undertook a massive nationalization program, claiming the major electricity, oil, and other companies for the state, and created state-run companies like PEMEX, the oil conglomerate still in existence today. In Chiapas, the federal government seized thousands of hectares of underutilized lands—the Great Depression had dried up demand for many of Mexico's export crops—and redistributed them to farmers and collective peasant organizations known as *ejidos*. The policies fomented a robust cycle of homegrown production and demand, and Mexico entered several decades of sustained growth dubbed The Mexican Miracle.

Cárdenas also founded a new government agency, the Department of Indian Protection, which would later become the powerful National Indianist Institute, or INI, and whose first director was Chiapas governor Erasto Urbina. Urbina, in turn, helped indigenous farmers in Chiapas obtain federal land

© LIZA PRADO

There are several autonomous Zapatista communities in Chiapas, where visitors have to show identification and answer questions from masked guards before being allowed in.

grants and established an indigenous workers' union to recruit and represent workers in the state's coffee plantations. While not done simply to curry political favor, these actions did have the effect of cementing indigenous support for the newly formed Institutional Revolutionary Party, or PRI. That support proved crucial, and surprisingly resilient, as the PRI consolidated power and morphed from the enlightened party of Lázaro Cárdenas to a so-called "perfect dictatorship"—deeply corrupt, and holding every major office in the federal government, and most state governments as well, for more than seven decades. Even today, voting for a non-PRI candidate (like joining a Protestant faith) is a grave offense in many indigenous communities; anyone discovered doing so can be immediately and permanently expelled from their home and the community. By the same token, many indigenous communities in Chiapas do not support the fiercely anti-PRI Zapatista movement.

In the 1960s and '70s, a boom in energy projects—namely oil drilling and dam construction—sent economic and social shockwaves through Chiapas, in much the same way timber and coffee production did a century prior. Two major dams were constructed on the Río Grijalva in the 1960s, and rising oil prices in the 1970s prompted PEMEX to greatly expand off-shore drilling along the Gulf coast. In Chiapas, as elsewhere, thousands of farmers left the countryside for construction and transport jobs on these massive projects. While the added income was a boon for those who got it, agricultural production fell dramatically nationwide, forcing Mexico to import corn and other staples. Perhaps more importantly, Mexico's energy boom altered the social and economic fabric of many indigenous villages. Incomes gaps emerged in longtime egalitarian communities, and traditional farming techniques—which among other things relied on neighbors helping harvest one another's fields—were disrupted; in severe cases, farmers were forced to sell their land or move to urban areas.

In the 1980s, after reaping huge profits from

oil exports during the oil crisis, the Mexican peso suddenly plunged, as much as 500 percent by 1982, prompting then president López Portillo to nationalize Mexico's banks. Under pressure from international financial institutions, Mexico adopted dramatic restructuring and austerity measures, including virtually eliminating agricultural subsidies to small farmers, like those in Chiapas. The federal government also began a concerted campaign, under the guise of economic restructuring, of undermining the agrarian reform laws dating to the Mexican Revolution. In 1992, president Carlos Salinas de Gortari succeeded in amending the constitution, eliminating the provision that committed the government to providing all farmers with land, and allowing for the privatization of communal *ejidos*. This unprecedented action—ending almost a century of land reform—and the adoption of the North American Free Trade Agreement (NAFTA) shortly thereafter, utterly demoralized many poor and landless farmers, especially in eastern Chiapas, and was a major catalyst for the Zapatista uprising, launched on January 1, 1994—the day NAFTA took effect.

A series of electoral reforms implemented in the late 1980s and through the 1990s paved the way for the historic 2000 presidential election, in which an opposition candidate— former Coca-Cola executive Vicente Fox of the right-of-center PAN—defeated the PRI, ending the latter's 70-year reign of power. Fox was succeeded in 2006 by another PAN member, Felipe Calderón Hinojosa, in an election in which the PRI finished a distant third. However, the election was marred by allegations of fraud and weeks of post-election demonstrations.

President Calderón's number one priority has been cracking down on drug cartels, an effort that has succeeded in hampering the drug trade, but has also sparked a cascade of violence among rival cartel members, the police, and military, with prosecutors and journalists being targeted for intimidation and even murder. While most of the violence related to the crackdown has been in the north, Chiapas has also seen increased military presence, particularly in the state's far east, which is sometimes used as a portal for drug shipments from South America. The eastern jungles are also where the EZLN (the Zapatista National Liberation Army) is strongest, though the Zapatistas do not appear to be involved in drug trafficking. By the same token, it seems unlikely, as some EZLN supporters claim, that the government is using drugs merely as an excuse to weaken their movement; that may be giving the struggling movement too much credit. For better or worse, the stalemate between the EZLN and the Mexican government shows little signs of change, let alone resolution, especially with Calderón and the country focused on the drug war, the economic crisis, and other matters.

In Chiapas, a number of major projects have moved steadily forward with state and federal support, including several related to tourism. Construction of a toll road between San Cristóbal de las Casas and Palenque began in 2009 (projected to be completed by 2014) and plans for an international airport in Palenque are gaining steam. Both changes could greatly increase tourism traffic to the state, but could also risk inflaming conflict between the government and small farmers and communities, whose lands may be affected.

Government and Economy

GOVERNMENT

Mexico enjoys a constitutional democracy modeled after that of the United States, including a president (who serves one six-year term), a two-house legislature, and a judiciary branch. For 66 years (until the year 2000), Mexico was controlled by one party, the so-called moderate Partido Revolucionario Institucional (PRI). A few cities and states elected candidates from the main opposition parties—the conservative Partido de Acción Nacional (PAN) and leftist Partido de la Revolución Democrática (PRD)—but the presidency and most of the important government positions were passed from one hand-picked PRI candidate to the next, amid rampant electoral fraud.

Indeed, fraud and corruption have been ugly mainstays of Mexican government for generations. In the 1988 presidential election, PRI candidate Carlos Salinas de Gortari officially garnered 51 percent of the vote, a dubious result judging from polls leading up to the election and rendered laughable after a mysterious "breakdown" in the election tallying system delayed the results for several days.

Salinas de Gortari, accused of having stolen millions of dollars from the federal government during his term, ended his term under the same heavy clouds of corruption and fraud that ushered him in. That said, Salinas pushed through changes such as increasing the number of senate seats and reorganizing the federal electoral commission that helped usher in freer and fairer elections. He also oversaw the adoption of NAFTA in 1993, which has sped up Mexico's manufacturing industry but seriously damaged other sectors, especially small farmers, many of whom are indigenous.

The 1994 presidential election was marred by the assassination in Tijuana of the PRI candidate, Luis Donaldo Colosio, the country's first major political assassination since 1928. Colosio's campaign manager, technocrat Ernesto Zedillo, was nominated to fill the candidacy and eventually elected. Zedillo continued with reforms, and in 2000, for the first time in almost seven decades, the opposition candidate officially won. PAN candidate Vicente Fox, a businessman and former Coca-Cola executive from Guanajuato, took the reigns promising continued electoral reforms, a stronger private sector, and closer relations with the United States. He knew U.S. president-elect George W. Bush personally, having worked with him on border issues during Bush's term as governor of Texas. Progress was being made until the terrorist attacks of September 11, 2001, pushed Mexico far down on the U.S. administration's priority list. With Mexico serving a term on the U.N. Security Council, Fox came under intense pressure from the United States to support an invasion of Iraq. He ultimately refused—Mexican people were overwhelmingly opposed to the idea—but it cost Fox dearly in his relationship with Bush. The reforms Fox once seemed so ideally poised to achieve were largely incomplete by the time his term ended.

The presidential elections of 2006 were bitterly contested, and created—or exposed—a deep schism in the country. The eventual winner was PAN candidate Felipe Calderón Hinojosa, a former secretary of energy under Fox. His main opponent, Andrés Manuel López Obrador, was a former mayor of Mexico City and member of the left-leaning PRD. Though fraught with accusations and low blows, the campaign also was a classic clash of ideals, with Calderón advocating increased foreign investment and free trade, and López Obrador assailing the neo-liberal model and calling for government action to reduce poverty and strengthen social services. Both men claimed victory after election day; when Calderón was declared the winner, López Obrador alleged widespread fraud and called for a total recount; his supporters blocked major thoroughfares throughout the country for weeks. The Mexican Electoral Commission did a selective recount and affirmed a Calderón victory; the official figures set the margin at under 244,000 votes out of 41 million cast, a difference of just 0.5 percent. Calderón's inauguration was further marred by legislators fist-fighting in the chamber, and the new president shouting his oath over jeers and general ruckus.

Calderón was confronted with a number of thorny problems upon inauguration, including a protest in Oaxaca that had turned violent, and spiraling corn prices that in turn drove up the cost of tortillas, the most basic of Mexican foods. While addressing those and other issues, he pressed forward with promised law-and-order reforms, raising police officers' wages and dispatching the Mexican military to staunch rampant gang and drug-related crime in cities like Tijuana and Cuidad Juárez. The effort sparked a veritable war between law-enforcement officials and the powerful drug cartels vying for shrinking territory. A staggering 5,300 people were murdered in Mexico in 2008—double the 2007 figure—most taking place in the northern border states and blamed on the drug war. The dead included a shocking number of police officers and prosecuting attorneys, as well as journalists targeted by the cartels for their coverage of the drug trade. For its part, the far eastern corner of Chiapas is a known drug-trafficking corridor—particularly as Colombian cartels look for alternatives to the now heavily patrolled Caribbean routes—but so far the state has seen very little drug-related violence, and virtually none targeted at tourists.

Chiapas produces nearly 15 percent of Mexico's corn, the nation's most vital and basic staple.

ECONOMY

Chiapas is one of the most resource-rich states in Mexico: It's the number-one producer of coffee, number two in overall agricultural production (mostly bananas, cacao, and corn), and number four in crude oil and natural gas, with massive untapped deposits believed to exist in the Lacandón jungle. Three massive dams in Chiapas—one of which is the country's largest—generate about 50 percent of Mexico's hydroelectric power, and the state contains 40 percent of the country's fresh water. Cattle ranching and timber harvesting have been significant activities since the 19th century, though both have come under fire for their environmental impact. Chiapas's archaeological, colonial, and natural attractions draw a growing number of tourists every year, and tourism development is a motivating factor for a number of current and proposed capital projects, including construction of a toll road between Palenque and San Cristóbal.

Despite its extraordinary natural resources, Chiapas still ranks as the poorest state in the union. Many families live on less than US$250 per month, and a staggering 94 of Chiapas's 118 municipalities are classified as being on or below the poverty line.

People and Culture

DEMOGRAPHY

Today, 75–80 percent of the Mexican population is estimated to be mestizo (a combination of the indigenous and Spanish-Caucasian races). Only 10–15 percent are considered to be indigenous peoples. (In comparison, as recently as 1870 the indigenous made up more than 50 percent of the population.) While there are important native communities throughout Mexico, the majority of the country's indigenous peoples live in Chiapas, Oaxaca, and the Yucatán.

Chiapas's indigenous population accounts for about 15 percent of the state population, though numerous municipalities are virtually 100 percent indigenous (albeit sparsely populated); the indigenous population is comprised of 12 different ethnic groups: Tzotzil, Tzeltal, Ch'ol, Zoque, Tojolabal, Kanjobal, Chuj, Mam, Jacalteco, Mochó, Cakchiquel, and Lacandón. Of these, the Tzotzil and Tzeltal make up the vast majority of the state's total indigenous population—36 percent and 35 percent respectively. Sadly, most of Chiapas's indigenous population lives on or below the poverty line and suffers from high illiteracy rates—in some communities it's nearly 50 percent—as well as elevated infant mortality rates.

RELIGION

While Mexico is predominantly Roman Catholic, a vigorous evangelical Protestant movement has earned hundreds of thousands of converts across the country, including Presbyterians, Baptists, Pentecostals, Jehovah Witnesses, Seventh Day Adventists, and Mormons. Nowhere are evangelical conversions as pronounced—or contentious—as in Chiapas, where over 36 percent of residents identify as non-Catholic Christians (compared to around 12 percent nationwide). There is even a small number of Muslim converts, around 300 in all, concentrated in the outskirts of San Cristóbal.

Religion is a particularly complex and contentious issue in Chiapas's indigenous communities. Most were converted to Catholicism early in the colonial era, though many pre-Hispanic beliefs and customs remain in wide use, often blended with standard Catholic mores. A number of traditional Maya beliefs are curiously similar to Christian ones, including a cross-like symbol—to the Maya, it represents a sacred ceiba tree connecting Earth to the upper and lower realms—and a chaotic five-day period known as the "lost days" that coincides almost exactly with Carnaval. In Chamula, a fiercely independent community near San Cristóbal, residents worship various Catholic saints, yet expelled the local priest when he tried to steer them away from certain Maya customs, including the use of shamans and healing ceremonies.

But practicing a syncretistic form of religion

© LIZA PRADO

Many indigenous children sell *artesanía* – and look after their younger siblings – in San Cristóbal's plazas and tourist areas.

PAPEL PICADO

Mexicans are famous for their celebrations – whether it's to honor a patron saint or to celebrate a neighbor's birthday, partying is part of the culture. Typically, fiestas feature great music, loads of food, fireworks, and brightly colored decorations, often including *papel picado* (literally, diced paper).

Dancing at the slightest breeze, *papel picado* is tissue paper cut or stamped with a design that is appropriate for the occasion: a manger scene at Christmas, church bells and doves for a wedding, skeletons in swooping hats for Day of the Dead. Once cut, row upon row of *papel picado* is strung across city streets, in front of churches, or in people's backyards.

After the celebration, few are inclined to take down the decorations. Wind and rain eventually do the job, leaving just the thin cord and a few bits of torn paper. Nowadays, *papel picado* is often made of plastic, especially for use outdoors, which isn't quite as attractive but lasts for months – a reminder of festivities past.

has not made indigenous communities or leaders more tolerant of religious diversity; to the contrary, those who convert to Protestantism often are summarily expelled from their home, land, and community. Thousands of desperately poor *expulsados* (expelled ones) live in slums around San Cristóbal; in some cases, entire towns have been founded by non-Catholics. Very few indigenous towns have (or would tolerate) both a Catholic and Protestant church—Tenejapa and Amatenango del Valle are two of the select few.

LANGUAGE

Though Spanish remains the dominant language, various Maya languages are spoken widely in northern, central, and eastern Chiapas. Tzotzil and Tzeltal have the most speakers statewide, concentrated in the central highlands including San Cristóbal and

surrounding villages. Both languages also are spoken in Palenque and the Río Usumacinta Valley, though Ch'ol is the dominant tongue there. The Lacandón, who number about a thousand and live in the state's central rainforest, speak a version of Yucatec Maya. Other language groups include Tojolabal, found mostly in the Lakes Region, and Zoque, a non-Maya language spoken in parts of northern and western Chiapas, as well as in Oaxaca, Tabasco, and Veracruz.

Many older Maya do not speak any (or much) Spanish, though the younger generations typically do. Only a small number of non-indigenous Chiapanecans learn the basics of one or more Maya languages; those who do are most often merchants who frequent indigenous markets and teachers working in rural areas.

ART

Mexico has an incredibly rich colonial and folk-art tradition. While not necessarily considered art by the people who make and use it, traditional indigenous clothing is beautiful and travelers and collectors are increasingly able to buy it in local shops and markets. Prices for these items can be high, for the simple fact that they are handwoven and can literally take months to complete. San Cristóbal de las Casas is an especially good place to purchase high-quality textiles from around the state; you'll also find a variety of beautiful pottery, wood carvings, and amber jewelry.

HOLIDAYS AND FESTIVALS

Mexicans take holidays—of their country, their saints, and their families—seriously. You'll be hard-pressed to find a two-week period when something or someone isn't being celebrated. On major holidays—Christmas, New Year's Day, and Easter—be prepared for crowds on the beaches, at the waterfalls and lakes, and at archaeological sites. Be sure to book your hotel and buy your bus tickets well in advance; during holidays, the travel industry is saturated with Mexican travelers.

In addition to officially recognized holidays, villages and cities hold numerous festivals and

REGIONAL HOLIDAYS AND CELEBRATIONS

- Jan. 1: **New Year's Day** and **anniversary of Zapatista uprising**

- Jan. 6: **Día de los Reyes Magos** (Three Kings Day – gifts exchanged)

- Jan. 8-22: **Festival de San Sebastián** (Festival in Chiapa de Corzo, featuring costumed *parachicos*)

- February: **Fiesta de San Caralampio** (month-long celebration, especially in Comitán)

- Feb. 2: **Virgen de la Candelaria** (religious candlelight processions light up several towns)

- Feb. 5: **Flag Day**

- Late Feb.: **Carnaval** (seven-day celebration before Ash Wednesday; celebrated especially vigorously in San Juan Chamula)

- Mar. 21: **Birthday of Benito Juárez** (president of Mexico for five terms; born in 1806)

- Late March/early April: **Semana Santa** (holy week, with various religious celebrations and reenactments culminating in Easter; also a major travel period for Mexicans)

- May 1: **Labor Day**

- May 3: **Day of the Holy Cross** (celebrated widely, notably in Zinacantán and Tenam Puente Archaeological Zone)

- May 5: **Battle of Puebla** (aka **Cinco de Mayo;** celebration of the 1862 defeat of the French)

- June: **Corpus Christi** (unique celebrations in Chiapas de Corzo and Suchiapa, outside Tuxtla)

- Sept. 16: **Independence Day** (celebrated on the night of the 15th)

- Sept. 24-Oct. 8: **Fiesta de San Francisco de Asís** (patron saint of Tonalá and Amatenango, which host large celebrations)

- Oct. 12: **Día de la Raza** (Day of the Race; celebrated in lieu of Columbus Day and observed on the same date)

- Nov. 1-2: **All Saints Day** and **Day of the Dead** (church ceremonies and graveside parties in honor of the deceased; some indigenous communities celebrate only on the 1st or 2nd)

- Nov. 20: **Día de la Revolución** (celebration of the beginning of the Mexican Revolution in 1910)

- Dec. 12: **Virgen de Guadalupe** (religious celebration in honor of Mexico's patron saint)

- Dec. 25: **Christmas** (celebrated on the night of the 24th)

celebrations: for patron saints, birthdays of officials, a good crop, a birth of a child. You name it, it's probably been celebrated. Festivals typically take place in and around the central plaza of a town with dancing, live music, colorful decorations, and fireworks. Temporary food booths are set up around the plaza and typically sell tacos, *churros* (fried dough dusted with sugar), tamales (both sweet and meat), and plenty of drinks.

ESSENTIALS

Getting There

For centuries, getting to Chiapas required harrowing and uncertain land treks limited to mule trains and narrow paths through the tangled jungle. Today, the state is easily accessible. Visitors arrive via airplane, a network of good highways, excellent bus service, and even by cruise ship.

AIR

The main airport in Chiapas is in **Tuxtla Gutiérrez (TGZ);** its service is almost exclusively limited to flights that are headed to or from Mexico City. Chiapas also has a second commercial airport, located in **Tapachula (TAP).** It's a convenient place to land if you're

planning to spend most of your trip along the Pacific coast or are headed to Central America.

Departure Tax

There is a US$38 departure tax to fly out of Mexico—most airlines incorporate the tax into their tickets, but it's worth setting aside some cash just in case.

BUS

Chiapas's main interstate bus hub is in **Tuxtla Gutiérrez,** with service to and from Mexico City, Oaxaca, Tabasco, Yucatán, and other major destinations in the country. There also are buses between Tapachula and cities in

© H.W. PRADO

Guatemala; travel agencies and tour operators in Palenque and San Cristóbal offer van service to destinations in Guatemala, including Flores, Quetzaltenango, Panajachel, Antigua, and Guatemala City.

CAR

Foreigners driving into Mexico are required to show a valid driver's license, title, registration, and proof of insurance for their vehicle. Mexican authorities do not recognize foreign-issued insurance; Mexican vehicle insurance is available at most border towns 24 hours a day and several companies also sell policies over the Internet. Do not cross the border with your car until you have obtained the proper papers.

CRUISE SHIP

A handful of cruise ships stop in Puerto Chiapas, just east of Tapachula, every year. Many sail out of San Diego, CA, stopping along the Mexican Pacific coast and continuing into Central America; others start in Fort Lauderdale, FL, and head through the Panama Canal before continuing north to Puerto Chiapas and beyond.

Prices are competitive and ships vary in services, amenities, activities, and entertainment. Pools, restaurants, nightclubs, and cinemas are commonplace. Fitness centers and shops also make ship life convenient. To hone in on the type of cruise you'd like to go on, research options on the Internet, in the travel section of your local newspaper, and by contacting your travel agent.

If your budget is tight, consider traveling standby. Ships want to sail full and are willing to cut their prices—sometimes up to 50 percent—to do so. Airfare usually is not included. Note: Once you're on the standby list, you likely will have no choice of cabin location or size.

NEIGHBORING COUNTRIES

Chiapas is Mexico's gateway to Guatemala; travel across the border is typically overland near

DRIVING DISTANCES FROM SAN CRISTÓBAL DE LAS CASAS

Location	Distance	Location	Distance
Airport (TGZ)	57 km (35 mi)	Ocosingo	88km (55 mi)
Amatenango	36 km (22 mi)	Palenque	203 km (126 mi)
Cancún	1,025 km (637 mi)	Puerto Arista	280 km (168 mi)
Chenalhó	32 km (20 mi)	San Juan Chamula	10 km (6 mi)
Chiapa de Corzo	70 km (44 mi)	Tapachula (via Motozintla)	330 km (198 mi)
Comitán	90 km (56 mi)	Tapachula (via Tonalá)	476 km (296 mi)
Lagunas de Montebello	145 km (90 mi)	Tenejapa	28 km (17 mi)
Mérida	735 km (457 mi)	Tonalá	256 km (154 mi)
Mexico City	1,065 km (662 mi)	Tuxtla Gutiérrez	85 km (51 mi)
Oaxaca City	625 km (388 mi)	Villahermosa	305 km (183 mi)
		Zinacantán	12 km (7 mi)

GETTING TO GUATEMALA

Chiapas is Mexico's only gateway to Guatemala; there are several ways to get there, using public transportation or private tour operators. All except for the smallest of border crossings have money changers and are open 24 hours daily. Plan on getting an early start, as immigration lines can be long and it's best to avoid traveling in border areas after dark.

FROM SAN CRISTÓBAL DE LAS CASAS

Agencia Chincultik (Real de Guadalupe 34, tel. 967/678-0957, 8 A.M.–9 P.M. daily) offers daily direct van service to Quetzaltenango/Xela (US$25, 7 hrs), Panajachel (US$25, 8 hrs), Antigua (US$35, 10 hrs), and Guatemala City (US$55, 11 hrs). Prices can fluctuate by season, and reservations are required a day in advance.

FROM PALENQUE

Several tour operators offer an overnight excursion that includes one-way transport to Flores, Guatemala, which is near Tikal Archaeological Zone. The trip includes visiting Bonampak and Yaxchilán archaeological sites on the first day, and spending the night near the border. The following morning, a 30-minute boat ride takes travelers to Betel, Guatemala, where a shuttle is waiting to take them to Flores (US$100-110 pp, including all transport, meals, and lodging).

Reliable operators include **Na Chan Kan** (next to Hotel Avenida, Av. Juárez s/n, tel. 916/345-0263, www.nachankan.com, 6 A.M.–10 P.M. daily), **Kukulcán Travel Agency** (next to the bus station, Av. Juárez 8, tel. 916/345-1506, www.kukulcantravel.com, 7 A.M.–10 P.M. daily), and **Transporte Chambalú** (Av. Miguel Hidalgo btwn. 3a and 4a Calle Pte. Nte., tel. 916/345-2849, 7 A.M.–9 P.M. daily).

FROM CIUDAD CUAUHTÉMOC

Ciudad Cuauhtémoc is four kilometers (2.5 miles) from the Guatemalan border at La Mesilla. Colectivo taxis (US$0.85) or private taxis (US$3.50) take travelers from town to the crossing, where you can walk to the other side. Once in Guatemala, mototaxis (US$0.25) ferry passengers to the bus station, where there is service to Guatemala City, Huehuetenango, and Quetzaltenango/Xela.

FROM TAPACHULA

Daily direct buses to Guatemala City (US$15-20, 5.5-6 hrs, 6 A.M., 7 A.M., 9:30 A.M., 2:30 P.M.) leave from Tapachula's first-class bus station (17a Calle Ote. at 3a Av. Nte., tel. 962/626-2881). Bus lines servicing this route include **TICA Bus** (tel. 962/626-2880, www.ticabus.com), **Linea Dorada** (Guatemala tel. 502/232-5506, tikalmayanworld.com), and **Trans Galgos Inter** (tel. 962/625-4588, www.transgalgosinter.com.gt).

If you're heading to western Guatemala (or just want to spend a bit less to get to Guatemala City), take a combi operated by **Unión y Progreso** (5a Calle Pte. near 12a Av. Nte., tel. 962/626-3379, US$0.85, every 10 mins 5 A.M.-10 P.M.) to the Talismán-El Carmen border, about 20 kilometers away (12.5 miles). There you can cross the border on foot, and then catch a bus or combi to Guatemala City (US$8.50, 6.5-7 hrs) or Quetzaltenango/Xela (via Coatepeque or Malacatán, US$4, 4.5-5 hrs).

Another option, albeit less recommended, is to cross at Ciudad Hidalgo, 37 kilometers away (23 miles); lines can be excruciatingly long here compared to Talismán, thanks to the higher number of commercial vehicles, though once you make it across you'll have more, and more frequent, onward bus service. To get to Ciudad Hidalgo from Tapachula, **Autotransportes Paulino Navarro** (7a Calle Pte. 5, tel. 962/626-1152) has combi service every 10 minutes 4:30 A.M.-9:30 P.M. daily (US$1.25, 50 mins). Once there, walk across the border to Ciudad Tecún Umán and jump on a combi or bus traveling into the interior of Guatemala.

Note: The Ciudad Hidalgo border is considered less safe than Talismán; keep a close eye on your belongings and beware of counterfeit bills if you exchange money.

Tapachula and Ciudad Cuatémoc. Travel agencies and tour operators in the towns of Palenque and San Cristóbal de las Casas also arrange transportation to various destinations in Guatemala.

At the time of research, citizens of the United States, Canada, and European countries did not need visas to enter Guatemala. Before you start the trek towards the border, though, call the Guatemalan consulate to confirm that visa requirements have not changed.

Getting Around

AIR

Since there are only two airports in Chiapas with regular commercial service—Tuxtla and Tapachula—there isn't much in-state air travel. Factor in the check-in process, security, and baggage claim, not to mention having to fly through Mexico City to get to either place, and it doesn't make much sense travel-wise.

If your time is tight and your budget can handle it, **Servicios Aéreos San Cristóbal** (Aérodromo Miguel Alemán, Carr. Comitán–Trinitaria Km. 1262, tel. 963/632-4662, toll-free Mex. tel. 800/523-4954, www.servicios aereossancristobal.com) regularly flies passengers to Palenque, Ocosingo, and Comitán; trips to other parts of the state also can be arranged.

BUS

Mexico's bus and public transportation system is one of the best in Latin America, if not the Western Hemisphere, and Chiapas's bus system is no exception. ADO and its affiliate bus lines practically have a monopoly, but that has not made bus travel any less efficient or less affordable. Dozens of buses cover every major route many times per day, and even smaller towns have frequent and reliable service. Buses come in three main categories:

First Class

First class—known as *primera clase* or sometimes *ejecutivo*—is the most common and the one travelers use most often. Buses have reclining seats and TVs where movies are played on long trips. First-class buses make some intermediate stops but only in large towns. The main first-class lines in Chiapas are OCC and ADO.

Deluxe Class

Deluxe class—usually called *lujo* (luxury)—is a step up; they are often slightly faster since they're typically nonstop. The main deluxe line is ADO-GL, which costs 10–25 percent more than regular ADO. ADO-GL buses have nicer seats and better televisions (with even more recent movies!). Sometimes there are even free bottles of water in a cooler at the back. Even nicer are UNO buses, which often charge twice as much as regular ADO. UNO offers cushy extra-wide seats (only three across instead of four), headphones, and sometimes a light meal like a sandwich and soda.

Second Class

Second class—*segunda clase*—is significantly slower and less comfortable than first class, and not all that much cheaper. Whenever possible, pay the dollar or two extra for first class. Second-class buses are handy in that you can flag them down anywhere on the roadside, but that is precisely the reason they're so slow. In smaller towns, second class may be the only service available, and it's fine for shorter trips. The main second-class lines in Chiapas are Rápidos del Sur, Mayab, and AEXA.

For overnight trips, definitely take first class or deluxe. Not only will you be much more comfortable, but second-class buses are sometimes targeted by roadside thieves since they drive on secondary roads and stop frequently.

Wherever bus service is thin, you can count on there being frequent *colectivos* or *combis*—vans or minibuses—that cover local routes. They can be flagged down anywhere along the road.

CAR

As great as Mexico's public transportation system is, a car is an excellent way to tour Chiapas. Many of the sights—ruins, indigenous villages, waterfalls, beaches, wildlife—are well outside of the region's cities, down long access roads, or on the way from one town to the next. Having a car also saves you the time and effort of walking or the cost of hiring a driver to get to all those "missing links"; it allows you to enjoy the sights for as much or as little time as you choose.

If you're here for a short time—a week or less—consider renting a car for the simple reason that you'll have the option of seeing and doing twice as much. While a car isn't necessary to visit Palenque, San Cristóbal de las Casas, or Tuxtla Gutiérrez themselves, consider renting one for select trips, like Aguacero and Sima de las Cotorras outside Tuxtla, the indigenous villages outside San Cristóbal, or the less-accessible parts of the Lakes Region.

Note: Though driving in Chiapas during the daytime is safe, not to mention incredibly beautiful, **driving at night is not recommended** due to the possibility of roadside robberies. This is especially a concern on the Palenque–San Cristóbal and Palenque–Frontera Corozal roads. (The far eastern elbow of the Carretera Fronteriza should be avoided at all times due to drug trafficking; take the Chajul–Pico de Oro cutoff instead.) Even late-night buses should be avoided whenever possible, as they are occasionally targeted as well. In the unlikely event you are stopped by bandits, do not resist. Give them whatever they ask for—usually any cash you have on hand—and they'll typically send you on your way.

Car Rental

International car rental chains like Europcar, Thrifty, and Hertz have a limited presence in Chiapas, mostly in Tuxtla plus a couple in Tapachula. They occasionally have online specials but otherwise tend to be expensive (US$50–90 per day). Mexican car rental agencies are few and far between—there's one in San Cristóbal—and often have older cars and similar rates to the international chains. Be aware that there are no car rental agencies in Palenque; the nearest ones are in Villahermosa, Tabasco, and one local agency in San Cristóbal.

Most credit cards offer free international car insurance; however, at the time of research, only Europcar offered lower prices for declining the company coverage. If you do use the agency's insurance, be sure to get the details: Is it partial or full coverage? How much is the deductible? Does it offer a zero-deductible plan? **Note:** You will be asked to leave a blank credit card imprint, ostensibly to cover the deductible if there is any damage. Be sure that this is returned to you when you bring back the car.

Before renting, have the attendant review the car for existing damage—definitely accompany him on this part and don't be shy about pointing out every nick, scratch, and ding. Other things to confirm before driving off include:

- There is a spare tire (preferably a full-size, not temporary one) and a working jack and tire iron.

- All the doors lock and unlock, including the trunk.

- The headlights, brake lights, and turn signals work.

- All the windows roll up and down properly.

- The proper—and current—car registration is in the car.

- The amount of gas in the tank—you'll have to return it with the same amount.

- There is a 24-hour telephone number for the car rental agency in case of an emergency.

Highways and Road Conditions

Improvements in Chiapas's roads and highways have made driving here much easier, safer, and quicker, and roadside robberies are quite rare, especially during the daytime. Most roads travelers are likely to drive are paved; notable exceptions are access roads to Aguacero, Sima de las Cotorras, Las Nubes, and parts of the

© LIZA PRADO

Chiapas's highways are generally in good condition, but stay alert for unexpected hazards, like this sinkhole on the road to Las Guacamayas.

Carretera Fronteriza, though all are passable in an ordinary car. More difficult, but still manageable, are the roads to Nahá and Metzabok, and along the Ruta del Café.

The state's main highways are Highway 199, which connects San Cristóbal and Palenque; Highway 190, which runs between Tapachula, San Cristóbal, and Tuxtla, continuing to Oaxaca; Highway 200, the coastal highway between Tonalá and Tapachula; and the Carretera Fronteriza, making a long backwards *C* along the Guatemala border between Palenque and Comitán. Highway 186 clips the top of Chiapas, running between Villahermosa and Campeche, while Highway 195 winds north of San Cristóbal, also bound for Villahermosa.

There are four *cuotas,* or toll roads, in Chiapas: between San Cristóbal and Tuxtla, between Tuxtla and Ocozocoatla, between Ocozocoatla and Puente Chiapas (near the Chiapas-Veracruz border), and between Arriaga and Tierra y Libertad, a steep mountain pass known as *la sepultura* (the grave). Another toll road, connecting

Palenque and San Cristóbal, is in the works. Toll roads are highly recommended over their *libre* (free) counterparts, for both speed and safety, and all cost less than US$5.

Perhaps the biggest annoyance (or hazard, depending how fast you're going) are *topes* (speed bumps). They are common on all roads and highways, except toll roads, and are typically placed near roadside towns. They vary in size, but many are big and burly and hitting them at even a slow speed can do a number on you, your passengers, and your car. As soon as you see a sign announcing an upcoming town or village, be ready to slow down. By the same token, few roads have much of a shoulder—watch for people and animals on the roads, especially around villages but even in places you don't expect.

Ángeles Verdes

If you break down or run out of gas on a main road during daylight hours, stay with your car. **Los Ángeles Verdes** (The Green Angels, toll-free Mex. tel. 078 or 800/903-9200), a government-sponsored tow truck and repair service, cruise many of these roads on the lookout for drivers in trouble. They carry a CB radio, gas, and small parts, and are prepared to fix tires. If you have a cellular phone—or happen to be near a pay phone—call your car rental agency; the Ángeles Verdes are a great backup. If you are on a remote road and don't have a phone, you're better off walking or hitching a ride to the nearest town.

Note: There is no Ángeles Verdes service on the road from Comitán to Lagunas de Montebello.

Driving Scams

Most travelers have heard horror stories about Mexican police and worry about being taken for all their money or being trundled off to jail without reason. In Chiapas, while there is certainly corruption among the police, they don't typically target tourists. As long as you are a careful and defensive driver, it is very unlikely you'll have any interaction with the police at all. Most travelers who are pulled over actually have done something wrong—speeding, running a stop sign, turning on red. In those situations, remain calm and polite. If you have an explanation, definitely give it; it is not uncommon to discuss a given situation with an officer. Who knows, you may even convince him you're right—it's happened to us!

Of real concern are gas station attendants.

Full service is the norm here—you pull up, tell the person how much you want, and he or she does the rest. A common scam is for one attendant to distract you with questions about wiper fluid or gas additives while another starts the pump at 50 or 100 pesos. Before you answer any questions, be sure the attendant "zeroes" the pump before starting it.

HITCHHIKING

Hitchhiking is not recommended for either men or women. That said, it sometimes can be hard to know what is a private vehicle and what is a *colectivo* (shared van). If there's no bus terminal nearby, your best bet is to look for locals who are waiting for public transportation and see which vans they take. If you have no choice but to hitch a ride, opt for a pickup truck, where you can sit in the back.

TOURS

Regional travel agents and tour operators in larger towns offer a vast range of organized trips around Chiapas. You pay more, of course, but all arrangements and reservations are made for you, from guides and transportation to hotels and meals. Special-interest trips also are common—archaeological tours, excursions to indigenous villages, plus bird-watching and eco-adventure trips. Ask around, surf the Internet, and you'll find a world of organized travel.

Visas and Officialdom

PASSPORTS

Gone are the days you can zip down to Mexico with just your driver's license and birth certificate. Since January 2007, all U.S. citizens returning from Mexico (and elsewhere) by air, land, or sea are required to have a passport. Canadians may travel to Mexico without a passport; they simply need an official photo ID and proof of citizenship, such as an original birth certificate. All other nationalities must have a valid passport.

VISAS AND TOURIST CARDS

Citizens of most countries, including the United States, Canada, and members of the E.U., do not need to obtain a visa to enter Mexico. All foreigners, however, are issued a white tourist card when they enter, with the number of days that they are permitted to stay in the county written at the bottom, typically 30–60 days. If you plan to stay for more than a month, politely ask the official to give you the amount of time you need; the maximum stay is 180 days.

Hold on to your tourist card! It must be returned to immigration officials when you leave Mexico. If you lose it, you'll be fined and may not be permitted to leave the country (much less the immigration office) until you pay.

To extend your stay up to 180 days, head to the nearest immigration office a week *before* your tourist card expires. Be sure to bring it along with your passport. There, you'll fill out several forms, go to a bank to pay the US$22 processing fee, make photocopies of all the paperwork (including your passport, entry stamp, tourist card, and credit card), and then return to the office to get the extension. For every extra 30 days requested, foreigners must prove that they have US$1,000 available, either in cash or travelers checks, or simply by showing a current credit card. The process can take anywhere from a couple hours to a week, depending on the office.

CUSTOMS

Plants and fresh foods are not allowed into Mexico and there are special limits on alcohol, tobacco, and electronic products. Archaeological artifacts, certain antiques, and colonial art cannot be exported from Mexico without special permission.

Above all, do not attempt to bring marijuana or any other narcotic in or out of Mexico. Jail is one place your trusty guidebook won't come in handy.

Returning home, you will be required to declare all items you bought in Mexico. Citizens of the United States are allowed to reenter with US$800 worth of purchases duty-free; the figure for other travelers varies by country.

CONSULATES

Guatemala is the only foreign country with representation in Chiapas. There are two **Guatemalan consulates** in Chiapas: one in Tapachula (5a Av. Nte., tel. 962/626-1252, 10 A.M.–3 P.M. and 4–6 P.M. Mon.–Fri.) and another in Comitán (1a Calle Sur Pte. near 3a Av. Sur Pte., tel. 963/632-2669, 9 A.M.–1 P.M. and 2–5 P.M. Mon.–Fri.) As of 2009, citizens of the United States, Canada, and European countries do not need a visa to enter Guatemala.

There are no U.S. (www.travel.state.gov), Canadian (www.canadainternational.gc.ca), or European consulates in Chiapas. If you are a citizen of one of these countries and need assistance with your passport (replacing a lost one, adding pages, etc.) or are in a serious or emergency situation, including hospitalization, assault, arrest, lawsuit, or death, you'll have to contact one of your representatives elsewhere in Mexico; check online to confirm the location of your country's nearest consulate.

UNDERAGE TRAVELERS

From the United States, anyone under 18 traveling internationally without *both* parents or legal guardians must present a signed, notarized letter from the parent(s) staying at home granting permission to leave the country. This requirement is aimed at preventing international abductions, but it causes frequent and major disruptions for vacationers.

Tips for Travelers

Chiapas is a big beautiful state, with a wide array of archaeological, colonial, cultural, and natural attractions; to see and do it all would take months, or more. That said, for most travelers seven days is enough to get a quick taste, while two to three weeks let you truly savor what the state has to offer.

Budget two to four days for Palenque and the Río Usumacinta Valley—one day for Palenque ruins, and another one to three days for outlying waterfalls and archaeological sites. San Cristóbal and the Lakes Region can easily occupy another three to six days—between San Cristóbal itself, the nearby indigenous villages, and outings to Comitán, Lagunas de Montebello, and beyond. Tuxtla Gutiérrez and the Pacific coast include a

CHIAPANECAN CUISINE

Traditional Chiapanecan food is one of Mexico's most unique, reflecting the influences of its Maya and European heritage. Some of the most popular – and notable – menu items include:

- **Butifarra:** Pork sausage prepared with walnut, ground pepper, and anis.

- **Café:** Coffee; Chiapas has world-class organically grown coffee.

- **Chipilín con Bolita:** Chipilín (a green, leafy plant) soup served with balls of corn dough that are stuffed with cheese.

- **Comida Grande:** Beef steak served with pumpkin-seed sauce.

- **Niguijuti:** Pork served in mole, a spicy chocolate-based sauce.

- **Nucú (aka Chicatana):** Grilled winged ants; the abdomen is typically eaten with lime and hot sauce.

- **Plátanos Fritos:** Fried plantains, often stuffed with cheese.

- **Pox:** Sugar cane liquor, typically home-brewed in indigenous villages.

- **Pozol:** A corn-based drink, often mixed with cacao, though salt and hot sauce are occasionally added instead; dates to pre-Hispanic times.

- **Queso:** Cheese; high-quality cheeses are produced throughout the state. Popular ones include *doble crema* (double cream) and *enchilados* (infused with hot peppers).

- **Rata de Campo:** Grilled rat, typically caught in the woods and served in soup; the intestines are believed to have medicinal properties.

- **Shispolá:** Flavorful soup made with beef, garbanzo beans, cabbage, and hot peppers.

© LIZA PRADO

Sauteed shrimp is a classic Pacific coast dish.

- **Sihuamonte:** Hearty stew typically made with armadillo, rabbit, beef, or chicken.

- **Sopa de Pan:** Bread soup made with chicken broth and layers of French bread, cooked onions, tomatoes, plantains, zucchini, squash, green beans, and boiled tomatoes – all topped with raisins and almonds.

- **Tamales:** Corn dough stuffed with a variety of fillings and wrapped in corn husks, banana leaves, or leaves of *hoja santa* (a licorice-flavored plant); Chiapas has over 40 different types of tamales ranging from *rajas con queso* (pickled jalapeños with cheese) and *bola* (pork with chile ancho) to *puchulu* (fresh flower petals) and *juacané* (dried shrimp heads, beans, and pumpkin seeds).

- **Tascalate:** Corn-based drink made with a mixture of chocolate, ground pine nuts, achiote, vanilla, and sugar.

handful of must-see sights—especially Cañón del Sumidero, near the town of Chiapa de Corzo—but otherwise are visited only by travelers with plenty of time or specific interests.

ACCOMMODATIONS

Lodging in Chiapas truly runs the gamut: camping, thatch-roofed bungalows, hostels, small hotels, bed-and-breakfasts, boutique hotels, ex-haciendas turned deluxe hotels, and chains.

Taxes on your hotel bill, referred to generally as IVA (value-added tax, pronounced EE-va), are usually 12 percent but can be as high as 17–22 percent. Be sure to ask if the rate you're quoted includes taxes (*¿Incluye impuestos?*); in many cases, especially at smaller hotels, the taxes are applied only if you pay by credit card.

You may be required to make a deposit in order to reserve a room, especially in popular areas during high season. However, in Mexico credit cards cannot be charged without a physical signature, so they aren't much help as a deposit. Many hotels utilize PayPal or a similar service; those that do not will give you the name of their bank and account number, and you must pass by a branch and make the deposit with the teller. Be sure to get a receipt, and notify the hotel after making the deposit.

Cancellation policies tend to be rather unforgiving, especially during high season; you may be required to give a month or more advance notice to receive even a partial refund. Trip insurance is a good idea if your plans are less than concrete.

CONDUCT AND CUSTOMS
Clothing

Perhaps the most common faux pas committed by foreign travelers in Mexico is wearing shorts when not appropriate. Mexicans rarely wear shorts outside the home or off the beach, while many foreign travelers seem to have packed nothing but. It's somewhat moot in San Cristóbal, where it's often too chilly for shorts anyway, and there's always a bit more flexibility along the coast. But in Palenque, Tuxtla, and elsewhere—and certainly when attending

© LIZA PRADO

Be sure to ask permission before taking any indigenous person's photograph, especially if you're interested in capturing his or her face.

any sort of performance or visiting a church or indigenous village—long pants are more appropriate and respectful than shorts, even when it's hot and muggy. Needless to say, topless and nude sunbathing is virtually unheard-of in Chiapas.

Photographing Locals

No one enjoys having a stranger take his or her picture for no good reason, and indigenous people are no different. The best policy is simply not to take these photographs unless you've first asked the person's permission and he or she has agreed.

Tip: If the potential subject of your photo is a vendor, buy something and *then* ask if you can take a photo—you're more likely to get a positive response.

Greetings

Even a small amount of Spanish can go a long way in showing respect and consideration for people you encounter. Make a point of learning basic greetings like *buenos días* and *buenas tardes* and using them in passing, or as a preface to a conversation; it is considered somewhat impolite to launch into a discussion without greeting the other person first.

OPPORTUNITIES FOR STUDY AND EMPLOYMENT

San Cristóbal has a number of language schools where you can learn not only Spanish, but Tzotzil and Tzeltal, the state's most common Maya languages. Language classes are offered at: **Instituto de Lenguas Jovel** (Francisco Madero 45, tel. 967/678-4069, www.instituto jovel.com), **El Puente Spanish Language School** (Calle Real de Guadalupe 55, tel. 967/678-3723, www.elpuenteweb.com), and **La Casa en el Árbol** (Calle Real de Mexicanos 10, tel. 967/674-5272, www.lacasaenelarbol.org).

ACCESS FOR TRAVELERS WITH DISABILITIES

While Mexico as a whole has made many improvements in access for the blind and those in wheelchairs, Chiapas is still a very hard place to navigate if you have a disability. Smaller towns are the most problematic, as their sidewalks can be narrow and even some main streets are not paved. Definitely ask for help—for what Mexico lacks in infrastructure, its people make up for in graciousness.

TRAVELING WITH CHILDREN

Chiapas is a good place to take kids, assuming they have an interest in outdoor activities and cultural experiences. There are no all-inclusive resorts or ecoparks (like, say, those in Cancún and the Riviera Maya), but there are a number of kid-friendly options: Tuxtla's zoo and science museum are near each other, and are both excellent, and there's also a large children's park for toddlers and younger kids; San Cristóbal's amber museum and Palenque's archaeological museum also are good options for tweens and teens, as are the archaeological zones, especially those nestled in the forest or that involve a lot of climbing and clambering—good ones include Yaxchilán (which includes a boat ride and the possibility of seeing monkeys and crocodiles), Plan de Ayutla, Toniná, and Tenam

Puente. Finally, Chiapas's many natural wonders are sure to wow most youngsters, especially El Chiflón waterfall (with a zip line and mist-drenched observation deck), Cañón del Sumidero, and Sima de las Cotorras. Perhaps best of all, Mexico is a country where family is paramount, so kids—even fussy ones—are welcome just about everywhere.

WOMEN TRAVELING ALONE

Solo women should expect a certain amount of unwanted attention, mostly in the form of whistles and catcalls. It typically happens as they walk down the street and sometimes comes from the most unlikely sources—we saw a man dressed as Bozo the Clown turn mid–balloon animal to whistle at a woman walking by. Two or more women walking together attract much less unwanted attention, and a woman and a man walking together will get none at all (at least of this sort—street vendors are a different story). While annoying and often unnerving, this sort of attention is almost always completely benign, and ignoring it is definitely the best response. Making eye contact or snapping a smart retort will only inspire more attention. Occasionally men will hustle alongside a woman trying to strike up a conversation—if you don't want to engage, a brief *no, gracias* should make that clear. To minimize unwanted attention, avoid wearing revealing clothing. Carrying a notebook—or creating the appearance of working—also helps.

SENIOR TRAVELERS

Seniors should feel very welcome and safe visiting Chiapas. Mexico is a country that affords great respect to its *personas de la tercer edad* (literally "people of the third age") and especially in tradition-minded Chiapas. But as anywhere, older travelers should take certain precautions. Palenque and Tuxtla, as well as the Pacific coast, are known to be extremely hot and humid, especially May–July. Seniors should take extra care to stay cool and hydrated. Exploring the Maya ruins also can be exhausting. Bring water and snacks, especially to smaller sites where they may not be commonly sold. Travelers with balance or mobility concerns should think twice about climbing any of the pyramids or other structures. They can be deceptively treacherous, with steps that are steep, uneven, and slick.

Tuxtla Gutiérrez and Tapachula have reputable hospitals, staffed by skilled doctors, nurses, and technicians; San Cristóbal and Comitán also have reliable service, though they may lack the equipment and staff for more complex medical matters. Outside those cities, health care is spotty at best. Most prescription medications are available in Mexico, often at discount prices. However, pharmacists are woefully under-trained and you should always double-check the active ingredients and dosage of any pills you buy here.

GAY AND LESBIAN TRAVELERS

While openly gay women are still rare in Mexico, gay men are increasingly visible in large cities and certain tourist areas. Nevertheless, many locals—even in large cities—are not accustomed to open displays of homosexuality and may react openly and negatively. Many hotel attendants also simply don't understand that two travel companions of the same gender may prefer one bed—in some cases they will outright refuse to grant the request. Some couples find it easier to book a room with two queen-size beds and just sleep in one.

TRAVELING WITH IMPORTANT DOCUMENTS

Make several copies of your passport, tourist card, and airline tickets. Whether you're traveling solo or with others, leave a copy with someone you trust at home. Store one copy in a separate bag and if you have a travel companion, give a copy to him or her. Be sure to carry a copy of your passport and tourist card in your purse or wallet and leave the originals in the hotel safe or locked in your bag; they're a lot more likely to be lost or stolen on the street than taken by hotel staff. When you move from place to place, carry your passport and important documents in a travel pouch, always under your clothing. Write down your credit card and ATM numbers and the 24-hour service numbers and keep those in a safe place.

Health and Safety

SUNBURN

Many travelers in Chiapas get sunburned unwittingly, especially in highland areas like San Cristóbal where the sun can be intense even while the temperature remains fairly cool. Use a billed hat, as well as waterproof and sweatproof sunscreen with a high SPF. Remember that redness from a sunburn takes several hours to appear—that is, you can be sunburned long before you *look* sunburned.

If you do get sunburned, treat it like any other burn by running cool water over it as long and as often as you can. Do not expose your skin to more sun. Re-burning the skin can result in painful blisters that can easily become infected. There are a number of products designed to relieve sunburns, most with aloe extracts. Be sure to drink plenty of water to keep your skin hydrated.

HEAT EXHAUSTION AND HEAT STROKE

Heat exhaustion and heat stroke sometimes strike at archaeological ruins, where travelers can spend hours climbing and walking in the open sun, often without drinking enough water; it's also a concern in hot humid areas like Tuxtla Gutiérrez and the Pacific coast. The symptoms of heat exhaustion are cool moist skin, profuse sweating, headache, fatigue, and drowsiness. You should get out of the sun, remove any tight or restrictive clothing, and sip a sports drink such as Gatorade. Cool compresses and raising your feet and legs helps too.

Heat exhaustion is not the same as heat stroke, which is distinguished by a high body temperature, a rapid pulse, and sometimes delirium or even unconsciousness. It is an extremely serious, potentially fatal condition and victims should be taken to the hospital immediately. In the meantime, wrap the victim in wet sheets, massage the arms and legs to increase circulation, and do not administer large amounts of liquids. Never give liquids if the victim is unconscious.

DIARRHEA

Diarrhea is not an illness in itself, but your body's attempt to get rid of something bad in a hurry; that something can be any one of a number of strains of bacteria, parasites, or amoebae that are often passed from contaminated water. No fun, it is usually accompanied by cramping, dehydration, fever, and of course, frequent trips to the bathroom.

If you get diarrhea, it should pass in a day or two. Anti-diarrheals such as Lomotil and Imodium A-D will plug you up but don't cure you—use them only if you can't be near a bathroom. The malaise you feel from diarrhea typically is from dehydration, not the actual infection, so be sure to drink plenty of fluids—a sports drink such as Gatorade is best. If it's especially bad, ask at your hotel for the nearest *laboratorio* (laboratory or clinic), where the staff can analyze a stool sample for around US$5 and tell you if you have a parasitic infection or a virus. If it's a common infection, the lab technician will tell you what medicine to take. Be aware that medicines for stomach infection are seriously potent, killing not only the bad stuff but the good stuff as well; they cure you but leave you vulnerable to another infection. Avoid alcohol and spicy foods for several days afterward.

A few tips for avoiding stomach problems include:

Only drink bottled water. Avoid using tap water even for brushing your teeth.

Avoid raw fruits or vegetables that you haven't disinfected and cut yourself. Lettuce is particularly dangerous since water is easily trapped in the leaves. Also, as tasty as they look, avoid the bags of sliced fruit sold from street carts.

Order your meat dishes well done, even if it's an upscale restaurant. If you've been to a market, you'll see that meat is handled very differently here.

INSECTS

Insects are not of particular concern in Chiapas, certainly not like they are in other parts of the tropics. Mosquitoes are common, but are not known to carry malaria. Dengue fever, also transmitted by mosquitoes, is somewhat more common, but still rare. Certain destinations are more likely to be buggy, like forested archaeological zones, coastal bird-watching areas, and coffee-growing zones; travelers definitely should bring and use insect repellent there, if only for extra comfort.

CRIME AND POLITICAL UNREST

Contrary to public perceptions, Chiapas is a very safe and tranquil place. The Zapatista uprising occurred more than 15 years ago— 15 years!—and certainly should not dissuade would-be visitors from coming. The drug-related violence plaguing Mexico, and widely reported in the international media, occurs primarily in the northern states, and in any case rarely involves tourists or other civilians. (That said, you should avoid the far eastern corner of Chiapas, along the Guatemala border, due to the presence of drug trafficking.) Illicit drugs are relatively easy to obtain in Palenque and San Cristóbal, but bear in mind that drug crimes, including simple possession, are prosecuted vigorously in Mexico and your country's embassy can do little or nothing to help you. In all areas, common-sense precautions are always recommended, such as taking a taxi at night instead of walking (especially if you've been drinking) and avoiding flashing your money and valuables, or leaving them unattended on the beach or elsewhere. Utilize the safety deposit box in your hotel room, if one is available; if you rent a car, get one with a trunk so your bags will not be visible through the window, and avoid driving on highways after dark.

Information and Services

MONEY
Currency and Exchange Rates

Mexico's official currency is the peso, divided into 100 centavos. At the time of research, US$1 was equal to MP$12, while the Canadian dollar exchanged at MP$10.5, and the euro at MP$15.0. However, the peso was undergoing severe fluctuations—after over a decade of being virtually rock solid—so it's worth double-checking all listed prices listed in this guidebook.

ATMs

Almost every town in Chiapas has an ATM, and they are without question the easiest, fastest, and best way to manage your money. The ATM may charge a small transaction fee (US$1–3 typically) and your home bank may as well, but you don't lose any more than you would by buying travelers checks and then exchanging them for a fee or at a bad rate.

Tip: Find out if your bank partners with a Mexican bank; if it does, use that bank's ATMs to avoid double transaction fees.

Travelers Checks

With the spread of ATMs, travelers checks have stopped being convenient for most travel, especially in a country as developed as Mexico. If you do bring them, you will have to exchange them at a bank or a *casa de cambio* (exchange booth).

Credit Cards

Visa and MasterCard are accepted at all large hotels and many medium-size ones, upscale restaurants, main bus terminals, travel agencies, and many shops throughout Mexico. American Express is accepted much less frequently. Some merchants tack on a 5–10 percent surcharge for any credit card purchase—ask before you pay.

Cash

It's a good idea to bring a small amount of U.S. cash, on the off chance that your ATM or credit cards suddenly stop working; US$200 is more than enough for a two-week visit. Stow it away with your other important documents, to be used only if necessary.

Tax

A 12 percent value-added tax (*IVA* in Spanish) applies to hotel rates, restaurant and bar tabs, and gift purchases. When checking in or making reservations at a hotel, ask if tax has already been added. In some cases, the tax is 22 percent.

Bargaining

Bargaining is common and expected in street and artisans' markets, but try not to be too aggressive. Some tourists derive immense and almost irrational pride from haggling over every last cent, and then turn around and spend several times that amount on beer or snacks. The fact is, most bargaining comes down to the difference of a few dollars or even less, and earning those extra dollars is a much bigger deal for most artisans than spending them is to most tourists.

Tipping

While tipping is always a choice, it is a key supplement to many workers' paychecks. In fact, for some—like baggers at the grocery store—the tip is the *only* pay they receive. And while dollars and euros are appreciated, pesos are preferred. (Note: Foreign coins can't be changed to pesos, so are useless to workers.) Average gratuities in the region include:

- Archaeological zone guides: 10–15 percent if you're satisfied with the service; for informal guides (typically boys who show you around the site) US$1–2 is customary.

- Gas station attendants: around US$0.50 if your windshield has been cleaned, tires have been filled, or the oil and water have been checked; no tip is expected for simply pumping gas.

- Grocery store baggers: US$0.25–0.50.
- Housekeepers: US$1–2 per day; either left daily or as a lump sum at the end of your stay.
- Porters: about US$1 per bag.
- Taxi drivers: Tipping is not customary.
- Tour guides: 10–15 percent; and don't forget the driver—US$1–2 is typical.
- Waiters: 10–15 percent; make sure the gratuity is not already included in the bill.

MEDIA AND COMMUNICATIONS
Postal Service

Mailing letters and postcards from Mexico is neither cheap nor necessarily reliable. Delivery times vary greatly, and letters get "lost" somewhat more than postcards. Letters (under 20 grams) and postcards cost US$1 to the United States and Canada; US$1.20 to South America; and US$1.35 to the rest of the world.

Telephone

Ladatel—Mexico's national phone company—maintains good public phones all over Chiapas and the country. Plastic phone cards with little chips in them are sold at most mini-marts and supermarkets in 30-, 50-, 100-, and 200-peso denominations. Ask for a *tarjeta* Ladatel—they are the size and stiffness of a credit card, as opposed to the thin cards used for cell phones, known as *fichas*. Insert the card into the phone, and the amount of credit is displayed on the screen. Rates and dialing instructions are inside the phone cabin. At the time of research, rates were US$0.25 for local calls of any length, US$0.35 per minute for national calls, and US$0.40 per minute for calls to the United States and Canada.

To call a cellular phone from a landline, dial 044 plus the area code and number. (If it's an out-of-area cell phone, dial 045 instead of 044.) Be aware that calling a cell phone, even a local one, costs the same as a domestic long-distance telephone call. If calling from a cell phone (or sending a text message), it's not necessary to dial 044 or 045.

USEFUL TELEPHONE NUMBERS

TRAVELER ASSISTANCE

- Emergencies: 060 or 066
- Ángeles Verdes (Green Angels): 078 or 800/903-9200
- Directory Assistance: 044

LONG-DISTANCE DIRECT DIALING

- Domestic long-distance: 01 + area code + number
- International long-distance (United States only): 001 + area code + number
- International long-distance (rest of the world): 00 + country code + area code + number

LONG-DISTANCE COLLECT CALLS

- Domestic long-distance operator: 02
- International long-distance operator (English-speaking): 09

A number of Internet cafés offer fairly inexpensive web-based phone service, especially in the larger cities where broadband connections make this sort of calling possible. Rates tend to be significantly lower than those of Ladatel, and you don't have to worry about your card running out.

If you've got an unlocked GSM cell phone, you can purchase a local SIM card for around US$15, including US$5 credit, for use during your trip. Calls are expensive, but text messaging is relatively cheap, including to the United States; having two local phones/chips can be especially useful for couples or families traveling together.

Beware of phones offering "free" collect or

credit card calls; far from being free, their rates are typically outrageous.

Internet Access

Internet cafés can be found in virtually every town in Chiapas; most charge around US$1 per hour. Most places also will burn digital photos onto a CD or DVD—they typically sell blank discs, but travelers should bring their own USB cable.

Wireless Internet also is becoming popular at hotels in all price ranges; if you need to stay connected while you're on the road and you're willing to travel with a laptop, it's easy—and free—to access the Internet.

Newspapers

The most popular daily newspapers in the Chiapas are *El Diario de Chiapas* and *Cuarto Poder;* the main national newspapers are also readily available in San Cristóbal de las Casas, Tuxtla Gutiérrez and Tapachula, including *Reforma, La Prensa,* and *La Jornada.* For news in English, you'll occasionally find magazines like *Newsweek* or *Time,* as well as the Mexico City–based newspaper *The News,* at large bookstores and magazine shops.

Radio and Television

Most large hotels and a number of midsize and small ones have cable or satellite TV, which usually includes CNN (though sometimes in Spanish only), MTV, and other U.S. channels. AM and FM radio options are surprisingly bland—you're more likely to find a good *rock en español* station in California than you are in Chiapas.

MAPS AND TOURIST INFORMATION
Maps

Most local tourist offices distribute maps to tourists free of charge, though quality varies considerably. Car rental agencies often have maps and some hotels create maps of nearby restaurants and sights for their guests.

Tourist Offices

Most cities in Chiapas have a tourist office. Some tourist offices are staffed with friendly and knowledgeable people and have a good sense of what tourists are looking for. At others, you'll seriously wonder how the people there were hired. It is certainly worth stopping in if you have a question—you may well get it answered, but don't be surprised if you don't.

Film, Photography, and Video

Digital cameras are as ubiquitous in Mexico as they are everywhere else, but memory sticks and other paraphernalia can be prohibitively expensive; bring a spare chip in case your primary one gets lost or damaged. If your chip's capacity is relatively small, and you're not bringing your laptop along, pack a couple blank DVDs and a USB cable to download and burn photos, which you can do at most Internet cafés.

Video is another great way to capture the color and movement of Chiapas. Be aware that all archaeological sites charge an additional US$3 to bring in a video camera; tripods are often prohibited.

WEIGHTS AND MEASURES
Measurements

Mexico uses the metric system, so distances are in kilometers, weights are in kilograms, gasoline is sold by the liter, and temperatures are given in Celsius. See the chart at the back of this book for conversions from the imperial system.

Time Zone

Chiapas is in U.S. Central Standard Time. Daylight Savings Time is observed April–October, though be aware that the hour switches on different days in Mexico and the United States.

Electricity

Mexico uses the 60-cycle, 110-volt AC current common in the United States. Bring a surge protector if you plan to plug in a laptop.

RESOURCES

Spanish Glossary

The form of Spanish spoken in Chiapas is quite clear and understandable, and far less clipped or colloquial than in other countries. That's good news for anyone new to the language, or those hoping to use their trip to learn more.

abarrotería grocery store

abierto open

adiós goodbye

agua water

alcalde mayor or municipal judge

alfarería pottery

alfarero, alfarera potter

amigo friend

andador walkway or strolling path

antojitos native Mexican snacks, such as huaraches, flautas, tacos, and quesadillas

árbol tree

artesanías handicrafts, as distinguished from **artesano, artesana,** the person who makes handicrafts

asiento seat

audiencia one of the royal executive-judicial panels sent to rule Mexico during the 16th century

ave bird

ayuntamiento either the town council or the building where it meets

bailar to dance

banco bank

baño bathroom

barco boat

barrio a neighborhood, typically of a colonial town

basura trash

bien good

bienes raices literally "good roots," but popularly, real estate

boleto ticket, boarding pass

bordado embroidery

borrego sheep

bosque forest

bucear, buzo to scuba dive, scuba diver

bueno good

caballero gentleman

caballo horse

cabecera head town of a municipal district, or headquarters in general

cacique chief or boss

café coffee

calentura fever

calesa early 1800s-style horse-drawn carriage; also called **calandria**

caliente hot (temperature)

calle street

cama bed

caminar to walk

camionera central central bus station; alternatively, *terminal camionera*

campesino country person; farm worker

canasta basket of woven reeds, with handle

caracol literally, a snail; in the Maya world, it represents the cycle of life and death; in Zapatista speak, an administrative center or village

cárcel jail or prison

carne meat

casa house

casa de huéspedes guesthouse, often operated in a family home

caudillo dictator or political chief

ceiba giant silk-cotton tree; in the Maya world, a

sacred tree connecting the Earth to the upper and lower realms

cena dinner

centro de salud health clinic

cerdo pig

cerrado closed

chile chile pepper, sometimes hot sauce

churrigueresque Spanish baroque architectural style incorporated into many Mexican colonial churches, named after the 17th-century Spanish architects and brothers José Benito, Joaquín, and Alberto Churriguera

cigarrillo cigarette

ciudad city

cofradía Catholic fraternal service association, either male or female, mainly in charge of financing and organizing religious festivals

colectivo a shared public taxi or minibus that picks up and deposits passengers along a designated route; alternatively, *combi*

colegio preparatory school or junior college

Coleto colloquial term for a person from San Cristóbal de las Casas

colonia city neighborhood or subdivision; similar to *fraccionamiento* or *barrio*

combi a shared public minibus; alternatively, *colectivo*

comedor small restaurant

comer to eat

comida food

correo post office

criollo person of all-Spanish descent born in the New World

cuadra city block

cuánto how much

Cuaresma Lent

cuota literally "toll," commonly refers to a toll highway

curandero, curandera indigenous medicine man or woman

dama lady

derecha right (directional)

desayuno breakfast

día day

diarrea diarrhea

Dios God

dolor pain

Domingo de Ramos Palm Sunday

Don, Doña title of respect, generally used for older man or woman

ejido a constitutional, government-sponsored form of community, with shared land ownership and cooperative decision-making

encomienda a Spanish grant of indigenous labor or tribute to colonist

español Spanish

EZLN Ejército Zapatista de Liberación Nacional (Zapatista National Liberation Army)

farmacia pharmacy; drugstore

fiebre fever

fiesta party

finca farm

foto photo

fraccionamiento city sector or subdivision; similar to *colonia* or *barrio*

frijol bean

frio cold

frito fried

fruta fruit

gasolinera gasoline station

gracias thank you

gratis free

gringo term referring to North American whites, sometimes derogatorily, sometimes not

grito a scream; *El Grito* commonly refers to Mexican Independence Day celebrations, from Hidalgo's *Grito de Dolores*

guía guide

hacienda large landed estate; also the government treasury

hola hello

hombre man

huipil traditional Maya woman's embroidered shirt

iglesia church

impuestos, IVA taxes, value-added tax (pronounced "EE-va)

INAH Instituto Nacional de Antropología e Historia (National Institute of Anthropology and History)

indígena indigenous or aboriginal inhabitant of all-native descent who speaks his or her native tongue; commonly, but incorrectly, an Indian *(indio)*

jabón soap

jaguar jaguar

jardín garden

jején "no-see-um" biting gnat

judiciales the federal or state police, best known to motorists for their highway checkpoint inspections; alternatively, *federales*

lago lake

lancha small motorboat; alternatively, *panga*

larga distancia long-distance telephone service, or the *caseta* (booth) where it's provided

licenciado title that indicates the receipt of an academic degree, approximately equivalent to a bachelor's degree (abbr. Lic.)

llave door key

lluvia rain

luna moon

machismo; macho exaggerated sense of maleness; person who holds such a sense of himself

maíz corn

mal bad

mañana morning; tomorrow

max monkey

médico doctor

mescal alcoholic beverage distilled from the fermented hearts of maguey (century plant)

mestizo person of mixed European and indigenous descent

milpa a farm plot, usually of corn, squash, and beans

mono monkey

mordida slang for bribe; literally, "little bite"

Mudejar architectural style developed by Moorish artisans in southern Spain

no no

noche night

nombre name

palapa thatched-roof structure, often open and shading a restaurant

panga small motorboat; alternatively, *lancha*

parque central town plaza or central square; alternatively, *zócalo*

pasajero passenger

PEMEX government gasoline station, acronym for Petróleos Mexicanos, Mexico's national oil corporation

peninsulares the Spanish-born ruling colonial elite

pescado fish

petate a mat, traditionally woven of palm leaf

picoso spicy

plan political manifesto, usually by a leader or group consolidating or seeking power

plaza town plaza; modern shopping mall

policía municipal police

pollo chicken

por favor please

Porfiriato the 34-year (1876–1910) ruling period of president-dictator Porfirio Díaz

pozol a corn-based drink, often mixed with cacao, though salt and hot sauce occasionally are added instead

pozole popular stew of hominy in broth, usually topped by shredded pork, cabbage, and diced onion

presidencia municipal the headquarters, like a U.S. city or county hall, of a Mexican *municipio*, a county-like local governmental unit

propina tip, as at a restaurant or hotel; alternatively, *servicio*

pueblo town or people

quinta a villa or country house

retablo carved and painted wood altarpiece

retorno highway turnaround

río river

ropa clothes

salsa picante hot sauce

selva jungle

semana week

Semana Santa literally Holy Week – the week before Easter, popular travel period for Mexicans

sendero walking path

sí yes

sol sun

tarde afternoon; late

tejido a weaving

temascal Maya steam bath

temporada season, as in *temporada alta/baja* (high/low season)

terminal camionera central bus station; alternatively, *camionera central*

zócalo town plaza or central square; alternatively, *parque central*

Abbreviations

Av. *avenida* (avenue)
Blvd. *bulevar* (boulevard)
Calz. *calzada* (thoroughfare, main road)
Carr. *carretera* (highway)

Col. *colonia* (neighborhood)
Nte. *norte* (north)
Ote. *oriente* (east)
Pte. *poniente* (west)
s/n *sin número* (no street number)

Tzotzil Maya Glossary

The Maya language family includes 30 distinct languages, together spoken by nearly six million people in Mexico, Guatemala, and Belize. Tzotzil is one of the most widely used Maya languages in Chiapas, spoken by over 35 percent of the state's indigenous population.

ac'ubal night
atimol bathroom
avocoluc please
bat me good-bye
bats'i c'obil right (directional)
be walking path
beq'uet meat
biil name
ca' horse
c'ac'al day; sun
c'a'ep trash
cajvel coffee
canava boat
caxlan chicken
caxlan-c'op Spanish
chenec' bean
chij sheep
ch'ilbil fried
chitom pig
ch'ivit town plaza
chon animal
chopol bad
chotlebal seat
choy fish
chucvanab jail or prison
ch'ulna church
c'oc' fever; hot (temperature)
colaval thank you
c'u'il clothes
c'uxi hello
c'u yepal how much

jabnaltic forest
jamal open
jbeiltasvanej guide
jcaxlan person of mixed European and indigenous descent
jch'ulme'tic moon
j'ilvanej indigenous medicine man or woman
jo' water; rain
jolob a weaving
jpoxtavanej doctor
jteclum town or people
juch'bil chichol hot sauce
jxcanvil passenger
ich chile pepper, sometimes hot sauce
ixim corn
lec good
lobajel fruit
loc'ol photograph
luch embroidery
macal closed
mal c'ac'al afternoon
mayol municipal police
moch basket of woven reeds, with handle
mo'oj no
muc' ta jteclum city
muc'tic jabnaltic jungle
mut bird
na house
nab lake
natil c'u'il huipil, traditional Maya woman's embroidered shirt
oc'ob morning
pinca farm
pop a mat, traditionally woven of palm leaf
pus temascal, Maya steam bath
q'uin party
Riox God
schi'il friend

sc'uxul pain

sic cold

syaveal door key

ta moton free

tana yes

tan-us "no-see-um" biting gnat

ta slajes to eat

ta x'ac'otaj to dance

ta xanav to walk

te' tree

tem bed

t'ot' literally, a snail; in the Maya world, it represents the cycle of life and death; in Zapatista speak, an administrative center or village

tsa'nel diarrhea

ts'et left (directional)

ts'ib bolom jaguar

ts'omol bank

ts'unbaltic garden

tuch'ich' early 1800s-style horse-drawn carriage

tulix cigarette

uch'omo popular *pozole* stew of hominy in broth, usually topped by shredded pork, cabbage, and diced onion

uc'um river

us mosquito

vaj tortilla

ve'el ta mal c'ac'al dinner

ve'lil food

ve'lil ta sob breakfast

vinic man

xavon soap

xemana week

ya spicy

yajval jteclum indigenous or aboriginal inhabitant of all-native descent who speaks his or her native tongue

yaxte' ceiba tree or giant silk-cotton tree; in the Maya world, a sacred tree connecting the Earth to the upper and lower realms

Tzotzil Maya Glossary adapted from *Diccionario Tzotzil de San Andrés.* Hidalgo, Mexico: Summer Institute of Linguistics, 1986.

Spanish Phrasebook

Whether you speak a little or a lot, using your Spanish will surely make your vacation a lot more fun. You'll soon see that Mexicans truly appreciate your efforts and your willingness to speak their language.

PRONUNCIATION

Spanish commonly uses 30 letters — the familiar English 26, plus four straightforward additions: ch, ll, ñ, and rr, which are explained in this phrasebook under "Consonants."

Once you learn them, Spanish pronunciation rules generally don't change, unlike in English and other languages. Spanish vowels generally sound softer than in English. (*Note:* The capitalized syllables below receive stronger accents.)

Vowels

a like ah, as in "hah": *agua* AH-gooah (water), *pan* PAHN (bread), and *casa* CAH-sah (house)

e like eh, as in "hem": *mesa* MEH-sah (table), *tela* TEH-lah (cloth), and *de* DEH (of, from)

i like ee, as in "need": *diez* dee-EHZ (ten), *comida* koh-MEE-dah (meal), and *fin* FEEN (end)

o like oh, as in "go": *peso* PEH-soh (weight), *ocho* OH-choh (eight), and *poco* POH-koh (a bit)

u like oo, as in "cool": *uno* OO-noh (one), *cuarto* KOOAHR-toh (room), and *usted* oos-TEHD (you); when it follows a "q" the u is silent; when it follows an "h" or has an umlaut, it's pronounced like "w"

Consonants

b, d, f, k, l, m, n, p, q, s, t, v, w, x, y, z, and ch

pronounced almost as in English; **h** occurs, but is silent.

c like k as in "keep": *cuarto* KOOAR-toh (room), Tepic the-PEEK (capital of Nayarit state); when it precedes "e" or "i," pronounce **c** like s, as in "sit": *cerveza* sehr-VEH-sah (beer), *encima* ehn-SEE-mah (atop).

g like g as in "gift" when it precedes "a," "o," "u," or a consonant: *gato* GAH-toh (cat), *hago* AH-goh (I do, make); otherwise, pronounce **g** like h as in "hat": *giro* HEE-roh (money order), *gente* HEN-teh (people)

j like h, as in "has": *jueves* HOOEH-vehs (Thursday), *mejor* meh-HOR (better)

ll like y, as in "yes": *toalla* toh-AH-yah (towel), *ellos* EH-yohs (they, them)

ñ like ny, as in "canyon": *año* AH-nyo (year), *señor* SEH-nyor (Mr., sir)

r is lightly trilled, with your tongue at the roof of your mouth like a very light English d, as in "ready": *pero* PEH-roh (but), *tres* TREHS (three), *cuatro* KOOAH-troh (four).

rr like a Spanish r, but with much more emphasis and trill. Let your tongue flap. Practice with *burro* (donkey), *carretera* (highway), and Carrillo (proper name), then really let go with *ferrocarril* (railroad).

Note: The single exception to the above is the pronunciation of **y** when it's being used as the Spanish word for "and," as in "Eva y Leo." In such case, pronounce it like the English ee, as in "keep": Eva "ee" Leo (Eva and Leo).

Accent

The rule for accent, the relative stress given to syllables within a given word, is straightforward. If a word ends in a vowel, an n, or an s, accent the next-to-last syllable; if not, accent the last syllable.

Pronounce *gracias* GRAH-seeahs (thank you), *orden* OHR-dehn (order), and *carretera* kah-reh-TEH-rah (highway) with the stress on the next-to-last syllable.

Otherwise, accent the last syllable: *venir* veh-NEER (to come), *ferrocarril* feh-roh-cah-REEL (railroad), and *edad* eh-DAHD (age).

Exceptions to the accent rule are always marked with an accent sign: (á, é, í, ó, or ú), such as *teléfono* teh-LEH-foh-noh (telephone), *jabón* hah-BON (soap), and *rápido* RAH-pee-doh (rapid).

BASIC AND COURTEOUS EXPRESSIONS

Most Spanish-speaking people consider formalities important. Whenever approaching anyone, do not forget the appropriate salutation – good morning, good evening, etc. Standing alone, the greeting *hola* (hello) can sound brusque.

Hello. *Hola.*
Good morning. *Buenos días.*
Good afternoon. *Buenas tardes.*
Good evening. *Buenas noches.*
How are you? *¿Cómo está Usted?*
Very well, thank you. *Muy bien, gracias.*
Okay; good. *Bien.*
Not okay; bad. *No muy bien; mal.*
So-so. *Más o menos.*
And you? *¿Y usted?*
Thank you. *Gracias.*
Thank you very much. *Muchas gracias.*
You're very kind. *Muy amable.*
You're welcome. *De nada.*
Good-bye. *Adiós.*
See you later. *Hasta luego.*
please *por favor*
yes *sí*
no *no*
I don't know. *No sé.*
Just a moment, please. *Un momentito, por favor.*
Excuse me, please (when you're trying to get attention). *Disculpe* or *Con permiso.*
Excuse me (when you've made a mistake). *Lo siento.*
Pleased to meet you. *Mucho gusto.*
How do you say...in Spanish? *¿Cómo se dice...en español?*
What is your name? *¿Cómo se llama Usted?*
Do you speak English? *¿Habla Usted inglés?*
Is English spoken here? *¿Se habla inglés?*
I don't speak Spanish well. *No hablo bien el español.*
I don't understand. *No entiendo.*
My name is . . . *Me llamo . . .*
Would you like . . . *¿Quisiera Usted . . .*
Let's go to . . . *Vamos a . . .*

TERMS OF ADDRESS

When in doubt, use the formal *Usted* (you) as a form of address.

I *yo*
you (formal) *Usted*
you (familiar) *tú*
he/him *él*
she/her *ella*
we/us *nosotros*
you (plural) *ustedes*
they/them *ellos* (all males or mixed gender); *ellas* (all females)
Mr., sir *señor*
Mrs., ma'am *señora*
miss, young lady *señorita*
wife *esposa*
husband *esposo*
friend *amigo* (male); *amiga* (female)
boyfriend; girlfriend *novio; novia*
son; daughter *hijo; hija*
brother; sister *hermano; hermana*
father; mother *padre; madre*
grandfather; grandmother *abuelo; abuela*

TRANSPORTATION

Where is...? *¿Dónde está...?*
How far is it to...? *¿A cuánto está...?*
from...to . . . *de...a . . .*
How many blocks? *¿Cuántas cuadras?*
Where (Which) is the way to...? *¿Dónde está el camino a...?*
the bus station *la terminal de autobuses*
the bus stop *la parada de autobuses*
Where is this bus going? *¿A dónde va este autobús?*
the taxi stand *la parada de taxis*
the train station *la estación de ferrocarril*
the boat *el barco* or *la lancha*
the airport *el aeropuerto*
I'd like a ticket to . . . *Quisiera un boleto a . . .*
first (second) class *primera (segunda) clase*
round-trip *ida y vuelta*
reservation *reservación*
baggage *equipaje*
Stop here, please. *Pare aquí, por favor.*
the entrance *la entrada*
the exit *la salida*

the ticket office *la taquilla*
(very) near; far *(muy) cerca; lejos*
to; toward *a*
by; through *por*
from *de*
the right *la derecha*
the left *la izquierda*
straight ahead *derecho; directo*
in front *en frente*
beside *al lado*
behind *atrás*
the corner *la esquina*
the stoplight *el semáforo*
a turn *una vuelta*
here *aquí*
somewhere around here *por aquí*
right there *allí*
somewhere around there *por allá*
street; boulevard *calle; bulevar*
highway *carretera*
bridge *puente*
toll *cuota*
address *dirección*
north; south *norte; sur*
east; west *oriente (este); poniente (oeste)*

ACCOMMODATIONS

hotel *hotel*
Is there a room? *¿Hay habitación?*
May I (may we) see it? *¿Podría (podríamos) verlo?*
What is the rate? *¿Cuál es la tarifa?*
Is that your best rate? *¿Es su mejor precio?*
Is there something cheaper? *¿Hay algo más económico?*
a single room *un cuarto sencillo*
a double room *un cuarto doble*
queen-size bed *cama matrimonial*
twin bed *cama individual*
with private bath *con baño privado*
hot water *agua caliente*
shower *regadera*
towels *toallas*
soap *jabón*
toilet paper *papel higiénico*
blanket *cobija*
sheets *sábanas*
air-conditioned *aire acondicionado*

fan *abanico; ventilador*
key *llave*
manager *gerente*

FOOD
I'm hungry. *Tengo hambre.*
I'm thirsty. *Tengo sed.*
menu *carta; menú*
order *orden*
glass *vaso*
fork *tenedor*
knife *cuchillo*
spoon *cuchara*
napkin *servilleta*
soft drink *refresco*
coffee *café*
tea *té*
drinking water *agua pura; agua potable*
carbonated water *agua mineral*
bottled uncarbonated water *agua sin gas*
beer *cerveza*
wine *vino*
milk *leche*
juice *jugo*
cream *crema*
sugar *azúcar*
cheese *queso*
snack *antojito; botana*
breakfast *desayuno*
lunch *almuerzo or comida*
daily lunch special *comida corrida*
dinner *cena*
the check *la cuenta*
eggs *huevos*
bread *pan*
salad *ensalada*
fruit *fruta*
mango *mango*
watermelon *sandía*
papaya *papaya*
banana *plátano*
apple *manzana*
orange *naranja*
lime *limón*
fish *pescado*
shellfish *mariscos*
shrimp *camarones*
meat (without) *(sin) carne*

chicken *pollo*
pork *puerco*
beef; steak *res; bistec*
bacon; ham *tocino; jamón*
fried *frito*
grilled *asada*
barbecue; barbecued *barbacoa; al carbón*

SHOPPING
money *dinero*
money-exchange bureau *casa de cambio*
I would like to exchange travelers
   checks. *Quisiera cambiar cheques de
   viajero.*
What is the exchange rate? *¿Cuál es el tipo
   de cambio?*
How much is the commission? *¿Cuánto
   cuesta la comisión?*
Do you accept credit cards? *¿Aceptan
   tarjetas de crédito?*
money order *giro*
How much does it cost? *¿Cuánto cuesta?*
What is your final price? *¿Cuál es su último
   precio?*
expensive *caro*
cheap *barato; económico*
more *más*
less *menos*
a little *un poco*
too much *demasiado*

HEALTH
Help me please. *Ayúdeme por favor.*
I am ill. *Estoy enfermo.*
Call a doctor. *Llame un doctor.*
Take me to ... *Lléveme a ...*
hospital *hospital; clínica médica*
drugstore *farmacia*
pain *dolor*
fever *fiebre*
headache *dolor de cabeza*
stomachache *dolor de estómago*
burn *quemadura*
cramp *calambre*
nausea *náusea*
vomiting *vomitar*
medicine *medicina*
antibiotic *antibiótico*

pill; tablet *pastilla*
aspirin *aspirina*
ointment; cream *pomada; crema*
bandage *venda*
cotton *algodón*
sanitary napkins *Kotex*
birth control pills *pastillas anticonceptivas*
contraceptive foam *espuma anticonceptiva*
condoms *preservativos; condones*
toothbrush *cepillo de dientes*
dental floss *hilo dental*
toothpaste *pasta de dientes*
dentist *dentista*
toothache *dolor de dientes*

POST OFFICE AND COMMUNICATIONS

long-distance telephone *teléfono de larga distancia*
I would like to call . . . *Quisiera llamar a . . .*
collect *por cobrar*
person to person *persona a persona*
credit card *tarjeta de crédito*
post office *correo*
letter *carta*
stamp *estampilla, timbre*
postcard *tarjeta postal*
air mail *correo aereo*
registered *registrado*
money order *giro*
package; box *paquete; caja*
string; tape *cuerda; cinta*

AT THE BORDER

border *frontera*
customs *aduana*
immigration *migración*
tourist card *tarjeta de turista*
inspection *inspección; revisión*
passport *pasaporte*
profession *profesión*
marital status *estado civil*
single *soltero*
married; divorced *casado; divorciado*
widower *viudo* (male); *vuida* (female)
insurance *seguro*
title *título*
driver's license *licencia de manejar*

AT THE GAS STATION

gas station *gasolinera*
gasoline *gasolina*
unleaded *sin plomo*
fill it up, please *lleno, por favor*
tire *llanta*
tire repair shop *vulcanizadora*
air *aire*
water *agua*
oil; oil change *aceite; cambio de aceite*
grease *grasa*
My...doesn't work. *Mi...no sirve.*
battery *batería*
radiator *radiador*
alternator *alternador*
generator *generador*
tow truck *grúa*
repair shop *taller mecánico*
tune-up *afinación*
auto parts store *refaccionería*

VERBS

Verbs are the key to getting along in Spanish. They employ mostly predictable forms and come in three classes, which end in *ar*, *er*, and *ir*. Note that the first-person *(yo)* verb form is often irregular.

to buy *comprar*
I buy, you (he, she, it) buys *compro, compra*
we buy, you (they) buy *compramos, compran*
to eat *comer*
I eat, you (he, she, it) eats *como, come*
we eat, you (they) eat *comemos, comen*
to climb *subir*
I climb, you (he, she, it) climbs *subo, sube*
we climb, you (they) climb *subimos, suben*
to do or make *hacer*
I do or make, you (he she, it) does or makes *hago, hace*
we do or make, you (they) do or make *hacemos, hacen*
to go *ir*
I go, you (he, she, it) goes *voy, va*
we go, you (they) go *vamos, van*
to go (walk) *andar*
to love *amar*

to **work** *trabajar*
to **want** *desear, querer*
to **need** *necesitar*
to **read** *leer*
to **write** *escribir*
to **repair** *reparar*
to **stop** *parar*
to **get off (the bus)** *bajar*
to **arrive** *llegar*
to **stay (remain)** *quedar*
to **stay (lodge)** *hospedar*
to **leave** *salir* (regular except for *salgo*, I leave)
to **look at** *mirar*
to **look for** *buscar*
to **give** *dar* (regular except for *doy*, I give)
to **carry** *llevar*
to **have** *tener* (irregular: *tengo, tiene, tenemos, tienen*)
to **come** *venir* (irregular: *vengo, viene, venimos, vienen*)

Spanish has two forms of "to be." Use *estar* when speaking of location or a temporary state of being: "I am at home." *"Estoy en casa."* "I'm sick." *"Estoy enfermo."* Use *ser* for a permanent state of being: "I am a doctor." *"Soy doctora."* *Estar* is regular except for *estoy*, I am. *Ser* is irregular:

to **be** *ser*
I am, you (he, she, it) is *soy, es*
we are, you (they) are *somos, son*

NUMBERS
zero *cero*
one *uno*
two *dos*
three *tres*
four *cuatro*
five *cinco*
six *seis*
seven *siete*
eight *ocho*
nine *nueve*
10 *diez*
11 *once*
12 *doce*

13 *trece*
14 *catorce*
15 *quince*
16 *dieciseis*
17 *diecisiete*
18 *dieciocho*
19 *diecinueve*
20 *veinte*
21 *veintiuno*
30 *treinta*
40 *cuarenta*
50 *cincuenta*
60 *sesenta*
70 *setenta*
80 *ochenta*
90 *noventa*
100 *cien*
101 *cientiuno*
200 *doscientos*
500 *quinientos*
1,000 *mil*
10,000 *diez mil*
100,000 *cien mil*
1,000,000 *millón*
one half *medio*
one third *un tercio*
one fourth *un cuarto*

TIME
What time is it? *¿Qué hora es?*
It's one o'clock. *Es la una.*
It's three in the afternoon. *Son las tres de la tarde.*
It's 4 A.M. *Son las cuatro de la mañana.*
six-thirty *seis y media*
a quarter till eleven *un cuarto para las once*
a quarter past five *las cinco y cuarto*
an hour *una hora*

DAYS AND MONTHS
Monday *lunes*
Tuesday *martes*
Wednesday *miércoles*
Thursday *jueves*
Friday *viernes*
Saturday *sábado*
Sunday *domingo*
today *hoy*

tomorrow *mañana*	**October** *octubre*
yesterday *ayer*	**November** *noviembre*
January *enero*	**December** *diciembre*
February *febrero*	**a week** *una semana*
March *marzo*	**a month** *un mes*
April *abril*	**after** *después*
May *mayo*	**before** *antes*
June *junio*	
July *julio*	Adapted from Bruce Whipperman's
August *agosto*	*Moon Pacific Mexico.*
September *septiembre*	

Suggested Reading

The following titles provide insight into Chiapas and the Maya people. A few of these books are more easily obtained in Mexico, but all of them will cost less in the United States. Most are nonfiction, though several are fiction and great to throw into your carry-on for a good read on the plane, or for when you're in a Chiapanecan mood. Happy reading.

Beletsky, Les. *Travellers' Wildlife Guides: Southern Mexico* Northampton: Interlink Books, 2007. A perfect companion guide if you plan on bird-watching, hiking, or canoeing your way through your vacation. Excellent illustrations.

Coe, Andrew. *Archaeological Mexico: A Traveler's Guide to Ancient Cities and Sacred Sites.* Emeryville: Avalon Travel Publishing, 2001.

Coe, Michael D. *Breaking the Maya Code.* New York: Thames and Hudson, 1999. A fascinating account of how epigraphers, linguists, and archaeologists succeeded in deciphering Maya hieroglyphics.

Coe, Michael D. *The Maya.* New York: Thames and Hudson, 1993. A well-illustrated, easy-to-read volume on the Maya people.

Collier, George (in collaboration with Elizabeth Lowery Quaratiello). *Basta: Land and the Zapatista Rebellion in Chiapas.* Chicago: First Food Books, 1999. A balanced and highly readable account of social, economic, and agrarian factors that led to the Zapatista uprising.

Cortés, Hernán. *Five Letters.* New York: Gordon Press, 1977. Cortés' letters to the king of Spain, telling of his accomplishments and justifying his actions in the New World.

Davies, Nigel. *The Ancient Kingdoms of Mexico.* New York: Penguin Books, 1991. An excellent study of the preconquest of the indigenous peoples of Mexico.

Díaz del Castillo, Bernal. *The Conquest of New Spain.* New York: Penguin Books, 1963. History straight from the adventurer's reminiscences, translated by J. M. Cohen.

Fehrenbach, T. R. *Fire and Blood: A History of Mexico.* New York: Collier Books, 1973. Over 3,000 years of Mexican history, related in a way that will keep you reading.

Ferguson, William M. *Maya Ruins of Mexico in Color.* Norman: University of Oklahoma Press, 1977. Good reading before you go, but too bulky to carry along. Oversized with excellent drawings and illustrations of the archaeological structures of the Maya.

Franz, Carl. *The People's Guide to Mexico*. Emeryville: Avalon Travel Publishing, 2006. A humorous guide filled with witty anecdotes and helpful general information for visitors to Mexico. Don't expect any specific city information, just nuts-and-bolts hints for traveling south of the border.

Greene, Graham. *The Power and the Glory*. New York: Penguin Books, 1977. A novel that takes place in the 1920s about a priest and the anti-church movement that gripped the country.

Grube, Nikolai. *Maya: Divine Kings of the Rain Forest*. Königswinter: Konemann, 2008. A beautifully compiled book of essays, photographs, and sketches relating to the Maya, past and present. Too heavy to take on the road but an excellent read.

Harvey, Neil. *The Chiapas Rebellion*. Durham and London: Duke University Press, 1998. A highly academic examination of the sociopolitical roots of the Zapatista uprising, especially prior peasant movements.

Hayden, Tom, Ed. *The Zapatista Reader*. New York: Thunder's Mouth Press/Nation Books, 2002. A wide-ranging collection of essays by leading writers, from Nobel Prize–winners Octavio Paz and José Saramago to journalists Naomi Klein and Andrew Kopkind, compiled by civil rights leader and former state senator Tom Hayden.

Heffern, Richard. *Secrets of the Mind-Altering Plants of Mexico*. New York: Pyramid Books, 1974. A fascinating study of many substances, from ancient ritual hallucinogens to today's medicines that are found in Mexico.

Laughlin, Robert M. *The People of the Bat*. Washington, DC: Smithsonian Institution Press, 1988. Maya tales and dreams as told by the Zinacantán Indians in Chiapas.

Meyer, Michael and William Sherman. *The Course of Mexican History*. New York: Oxford University Press, 2006. A concise one-volume history of Mexico.

Nelson, Ralph. *Popul Vuh: The Great Mythological Book of the Ancient Maya*. Boston: Houghton Mifflin, 1974. An easy-to-read translation of myths handed down orally by the Quiche Maya, family to family, until written down after the Spanish conquest.

Perry, Richard and Rosalind. *More Maya Missions: Exploring Colonial Chiapas*. Santa Barbara: Espadaña Press, 1994. Detailed and informative guide, including excellent hand-drawn illustrations, about numerous colonial missions and structures in Chiapas.

Riding, Alan. *Distant Neighbors*. New York: Vintage Books, 1989. A widely-read account of modern Mexico and U.S.-Mexico relations, updated and reissued numerous times.

Sodi, Demetrio M. (in collaboration with Adela Fernández). *The Mayas*. Mexico: Panama Editorial S.A., 1987. This small pocketbook presents a fictionalized account of life among the Mayas before the conquest. Easy reading for anyone who enjoys fantasizing about what life *might* have been like.

Stephens, John L. *Incidents of Travel in Central America, Chiapas, and Yucatán*. 2 vols. New York: Dover Publications, 1969. Good companions to refer to when traveling in the area. Stephens and illustrator Frederick Catherwood rediscovered many of the Maya ruins on their treks that took place in the mid-1800s. Easy reading.

Thompson, J. Eric. *Maya Archaeologist*. Norman: University of Oklahoma Press, 1963. Thompson, a noted Maya scholar, traveled and worked at many of the Maya ruins in the 1930s.

Thompson, J. Eric. *The Rise and Fall of the Maya Civilization.* Norman: University of Oklahoma Press, 1973. One man's story of the Maya. Excellent reading.

Webster, David. *The Fall of the Ancient Maya.* New York: Thames and Hudson, 2002. A careful and thorough examination of the possible causes of one of archaeology's great unsolved mysteries—the collapse of the Classic Maya in the 9th and 10th centuries.

Werner, David. *Where There Is No Doctor.* Palo Alto, California: The Hesperian Foundation, 1992. This is an invaluable medical aid to anyone traveling not only to isolated parts of Mexico but to any place in the world where there's not a doctor.

Wilson, Carter. *Crazy February: Death and Life in the Maya Highland of Mexico.* Berkeley: University of California Press, 1974. A fascinating ethnographic novel set in a fictional Maya town modeled on San Juan Chamula, where the author spent extended periods.

Wolf, Eric. *Sons of the Shaking Earth.* University of Chicago Press, 1962. An anthropological study of the indigenous and mestizo people of Mexico and Guatemala.

Wright, Ronald. *Time Among the Maya.* New York: Weidenfeld and Nicolson, 1989. A narrative that takes the reader through the Maya country of today with historical comments that help put the puzzle together.

Internet Resources

www.asieschiapas.gob.mx
Official state government website providing a general overview of Chiapanecan culture, life, and history.

www.cdi.gob.mx/ecoturismo
Official website of La Comisión Nacional para el Desarrollo de los Pueblos Indígenas (CDI), a federally funded program dedicated to promoting Mexico's indigenous-run tourism sites; extensive coverage of offerings in Chiapas is included.

www.colonial-mexico.com
Photos and text on colonial Mexico by Richard and Rosalind Perry, authors of the *More Maya Missions* handbook.

www.ezln.org.mx
Official website of the EZLN, with links to related websites.

www.geocities.com/ RainForest/3134/
Informative website for and about the Lacandón indigenous group.

www.mesoweb.com
Website relating to Mesoamerican cultures, including detailed reports and photos of past and current archaeological digs.

www.mostlymaya.com
Eclectic but informative website on various Maya topics; especially useful for info on Maya languages.

www.mundochiapas.com
Spanish- language website dedicated to everything Chiapas, from the sights and attractions to hotel reservations and car rentals.

www.palenque.com.mx
The city of Palenque's bilingual (Spanish and English) website with information about the area's points of interest.

www.sectur.gob.mx
Official website of Mexico's national tourism board, including detailed information about Chiapas.

www.turismochiapas.gob.mx
Official website of the Chiapas' state tourism board.

Index

List of Maps

Acknowledgments

To Vicky, Ana Luisa, Magdalena, Teresa, Chio, and Sandra, for their loving care of our daughter, without which we never would have completed this book.

Para Vicky, Ana Luisa, Magdalena, Teresa, Chio, y Sandra, por su cariòño y las atenciones que le dieron a nuestra hija, sin el cual nunca hubieramos terminado este libro.

Thank you, first, to the hundreds of everyday residents of Chiapas—from friendly bus drivers to helpful hotel receptionists to patient passersby—whose names we never learned but whose assistance was essential to the research of this book. We're also very grateful to the many ex-patriots and fellow travelers we met along the way, and those who wrote letters and emails, for their tips and suggestions.

In San Cristóbal de las Casas, special thanks go to Jack Nelson at Museo/Galería de Arte Contemporeano Elisa Burkhard, and David and Nancy Orr at Casa Felipe Flores, for their considerable help and valued friendship. We're also very grateful to Dana Gay Burton at La Pared bookstore, Bela Wood at Bela's B&B, and Cisco Dietz at Sol y Luna Guest Inn for their guidance and goodwill, and to Tim Trench for information and insight on the Selva Lacandona. Thank you, too, to Linda and Andrew (of SanCrisRentals.com), and Meghan and John (master frog hunters) for helping make San Cristóbal a home away from home.

We are fortunate to have such excellent editorial and production support from everyone at Moon Handbooks. Thanks to Grace Fujimoto for sending us off, and to Sabrina Young for her sharp editing. Thank you as well to Brice Ticen and the cartography department, and Kathryn Osgood and the graphics department, for making this book look so great, inside and out.

Thank you so much to Mom and Dad Prado, Mom and Dad Chandler, Ellen, Elyse, Carlitos, Lalo, Abuelita Trini, Amy (plus one), and Michael for visiting us in Chiapas, and for your unwavering love and support, and to Kelly, Dan, Joey, Sue, Katy, Kyle, Javier, Debbie, David, all the little guys, as well as all of our friends, for rooting for us back home—it truly makes a world of difference.

Finally, special thanks to H. W. Prado (Dad or *Suegro*, Tata) for his beautiful photographs, and of course to Eva Quetzal, consummate travel companion, and the love of our lives.

www.moon.com

DESTINATIONS | ACTIVITIES | BLOGS | MAPS | BOOKS

MOON.COM is all new, and ready to help plan your next trip! Filled with fresh trip ideas and strategies, author interviews, informative blogs, a detailed map library, and descriptions of all the Moon guidebooks, Moon.com is all you need to get out and explore the world—or even places in your own backyard. As always, when you travel with Moon, expect an experience that is uncommon and truly unique.

MAP SYMBOLS

▦ Expressway	🄲	Highlight	✗	Airfield	⚑	Golf Course	
Primary Road	○	City/Town	✈	Airport	🄿	Parking Area	
Secondary Road	◉	State Capital	▲	Mountain	◬	Archaeological Site	
Unpaved Road	⊛	National Capital	✚	Unique Natural Feature	⬧	Church	
Trail	★	Point of Interest					
Ferry	●	Accommodation	〽	Waterfall	🛢	Gas Station	
Railroad	▼	Restaurant/Bar	▲	Park	🗺	Glacier	
Pedestrian Walkway	■	Other Location	🄣	Trailhead		Mangrove	
Stairs	⋀	Campground	🎿	Skiing Area		Reef	
						Swamp	

CONVERSION TABLES

°C = (°F - 32) / 1.8
°F = (°C x 1.8) + 32
1 inch = 2.54 centimeters (cm)
1 foot = 0.304 meters (m)
1 yard = 0.914 meters
1 mile = 1.6093 kilometers (km)
1 km = 0.6214 miles
1 fathom = 1.8288 m
1 chain = 20.1168 m
1 furlong = 201.168 m
1 acre = 0.4047 hectares
1 sq km = 100 hectares
1 sq mile = 2.59 square km
1 ounce = 28.35 grams
1 pound = 0.4536 kilograms
1 short ton = 0.90718 metric ton
1 short ton = 2,000 pounds
1 long ton = 1.016 metric tons
1 long ton = 2,240 pounds
1 metric ton = 1,000 kilograms
1 quart = 0.94635 liters
1 US gallon = 3.7854 liters
1 Imperial gallon = 4.5459 liters
1 nautical mile = 1.852 km

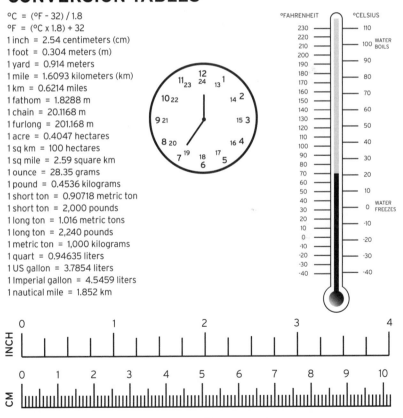

MOON CHIAPAS

Avalon Travel
a member of the Perseus Books Group
1700 Fourth Street
Berkeley, CA 94710, USA
www.moon.com

Editor: Sabrina Young
Series Manager: Kathryn Ettinger
Copy Editor: Amy Scott
Graphics Coordinator: Kathryn Osgood
Production Coordinator: Darren Alessi
Cover Designer: Kathryn Osgood
Map Editor: Brice Ticen
Cartographers: Chris Markiewicz, Kat Bennett
Indexer: Jean Mooney

ISBN: 978-1-59880-242-9
ISSN: 1947-6582

Printing History
1st Edition – November 2009
5 4 3 2 1

Printed in Canada by Friesens Corp.

KEEPING CURRENT

If you have a favorite gem you'd like to see included in the next edition, or see anything that needs updating, clarification, or correction, please drop us a line. Send your comments via email to feedback@moon.com, or use the address above.